The English-Chinese Handbook of Museum Collection Conservation Technical Terms

博物馆藏品保护英汉词汇手册

中国博物馆协会　编

文物出版社

图书在版编目（CIP）数据

博物馆藏品保护英汉词汇手册／中国博物馆协会编.—北京：文物出版社，2021.5

ISBN 978－7－5010－7078－7

Ⅰ.①博…　Ⅱ.①中…　Ⅲ.①文物—藏品保管（博物馆）—词汇—英、汉—手册　Ⅳ.①G264.2－62

中国版本图书馆 CIP 数据核字（2021）第 026483 号

博物馆藏品保护英汉词汇手册

编　　者：中国博物馆协会

责任编辑：宋　丹　李　睿
责任印制：苏　林
封面设计：新　知

出版发行：文物出版社
社　　址：北京市东直门内北小街 2 号楼
邮　　编：100007
网　　址：http：//www.wenwu.com
经　　销：新华书店
印　　刷：宝蕾元仁浩（天津）印刷有限公司
开　　本：710mm×1000mm　1/16
印　　张：22.5
版　　次：2021 年 5 月第 1 版
印　　次：2021 年 5 月第 1 次印刷
书　　号：ISBN 978－7－5010－7078－7
定　　价：168.00 元

各章审核专家

序号	章节名称	审核专家	所在单位
1	基本概念	马清林	山东大学
2	藏品管理	张欢	广东省博物馆
3	绘画	苏伯民、韩霈泽	敦煌研究院
4	纸本、档案和书籍	周旸	中国丝绸博物馆
5	织物	赵丰	中国丝绸博物馆
6	视听	李佐文	中国传媒大学
7	金属	陈坤龙	北京科技大学
8	陶瓷、玻璃和石制品	陈坤龙 薛吕 解立	北京科技大学 上海玻璃博物馆 中国古迹遗址保护协会
9	建筑	解立	中国古迹遗址保护协会
10	动植物材料	周旸	中国丝绸博物馆
11	修复材料	潘路	中国国家博物馆
12	修复方法与工具	沈大娲	中国文化遗产研究院
13	分析方法	雷勇	故宫博物院
14	其他	艾静芳	中国博物馆协会

《博物馆藏品保护英汉词汇手册》
编辑工作组

顾　问：马清林

主　编：艾静芳

编　辑：刘诗琦

校　对：龙莎莎　阚颖浩

序　言

　　近年来，中国经济和社会的飞速发展带来了博物馆的数量和质量上的巨变。截至2019年底，全国已备案博物馆达5535家，博物馆体系日益完善，功能质量逐步提升，社会影响力不断增强。这一高质量发展的动力是党和国家的高度重视，各界公众的广泛关注，同时也离不开中国博物馆界与国际博物馆界不断深化的国际交流与合作。

　　2021年5月，国际博物馆协会藏品保护委员会第19届大会将在中国举办。ICOM-CC大会是国际藏品保护人员、专家学者及机构重要的学术和技术交流平台。此次大会是继2010年上海国际博协第22届大会之后，中国举办的又一次水平高、规模大、参与广、影响力强的国际博物馆专业盛会，对于提升我国文物保护特别是馆藏文物的保护水平有重大意义。

　　适逢此次大会，《博物馆藏品保护英汉词汇手册》的出版，将为我国文物保护工作者更好地参与国际学术交流提供帮助。希望广大文物保护工作者能够通过对术语的把握，在学习国外先进经验的同时，把我国成功的文物保护经验向国际同行宣传交流，增强中华文化国际传播力、影响力，以更加专业的语言讲好中国故事！

关强

国家文物局副局长

2021年3月

目录
CONTENTS

01

基本概念
General

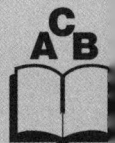

abraded 刮擦	The surface layer of an object is abraded when there is loss or damage to it as a result of mechanical action. 刮擦是指因外力作用对物体表面造成的缺失或损伤。
abrasion (1) 磨损 (1)	Abrasion is the loss or damage of a surface layer of an object caused by mechanical action. 磨损是由于外力作用导致的物体表层的缺失或损伤。
abrasion (2) 磨损 (2)	Abrasion is the loss of material on the surface of a painting or object caused by wearing, rubbing or scraping. Underlying layers may be exposed. 磨损是指绘画或物体表面因为摩擦或刮擦而导致的材料损失，严重的话基层都可能裸露出来。
abrasive 研磨料	An abrasive is a material or substance which causes abrasion. 研磨料是具有研磨作用的材料或物质。
accelerated ageing 加速老化	Accelerated ageing is the process of decreasing the deterioration time of a sample by exposing it to more extreme conditions than are normally experienced, such as increased humidity, temperature or air pollutant concentrations. 加速老化指将样品暴露在比正常情况更恶劣的条件下（例如提高湿度，温度或空气污染物浓度），以加快样品老化的过程。
acclimatise 适应	An object will acclimatise when it interacts with and adjusts to the prevailing environmental conditions. 当对象与环境产生互动，并对自身做出适当调整时，它就在适应环境。
acclimatised 环境适应性	An object becomes acclimatised as it adjusts its properties in response to the prevailing environmental conditions. 对象根据当下主要的环境条件调整其属性时，它就会逐渐适应环境。
accredit 资质认证	A professional or regulatory body will accredit a practitioner as a formal declaration that this person is competent and will work to an acceptable standard. 专业或监管机构向从业人员进行资质认证，证明该人具有相关能力并符合工作的标准要求。
accreditation 认证	The accreditation of a practitioner is the formal recognition, by a professional or regulatory body, that this person is competent and will work to an acceptable standard. 从业人员的认证是专业人员或监管机构颁发的正式认证，表明此人具有专业能力，符合工作标准。
accretion 沉积物	An accretion is an unwanted deposit on the surface of an object or painting. These can be for example, insect deposits, dirt and salts. 沉积物指物体或绘画表面上多余的物质，如昆虫留下的沉淀物、污垢和盐分等。
acetate 乙酸	Acetate is a shortened name for cellulose diacetate. The degree of polymerisation of about 130 is lesser than triacetate. Acetate has been made into fibres since 1921. See also cellulose acetate. 乙酸是二乙酸纤维素的简称，其聚合度约为130，小于三乙酸酯的聚合度。1921年以来，乙酸已用于制作纤维。另见醋酸纤维素。

acid-free 无酸的	An acid-free material or environment is pH neutral or has been buffered to prevent acidic degradation. 无酸材料或无酸环境的pH值呈中性，或者做了缓冲处理以防止酸性降解。
active corrosion 腐蚀活跃	A material is undergoing active corrosion if the reaction is occuring at the time of observation. 正值观察时期材料发生反应，说明此时腐蚀活跃正在发生。
adhere 粘合	When you adhere two or more parts of an object, you join them together using an adhesive. 粘合是指将物体的两个或多个部分使用粘合剂连接在一起。
adherend 粘附体	An adherend is the piece of an object to which an adhesive is bonded. Two adherends and an adhesive make up the join. 粘附体是指通过粘合剂粘接上的物体。连接点由两个粘附体和粘合剂组成。
adhesion 粘结	Adhesion is the result of intermolecular forces which hold an adhesive to a surface. 粘结是粘合剂分子间的作用后黏附在物体表面的结果。
adhesive 胶粘剂	a. An adhesive is the liquid material initially applied to the parts of an object that are going to be bonded together. b. An adhesive is the material resulting from the setting process that forms the final bond between two or more parts of an object. a.胶粘剂最初是将要粘合的物体零件粘在一起的液体材料。b.胶粘剂是在组装过程中将物体的两个或更多部分粘合在一起，并最终形成完整形状的物质。
adsorbant 吸附剂	An adsorbant is a solid material whose surface reacts with another substance. The reaction may be reversible by making and breaking of informal bonds or may become irreversible as a result of a chemical reaction. 吸附剂是一种固体材料，其表面可与另一种物质发生反应。通过形成和破坏非化学键，这一反应具有可逆性，或者由于化学反应可以变得不可逆。
aesthetic 美学的	The aesthetic quality of an object is people's appreciation of its appearance and beauty. 器物的美学品质是人对其外观及美学特质的鉴赏。
ageing 老化	Ageing is the gradual change over time in the properties of a material, usually due to environmental influences rather than deliberate human intervention. 老化指材料特性随时间逐渐变化，通常是由环境影响而非人为干预所致。
air changes/day 换气次数／天	The air changes/day (acd) of a cabinet or room are the number of times that air with the volume of the sealed space has entered (and left) the space. The acd of a space is an indication of the leakiness of the space. 橱柜或房间的每日换气次数（缩写：acd）指在密封空间内，空气进入（和离开）同一空间的次数，该数值用于表示空间的密闭程度。

algae 藻类	Algae is a classification of a large number of different plants which grow in water. Algae are pests present in damp places in buildings and during storage of waterlogged objects. They may form coloured stains on objects. 藻类是大量水生植物的一类。藻类是潮湿环境中的建筑物和浸水物体储存时的有害物质，可能会在物体上留下带有颜色的污渍。
alteration 改动	An alteration is a change made to an object when it is still in use and before it becomes an historical object. Alterations include removing or adding parts from or to an object. 改动指在物体未成为历史遗产前，对仍处于使用中的物体进行调整，包括零件进行增加和删除。
anionic surfactant 阴离子型表面 活性剂	An anionic surfactant is one whose hydrophilic portion is a negative ion. 阴离子表面活性剂的亲水部分为负离子。
antichlor 脱氯剂	An antichlor is a chemical substance used to remove residues of chlorine-based bleaching agents. 脱氯剂是一种用于去除氯基漂白剂残留物的化学物质。
antistatic 抗静电	An antistatic material is one which reduces the build-up of electrical charge on the surface. It does this by allowing the charge to drain away, for instance by being electrically conductive or by adding a hygroscopic coating. 抗静电材料可以减少物体表面的电荷堆积，通过导电或涂上吸湿涂层，可以导致电流流失。
aqueous 水溶性物质	An aqueous substance is one that can be dissolved in water. 水溶性物质是指可溶于水的物质。
archive (2) 档案 (2)	The archive of an object, collection, building or site is the preserved documentation associated with it. 某一器物、藏品、建筑物或遗址的档案是指与之关联成为一体的留存记录。
armature 支架	The armature of an object is an internal, usually metal, framework of support which was used in the original construction or later repair. 器物的支架通常是金属制成的内部支撑框架，用于初期构造或后期维修。
authenticity 真品	An object has authenticity when it is accepted as having undisputed origin or being genuine. 当文物具有无可争议的来源或真实性时，它可被称为真品。
backing (2) 衬底	See substrate (1). 见基材。
barrier (2) 屏蔽设施 (2)	A barrier is a cultural construct which prevents an audience from being receptive to a message. 屏蔽设施是一种阻碍观众获取信息的文化设施。

bevelled edge 斜角侧边	A bevelled edge is one that is sloping. The face of a stretcher that touches the back of a painting canvas usually has a bevelled edge. 斜角侧边是具有斜坡的边缘。内框表面与画布背面接触的地方，通常就有斜角侧边。
binder 粘结剂	A binder is a polymer which is used to hold together particles on a substrate. In a photographic emulsion, a binder consists of polymers such as albumen, starch, gelatin, gum arabic, or poly(vinyl alcohol) which hold the image forming substance in place. 粘结剂是将颗粒粘合在基体上的聚合物。在照相乳剂中，粘合剂由如蛋白、淀粉、明胶、阿拉伯树胶或聚乙烯醇等聚合物组成，这些聚合物可以将形成图像的物质保持在适当位置。
binding agent (1) 粘合剂 (1)	A binding agent is an agent that adheres the component parts of a mixture into a coherent mass. 粘合剂是将混合物的组成部分粘合成一体的试剂。
bioalteration 生物蚀变	Bioalteration is biological action on the chemical and/or physical properties of objects. 生物蚀变是对物体的化学和/或物理性质的生物作用。
biodegradation 生物降解	Biodegradation is any biological breakdown mechanism which causes damage to an object. 生物降解是指会对物体造成损害的任何生物分解机制。
biodeterioration 生物劣化	Biodeterioration is the damage caused to an object by non-human living organisms, such as bacteria, fungi, insects or rodents. 生物劣化是指由细菌、真菌、昆虫或啮齿动物等非人类生命体对物体造成的伤害。
biological attack 生物侵袭	Biological attack is decay caused by the action of living organisms such as bacteria, fungi or animals. 生物侵袭是指因细菌、真菌或动物等生物体的作用而引起的腐坏。
blanch 漂白	When a surface coating blanches, a white area forms within the thickness of the coating. 当表面涂层变白时，会在涂层的厚度范围内形成白色区域。
bleach (2) 漂白剂 (2)	When you bleach a colourant, you reduce or remove it by exposing it to sunlight or by adding chemicals. 漂白染料时，可以将其暴露在光照下或加入化学物品以减少颜色或使其脱色。
blister (1) 鼓泡 (1)	A blister is a raised area of the surface layer of an object, which is caused by chemical action or excess heat. Blisters are often empty underneath and attached to the substrate around their circumference. 鼓泡指物体表面的凸起部分，是化学作用或环境过热造成的结果。鼓泡底部都为空心，附着在环绕其周围的基材上。

bond 粘结点	A bond is the join between two or more fragments of an object using an adhesive. 粘结点是用粘合剂将物体的两个或多个部分连接在一起的节点。
break 裂缝	A break is the line along which a material of an object has separated by its cohesive failure into two fragments. In a break, the fragments are completely detached from each other. 裂缝指器物由于内部受损沿某条线而分裂成两个部分。在断裂状态下，器物的两个部分完全相互脱离。
break edge 断面	A break edge is the new surface that is created by a break. 断面指由于断裂而产生的新截面。
brittle 脆性的	A material is brittle if it is apt to break due to inherent hardness and lack of toughness. 材料变脆指因材料内部硬度强但却缺乏韧性，所以易于断裂。
brittleness (1) 脆性 (1)	Brittleness is damage caused by a breakdown of long polymer molecule chains due to loss of moisture or plasticizers. 脆性指由于水分或增塑剂流失而导致的长聚合物分子链断裂，从而引起的损坏。
browning 褐变	Browning is the visible darkening of a material or surface layer due to exposure to light or chemical action. 褐变指由于暴露在光照或化学作用下，材料表面发生可见变黑。
buckle (2) 弯曲 (2)	When a material buckles, it becomes unevenly deformed in several directions. This is caused by mechanical forces, inbuilt stresses and/or climatic changes. 当材料发生弯曲时，它在多个方向上出现不均匀变形，通常是由机械力，内部压力和/或气候变化引起。
buffering agent 缓冲剂	A buffering agent is a salt of an alkali which is able to absorb large quantities of hydrogen ions in solution. It is used to treat acidity in textiles and paper objects. 缓冲剂是一种碱盐，能吸收溶液中大量的氢离子，常用于调整纺织品和纸制品中的酸度。
bulking agent (1) 填充剂 (1)	A bulking agent is an impregnant which fills the voids in an object, and then solidifies, so providing mechanical reinforcement. 填充剂可以填补物体中的空洞部分，然后加固，从而加强物体的稳定性。
burial environment 埋藏环境	The burial environment is the external conditions surrounding an object deposited in the ground. 埋藏环境指围绕埋藏在地下的物体的外部环境。
burn blister 起疱	See blister. 见鼓泡。

calcium carbonate **碳酸钙**	Calcium carbonate,CaCO$_3$, is the result of a reaction between calcium oxide and carbon dioxide, and is a major component of chalk and limestone. Calcium carbonate is used as a buffer that is added to paper in order to reduce the likelihood of decrease in pH. 氧化钙与二氧化碳反应可得到碳酸钙CaCO$_3$。碳酸钙是白垩和石灰石的主要成分，可用作缓冲剂，在纸张中添加碳酸钙可以降低pH值。
cameo **浮雕**	A cameo is an object made from material of different coloured layers carved or moulded in low relief to show the design and background in contrast colours. Originally, stone or shell were used, but the same technique exists in glassware to make cameo glass. Jasperware is a famous ceramic example. 浮雕指由浅浮雕刻或模制的不同色层材料制成的物体，以便通过对比色显示出作品的设计和背景。最初人们使用石头或贝壳，后来在玻璃器皿中也会使用相同的技术来制作浮雕玻璃（Jasperware）则为典型实例。
casein **酪蛋白**	Casein is a protein found in milk which dissolves in alkaline solutions. It is used as an adhesive or consolidant, especially when cross-linked with calcium salts, which cause the polymer to be insoluble. 酪蛋白是牛奶中的一种蛋白质，可溶于碱性溶液。酪蛋白可用作粘合剂或固结剂，尤其是与钙盐发生交联时，会使聚合物变得不可溶。
cavity **腔、洞**	A cavity is a small hollow space, usually closed, within a solid body. 空腔是实心物体内部小的封闭空间。
cellulose **纤维素**	Cellulose is a linear polysaccharide of glucose with a chemical composition of $(C_6H_{10}O_5)$n, where n can be up to 15,000 units. It is the major structural material of plants. 纤维素是葡萄糖的线性多糖，化学成分为（C$_6$H$_{10}$O$_5$）n，其中n最高可为15,000，是植物的主要结构材料。
cellulose fibre **纤维素纤维**	A cellulose fibre consists primarily of cellulose, a polymer of glucose monomer units. Cellulose fibres are derived from plant materials such as seed hairs, stems or leaves. They can also be extruded as regenerated cellulose. The major natural cellulose fibres are cotton and linen. In textile conservation, they are used in the form of fabrics and threads to repair, reconstruct, consolidate or support textile objects. 纤维素纤维主要由纤维素（葡萄糖单体单元的聚合物）组成。纤维素纤维源自植物材料，如种子毛，茎或叶等，它们还可以制成再生纤维素。天然纤维素纤维主要是棉和亚麻。在织物的保护中，它们以织物和织线的形式修复、重塑、加固或支撑织物。
change **改变**	A change is any observable or measurable alteration in a material, object or its environment. 改变是指材料，器物或其所处环境中的任何一个可识别或可测量的变化。

chelating agent 螯合剂	A chelating agent such as ethylenediamine tetraacetate (EDTA) is a ligand which forms a very stable complex with a metal ion through multiple links. In conservation chelating agents are sometimes used to dissolve metal salts at near neutral pH. See also sequestering agent. 螯合剂如乙二胺四乙酸酯（EDTA）是一种配体物质，通过与金属离子形成螯合环而形成非常稳定的复合物。在修复领域中，当pH值接近中性的条件下，有时会用螯合剂溶解金属盐。另螯合剂。
chemical cleaning 化学清洁	Chemical cleaning is a treatment using added chemicals to react with and dissolve or disrupt unwanted materials on an object. 化学清洁是指加入化学物质同物体发生反应，进而溶解或消除物体中有害物质的处理方法。
chip 缺口	A chip is a flake of material lost from a surface or edge of a brittle object, usually resulting from a blow or pressure. 缺口指脆性物体表面或边缘缺失的小薄片，通常由风吹或压力所致。
chipped 受切损的	If an object is chipped, a fragment has been broken off from its surface or edge. 若物体有缺口，说明已经有碎片从其表面或边缘脱落。
chromogenic 显色剂	A substance is chromogenic when it creates colour. 显色剂是指能产生颜色的物质。
clean 清洁	When you clean an object, you remove undesirable material from it, which is usually not part of the original object. This material may be harmful, such as salts on ceramics, disfiguring or may conceal information, in which case cleaning may clarify form of the information 清洁是指去除器物上不需要的材料。这些材料通常不属于器物本身，并可能对器物造成危害，如陶瓷上的盐渍会损害或掩盖器物本身的信息。因此清洁可以起到恢复信息的作用。
cleavage 裂缝	Cleavage is the split along a line of weakness in a rigid material such as laminated stone. 裂缝指坚硬材料（如积层岩）中沿线裂开的部分。
coat 涂层	A coat is a layer of a material (such as paint, render or plaster) applied to a prepared surface, for example, a coat of paint. 涂层指涂在器物表面上的一层材料（如油漆，抹灰或灰泥），例如油漆涂层等。
coating 涂层	See coat. 见涂层。
code of conduct 行业规范 / 行业行为准则	Each regulatory or profesional body issues a code of conduct which contains guidelines for acceptable professional behaviour. 相关监管或专业机构发布的规范从业人员行为的规则。
code of ethics 道德规范	A code of ethics usually underpins a code of conduct which inform professional behaviour. 道德规范是行业规范/行业行为准则的基础，规定了相关人员的职业行为。

cohesive failure 内聚破坏	Cohesive failure is the internal separation of a material due to an external force. This failure can occur in an adhesive or the adherend during the breaking of a bond. 内聚破坏指由外力导致的材料内部脱离。当粘接过程遭到破坏时，粘合剂或被粘物可能会发生这种情况。
compatible 兼容	Two or more materials are compatible if they can be placed together or in close proximity without detriment to any of them. 如果两种或多种材料紧贴或相邻放置，且它们之中的任何一种物质都没有受到损害，那么它们就是可兼容的。
composite 复合的	A composite object is one that is made up of two or more materials. 复合物体是由两种或两种以上的材料组成的物体。
condition 现状	The condition of an object or building is its state of completeness and the amount of deterioration it has undergone. 物体或建筑物的现状指其保存的完整程度和其遭受破坏的程度。
condition report 现状评估报告	A condition report records the condition of an object, and is principally used to assess conservation needs and provide evidence in order to monitor deterioration. 现状评估报告是文物保存状况的记录，该记录原则上用于保护需求评估，并为文物的劣化监控提供依据。
conservation 保护／修复	Conservation is any action undertaken to preserve both the physical state and the contained information in an object for posterity. The action must be underpinned by appropriate understanding, documentation of deterioration, potential treatments and long term care of the object. 保护是为后世对目标对象的外形及其所含信息而采取的任何保存和维护措施。这一行为必须以人们对目标对象的合理认识，病害的记录，潜在的修复手段和长期的维护为基础。
conservation archaeology 考古保护	Conservation archaeology applies archaeological techniques to the study and conservation of historic buildings and monuments. 考古保护是将考古技术应用到对历史建筑和古迹的研究和保护中。
conservation ethics 保护原则	Conservation ethics are the moral principles or approach that guide the implementation of works undertaken to objects, buildings and monuments. 保护原则是指导相关文物、建筑和古迹进行保护的规范标准及方法。
conservation scientist 文物保护科学家	A conservation scientist applies scientific research and methods to the understanding of the conservation of objects or buildings. 从事修复的科学家将科学的研究和方法应用于器物或建筑物的保护修复中。
conservation survey 保护需求调查	A conservation survey is a study of a group of objects or a building with the aim to assess conservation requirements. 保存状况调查指为评估保护需求而对一组对象或建筑物开展的研究。

conservation technician 修复技师	A conservation technician is a person who is trained in the techniques of conservation and who works under the supervision of a conservator. 修复技术员指接受过文物修护技术培训，并在文物修复师监督下开展修复工作的相关人员。
conservationist 环保主义者	A conservationist is a person who aims to achieve the survival of natural habitats and wildlife. 环保主义者致力于保护自然栖息地和野生动植物。
conservator 文物保护专业人员	A conservator is an appropriately trained, experienced, qualified or accredited professional responsible for the conservation of objects. See conservator-restorer 文物保护专业人员是指经过相关文物保护培训，具有一定经验，并通过资格认证专门从事文物保护工作的相关人员。另见 conservator-restorer
conservator-restorer 文物保护专业人员	A conservator-restorer is a person professionally qualified to carry out interventions on cultural property in order to achieve their conservation and restoration. The term conservator-restorer is a European one encompassing the different cultural and linguistic traditions in the use of conservator and restorer which describe the same role in different countries. 文物保护专业人员是指为了保护和修复文物，对其进行干预来达到保护和修复目的的专业人员。该词是"Conservator"的欧洲专用术语，它包含了不同的文化和语言传统。
construction 构造	The construction of an object is the materials and method used in its making. 物体构造指制造该物体时使用的材料和方法。
contamination 污染	Contamination is the introduction of a contaminant to an object or sample. 污染是指将污染物带入物体或者样品中。
contraction 缩裂	Contraction is deterioration where parts of the painting shrink and cause the paint layers and ground layer to crack and show cleavage. 缩裂是指当部分颜料收缩并引起颜料层和底层裂化并出现开裂所发生的劣化过程。
controlled drying 可控干燥	Controlled drying of a wet object allows the water to evaporate in a controlled humidity environment. 对潮湿物体进行可控干燥是将水从湿度可控的环境中蒸发的过程。
corrosion 腐蚀	Corrosion of a material is deterioration of the material caused by chemical reactions with components of the environment. Corrosion normally refers to deterioration related to metals, stone and glass. Corrosion of a metal involves its oxidation. 腐蚀指材料与环境发生化学反应从而导致的材料劣化。腐蚀通常指与金属，石材和玻璃有关的劣化。金属腐蚀包含氧化反应。
corrosion product 腐蚀产物	A corrosion product is the material formed when a material reacts with, for instance, oxygen, water, electrolytes or bacteria. 腐蚀产物是材料与如氧气，水，电解质或细菌反应时生成的产物。

crack 裂纹	A crack is a fissure in a rigid substance. Cracks can form a network and be caused by internal or external forces. 裂纹指刚性物质的裂缝，通常由内力或外力引起，可以连成一片网状结构。
cracking 裂解	Cracking is the development of fissures in a material due to mechanical stresses as the surface shrinks more than the core of the material. 裂纹指由机械应力所致的材料上的裂纹，这是因为物体表面的收缩程度大于材料本身的收缩程度。
crackle 裂纹	a. Crackle is a network of fine cracks that can occur in paintings, glass and ceramics. See also crazing. b. The crackle in a ceramic glaze is a pattern of fine cracks normally formed deliberately by the potter using a body and glaze that slightly mismata. a.裂纹是出现在书画，玻璃和陶瓷中细致入微的网状裂纹。另见开片。 b.瓷釉上的精细的裂纹通常是陶瓷工匠故意之作，他们将陶瓷本体和釉故意不相溶从而造成了这种图案。
crazing 开片	Crazing is the formation on ageing of fine, randomly distributed cracks in the surface layer of an object, such as varnish on a painting and glaze on a ceramic. 开片是物体老化后，在其表层形成了随机分布的细小裂纹（如绘画上光油层和陶瓷上的釉层）。
crease 折痕	A crease is a linear distortion caused accidentally by pressure along a fold in an object. Creasing is formed in the course of normal use, careless handling or poor storage. Creasing patterns in an object can be studied to trace its history and use. 折痕是由沿物体折痕偶然引发的线性变形。在正常使用、搬运不够小心或存放不当的情况下都会给物体造成折痕。通过研究物体上的折痕形状，能够追踪其使用历史和用途。
creep 蠕变	Creep in a plastic material is its slow flow by viscoelastic distortion. 塑料材料的蠕变是由粘弹性变形引发的缓慢流动。
cross-link 交联	Polymer chains cross-link when bonds form between the chains. 当链与链之间形成键时，高分子链发生了交联反应。
crumbling 剥落	A crumbling material is one whose surface or internal structure has weakened sufficiently that crumbs of the material are falling off as a result of chemical, physical or biological deterioration. 剥落指物体表面或内部结构足够衰弱而发生的碎屑脱落现象，通常由化学，物理或生物降解导致。
cultural heritage 文化遗产	Cultural heritage is the surviving material and non-material evidence and practices that are of significance to a particular population group. 文化遗产指对特定人群具有重要意义且存留至今的物质和非物质的证据与实践。
cultural resource 文化资源	A cultural resource is a building, object or collection viewed as an asset to a community. 文化资源，即社区群体中的资产，包括建筑、实物或收藏品。

cupping 碟状起甲	Cupping is damage in the paint and ground layers. Individual paint flakes attached in the middle to the substrate and separated by cracks with uplifting edges, with each flake forming a saucer shape. 碟状起甲是指颜料层和底层发生损坏。单个颜料薄片附着在基底中间，因边缘隆起产生裂缝而分开，每个薄片呈碟形。
damage 损害	Damage to an object is an unwanted change that results in a reduction in the object's value. Damage is usually the result of a physical change in the object but may result from a change in its environment or a loss of an intagible attribute. 物体损伤会降低其价值。通常情况下，损伤由某些物理变化引发，也可能因为物体所处环境发生改变或失去其可识别特性导致。
darken 变暗	A surface darkens when it changes in colour to a deeper hue due to exposure to light, storage in the dark or chemical action. 物体表面颜色变暗可以由多种原因造成，如暴露在光线之中、储存在暗处或化学作用等。
dating 断定年代	Dating is the process of assigning to an object a period or age at which it was originally constructed. 断定年代指判断对象最初建造的时期或年代的过程。
deacidification 脱酸	Deacidification is the process of increasing the pH value of an object or material by washing or use of an alkaline reagent. 脱酸是指通过清洗或使用碱性试剂来提高物体或材料的pH值。
decay 降解	Decay is the breakdown of an organic substance by biological mechanisms. 降解是有机物质通过生物机制发生的分解。
decay product 劣化产物	A decay product is a material that is produced by alteration of the materials of the object. 劣化产物是因物体的材料发生变化所产生的物质。
decomposition 分解	Decomposition of an organic material is its total breakdown and loss through the action of bacteria or fungi. 有机材料的分解是在细菌或真菌的作用下发生的完全分解和亏损。
deformation 变形	Deformation is a distortion in the plane of the stat object. 变形是静态物体平面上发生的变形。
degrade 降解	A material degrades when it loses smaller fragments by molecular or physical breakdown. 当材料因分子或物理原因分解，损失了较小的碎片后，材料就会发生降解。
dehydrated 脱水	An object is dehydrated when water is lost or removed from it by a physical process. A substance can be dehydrated when water is removed from it by a chemical process, for instance in some polymerisation reactions. 物体脱水指通过物理过程将物体的水分除去的过程。通过化学方法也能除去物质中的水分，如某些聚合反应。

dehydration 脱水	Dehydration of a material is the release of water from the structure of the material. This can involve a chemical reaction or be a physical process. 脱水是指将材料结构中的水释放出来，该过程涉及化学反应或物理过程。
delaminate 分层	A composite object delaminates when it deteriorates by separation and loss of material in thin layers. 由于薄层中材料的缺失和分离，复合物会退化，发生分层现象。
delamination (1) 分层过程 (1)	Delamination is a deterioration process where materials lose their internal bonding and break up into the layers of which they were originally composed. 分层是一种退化过程，在此过程中，材料内部各层间的粘合力减弱，逐渐分解成最初的层次。
delamination (2) 揭取 (2)	Delamination is the removal of a lamination layer from a document or binding. 揭取指文档或装订书籍叠合层的分离。
deliquescent 易潮解的	A deliquescent material absorbs water vapour from the air to form a solution. The water vapour pressure of the material must be less than that of the ambient air for this to occur. 易潮解材料会从空气中吸收水蒸气形成溶液。材料的水蒸气压力须低于周围空气的压力时才会发生此类情况。
dent 凹痕	A dent is a concave depression in a material such as canvas. 凹痕是类似帆布等材料中的凹陷部分。
deposit (1) 沉积物（1）	A deposit is an accumulation of extraneous matter on the surface or in the pores of an object. 沉积物是异物在物体表面或孔隙中积聚下来的物质。
deposit (2) 存放	A deposit is deliberate placing of one or more objects for later recovery or in a culturally significant place. 存放是有意安放一个或多个物品以待后期回收，或存放于具有文化意义的场所。
description 描述	A description is a textual record, usually illustrated, which contains details of all visible or discernable features and authenticated information about a given object. 描述是文字记录，通常配有图例说明，包含文物的所有可见或可识别的详细信息。
desiccated 干燥剂	An object, material or environment is desiccated when most or all of the water has been removed, usually by a dessicant which absorbs water. 通常使用吸水的干燥剂除去大部分或者全部水分后，物体、材料或者环境就会变得干燥。
destruction 毁坏	Destruction is the breakdown of the structure or total loss of an object or building. It is a completely irrecoverable process. 毁坏指物体或建筑物的结构整体坍塌或缺损，该过程根本无法恢复。
detached 脱离	A fragment of an object becomes detached when it has separated from it. 脱离指物体一部分离开原位。

deteriorate 劣化	An object deteriorates when its information content reduces as a result of a worsening of condition due to biological, chemical or mechanical action. 物体劣化是指，因生物、化学或机械作用使状况恶化引起信息量减少。
deterioration 劣化现象	Deterioration is a process that makes an object or building less useful, pleasing or valuable. It can be caused by climate changes, chemical, physical and/or biological processes. See also ageing. 实物或建筑的可用性、观赏性与价值逐渐降低的过程即为劣化。引起其劣化的因素有：气候变化、化学、物理和/或生物过程。另见老化。
dirt 尘污	Dirt is any extraneous matter, such as dust, grit or grime, on an object. 尘污是物体上多余的物质，例如灰尘，沙子或污垢等。
disassemble 拆解	When you disassemble an object, you take apart bonds that had been made in a previous repair or conservation treatment. 拆解对象时，需要将先拆除之前在修复或保护处理中粘合的部分。
discolouration 变色	Discolouration of an object is an unwanted change of colour caused by the addition of another substance or chemical reactions from the effects of oxygen, chemicals, light or heat. 物体变色指由添加额外物质或由氧气、化学物质，光或热气作用而引发化学反应的结果。
disintegrate 瓦解	An object disintegrates when it deteriorates by separation into component parts or fragments which lose cohesion. 当物体分解成碎片或碎片间的粘着力失效时，就会发生瓦解。
dismantle 拆卸	When you dismantle a composite object, you separate the parts that were originally used to make it. 拆卸一个组合物件时，需要将最初组合在一起的零件进行拆分。
distorted 变形的	An object is distorted when it has undergone an unwanted change in shape or in the alignment of component parts. 当物体形状或其组成部分的排位发生不必要的变化时，就会发生变形。
distortion 变形	Distortion of an object is an unwanted change in shape. 物体变形是指其形状上的不必要改变。
distressed 表面磨损	A distressed surface is one that has been deliberately damaged, physically or chemically, frequently in order to fake its age. For instance, on a frame, some of the gilt surface may be rubbed off to reveal some of the underlying surface. 表面磨损是指为了伪造物体年代，对物体的物理或化学性质进行人为破坏的结果，如摩擦物体的框架或镀金表面，以露出其底层部分。
document 记录	When you document new acquisitions and existing collections, you make a record of their condition and treatment in line with appropriate professional standards and internal convention. 当记录新购置和现有藏品时，需根据专业标准和业内惯例记录藏品的状况和修复情况。

dowel 销钉	A dowel is a peg or pin which is used to join detached parts of an object. The dowel, made of wood, perspex or metal, is fitted into opposing holes drilled into each part and the two parts are usually bonded with an adhesive. 销钉是连接器物本身和其脱落部分的销钉或大头针。由木头、有机玻璃或金属制成的暗钉，被钻入相对一方脱落部分的孔中，一般用粘合剂将两个部分粘结在一起。
dry rot 干腐病	Dry rot is a fungal attack caused by Serpula lacrymans. It is an unusual kind of rot in that it does not need a local water supply. This brown rot causes considerable loss of cellulose and physical damage seen as shrinkage and cuboid cracking. 干腐病是由干腐菌引起的真菌侵袭，是一类无需局部水供应的不常见的腐蚀。该褐腐病会引起严重的纤维素损失和物理性损坏，如收缩和呈长方体开裂。
dyeing 染色	Dyeing is the process of applying dyes to a substrate. 染色是指将染料涂或浸到某些材质上的过程。
ecofact 生态产物	An ecofact is an object or feature that has been produced by natural processes or activity. 生态产物是通过自然过程或活动生产出的物体或特征。
education 教育	Education of a person provides a broad base of cultural insights and technical information. 教育为个体提供了更为广泛的文化见识和技术信息。
embrittlement 脆化现象	A flexible object undergoes embrittlement when it becomes brittle, usually as the result of deterioration. 当柔性物体通常因劣化而变脆时，其会发生脆化现象。
encapsulate 封装	You encapsulate a thin sheet of a material by enclosing it in a transparent jacket or envelope sealed on all four sides. 封装材料薄片是指将材料薄片封装在四面密封的透明外套或信封中。
encrustation 结壳	An encrustation on an object is a compact and coherent deposit resulting from chemical, physical or biological action. 物体结壳是在化学，物理或生物作用下产生的致密黏着的沉积物。
engraved 刻槽	See incised. 见有锯齿状边缘的。
erosion 侵蚀	Erosion is the surface attrition or wear of a material caused by natural physical action. 侵蚀是指由自然物理作用引起的材料表面的磨损。
evaporation 蒸发	Evaporation is the conversion of a liquid into its gaseous state. 蒸发是指液体转化成气态的过程。

examination technique 检测技术	Examination technique is the process undertaken prior to and during conservation to elicit information which may be historical or technical and used to inform further action or treatment. 在文物修复前和修复时，需要利用技术检测获取历史或技术信息，以便实施下一步的措施或处理。
excavation 发掘	The excavation of an object is the controlled and documented removal of obscuring soil or debris. This may happen on an archaeological site where the object is discovered, or in the laboratory when the details of the object are revealed. 对物体进行发掘是指清除遮盖的土壤或碎屑，并进行可控记录的过程。这可能出现在考古现场，或是分析该物体细节的实验室。
exfoliate 片状剥落	A material exfoliates when it degrades by the loss of flakes, scales or layers, for instance the detachment of layers of corrosion products from the surface of iron alloys. 当材料由于薄片脱落，水垢或层级缺失而发生降解时，就会发生片状剥落，如铁合金表面的腐蚀产物层脱落。
exfoliation (1) 剥落（1）	Exfoliation is the separation of layers. An example of exfoliation is the separation of the silver coating from the copper base in daguerreotypes. 剥落指层之间分离。比如，在银版照相法中镀银层从铜基上分离。
expansion 扩幅	In painting conservation, expansion is the increase in dimension of the support. 在绘画修复中，扩幅是指增加背纸的尺寸。
expertise 专业知识	A person who has expertise demonstrates relevant and recognised professional skills and underpinning knowledge needed to undertake a specific task. 专业技能是掌握某一领域专业知识的相关人员所拥有的技能，他们能根据其知识储备完成特定的工作任务。
exploded diagram 分解示意图	An exploded diagram is a drawing of a fragmented ceramic objects indicating the correct positioning of each sherd. 分解示意图指陶瓷残片的分解示意图，图中残片位置代表其在器物中实际位置。
facing 覆面层/饰面	a. A facing is a layer of material adhered to an object's surface in order to protect and strengthen it. Facings are intended to be easily removed at a later stage in treatment. The added facing may be soft tissue paper, Japan paper or fine fabric. b. facing is the process of applying a protective material to a surface. a. 覆面层是指附着在物体表面起保护和加强作用的材料层，在后续处理阶段易于清除。附加的面层可能是柔软的薄纸、和纸或细薄织物。 b. 饰面是将保护材料涂在表面上的过程。
facsimile 复制品	A facsimile is an exact copy that uses a technology (often the same photographic process as the original) to resemble the optical and physical object properties as close as possible. It is acknowledged as not being the original object. 复制品指使用原始技术（通常与原作相同的技术）使作品在视觉和外观上尽可能相近。如非真品，应进行标识其非真品。

fast 稳定性	A colourant that is fast to a potential deleterious influence is resistant to change. See also light fastness and wash fastness. 如果某种着色剂能抵抗潜在的有害影响，那么这个着色剂就是不易褪色的。另见耐晒牢度和耐洗牢度。
fast colour 不褪色剂	A fast colour is a colourant that does not change under a specific influence, such as that of light, acids or alkalis. 不褪色剂指在特定影响下（如光照或酸碱度）不会发生改变的着色剂。
fibre 纤维	A fibre is single unit of matter which is usually 100 times longer than it is thick. The average length of a fibre depends on the type, with most organic textile fibres varying in length from 15 to 150 millimetres. Most synthetic fibres can be made as long as desired. 纤维是单一物质单位，它的长度通常是其厚度的100倍。纤维的平均长度取决于它的类型，大多数有机的纺织纤维长度在15到150毫米之间。大多数合成纤维可以按照意愿制成想要的长度。
fibril 原纤维	A fibril is a physical building element of cellulose and protein fibres. Fibrils have a threadlike structure and are formed of bundles of long chains of molecules. 原纤维是纤维素和蛋白质纤维构成的物理成分。原纤维具有线状结构，并由分子长链构成。
field 领域	A field of activity is a specialist subject. 从事领域是指一门由专业人士从事的研究领域。
fill 充填体	A fill is a material used to replace or simulate lost areas of an object. 充填体是指替换或仿照原物体缺失部分而制成的材料。
filler (1) 填料 (1)	A filler is material added to a synthetic resin to modify its properties and to impart specific qualities, such as opacity, colour and texture. 填料是添加到合成树脂中的材料，可以改变其性能并赋予特定的品质，如不透明度、颜色和质地等。
filling 填充	See fill. 见填满。
film 薄膜	A film is a thin transparent sheet of a polymer. 薄膜是一张由聚合物制成的透明薄片。
Filoform 乳液法聚氯乙烯	Filoform is a poly(vinyl chloride). In the past it has been used in solution for the consolidation of wood and for lifting archaeological objects. 乳液法聚氯乙烯是一种聚氯乙烯，以前被用来加固木材和提取发掘出来的考古物品。
find 遗物	An archaeological find is an object retrieved from archaeological excavation. 遗物是从考古发掘中获取的文物。
finish (2) 抛光 (2)	The finish of a surface is its quality such as gloss or impasto. 表面的抛光程度是指物体具有某种品质，如富有光泽或具有厚重的颜料涂层。

finish (3) 修饰 (3)	When you finish a surface, you undertake a treatment to produce a specific surface quality, such as polishing a fill. 最后的修饰阶段时，人们往往会对物体表面进行特别处理，如抛光等。
finishing (4) 整理	The finishing of a textile involves the application of a substance or process to improve its appearance and or properties. There are two classifications: mechanical, involving heat, moisture and pressure; and chemical, involving the application of substances. Finishing takes place after the manufacture of the textile. When a textile is finished, it has not necessarily been made into a textile object. There are many types of finishes such as sizing, crease resistant (easy-care), waterproof, flame-proof, or anti-static. 纺织品的整理是指应用某种物质或工艺来改善其外观和或性能。有两类：机械整理，包括热、湿和压力；化学整理，涉及物质的应用。整理是纺织品生产完成后的最后一道工序。当纺织品被整理后，它不一定被制成产品。有许多类型的整理方法，如上浆、防皱（易于护理）、防水、阻燃或防静电。
fire gilding 火法镀金	Fire gilding is gold applied to an object in a medium which is burnt off in the kiln, such as in honey gilding. 火法镀金指在窑炉中燃烧掉介质后，进而在物体表面留下的金黄色镀层。
first aid 抢救性处理	First aid is given to an object or building as an emergency treatment to prevent further deterioration. It is often undertaken in situ and prior to full conservation. 抢救性处理是指为防止进一步恶化，而对物体或建筑物进行的处理，它通常在现场开展，之后再进行全面修复。
fissure 裂缝	A fissure is a cleft or split in the original material of the object, such as in building stone. 裂缝是物体原始材料（如建筑石材）上的开裂或裂缝。
fix 固定	You fix loose paint or particles by adhering it to its substrate. 通过将涂料和颗粒粘在基材上，来固定松动的涂料或颗粒。
fixative (1) 加固剂	A fixative is a surface consolidant used to secure loose particles, such as friable pigment. 加固剂是可用于加固物体表面，防止颗粒松散（如易碎颜料）。
flake 起甲	A flake is a thin scale which is the result of surface degradation causing the detachment of the scale. If the detachment is partial, the flake is held at only one small area of contact. 起甲指因材料表面发生降解从而导致剥落的小薄片。如果是部分脱离，则这种剥落仅发生在有限的相关区域。
flaking 起甲的	A flaking surface is one that is losing material in flakes. 起甲指物体表面材料发生薄片脱落的现象。
fold line 折叠线	A fold line is a linear distortion caused deliberately by pressure along a fold in an object. 折叠线是沿物体折叠方向施压，人为造成的线性变形。

fragile 易碎的	A fragile object is one that is delicate and can be easily broken or damaged. 易碎物品指容易易折断或损坏的物体。
fragment 碎片	A fragment of an object is a part of the original which has become detached. 碎片指已脱离物体本体的部分。
freeze 冷冻	When you freeze an object, you place it in a deep freezer, usually with a temperature of less than -20℃. When freezing is used to destroy insects, the object is first sealed into a plastic bag, in order to prevent moisture content changes and consequent distortion, then cooled to less than -30℃. Freezing is the first stage in carrying out the freeze-drying of water-damaged and water-logged archaeological organic materials. 冷冻时，通常需要将其物体置于低于20℃的冷藏器中。用冷冻法消灭昆虫时，首先要将物体密封在一个塑料袋中，以防止水分含量变化和随之而来的变形，然后冷却至-30℃以下。冷冻是对遇水损害、饱水考古有机材料冷冻干燥的第一步。
freeze drying 冷冻干燥	Freeze drying an object is a treatment used to remove water from a waterlogged object or small natural history specimens. The process involves freezing the water in the object followed by sublimation of the ice. 冷冻干燥是指将饱水物体或小型自然历史标本中的水除掉的过程，其中包括将物体中的水冷冻成冰，再升华等。
friable 易碎的	A friable material is one that is fragile and liable to powdering or crumbling due to lack of cohesion between particles. 脆性材料非常脆弱，由于缺乏颗粒之间的内聚力而易于粉化或剥落。
fugitive 易褪色的	A fugitive colourant is a colourant that is impermanent under specified conditions. An example of a fugitive colourant is a dye which would be dissolved out of an object by water. 易褪色染色剂指特定条件下，无法永久保持颜色的染色剂。例如，某种由可褪色染料浸染的器物，当人们把它放入水中后，颜色能水被溶解后析出。
fungal activity 真菌活性	Fungal activity is the development of a destructive plant-like organism as furry growths (hyphae) from which stems a spore-producing, fruiting body. 真菌活性指一种破坏性植物状生物体（如菌丝）产出的芽孢的子实体。
fungus 真菌	A fungus is one of a group of thallophytes, including mould and mildew, which feed on organic matter. 真菌是一组以有机物为食的藻生植物，包括霉菌和霉菌。
gap filling 填充缝隙	See fill. 见填满。
gild 镀金	When you gild a surface such as metal or wood, you apply a thin layer of gold leaf to it. 镀金指为金属或木材等材质的表面涂上一层薄薄的金箔。
gilding 贴金法	See water gilding or mordant gilding. 见水溶粘接剂贴金箔法或粘结剂贴金箔法。

glaze (3) 上釉 (3)	You glaze a surface when you apply a hard, glossy finish or coating. 上釉指用坚固带有光泽的涂料对表面进行处理。
gold leaf 金箔	A gold leaf is an alloy of gold beaten and/or rolled to a sheet with a thickness of approximately 0,0007 to 0,00001mm. It is usually 8cm × 8 cm in size with a colour dependent on the alloy use. 金箔是经打磨和/或捶制成的厚度约为 0.0007 至 0.0001 毫米的合金薄片，尺寸一般为 8 厘米 × 8 厘米，其颜色取决于其用途。
grain (1) 纹理 (1)	The grain of a material is the direction in which most fibres are orientated. 材料的纹理指大多数的纤维朝向。
grain direction 材料纹理）	See grain (1). 见纹理（1）.
grime 污垢	Grime is undesireable particulate material which is ingrained in the structure of an object. 污垢是扎根在物体结构中的不被需要的微粒材料。
ground (2) 底层	A ground is a layer, usually a gesso-like material, below a decorative surface such as paint gilding or varnish. 底层是颜料层（如烫金或光油层）的下一层，通常使用类似石膏的材料打底。
haze 光雾	The haze in an otherwise transparent material is a slight diffusion of light caused by particles or physical distortion of the material. 透明材料的光雾是指由颗粒或材料的物理变形引发的光的轻微扩散。
history file 历史文件	A history file holds all records relevant to a specific object which fall outside the museum's standard documentation. The file may include letters, press-cuttings and photographs of the object in use. 历史文件指与特定文物相关的所有记录，该记录甚至包含了博物馆标准文档以外的资料，这些文件可能包含信件，与文物有关的媒体剪报和照片等。
hole 孔隙	A hole is an interruption in the continuity of a surface characterised by a loss of material 孔隙是由材料损失引发的材料连续性中断。
HPC 羟丙基纤维素	See hydroxypropylcellulose. 见羟丙基纤维素。
hydration 水合作用	Hydration of a material is the absorption of water into the structure of the material. This can involve a chemical reaction or be a physical process. 材料的水合作用指水分被吸收进材料结构中的过程，其中涉及化学反应或物理过程。
hydrolysis (1) 水解 (1)	Hydrolysis is degradation of a polymer caused by reaction with water, usually with an acid or alkali catalyst. In hydrolysis, ester or amide groups within the polymer break, resulting in weakening of the fibre or film. 水解是聚合物与水（通常需要酸或碱性催化剂）反应而发生的降解。在水解过程中，聚合物内的酯或酰胺基团断裂，导致纤维或薄膜变弱。

hydrophilic 亲水	A hydrophilic material is one which interacts strongly with water. 亲水性材料指极易与水发生相互作用的材料。
hydrophobic 疏水	A hydrophobic material is one which repels water. 疏水性材料是排斥水的材料。
hydroxypropylcellu-lose 羟丙基纤维素	Hydroxypropylcellulose (HPC) is a cellulose ether. It is a non-ionic and thermoplastic polymer. The white powder is soluble in polar solvents and in water below 45℃. It is used as an adhesive, flocculant, wetting agent, thickener, consolidant, fixative, binder and in antistatic coatings 羟丙基纤维素（HPC）是一种纤维素醚，非离子热塑性聚合物。这种白色粉末，可溶于极性溶剂和45℃以下的水中。可用作粘合剂、凝聚剂、润湿剂、增稠剂、固化剂、固定剂，粘结剂和抗静电涂料。
imitation 仿制品	An imitation is a copy of an original object that is not intended to be taken as genuine. 仿制品是原作的复制品，不被视为真品。
immovable 不可移动的	An immovable object, such as a monument, is fixed in a specific situation and cannot be taken to another position. 不可移动的物体（如纪念碑）被固定在特定环境中，无法转移到其他位置。
impurity 杂质	Impurity is the presence of a very small amount of an unwanted substance in another. 杂质指另一种物质中存量极少的有害物质。
incised 有锯齿状边缘的	An incised surface of an object is one cut with lines. 物体的切割面是指用线条切割成的面。
incising 雕饰	Incising is cutting or carving the marked lines of the motive into the surface or ground. 雕饰指将图案线条切割或雕刻在物体表面或平面上。
inclusion 夹杂物	An inclusion is a particle of a different material found within the body of another, such as carbon in steel or crushed shell in ceramics. 夹杂物是另一个物体内部的与其不同材料的颗粒，如钢铁中的碳，或陶瓷中的碎壳等。
indigenous 原生的	An indigenous object is one that has been found or been kept in the geographic location where it was originally produced. 原生器物指那些从初始制作地出土或被保存下来的物品。
inherent vice 固有缺陷	An inherent vice is a structural problem of a painting due to the materials used or the way the materials were applied. 固有缺陷是指因材料使用或者材料应用方法引起涂料的结构问题。
inlaying 镶嵌	Inlaying is a decorative technique where materials of different colour or texture are fitted into cut depressions in a surface. 镶嵌是一种装饰技术，将不同颜色或质地的材料嵌入表面的凹陷处。

inscription 铭文	An inscription is text written on a monument or object during its production or usage. 铭文是在生产或使用过程中，写在纪念碑或物体上面的文字。
intangible attribute 无形属性	An intangible attribute of an object is a non-material aspect of its appreciation. The aspects can include social relationships, history of use, beliefs, and rituals. 无形属性是文物可以鉴赏的非物质特性，包括社会关系、使用历史、信仰和仪式方面的各个方面。
integrity 完整性	The integrity of an object is the state of surviving in a condition with no deliberate or accidental changes that detract from its perception as being original. 器物完整性指物体处在最初的状态，没有被刻意或偶然改变过。
interdisciplinary 跨学科	An interdisciplinary project or other activity involves a number of people with different disciplines. For example, a museum project comprises curators, conservators and designers. 跨学科项目或其他活动通常涉及不同学科的多种人才。例如，一个博物馆项目一般包括策展人，文物保护专业人员和设计师。
intern 实习生	An intern is a recently qualified graduate who undertakes a structured, supervised appointment, usually for a fixed term, with clear aims for professional development. 实习生是指近期通过考核的毕业生，他们具备清晰的职业发展目标，能在规定限期内在他人监督下完成结构化的工作任务。
internal stress 内应力	Internal stress is the forces within a material that may cause distortion or separation. 内应力指材料内部可能导致变形或分解的力。
iridescent 虹彩色的	An iridescent surface reflects light with a range of spectral colours due to interference effects, which vary with the angle of viewing. 由于干涉效应，虹彩色的表面会反射出整个光谱颜色的光，并随视角的变化而变化。
Japanese tissue paper 日本纸	Japanese tissue paper is a fine strong fibred paper made from the fibres of trees and plants. It is often used as a facing material in the conservation of paintings and polychrome sculpture. 日本纸是由树木和植物纤维制成的优质高纤维纸张，在绘画和彩色雕塑的修复中常被用作饰面材料。
judgement 判断	A judgement is a decision made after weighing of incomplete knowledge. 判断指在对不完全的依据进行考量后做出的决定。
lacuna 腔隙	A lacuna is a missing portion, cavity or loss from an object. 腔隙是物体的缺失、空腔或丢失的部分。
lamella 薄片	A lamella is a thin plate, scale, layer or film. 薄的板、鳞片、层或膜。

laminate (1) 复合结构（1）	A laminate is a natural or man-made structure composed of layers of different materials joined together. 由不同材料层结合在一起的天然或人造结构。
laser cleaning 激光清洗	Laser cleaning is a surface treatment which uses powerful radiation of selected wavelength to disrupt dirt on stone, parchment or glass. 激光清洗是一种表面处理方法，使用选定波长的强辐射来去除石制品、羊皮纸或玻璃上的灰尘。
layer (1) 层（1）	A layer is material making up an object that covers all or some of the area of the object, such as a coating or covering. 构成物体的材料，覆盖了物体的全部或部分区域，如涂层或覆盖物。
leaching 浸出	Leaching is the movement of soluble substances from their original position on a historic object to another or into an adjacent material. 浸出指可溶性物质从文物的原始位置向另一物体或相邻材料转移的行为。
life expectancy 预期寿命	Life expectancy is the period of time an object is considered useful before its changes in colour and density due to ageing are no longer tolerated. 预期寿命是指由于老化导致颜色和密度发生变化之前，可发挥其用途的时间段。
lift 抬升	You lift a fragile object from its burial environment using an artificial support to prevent further damage. 利用人工支撑物将易碎物品从其的埋葬环境中抬升，以防止其受到进一步损坏。
lifting 起翘	A surface layer on an object is lifting where areas have become partially detached from the substrate. 物体表面起翘指某些部分脱离基材的现象。
light damage 光退化	See photo-chemical degradation. 见光化学降解。
literature 已发表文献	The literature of a subject is its published body of knowledge. 某个主题的已发表文献是指与该主题相关的、已经发表的相关知识。
local treatment 局部修复	Local treatment is a conservation treatment on a small area of an object rather than on the whole object. 局部修复是针对修复对象的一小部分区域而非整体所进行的保护性处理。
long-term stability 长期稳定	Long-term stability denotes the durability of a material or object over a period of many years or decades. 若材料或物体在未来多年或数十年内的具有耐久稳定的状态，那么就是长期稳定的。
loss (1) 缺失 (1)	An object suffers loss when a part of the original material is missing. 缺失指物体的初始材料发生的减损。

lustre **光泽**	Lustre is the quality of light that is reflected from a surface. The lustre can vary: "splendent" from highly glossy opaque material such as polished haematite; "adamantine" from highly glossy transparent material such as diamond; "metallic", "vitreous","silky" and "dull" are descriptions of decreasingly brilliant lustre. On a ceramic, lustre is an iridescent glaze. 光泽是自器物表面反射出光的质感。不同物体光泽也不同：有的"灿烂光彩"来自不透明材料，如经过抛光的赤铁矿；有的"金刚石般的光泽"来自透明材料如钻石；使用"金属光泽"，"玻璃光泽"，"绢丝光泽"和"暗淡的"用以描述逐渐减少的光泽感。在陶瓷器表面上，呈现出虹彩玻璃光泽。
macromolecule 高分子	See polymer. 见聚合物。
macrophotography 宏观摄影	Macrophotography is a photographic method of documentation at moderate enlargement, between × 0.5 and 10. It is used to record a surface. 宏观摄影是放大倍率在0.5到10之间的摄影记录方法，主要用于记录器物表面状态。
manual dexterity 动手能力	Manual dexterity is hand skills demonstrated through practical work. 动手能力是通过实践显现出的手工技巧。
mark (1) 标识（1）	A mark is a symbol on an object which signifies its maker. 标识是器物上表明制造者信息的标志。
matrix 基质	The matrix of an object is the original extraneous matter in which it is embedded. The term is used especially of geological and archaeological specimens. 一个物体的基质是其内含的原始无关物质。这个术语特别用于地质和考古标本。
matte 哑光面	A matte surface is one that has a low gloss level. 哑光面指具有低光泽度的表面。
mechanical crack 机械裂纹	A mechanical crack is similar in appearance to an age crack. It is caused by external forces acting on a painting. 机械裂纹是外力作用对绘画作品引起的损伤，其外观与由老化造成的裂纹很相似。
mechanical damage 机械损伤	Mechanical damage is damage caused by physical factors and is usually the result of accidents, vandalism or normal use. In textiles, mechanical damage refers to cutting, tearing, fraying and abrasion. 机械性损伤是由物理因素引发的损伤，是意外事故、人为破坏或正常使用的结果。在纺织品中，机械损伤指切割，撕裂，磨损和擦伤。
mending 修补	a. Mending is the process of making minor repairs to a book without taking it apart or replacing any material. b. Mending is the process of making small repairs to sheets of paper, primarily to protect its structural integrity. a.修补是指对书籍进行细微修复，不拆散或替换书中任何材料的过程。 b.修补是指对纸张进行小修的过程，目的在于保护其结构完整性。

metal stain 金属污渍	A metal stain is an area of discolouration on the surface or within an object caused by contamination with metal corrosion products. For example, a metal stain can occur on a ceramic object caused by contact with a rusting iron rivet. 金属污渍是金属腐蚀产物污染了物体表面或内部区域所留下的变色区域。例如，与生锈的铁铆钉接触，陶瓷物体上会附着上金属污渍。
mentor 导师	A mentor is a senior member of the profession who provides guidance within a formal arrangement to a more junior member. 导师是指在某一领域中高级从业人员，经专门安排为初级人员提供职业指导。
micrograph 显微照片	A micrograph is a photograph taken through a microscope. 显微照片指通过显微镜拍摄出来的照片。
migration 迁移	Migration is the movement of ions, colour or stain within a material. 迁移是指材料内离子、颜色或者污渍的变化移动。
mottling 斑点状病害	Mottling on an object is damage that appears as patches or streaks of different colours. It is often caused by fungal or bacterial decay. 斑点通常由真菌或细菌腐烂引发，是一种病害，表现为物体上不同颜色的斑点或条纹。
multidisciplinary 多学科的	A multidisciplinary project is one that has more than one field of expertise involved. 多学科项目是涉及多个专业领域知识的项目。
museum standard retouch 博物馆修复标准	Museum standard retouch is a treatment used in cases where the original material should be readily distinguishable from any restoration, whilst allowing the viewer an appreciation of the object as a visual whole. 博物馆修复标准要求是指在修复过程中，使用的修复材料应与原始材料易于区分，并在同时照顾到观众欣赏物体时的整体视觉效果。
narrower term 狭义词	A narrower term is a term which has a more limited meaning than that covered by a wider term in a hierarchical taxonomy. For example a hammer (narrower term) is one type of hand tool (wider term). 狭义词是分层分类法中比广义词的含义更为狭义的术语。例如，锤子（狭义词）指一种手工工具（广义词）。
natural fibre 天然纤维	Natural fibres are fibres obtained from naturally occurring organic and inorganic materials. 天然纤维是从天然的有机和无机材料中获取的纤维。
natural light 自然光线	When you illuminate an object with natural light, the initial light source is daylight usually modified by reflection or filtering using a neutral coloured material. 当用自然光照明物体时，人们通过利用反射或使用中性色材料对初始光（通常为日光）进行调整。

neutralisation 中和作用	See deacidification. 见脱酸。
non-aqueous 非水的	A non-aqueous substance is one that is dissolved in a solvent other than water. 非水物质指溶于除水以外的溶剂中的物质。
non-ionic surfactant 非离子表面活性剂	A non-ionic surfactant is one in which the hydrophilic part contains no ions but interacts primarily through hydrogen bonds. 非离子表面活性剂是亲水部分不含离子，主要通过氢键发生相互作用的表面活性剂。
open pore 连通孔隙	An open pore in an object is a pore which is interconnected to others so as to allow infiltration by liquid or gases. 物体中的连通孔隙是指同其他孔隙相互连接，以便允许液体或气体渗透的孔隙。
operation 操作	An operation is a single step in a conservation treatment. 操作是修复流程中的一个环节。
oxidation 氧化	A material undergoes oxidation when it reacts chemically with oxygen. Both metals and organic materials undergo oxidation, frequently as part of a deterioration process. 当材料与氧气发生化学反应时，就会发生氧化反应。金属和有机材料都会发生氧化反应，通常也是物体劣化过程的步骤之一。
oxidising agent 氧化剂	An oxidising agent is a substance that provides oxygen to a substrate and removes hydrogen in the chemical reaction of oxidation. Oxidising agents react with the chromophores causing discoloration, rendering them colourless. 氧化剂是在氧化反应过程中向底物提供氧，并去除氢的物质。氧化剂与生色团反应导致其褪色。
oxygen scavenger 除氧剂	An oxygen scavenger is a substance which absorbs oxygen at low concentrations. It is used to keep enclosed areas, such as showcases and packaging, free of oxygen. Both iron oxide and zeolites are used as oxygen scavengers. 除氧剂是用来吸收低浓度氧气的物质，用于去除密闭区域中的氧气（如展示柜和包装盒）。氧化铁和沸石都可当作除氧剂。
pack 敷贴	See poultice. 见湿敷剂。
paste (1) 浆糊	Paste is a more or less viscous adhesive made by heating a water-starch mixture above its gelatinisation temperature (ca 85-90℃) for a prolonged period. Paste used for conservation purposes is mostly made from wheat or rice starch. 浆糊是一种粘性粘合剂，通过将水和淀粉混合物在一定时间内加热至超过糊化温度（约85-90℃）而制成。浆糊主要由小麦或大米淀粉制成，可用于修复。

paste (2) 粘贴 (2)	When you paste a material on an object, you apply paste or a pastelike adhesive to it, usually by using a brush, in order to bond it to the object. 粘贴材料时，通常使用刷子将浆糊或糊状粘合剂附着到材料上，以便将其粘在物体上。
patina 铜绿锈	a. A patina is a degraded surface of a material valued for its aesthetic qualities. b. Patina is a stable corrosion layer on a metal or other aged surface. It is often highly regarded by art collectors. a.铜绿锈是因其美学价值而备受重视的材料的腐蚀表层。b.铜绿锈是金属或其他表面老化后形成的稳定腐蚀层，它经常受到艺术品收藏家的推崇。
peeling 剥落	A surface that is peeling is deteriorating by losing layers. 表面剥落指器物因表层剥落缺失而导致的劣化现象。
penetration 渗透性	The penetration of a solution is the extent to which it passes into a historic material. This is important for solutions carrying consolidants and corrosion inhibitors. 溶液的渗透性是指其渗入文物材质的程度。这对含有加固材料和缓蚀剂的溶液非常重要。
permanent 耐久的	A material is permanent if it can withstand the influence of deteriorating agents indefinitely. 如果某种材料可以永远不受劣化剂的影响，那么它就是耐久的。
permeability 渗透性	Permeability is the rate of diffusion of a vapour through a specified film, usually expressed in gram per square metre per day $(g/m^2 \cdot d)$. 渗透性是水蒸气通过特定薄膜的渗透速率，通常以克每平方米每天（$g/m^2 \cdot d$）表示。
pesticide 杀虫剂	A pesticide is a substance that is used to kill pests, particularly insects and mammals. 杀虫剂指用于杀死害虫的一种物质，特别是一些昆虫和哺乳动物。
petrolatum 凡士林	Petrolatum is a mixture of mineral oils and waxes which forms a paste used as a lubricant and water repellent. 凡士林是矿物油和蜡的混合物，可用作润滑剂和防水剂。
pH-value pH 值	The pH-value of an aqueous solution is a measure of the acidity or alkalinity of the solution. It is expressed in a logarithmic scale of the hydrogen ions present in the solution -log[H+]. The scale ranges from 1 (acid) via 7 (neutral) to 14 (alkaline). 水溶液的 pH 值可用来衡量溶液的酸碱度，并用溶液中氢离子的对数来表示，范围从 1（酸）到 7（中性）再到 14（碱性）。
phase transition 相变	Phase transition denotes a change of crystalline structure of solids, or the conversion between solid, liquid or gaseous state. 相变表示固体的晶体结构变化，或表示固态，液态或气态之间的转化。

photo-chemical degradation 光化学降解	Photo-chemical degradation is chemical damage initiated by the energy of electromagnetic radiation. As a rule of thumb for solar radiation, half the damage results from UV and half from light. In textiles, the damage affects the chemical structure of the polymers and dyes. 光化学降解是由电磁辐射能量引发的化学损伤。根据太阳辐射的经验法则,一半的伤害来自紫外线,一半来自光。在纺织品中,降解会影响聚合物和染料的化学结构。
photodegradation 光降解	Photodegradation is the breakdown of a material following the absorption of light or UV radiation whose energy causes a chemical reaction. See also photo-chemical degradation. 光降解指材料在吸收光线或紫外线辐射后,能量变化引起化学反应,然后发生降解的过程。另见光化学降解。
photo-oxidation 光氧化	Photo-oxidation is the oxidation of a material under the influence of light or UV radiation. 光氧化指在光或紫外线照射下材料的氧化。
physical characteristics 物理特性	The physical characteristics of a material include strength, colour, density, magnetism and other properties that are exhibited without change of chemical structure. 材料的物理特性包括强度,颜色,密度,磁性和在不改变其化学结构的情况下展现出的其他特性。
pigment 颜料	A pigment is an insoluble fine powder that is used for colouring paints and other materials such as plastics and cement. 颜料是一种不溶性精细粉末,可为绘画作品和其他材料(如塑料和水泥)上色。
pit 坑	A pit is a small hemispherical loss from the surface of an object. 坑是指物体表面较小的半球状缺失。
pitting 点蚀	Pitting is a surface deterioration manifesting itself in the form of small, hemispherical losses. 点蚀是指以小的半球状缺失形式显现出的表面劣化。
plaster (1) 石膏 (1)	Plaster is a mixture in water of a binding agent (such as lime) and fillers which is applied as a covering to ceilings and walls. Plaster is frequently made with sands, aggregates or fibrous materials to provide reinforcement. 石膏是粘合剂(如石灰)和填料同水的混合物,可涂于天花板和墙壁表面。通常用沙子,骨料或纤维材料对石膏进行加固。
plaster of Paris 熟石膏	Plaster of Paris is made by partly dehydrating gypsum at ca $250℃$ to form the mineral bassanite $CaSO_4 \cdot 0.5H_2O$ which sets by hydration rapidly with the addition of water. Plaster of Paris is used for making casts and modelling. 熟石膏是将生石膏在$250℃$左右部分脱水,通过迅速加水发生水合作用而形成矿物$CaSO_4 \cdot 0.5H_2O$。熟石膏可用于制作铸型和石膏模型。

plastic (2) 可塑的 (2)	A plastic material is one that can be formed into a new shape that is retained in use. Examples are clay, horn, polyethene. 可塑材料是一种可塑化成型，形状保持不变的材料，如粘土，牛角，聚乙烯等。
polar solvent 极性溶剂	A polar solvent is one which interacts strongly with polar materials such as water. 极性溶剂是一种与极性材料（如水）发生强烈反应的溶剂。
polish (1) 抛光剂 (1)	A polish is a material that is rubbed into the surface of an object to make it glossy. 抛光剂指涂在物体表面，使其变得具有光泽的材料。
polish (2) 抛光	You polish a surface when you make it smooth or glossy by rubbing or fine abrasion. 对物体表面进行抛光是指通过摩擦或细磨物体使得其表面光滑或富有光泽。
pollutant 污染物	A pollutant is a contaminant of the normal clean environment. It may be a gas, liquid or solid. Some pollutants are damaging to historic materials, others are damaging to people, while others are damaging to the environment. 污染物是常规环境下的致污物。污染物可以是气体、液体或固体。有些污染物危害文物或危害人类健康，有些则会破坏环境。
polyester 聚酯	A polyester is a polymer made by reacting alcohol and organic acids together. Very high molecular weight poly(ethene terephthalate) PET, is used in the production of textile fibres, such as Terylene, and transparent films, such as Melinex. 聚酯是醇和有机酸的聚合物。高分子量的聚对苯二甲酸乙二酯PET可用于生产纺织纤维（如涤纶）和透明薄膜（如Melinex）。
polyester film 聚酯薄膜	A polyester film is an extruded film of polyethylene terephthalate (PET) made in different widths and thicknesses. It is highly transparent, strong (although easy to tear), durable, inert and chemically stable. 聚酯薄膜是以聚对苯二甲酸乙二醇酯（PET）为原料，采用挤出法制成的具有不同宽度和厚度的薄膜材料，具有高透明度、高强度（即使易于撕裂）、良好的耐久性、惰性和化学稳定性。
polyester resin 聚酯树脂	A polyester resin is formed from a mixture of a viyl monomer such as styrene with a polyester oligomer which contains reactive vinyl groups. The reaction between these is initiated with a peroxide radical source and is frequently catalysed with a cobalt compound. polyester resins are used for casting and for filling stone, glass and ceramics. 聚酯树脂由乙烯基单体（如苯乙烯）与含有反应性乙烯基团的聚酯齐聚物混合形成。这一反应由过氧化物自由基源引发，并且经常由钴化合物催化。聚酯树脂用于铸造以及填充石材，玻璃和陶瓷。

polymer 聚合物	A polymer is a molecule made up of many units of smaller molecules called monomers which are reacted together by polymerisation. There are a number of different reaction mechanisms used for polymerisation, such as condensation, free radial chain reaction, and oxidation. 高分子聚合物是由许多单体低分子通过聚合反应组成的分子。聚合反应包含有很多不同的反应机制，如缩合、自由基链反应和氧化等。
poor stability 稳定性差	Poor stability of an object denotes that without appropriate treatment the condition of the object is likely to deteriorate significantly within a short period of time. 物体的稳定性差意味着未经适当处理，物体的状态有可能会在短期内发生明显恶化。
pore 孔隙	A pore is a minute cavity in the body of an object or on its surface. The pore may be open, so allowing fluids to pass through, or closed. 孔隙是物体内部或表面上的微小空腔。孔隙可以是封闭的，也可以是允许液体流通的。
pore structure 孔隙结构	The pore structure of an object is the distribution of pores in the body. 物体的孔隙结构是物体内孔隙的分布状态。
porosity 孔隙率	The porosity of a material is the volume of its pores as a proportion of the gross volume of the material. 材料的孔隙率指材料中孔隙体积与材料总体积的比例。
portfolio (2) 文件夹 (2)	A portfolio is a portable case for presenting photographs, drawings and explanatory text used to demonstrate past work. 文件夹是用于展示过去工作中的照片，图片和说明性文字的便携式夹子。
poultice 湿敷剂	A poultice is a paste-like mixture used to draw out salts or stains from a porous body by capillary action and controlled evaporation. It is usually made by mixing an inert absorbent material with water or a chosen solvent. 湿敷剂是一种糊状混合物，通过毛细作用和可控的蒸发作用将多孔体中的盐或污渍吸出。湿敷剂通常由惰性吸收材料与水或选定的溶剂混合制成。
powdering 粉化	A surface is powdering when it is disintegrating into powder. 表面粉化指其崩解为粉末。
ppm ppm	1 ppm is a concentration of 1 part per million (0.0001 %). 1 ppm是百万分之一（0.0001%）的浓度。
preservation (1) 保存 (1)	The preservation of an object involves safeguarding its original or current state. 保存是指对物体进行修复和保护，使其处于最初状态或维持在当前状态。
primary material 原料	The primary material of an object is the substance used in its original construction. 原料是指器物在制作之初使用的材料。
priming (2) 底层	See ground (2). 见底层（2）。

pumice 浮石	A pumice is a porous volcanic rock used for polishing. It is used as a polishing stone. 浮石是用于抛光的多孔火山岩，可用作抛光石。
putty 腻子 / 油灰	a. Putty is a plastic material based on linseed oil and ground chalk, which is used as a filler and building material. It hardens over time. b. Putty is any synthetic material which has similar properties and uses to putty (a), such as epoxy putty. a.油灰是一种以亚麻籽油和白垩粉为基底的可塑材料，可用作填充料和建筑材料，并且随时间长度逐渐变硬。b.腻子指与油灰（a）具有类似属性和用途的合成材料，例如环氧腻子。
qualification 资质	A qualification is a formal award by an examining body that entitles a person to carry out a professional activity. 资质由审查机构正式授予，证明相关人员具备从事相关职业的正式资格。
reactivate 激发	You reactivate a latent adhesive by using heat or a solvent which makes the solid material tacky and able to form an adhesive bond with an object. Some latent adhesives are supplied as a free or supported film of material. 激发潜在粘合剂是指通过加热或使用能够让固体材料发粘的溶剂，激活粘合特性，使其与物体粘合在一起的过程。一些潜在的粘合剂通常以游离或载体薄膜的形式存在。
reassemble 重组	When you reassemble an object, you put back together the separated parts of the object in order to achieve the complete original construction. The separated parts may be treated or untreated. 重组需将对象的各部分拼接在一起，以达到其原始结构状态。实施对象的各个部分可以是经过修复处理或未处理的。
reconstruct 重建	When you reconstruct an object, you fill in a missing part of the object with new material to achieve an authentic appearance for the benefit of the public. 重建某一物体会对原始对象的缺失部分进行填充以呈现其真实外观，供大众欣赏。
reconstruction 重建	The reconstruction of an object is the creation of an imagined original state of the object based on documentary or material evidence of original attributes. The reconstruction may incorporate some of the original materials and may be in 2- or 3- dimensional form. Reconstructions aim to be easily reversible and detectable by experts. 重建是指根据原始文献或材料中对建造对象想象中的状态和特性描述来创建实体。重建可能会包含一些二维或三维形式的原始材料。重建应力争具有可逆性和检测性。
reducing agent 还原剂	A reducing agent is a substance which provides hydrogen and removes oxygen in the substrate in the chemical reaction of reduction. Reducing agents are used for bleaching. They react with some chromophores, rendering them colourless. 还原剂是在还原反应中为底物提供氢并去除氧的物质。还原剂可用于漂白，与某些生色团发生反应使其变为无色。

refractive index 折射率	The refractive index of a material is the ratio of the velocity of light in a vacuum to its velocity in the material. 折射率指光在真空中的传播速度与光在该介质中的传播速度之比。
reinforce 加强	You reinforce an object or a component part by the addition of a new material which is attached to the original in order to strengthen or support it. 加固是指在原始材料上填补新材料以加固物体本身或其组件，以增强并给予物体支撑。
reinforcement 加固	Reinforcement of a material is any treatment that strengthens this material. Some of the main types of reinforcement are stitching, repairing, mending, lining, lamination, or encapsulation. 材料加固是指能够提高材料强度的任何处理方法。一些主要的加固类型有缝合、修补、打补丁、托背纸、层压或封装等。
release agent 脱模剂	A release agent is an agent used during casting or moulding to prevent the liquid material from adhering to the mould during setting. Release agents are typically oily or hydrophilic materials which are chosen to have little cohesive strength or to have poor adhesion to the mould or casting medium. 脱模剂是在铸造或制模过程中为防止液体材料在定型时中粘附到模具上的一种试剂。脱模剂通常为油性或亲水性材料，具有很小的内聚强度或与模具或铸造介质的附着力差。
render 灰泥	See stucco. 见灰泥。
repair 进行修复	A building or object which cannot fulfil its designated function is repaired when the defects, damage or decay are remedied with the intention of returning a building or object to a previous condition or use. 当建筑物或某个物体无法发挥其最初功能时，就需要对其缺失，损坏或腐烂的地方进行修复，达到恢复其最初状态的目的。
repairing 修补	In paper conservation, repairing is a treatment of mechanical damage, which is applied with the aim of strengthening a piece of paper, a book cover or its pages. Repairing can be in the form of mending tears and/or filling in losses. 在纸张修复中，修补是一种应对外力损伤的处理方法，目的在于提高纸张，封皮或书本页面的强度。修复手段包含修补断裂或残损缺失等形式。
reshaping 重塑	Reshaping is work aiming at returning an object to its original form following distortion. 重塑是指将变形后的对象修复到原始形状的工作。
resin (1) 树脂 (1)	A plant resin is a viscous liquid exuded from a plant which hardens on exposure to air to become an amorphous, generally brittle, solid. This solid is insoluble in water and some fossil resins are also insoluble in organic solvents. Most plant resins are composed primarily of low molecular weight terpenoid compounds. Examples are colophony, dammar and mastic. 植物树脂是从植物中渗出的粘性液体，暴露于空气后会逐渐逐硬，变成无定形的脆性固体。固体树脂不溶于水，某些化石树脂也不溶于有机溶剂。大多数植物树脂主要是由低分子量萜类化合物构成。例如松香，达马(树)脂和乳香。

restoration (1) 修复 (1)	Restoration is the treatment of an object that adds material in order to create the semblance of its original appearance or structure. This is carried out to aid interpretation, use or aesthetic appreciation. 修复即对物体填补材料以恢复其初始外观或结构，从而更好诠释其内涵，应用或艺术美感。
restore 复原	When you restore an object, you replace missing or damaged parts of the object in order to recreate the original appearance and function of the object. 当复原物体时，需要对物体缺失或损坏的部分进行修复，以恢复物体最初的面貌和功能。
reversibility 可逆性	a. Reversibility is the extent to which the effect of a treatment can be undone. b. Reversibility is the ability of an applied material to be (largely) removed without damaging the object it was applied to. a.可逆性是指能够取消修复效果的程度。b.可逆性指（很大程度上）将施加在物体上的材料去除，对物体也不会造成损坏。
rinsing 冲洗	In paper conservation, rinsing is a treatment where an object containing unwanted chemicals is soaked in water in order for the chemicals to dissolve and be eliminated. The unwanted chemicals may be part of the dirt or may have been added to the object during an earlier treatment. 在纸张修复中，冲洗是指将含有多余化学物质的物体浸入水中，使化学物质溶解进而消除的处理方法。这些多余的化学物质可能是污垢的一部分，或者也可能是早期修复过程中导致纸张残留的物质。
rip 撕裂	See tear. 见撕破。
rodent attack 鼠类病害	Rodent attack is damage caused by mice or rats. Rodents chew pieces of nest material out of objects and soil them with urine and faeces. 鼠类病害至鼠类引起的病害。鼠类将文物咬碎筑巢，其排泄分泌物还对文物造成污染。
sand blasting 喷砂	Sand blasting is a powerful method of air abrasion using sand. 喷砂是指以空气为动力用砂子对物体表面进行处理的一种方法。
sand tray 砂盘	A sand tray is a container filled with granular material, usually sand, used to support fragments in the correct alignment during adhesion. The fragments are balanced on each other so allowing the action of gravity to close the join in a non-invasive manner 砂盘是一个含有颗粒（通常为沙子）的容器，在粘合时以正确的对齐方式支撑碎片。碎片彼此处于平衡状态，因此在重力作用下可以用非侵入性的方法连接结合点。
saturated pore 饱和孔隙	A saturated pore is a pore that is filled with fluid. 饱和孔隙是指充满液体的孔隙。
scalloping 扇形饰边	See stress garlands. 见模压花边。

scraping 刮除	When you clean a surface by scraping, you remove material by carefully drawing a blade across the surface. Overpaint and insoluble deposits are removed this way. 使用刀片刮除物体表面附着物，可用来清除掉多余的绘料和难溶的沉积物。
scratch 刮痕	A scratch is a shallow cut in a surface caused by something sharp. A scratch may be a form of damage or may be an intentional mark, for instance in certain decorative processes, such as scraffito. 划痕是锋利物体对物体表面造成的较浅的切口。划痕可以是一种损伤形式，也可以有意而为的痕迹，诸如刮涂等装饰过程中人为制造的痕迹。
screen printing 丝网印刷	Screen printing is a decorative technique involving a "screen", which is a fine mesh fixed on a frame. A design is made on a stencil which can be made of various materials: paper, plastic film or resin. 丝网印刷是一种涉及"丝网"的装饰性技术，是固定在框架上的细网，可由多种材料制成；可在纸张，塑料薄膜或树脂的模板上进行设计。
secondary material 二次添加材料	The secondary material of an object is substance deliberately added to the object during its working life. 二次添加材料是器物在使用过程中再次专门添加的材料。
sequestering agent 螯合剂	A sequestering agent is an chemical that forms a complex with a metal ion in solution so that the metal ion cannot react. See also chelating agent. 螯合剂是一种与溶液中的金属离子形成络合物的化学物质，与金属离子不发生反应。另见螯合剂。
set 固化	A medium sets when it converts from its liquid to solid state, for example by loss of solvent or by freezing. 当介质从液体状态转变为固态状态时（如溶剂流失或被冷冻），介质就会凝固。
shellac 虫胶	Shellac is a partly refined yellowish natural resin secreted by the lac insect (Lacifer lacca). Shellac produces a smooth durable film when deposited from alcohol solution and is used in varnishes, polishes and leather dressings. 虫胶是由紫胶虫（Lacifer lacca）分泌物精制的淡黄色天然树脂。其溶液在酒精挥发后，可产生光滑耐用的薄膜，用于上光油、抛光和皮革敷料中。
shrinkage (1) 收缩 (1)	Shrinkage is the reduction of volume or linear dimension. This may occur as a result of drying or setting of an adhesive. 收缩指体积或线性尺寸的缩小，这可能是由粘合剂干燥或凝固导致的结果。
shrinkage temperature 收缩温度	The shrinkage temperature of a collagen structure is the temperature at which the protein molecules denature and contract, causing a permanent shrinkage. The shrinkage temperature reduces as the collagen degrades and is used to diagnose the state of the structure of leather. 胶原蛋白结构的收缩温度是指蛋白质分子变性和收缩，并引起永久性收缩的温度。当胶原蛋白降解时，收缩温度会降低，这可用于诊断皮革结构状态。

silicone release paper 有机硅防粘纸	Silicone release paper is usually used as in interlayer to prevent adhesion to the underlying substrate because of the silicone coating. It is used commonly in processes such as heat sealing, where the paper separates the heating surface from adhering to other objects. 有机硅防粘纸通常作为中间层，防止硅酮涂层粘附到下面的材质。它通常用于热封，在此过程中，防粘纸能将受热物体的表面隔离开，防止其粘附其他物体上。
site 遗址	A site is a place in which there are identified archaeological remains, a historic property or features of special scientific interest. 遗址指已发现的考古遗址、历史遗迹或具有特殊科学价值特征的地方。
size (1) 胶料 (1)	Size is a substance used to improve the resistance of a material to the penetration of liquids such as water or ink. Main types are gelatin, glue, starch, rosin, modified celluloses, casein, or synthetic resins. 胶料是用于提升材料对水或墨水等液体渗透抵抗力的物质，主要类型为明胶，胶水，淀粉，松香，改性纤维素，酪蛋白或合成树脂。
soak (1) 浸泡 (1)	You soak an object when you place it into a liquid for an extended period as part of a treatment. 浸泡指将物体长时间放置在液体中的一种处理手段。
soap 肥皂	Soap is an anionic surfactant which is an alkali salt of a fatty acid. It is produced by hydrolysing triglycerides from animal and vegetable fats and oils with an alkali. 肥皂是一种阴离子表面活性剂，是脂肪酸的碱盐。它由动植物油脂中的甘油三酸酯和碱水解制成。
softened water 软化水	Softened water is water in which the soluble calcium and magnesium ions causing hardness have been made inactive. This can be achieved either by ion exchange, using a water softening apparatus, or by adding a chelating agent. See also purified water. 水的可溶性钙和镁离子影响了水的硬度。软化水指把水中的可溶性钙和镁离子去除后的水。软化水可通过水软化设备的离子交换或添加螯合剂而制成。另见纯净水。
soil 沾污	See dirt. 见污垢。
soiling 污染	Soiling is the accumulation of unwanted material on an object caused, for instance, by the accretion of atmospheric pollution or oils from manipulation. It usually refers to damage to historical objects, as opposed to objects in the ground. 污染指器物上因特殊原因造成多余物质的堆积，如因大气污染物累积或人工操作造成的油脂堆积。它通常指对文物的污损，而不是地下所有物件。
solvent 溶剂	A solvent is a liquid that can dissolve another substance, solid, liquid or gas. 溶剂是能够溶解另一种物质（固体，液体或气体）的液体。

solvent cleaning 溶剂清洗	Solvent cleaning of textiles is cleaning using non-aqueous solutions. Solvent cleaning is used when dirt and grime are insoluble in water or when there are materials present such as dyes which bleed in water. 通常对纺织品使用非水溶液进行溶剂清洗。当污垢不溶于水或（物体或材料中）存在易在水中渗出的物质时，例如染料，则使用溶剂清洗。
spalling 剥离	Spalling is the surface detachment and loss of chips from an object, caused by chemical, physical or biological action. The chips usually leave a conchoidal depression in the material of the object. 剥离是由于化学，物理或生物作用引起的物体表面剥落或物体的碎屑脱落。碎屑脱落通常会在材料上留下贝壳状的凹陷。
splitting 分裂	Splitting is deterioration resulting from separation of laminations in a material such as stone caused by chemical, physical or biological action. 分裂指在化学，物理或生物作用下，材料（如石材）中薄片脱落的劣化现象。
stabilised 稳定处理	An object which has been stabilised has received a treatment that prevents deterioration which had been occurring previously. 稳定处理后可以让物体免受先前发生的病害。
stable 稳定的	A stable object is one that will not change in the conditions it is likely to experience. 物体稳定是指在可能遭遇的情况下，也不会发生改变的物体。
stable colour 显色稳定	a. A stable colour is a colourant that will not bleed when submerged in an aqueous or solvent solution. b. See fast colour. a.显色稳定指当色剂与水溶液或溶剂相遇后，不会掺混其他颜色的现象。b.另见不褪色剂。
stain (2) 污渍 (2)	A stain is a discolouration of an object caused by the deposition of a contaminant from a solution. The stain can be fixed to the object like a dye. 污渍是指因溶液中污染物的沉积引起的物体变色。污渍像染色一样固定在物体上。
starch adhesive 淀粉粘合剂	Starch adhesive is an adhesive which is made from starch. In textile conservation, starch adhesives are used to attach backings to textiles. 淀粉粘合剂是由淀粉制成，在纺织品修复中，淀粉粘合剂可以将背衬与纺织品粘粘在一起。
starch paste 浆糊	See paste and starch adhesive. 见糨糊和淀粉粘合剂。
steam cleaning 蒸汽清洗	Steam cleaning is cleaning that uses steam to soften deposits and assist their removal from wall and other surfaces. Sometimes high-pressure steam is used in order to force off stubborn deposits such as chewing gum. 蒸汽清洁是指使用蒸汽来软化沉积物，并将其从墙壁和其他表面清除掉的一种清洁方式，有时还会使用高压蒸汽来清除顽固性沉淀物，例如口香糖等。

steaming 汽蒸法	Steaming is a treatment that uses steam to humidify organic materials, such as basketry, in order to make them more plastic and enable the object to be re-shaped. 汽蒸法是指用蒸汽对有机材料（例如编织品）进行加湿的处理方法，这样可使物体变得柔软，易于重新塑形。
sterilise 灭菌处理	You sterilise an object by killing all the micro-organisms, such as bacteria and fungi, in the object by the use of high temperature, chemicals or radiation. 通过使用高温，化学物品或辐射等手段对物体进行灭菌处理，杀除物体含有的微生物（例如细菌和真菌）。
strain 应变	Strain is the deformation of a material due to stress. It is expressed as the ratio of the distortion divided by original length. 应变是由应力导致的材料变形，表现为变形长度与原始长度的比率。
strain cracking 应变开裂	Strain cracking is cracking caused by the strain on an object. 应变开裂是由物体应力引起的开裂。
stress 压力	Stress is the force acting in or on an object and tending to deform it. The stress is expressed as the force divided by the area over which it is applied. 压力是作用在物体上或物体中使之变形的力。计算方法是压强除以受力面积。
striation 擦痕	A surface with striations is one which is marked with parallel scratches or grooves. 擦痕指物体表面上的平行划痕或凹槽。
structural consolidation 结构性加固	Structural consolidation of an object is the addition of a consolidant in order to increase the ability of the object to resist gravitational and major disruptive forces. 结构性加固是指注入加固剂，以增加物体抵抗重力和其他主要破坏力的能力。
stucco 灰泥	Stucco is a traditional decorative plaster based on lime. Its surface may be lined out in imitation of ashlar stone. 灰泥是以石灰为主的传统性装饰石膏，它可以像方石一样排列。
sturgeon glue 鱼鳔胶	Sturgeon glue is a glue made from the swim bladders of sturgeon. 鱼鳔胶是鲟鱼鳔制成的胶。
substrate (1) 基材（1）	The substrate is the material which forms the main structure of the object, such as the wooden core of a polychrome sculpture. 基材指形成物体主要结构的材料，如彩色雕塑的木芯。
sulfide gases 硫化气体	Sulfide gases, such as hydrogen sulfide and carbonyl sulfide, are pollutant gases derived from biological and geochemical sources. 诸如硫化氢和羰基硫之类的硫化物气体，源自生物和地球化学来源的污染物气体。

surface dirt 表面污垢	Surface dirt or debris is dirt which is loosely adhered to the surface of an object and thus easily removed. 表面污垢或碎屑指松散地黏着在物体表面，且易于清除的污垢。
swelling 溶胀	Swelling is the vertical expansion of a colloid due to the incorporation of a liquid. It is used to create images in a variety of processes, like carbon transfer and carbro, dye transfer, oil and bromoil, or Technicolor. 溶胀指由于掺入液体而引起的胶体的纵向扩张。溶胀经一系列处理后可用于创建图像，比如碳纸晒印和碳溴印相、染料转移，油和溴化油印相法或彩色印片法等。
tape (1) 带 (1)	A tape is a narrow band of a flexible material. It can consist of a woven fabric, paper, leather, parchment or plastic. 带是一条柔性材料组成的窄带子，可以由机织织物、纸张、皮革、羊皮纸或塑料制成。
taxonomy 分类法	Taxonomy is a systematic classification of a category of things, typically plants and animals, by comparing their similarities. 分类法是通过比较相近特征的不同，对一类事物进行系统分类，在分析动植物的时候经常使用该法。
tear 撕裂	A tear is a split or rent in a flexible material, such as paper or textile, which results in no loss of material and little distortion. It is a mechanical damage usually caused by the forcible pulling apart of the flexible material. 撕裂是指柔性材料（如纸张或纺织品）中的裂痕或碎片，不会导致材料缺失，但是会发生轻微变形。撕裂通常是将柔性材料强行拉开而引起的机械损伤。
tension 张力	Tension is a force that stretches an object. Excessive tension on textiles results in mechanical damage such as deformation, splits and tears. 张力代表拉伸物体的力。如果纺织品的张力过大，会导致机械性损伤，如变形，开裂和撕裂等。
terrestrial artefacts 地上文物	Terrestrial artefacts are archaeological finds from land sites (as opposed to water). 地上文物文物是指在陆地上（与水下相对）的考古发现。
translucent 半透明的	A translucent material is one that transmits and diffuses light but does not allow a well defined image to be seen through it. 半透明材料是指能传播和漫射光线，但不能通过它看到清晰图像的一种材料。
transparent coatings 透明涂料	Transparent coatings are visually inobtrusive transparent varnish coatings which are sometimes applied to metal surfaces such as silver for corrosion protection. 透明涂料指视觉上不引人注目的透明清光油层，有时应用于金属表面（如银）以防腐蚀。
unstable 不稳定的	An unstable object or material is one that is liable to deterioration under specified conditions. 物体或材料不稳定指在特定条件下易于劣化的物体或材料。

unstable colour 不稳定着色剂	a. An unstable colour is a colourant that will bleed when submerged in an aqueous or solvent solution. b. An unstable colour is a colourant that changes under a specific influence, such as that of light, acids or alkalis. a.不稳定着色剂指在浸没于水溶液或其他溶液时，会渗出的着色剂。b.不稳定着色剂指在遇光照、酸或碱等情况下，会产生变化的着色剂。
vacuum cleaning 真空除尘	Vacuum cleaning is a type of cleaning that removes dust or loosely attached dirt and debris from the surface of an object by using a machine which sucks up air and the entrained dirt. 真空除尘是一种通过使用能吸出空气及其附带污垢的机器，去除物体的表面灰尘或附着在表面的松散污垢和碎屑的清洁方式。
vacuum impregnate 真空浸渍	You vacuum impregnate an object when you introduce a fluid material into an object by extracting the air from it before or after placing the material. 真空浸渍指在将流体材料引入物体中之前，通过抽出物体内部空气后再对其进行浸渍处理。
vacuum tweezer 真空镊子	A vacuum tweezer is a tool for manipulating small pieces of material, using suction from a vacuum pump through a nozzle on which the piece is held by air pressure. 真空镊子是处理小件材料的工具，在气压作用下利用真空泵的吸力通过喷嘴吸住物体。
vapour bath 蒸气浴	A vapour bath is a micro-climate containing solvent vapour used to soften an adhesive in a previously repaired object. 蒸气浴是含有溶剂蒸汽的微气候，可将之前修复过的物体中的粘合剂软化。
vapour phase deacidification 气相脱酸	Vapour phase deacidification is a chemical treatment used to neutralise unwanted acids present in an object by subjecting it to a gaseous or vapour deacidification agent that reacts with the unwanted acids. 气相脱酸是一种化学处理，通过将物体中与气态或蒸气的脱酸剂发生反应来中和物体中的有害酸成分。
vapour treatment 蒸气处理	A vapour treatment is the use of solvent vapour to soften a component of an object. This is achieved by letting the vapour slowly penetrate the object. See also humidification. 蒸气处理指使用溶剂蒸气来软化物体成分的方法，蒸气会缓慢渗透进物体，从而达到软化效果。另见加湿。
varnish 清漆 / 光油	a. A varnish is a solution of a film forming material which dries to a hard shiny layer. b. A varnish is a transparent coating that protects or enhances the appearance of a surface. a.清漆是成膜材料的溶剂干燥后成为坚韧的光泽层。b.光油是一种透明涂层，可保护或改善外观。
veneer 饰面薄板	A veneer is a decorative or wearing layer applied to a structural or utilitarian substrate, usually of wood. 饰面薄板是通常用于木材结构或实用性基底的装饰层或耐磨层。

vermin 有害动物	Vermin are mammal pests, such as mice and rats, which attack collections of historic material. 有害动物一般为哺乳类，如鼠类，它们会啃咬文物。
vibration stress 振动应力	Vibration stress is the internal forces caused by vibration in a material or element of construction, which can lead to damage. 振动应力是由建筑材料或结构中的振动引发的导致物体损伤的内力。
vinyl resin 乙烯基树脂	A vinyl resin is a thermoplastic formed from vinyl monomers, such as H2C=CH-. 乙烯基树脂是由乙烯基单体形成的热塑性材料，例如 H 2 C ＝ CH-。
void 孔洞	A void in a material is a hole, space, cavity or pore. 孔洞是物料上有孔，空间，空腔或孔的地方。
warp (2) 卷翘 (2)	When a flat object warps, it distorts out of plane. This is used generally of wooden objects that deteriorate due to heat or humidity changes. 当平面物体卷翘时，其会在平面外扭曲。通常为木制品因热度或湿度变化时发生的劣化。
wash fastness 耐洗性	Wash fastness is the ability of coloured materials to resist loss of colour under wet cleaning. 耐洗性指有色材料在湿法清洗下抵抗褪色的能力。
washing 清洗	Washing is a cleaning process where the object is immersed in an aqueous solution of a surfactant (detergent) and/or other additives. Washing is normally followed by rinsing. 清洗是指将物体浸入表面活性剂（洗涤剂）和/或其他添加剂的水溶液中的一种清洁程序，清洗过后往往会开始冲洗的步骤。
water 水	Water is a clear volatile liquid. Water usually contains impurities which can be more or less removed by various methods such as distillation, ion exchange or adsorption. 水是透明的挥发性液体，或多或少含有些许杂质，但是可以通过各种方法（例如蒸馏、离子交换或吸附）将杂质去除。
water damage 水害	Water damage on an object is deterioration caused by previous contact with water. The effects on organic materials are characteristic and identifiable. 水害是因文物此前与水接触而发生的劣化现象。水害对有机材料的危害严重，易于识别。
water mist 水雾	A water mist is a fine water spray used for the gentle cleaning of masonry surfaces and buildings by keeping the dirt wet, softening it and enabling it to be washed off. 水雾是通过喷水雾的方式，润湿、软化和冲掉污垢的方法，目的在于较为温和地清洁砖石建筑和其他建筑物的表面。
water repellent 防水剂	A water repellent is a material applied to a surface that ensures water is shed from the surface. Porous building materials such as brick and stone are treated with water repellents like waxes or silicone oils, which prevent the penetration of water. 防水剂是一种应用于表面的材料，可确保水从表面滑落。多孔建筑材料（例如砖块和石材）用防水剂（如蜡或硅油）处理，以防止水渗透。

waterlogged 饱水的	A waterlogged material is one that has all its pores and internal volume saturated with water, due to prolonged submersion in water. This is usually accompanied by a breakdown of the cell walls of the organic material, which leaves it fragile and easily damaged. 饱水材料指由于长时间浸在水中，物体的所有孔和内部体积都充满了水，这通常伴随有机材料细胞壁破裂，使其变得易碎和容易损坏。
waterproof 防水	You waterproof the surface of a porous material by applying a treatment that makes the surface hydrophobic, using a coating or a surface alteration. This is carried out in order to improve water repellency and weather resistance. 通过使用涂层或对多孔材料表面进行防水处理，可以使物体表面不易被水沾湿，这样做能提高防水性和耐候性。
wax 蜡	Wax is a solid or semi-solid organic thermoplastic substance that is produced by an animal or plant, such as beeswax or carnauba, or a high molecular weight (C20-C40) hydrocarbon extracted from mineral oil with similar characteristics, such as microcrystalline wax. 蜡是一种动植物生成的固体或半固体的有机热塑性物质，如蜂蜡和巴西棕榈，或是从具有类似特性的矿物油中提取的高分子量（C20-C40）碳氢化合物。
wax mould 蜡模	A wax mould is a negative shape made from an object that is copied as a positive. 蜡模为阴模，即从物体复制品阳模翻制而成。
wear 磨损	An object wears when parts erode or rub away because of use. 当使用中的零件发生腐蚀或摩擦时，就会发生磨损。
wear and tear 磨损和撕裂	Wear and tear is the damage or deterioration of an object caused by normal usage. 磨损和撕裂指由于正常使用而导致的物体损伤或劣变。
weathering (1) 风化作用 (1)	The weathering of an object or building is the damage caused by exposure to the external environment resulting in surface erosion and decay. 物体或建筑物的风化是一种由于暴露在外部环境而导致的表面腐蚀和腐烂的损害。
weeping iron 渗液状铁器	Weeping iron is a phenomenon indicating active corrosion of archaeological iron which contains chloride concentrations. 渗液状铁器是含有较高氯离子浓度的考古铸铁的活性腐蚀现象。
wet 润湿	When a liquid wets a surface, the liquid flows more or less spontaneously onver the surface. The extent of wetting depends on the relative surface tensions, the viscosity of the liquid and the time allowed for flow. Increased wetting improves, for example the cleaning effect of a solution, and the colour saturation of a pigment by a medium. 当液体润湿物体表面时，液体或多或少会在表面流动，而润湿程度取决于相对的表面张力、液体粘度和流动时间。湿度的增加可以提高溶液的清洁效果以及颜料在介质中的色饱和度。

wet pack 湿敷贴	See poultice. 见湿敷剂。
wettability 润湿性	Wettability refers to a surface being either hydrophobic (water runs off in drops) or hydrophilic (water forms a continuous film). 润湿性指物体表面是疏水（水流成滴状）还是亲水（水形成连续膜）。
whiskers 高强度单晶细丝	Whiskers are high strength single crystal filaments used, for example, in fibre-reinforced materials. 高强度单晶细丝，可用于纤维增强材料等。
wider term 广义词	A wider term is a term that includes a number of related concepts in a hierarchical taxonomy. See also narrower term. 广义词是分层分类法中涵盖多个相关概念的术语。另见狭义词。
wollastonite 硅灰石	Wollastonite is a product found on devitritified glass. 硅灰石是玻璃质脱玻化后的产物。
working life (1) 使用寿命 (1)	The working life of an object is the period from its original manufacture, through modification to its being discarded. 器物的使用寿命指其从最初制造生产、改进再到被废弃的时间区段。
yellowing 泛黄的	Yellowing of a material is a colour change to yellow or yellow-brown. It is chemical damage caused by some deterioration mechanisms usually involving oxidation and is often associated with deterioration and brittleness. The yellow colour is due to the increase in blue light absorption by the chromophores which are created during the reactions. Yellowing of paper occurs under the influence of light and/or physical/chemical deterioration processes. Yellowing of oil paints is the creation of chromophores during oxidation in the dark. 材料泛黄指颜色变为黄色或黄棕色。它是一种由包括氧化的劣化机制引发的化学损害，一般与劣化反应和脆性相关。黄色是由于反应过程中产生的发色团对蓝光的吸收增加所致。纸张泛黄是在光和/或物理/化学变质过程的影响下发生的。油画黄化是由于黑暗环境中氧化过程产生了发色基团。

02

藏品管理
Collection Management

absolute humidity 绝对湿度	Absolute humidity is the amount of water vapour that is held in a given sample of air. 绝对湿度指给定空气样本中保持的水蒸气量。
accession 接收与登账	When you accession an object or collection, you accept it formally into a museum collection by a process of registration and documentation. 器物或藏品的接收与登账，是通过登记和入账的流程将其正式确定为博物馆藏品。
accommodation 存储处	Accommodation is the designated space for a specific purpose such as storage or a laboratory. 存储处指用于特定目的的指定空间，如库房或实验室。
acd 换气次数/天	See air changes/day. 见换气次数/天。
acid precipitation 酸性降水	Acid precipitation is rain, snow or mist contaminated by the reaction of atmospheric moisture with sulphur dioxide and oxides of nitrogen from industrial and vehicle emissions. 酸性降水是指大气中的水分与工业和汽车排放物中的二氧化硫和氮氧化物反应而污染的雨、雪或雾。
acid rain 酸雨	See acid precipitation. 见酸雨。
acid-free paper 无酸纸	Acid-free paper is paper that has a pH of 7 or above and may contain acid absorbing materials such as calcium carbonate. Acid-free paper is widely used both for wrapping and added as a conservation material. 无酸纸是指pH值为7或更高的纸，其中可能包含碳酸钙等吸酸材料。无酸纸广泛用于包装和文物保护。
acquisition 征集	An acquisition is an object (or group of objects) which has been added to a collection by gift, loan, purchase or fieldwork. If appropriate, this object will then be accessioned. 藏品征集是通过捐赠、租借、购买或田野考古与调查的方式将器物（或一组器物）添加到藏品中。如果合适，该器物将被正式登入入藏。
acquisition policy 藏品征集制度	The acquisition policy of an organisation is a formal document which defines the categories and the process of acceptance of additional material. 某机构的藏品征集制度是机构定义需要征集藏品的类别和其入馆手续的正式文件。
advocacy 宣传	Advocacy is the active support of a cause such as by giving presentations about conservation to lay audiences. 宣传是对事业的积极支持，例如，通过向非专业观众进行有关文物保护的演讲。
aerosol 气溶胶	An aerosol is a stable dispersion of airborne solid or liquid. This can deposit when it comes into contact with the materials of a building or object. 气溶胶是指悬浮在气体中的固态或液态颗粒所组成的稳定分散系统。当它与建筑物或器物的材料接触时，其可能会发生沉积。

Airbrasive®unit	An Airbrasive® unit is equipment manufactured to control air abrasive treatment Airbrasive®装置（商标名）是用于控制空气研磨处理的设备
air conditioning 空气调控	Air conditioning is the control of various qualities of the air, such as temperature, humidity and pollutants. This is usually achieved by mechanically circulating air through various components. 空气调控是对各种空气质量的控制，如温度，湿度和污染物。这通常是通过使空气机械循环通过各种组件来实现的。这通常是通过各个组件机械循环空气来实现的。
air pollution 空气污染	Air pollution is airborne gaseous and particulate matter that is not a component of normal clean air. Depending on type of pollutant, air pollution may be damaging to objects or people. 空气污染是指空气中的气态和微粒物质，它们不属于正常清洁空气的组成部分。不同的污染物，可能会损害器物或人。
air purification 空气净化	Air purification is the process of filtering or absorbing pollutants from a building or cabinet by using ducted air from mechanical plants. 空气净化是利用来自机械设备的风管过滤或吸收建筑物或展柜中污染物的过程。
airtight cabinet 气密柜	An airtight cabinet is one that has a very low rate of air exchange with the surrounding atmosphere, typically less than 0.1 air changes/day. 气密柜是一种与周围大气的空气交换速率非常低的柜，通常每天少于0.1次换气。
alphabetical catalogue 字母目录	An alphabetical catalogue is one that lists all objects in a collection or exhibition in alphabetical order. 字母目录是按字母顺序列出藏品或展览中所有器物的目录。
amenity group 便利设施组织	An amenity group is a national group or society that promotes a greater understanding for a particular period of history, together with its associated architecture and decorative arts. It often fulfills the role of statutory consultee in legislative processes. 便利设施组织指为促进对某段历史及其相关建筑和装饰艺术的认识而成立的社团。它们通常在特定立法过程中履行法定顾问的角色。
Arboflex 500®	Arboflex 500 is a butyl rubber and one of the more stable hydrocarbon elastomers. It resembles modelling clay in consistency and is used to fill the gap between the glass and the lead in stained glass panels. It does not set but will become brittle over t Arboflex 500®（商标名）是一种丁基橡胶，是较为稳定的碳氢化合物弹性体之一。在一致性上类似于造型粘土，用于填充彩色玻璃面板中玻璃和铅之间的间隙。它不会凝固，
anaerobic 厌氧的	An anaerobic environment is one that has very low oxygen levels. 厌氧环境是氧气含量极低的环境。

archive (1) 档案 (1)	An archive is a collection of public or historical records intended to survive in perpetuity. 档案是旨在永久保存的公共或历史记录。
archivist 档案管理员	An archivist works on, and/or has responsibility for, a collection of public or historical records. 档案管理员从事公共记录或历史记录管理工作，并对其负责。
artefact (1) 人工制品 (1)	An artefact is an object or feature that has been produced by human workmanship or activity. 人工制品是由人类加工制作或人类活动产生的遗物或遗迹。
artificial light 人造光源	Artificial light is a light that comes from a light source other than natural daylight. 人造光源是自然光源以外的光源。
assessment 评估	An assessment is the evaluation of an object or collection for conservation needs. 评估是出于保护需求而针对器物或藏品的评价。
atmosphere 大气 / 空气环境	The atmosphere of an object is the air surrounding it. 器物所处大气环境指其周围的空气。
attendance 参观人数	Attendance is the number of visitors to a museum or historic property. 参观人数是参观博物馆或历史古迹的人数。
attribution 归属 / 鉴定	Attribution is a judgement associating a historic object or work of art with a particular artist, maker or school. 归属是将历史器物或艺术品与特定艺术家、制造者或学派联系起来的判断。
Audience 受众	An audience is the recipients or prospective recipients of a particular activity, such as an exhibition or publication. 受众是特定活动（如展览或出版）的接收者或预期接收者。
automated **surveillance** 自动监测	Automated surveillance is surveillance that is provided by electronic security devices, such as close circuit television. 自动监测是由电子安全设备（如闭路电视）提供的监测。
backlog 积压工作	A backlog of work is the amount of work that has not been completed to schedule or remains unfinished. 积压工作是指尚未按计划完成的工作或尚未完成的工作量。
barrier (1) 防护栏	A barrier is a physical structure which deters or prevents visitors from touching objects on display. 防护栏是一种可以阻止或防止观众触摸展品的物理结构。
borrower （藏品）借用方	A borrower is an individual or an institution that receives an item or collection on loan. （藏品）借用方指通过借用（借展）的方式获得器物或藏品的个人或机构。

buffer (1) 缓冲物（1）	A buffer is any material addition to an object that counteracts mechanical or chemical deterioration of that object. The buffer thus prolongs the life-cycle of that object, while it is sacrificed in the process and has to be replaced or added again when it is worn out or exhausted. 缓冲物是为抵消机械或化学劣化而为器物添加的材料。缓冲物通过自身损耗起到延长器物的寿命的作用，当缓冲物被损耗或耗尽时，可以更换或再次添加。
buffer (4) 缓冲剂 (4)	A buffer is a material, such as silica gel, that can absorb or desorb moisture in order to stabilise the climate in the space in which it is present. 缓冲剂是一种可以吸收或释放水分的材料（如硅胶），以稳定其所存在空间的气候。
cabinet 储藏柜架	A cabinet is a case or cupboard with drawers or shelves used for storing or displaying objects. 储藏柜架是用于存放或展示器物的箱柜、抽屉柜、架子等。
catalogue (1) 藏品／展品目录	A catalogue lists all objects in a collection or exhibition. 藏品／展品目录列出了一类藏品或一个展览中的所有器物。
catalogue (2) 编制藏品目录 (2)	You catalogue a collection by producing a list of all the objects pertaining to this collection. 编制藏品目录指制作属于这一类藏品的所有器物的清单。
classification 分类	A classification sub-divides a collection into categories with identified common characteristics. 分类是将藏品细分为具有已识别共同特征的类别。
clean air 清洁空气	Clean air is air that contains nitrogen (78 %) and oxygen (21%). Trace levels of other gases (argon 1%, carbon dioxide, neon, etc.) are also present along with varying amounts of water vapour. 清洁空气指含氮量和含氧量分别为78%和21%的空气。剩余部分则为痕量水平的其他气体（1%的氩气、二氧化碳和氖气等）以及不同量的水蒸气。
climate control 气候控制	Climate control ensures that the environmental conditions surrounding an object or collection remain within requirements. 气候控制可确保器物或藏品周围的环境条件保持在要求的范围内。
collection 藏品	A collection is a group of acquired objects for the selection of which specific criteria have been used. 藏品是按照特定入藏标准鉴选的器物。
collection policy 藏品政策／制度	Institutions frequently issue a collection policy which sets out the criteria used in the acquisition of objects. A collection policy usually determines what is to be collected, how it is to be collected and the reasons for an object's inclusion in the collection. 机构发布藏品征集消息时，常使用藏品政策作为标准。藏品政策是决定性文件，通常包含收藏的内容、方式以及决定收藏的原因。

collections management 藏品管理	Collections management is the application of institutional policies and procedures concerned with acquisition, accessioning, control, cataloguing, use and disposal of objects. Collections management is the efficient auditing, arrangement, storage and documentation of collections and may also encompass all aspects of collections care including preventive conservation. 藏品管理是机构对于藏品的管理，包括制定藏品的征集、接收及登账、管理、编目、提用和注销的政策和实施相关程序。 藏品管理是有关藏品的全流程监管、利用、保管和记录，也可包括预防性保护在内的涉及藏品维护保养的各个方面。
collections manager 藏品主管	A collections manager is the person responsible for managing a collection. The responsibility usually relates primarily to physical (rather than academic) aspects. 藏品主管是负责管理藏品的人员。其职责通常主要涉及实物管理而非学术研究。
compactor 密集柜	A compactor is the placing of storage cabinets or racking on a number of trolleys running on rails. The trolleys are rolled together to allow a corridor to be opened between a pair of trolleys. This arrangement is used to save the space of a number of corridors is a store room. 密集柜就是把一组带滑轮的储藏柜架安装在导轨上。各组滑轮储藏柜架可在滑轨上移动贴合，为两组柜架之间留出过道。这种布置，可减少库房里的（常规固定式柜架之间）过道，节省库房空间。
competence 能力	A person's competence is the appropriate knowledge and skills necessary to perform a task to an acceptable standard. 能力是个人按照（社会、行业等）认可的标准，在执行任务时所必需的专门知识和技能。
conservation department （文物藏品） 保护部门	Within an institution, a conservation department specialises in conservation activities, training or research. （文物藏品）保护部门是机构中专门从事（文物藏品）保护活动、培训或研究的部门。
conservation laboratory （文物藏品） 保护实验室	A conservation laboratory is the area of an institution where conservation treatments are carried out. Depending on the institution, this area may also be called a workshop or a studio. （文物藏品）保护实验室是机构中开展保护处理的地方。根据机构的不同，该地方亦称为工作坊或工作室。
conservation plan 保护方案 / 保护规划	a. A conservation plan is a formal plan of action for a conservation process. b. A conservation plan sets out the significance and value of a heritage asset (such as a building) as a means of understanding and managing its history, use(s) and future conservation. a. 保护方案是关于保护流程的正式实施方案。b. 保护规划以遗产（如建筑物）的重要性和价值作为出发点，通过理解和管理该遗产的历史、用途和其未来保护状况对其实施规划。

conservation policy 保护政策 / 制度	A conservation policy sets out the principles intended to secure the survival or preservation of historic objects, buildings, monuments or areas for the future. 保护制度是旨在确保历史文物、建筑物或古迹能够留存下来或对其实施保护的原则。
context 背景	The context of an object is those external attributes which determine the significance of an object. The attributes can be geographic, spiritual, historic or cultural. 器物的背景指确定其重要性的外部属性。这些属性可以是地理、精神、历史或文化方面的。
control 控制	You control a situation or process when you manage or reduce potentially adverse influences on an object, a collection or its environment. 控制情况或流程是指控制或减少对器物、藏品或其环境的潜在不利影响。
core collection 核心藏品	a. The core collection of a museum is a group of objects fundamental to the aims stated in the collections policy of this museum. b. A core collection is the original collection around which a museum was founded. a. 博物馆的核心藏品指符合该博物馆收藏制度所规定基本目的的一组器物。b. 核心藏品指博物馆赖以建立的原始收藏。
corner pad 角垫	A corner pad is a pad placed on a vulnerable edge of an object such as a picture frame, to protect it against knocking. 角垫是指放置在如相框之类器物脆弱边缘上以防止其被撞击的垫子。
cultural property 文化财产	Cultural property is the surviving material evidence that is of significance to a particular population group. 文化财产是对特定人群具有重要意义的现存物证。
curator 策展人	a. A curator of a collection is a member of the museum staff who has responsibility for some or all of the actions relating to the collection's acquisition, documentation, preservation and interpretation. b. A curator of an exhibition is the person who is responsible for the selection and organisation of the objects. a. 藏品的策展人是博物馆负责与藏品的征集、记录、保存和阐释有关的部分或全部工作的人员。b. 展览的策展人负责藏品的挑选和组织。
custodian 保管员	A custodian is the person who is responsible for the safekeeping of a collection, building or site. 保管员是负责保管藏品、建筑物或遗址的人。
de-accessioning 注销	De-accessioning is the formal removal of an acquisition from a museum collection prior to disposal, for example by destruction, exchange or sale. 藏品注销是指从博物馆藏品中正式移除某件藏品。藏品注销之后，才能进行销毁、交换或出售等后续处置。
decision 决定	A decision is a professional judgement based on an accepted body of knowledge. 决定是基于公认知识体系所作出的专业判断。
dehumidifier 除湿器	A dehumidifier is a piece of machinery which removes moisture from an atmosphere. 除湿器是从大气中除去水分的机器。

destaticiser 除静电剂	A destaticiser is a substance which reduces the tendency for the surface of a material to become electrostatically discharged. 除静电剂是一种可以减少材料表面静电放电倾向的物质。
direct lighting 直接照明	Direct lighting is lighting with no barriers between the object and the light source. 直接照明指在器物和光源之间没有障碍的照明方式。
disaster plan 灾害应急计划	A disaster plan is a plan that determines the first steps that have to be undertaken (and who is to undertake them) in order to minimise the immediate results of occurring disasters such as fire, flooding, heavy storms, earthquakes, water leakage, burglar and/or vandalism. See also salvage plan. 灾害应急计划是为最大程度地减少灾难（如火灾、水灾、暴风雨、地震、漏水、盗窃和/或故意破坏）直接后果所采取的第一步必要措施的计划（包括实施主体）。另请参阅救助计划。
discipline 学科	A conservation discipline is a branch or specialism dealing with the care of historic material. 文物保护学科是专门研究历史材料保护的分支学科。
display 展览 / 展示	A museum display presents and interprets objects to its visitors, usually by incorporating text and graphics. 博物馆展览通常通过图文结合的方式来向参观者展示和阐释器物。
dry pipe system 干管系统	A dry pipe system is a water sprinkler whose pipes are filled only when a sensor detects fire. This technique reduces the likelihood of leaks and failure of sensor valves. 干管系统是一种仅在传感器检测到火情时，水管才被注满水的洒水器。该技术减少了传感器阀泄漏和发生故障的可能性。
drying stress 干燥应力	As a material loses water and shrinks, the drying stress is the force exerted on the material which causes distortion or other mechanical damage. 干燥应力就是当材料失去水分并收缩时，施加在材料上并会导致变形或其他机械损坏的力。
durability 耐久性	Durability of a material or construction is its ability to withstand decay or deterioration caused by chemical, physical and/or climatic factors. 材料或结构的耐久性是其承受由化学，物理和 / 或气候因素引起的降解或劣化的能力。
dust 灰尘	Dust is loose, airborne dirt which lands on objects. Dust particles are solid particles, 0.01 to above 15 microns in diameter. These deposit on objects, by gravity if above 15 micron, or by impact and adhesion if less, and can include human skin cells, animal hairs and soot. It can be acidic. Under humid conditions, dust can be a food source for mould and moths or become corrosive. 灰尘是散布在空气中的尘埃，会落在器物上。灰尘颗粒属固体颗粒，直径为0.01至15微米以上。直径超过15微米的灰尘会在重力的作用下沉积在器物上，而直径小于15微米的则通过冲击和粘附而沉积在器物上，可包括人体皮肤细胞、动物毛发和烟灰。它可以是酸性的。在潮湿的条件下，灰尘可能是霉菌和蛀虫的食物来源，或者会变得具有腐蚀性。

eco-museum 生态博物馆	An eco-museum is one that reflects a local environment, both man-made and natural. 生态博物馆是一种反映当地人文环境和自然环境的博物馆。
effloresce 粉化	A solution or hydrated mineral will effloresce when it loses water to form a new salt as a deposit on a surface. 粉化是溶液或水合矿物质失去水分后，表面形成的粉状新盐颗粒。
emergency plan 应急预案	An emergency plan formulated by a museum sets out the actions taken in anticipating, preventing and reacting to an emergency or disaster. 博物馆制定的应急预案详细说明了在预见、预防和应对紧急情况或灾难时，博物馆应采取的行动。
enter 入藏	An object is entered into a collection when it is physically received. 器物以实物方式纳入为藏品称之为入藏。
environment 环境	a. The environment of an object or a collection is the atmosphere surrounding it. b. The environment in a building is the atmosphere inside it. c. The environment of an area is the natural and man-made features of this area. a. 器物或藏品的环境指其周围的空气状况。b. 建筑的环境指其内部的氛围。C. 区域环境指该区域的自然和人为风貌。
Ethafoam® Ethafoam®	Ethafoam is a durable, tough, closed-cell, expanded foam made of polyethene. It is used to make supports and mounts for three dimensional objects. Ethafoam是由聚乙烯制成的耐用、坚韧、闭孔的膨胀泡沫。它用于制作三维器物的支撑和安装件。商标名。
ethics 文物保护基本原则	Ethics are the agreed tenets which guide conservation practice in a wider cultural context. 文物保护基本原则是可在更广泛的文化背景下，指导文物保护实践的公认原则。
ethnographic 民族志的	Ethnographic objects are the objects made by historical and present day indigenous peoples, which are studied by a different culture. 民族志的器物是由历史和当今土著民族制造的器物，它们是从不同的文化角度进行研究的。
ethnography 民族志	Ethnography is the study of historical and present day indigenous peoples by a different culture. This term is used differently in various European countries. 民族志是从不同的文化角度对土著民族历史和现状的研究。此术语在欧洲各个国家用法不同。
evacuate (1) 撤离 (1)	When you evacuate a collection, you remove the collection from a place where it is an imminent risk. 藏品撤离指从即将发生危险的地方撤离藏品。
exhibition 陈列/展览	An exhibition is a display of objects which is open to the public. 陈列/展览是公开陈列器物。

expanded polystyrene 发泡聚苯乙烯	Expanded polystyrene is a very light polystyrene foam that is used for packaging and cushioning. It is available in a number of densities and hardnesses. 发泡聚苯乙烯是一种非常轻的用于包装和缓冲的聚苯乙烯泡沫。它具有多种密度和硬度。
expendable 消耗性的（教育活动辅助用）	An expendable object in a collection is one which the custodian considers to be replaceable. Expendable objects are used in displays that cause damage to objects or for handling in education. 消耗性的展品指保管员认为可以被替代和更换的普通器物。一般作为教育活动辅助展品，主要被用于教育活动中的近距离接触互动展示，或可能造成器物损坏的展示。
exposed (1) 公开亮相（1）	A collection or object is exposed when it is displayed to a viewing public or given publicity. 藏品或器物的公开亮相是指向公众公开展示藏品或器物，或专门宣传该藏品或器物。
exposed (2) 暴露 (2)	An object is exposed to harm when subjected to a harmful agent, such as light on a watercolour. 当器物暴露于有害物质（例如水彩画暴露在光下）时会受到伤害。
external 外部的	An external environment or influence is one which is experienced outside a building. 外部环境或影响指在建筑物外部的环境或其所受影响。
facilities management 设施管理	Facilities management includes all those activities ensuring effectiveness in building maintenance, environmental and associated technical operations. 设施管理包括所有确保建筑物维护、环境和相关技术操作有效开展的活动。
fade 褪色	A colour fades when it loses intensity due to light and/or chemical action. 褪色是颜色由于光线和/或化学作用而变淡的过程。
fading 退化	Fading is loss of density due to ageing. 退化是由于老化而导致的密度损失。
fake 赝品	A fake is a copy of an original object produced with the intention that it will be taken as genuine. 赝品是指以假充真的物品。
feasibility study 可行性研究	A feasibility study is carried out to examine specific options (including condition, costs, values, opportunities) in advance of agreeing future action relating to an object, collection, building or group of buildings. 进行可行性研究是为了在就某器物、藏品、建筑物或建筑物群将来所要采取的行动达成一致意见前，对其进行的特定检查（包括条件、费用、价值和机会）。
fibre optic lighting 光纤照明	Fibre optic lighting is the illumination of an object using glass fibres to carry and deliver the light from a remote light source. 光纤照明是将远程光源的光通过玻璃纤维传输的照明方式。

flood 水害	A flood is the ingress of water to an area holding objects. 水害指水进入保存器物的区域。
fluorescent lamp 荧光灯	A fluorescent lamp emits light largely by fluorescence, in which a phosphor on the inside surface of the tube is made to fluoresce by ultra violet radiation from mercury vapour. 荧光灯主要通过荧光发光，管内表面的荧光粉通过汞蒸气的紫外线辐射而发出荧光。
foam system 泡沫系统	A foam system of fire control is the release of a high expansion foam when fire is detected. 防火控制的泡沫系统是在发现火情时释放高膨胀泡沫的系统。
Fome-Core® Fome-Core®	Fome-Core is a lightweight, stable board made up of a core of extruded polystyrene foam that is laminated on both sides with sheets of thin cardboard. It is available with acid free cardboard. It is used to make mounts for flat textiles and storage. Fome-Core是以聚苯乙烯泡沫塑料为芯，两面均压制一种轻巧、稳定的纸板。它可与无酸纸板一起使用。用于制作展示纺织品的安装架和其储存架。商标名。
framework 框架	A framework is a system of organising information used in collections management. 框架是用于组织藏品管理信息的系统。
functional object 实用器物 / 功能性器物	See living object. 见活体。
funding 专项资金	The funding of a specific project or task is the money that has been made available for it. 专项资金指为特定项目或任务提供的可用资金。
gallery (2) 展厅	A gallery is a display space, either a room or building, for exhibiting works of art or museum collections. 展厅是用于陈列艺术品或博物馆藏品的展示空间，可以是房间或建筑物。
gas system 气体系统	A gas system of fire control is the release of a gas such as Halon or carbon dioxide when fire is detected. Both these act as asphyxiants and can be dangerous to people trapped in a fire zone. 火灾控制的气体系统是在检测到起火时释放卤代烷或二氧化碳等气体的系统。这两种气体均具有窒息作用，对被困在火区的人员可能会构成危险。
glaze (2) 装玻璃隔板	You glaze a picture frame, cabinet, showcase or window when putting in a protective glass sheet. 装玻璃隔板指将相（画）框，储藏柜，陈列柜或展示橱窗放入保护性玻璃板。

grant 资助	A grant is financial support provided by an external body which does not wish to derive benefit from the transaction. 资助是外部机构提供的一种财务支持，他们不期望从资助中获得利益。
guideline 指南	A guideline is advice on the implementation of a policy. 指南是有关政策落地实施的建议。
handling 藏品操作	Handling is the entire process of lifting, supporting and carrying an object during examination, treatment, transportation, storage and display with due regard to its physical, chemical and biological safety. 藏品操作是在检查、保护处理、运输，保管和展示过程中，在充分考虑器物的物理、化学和生物安全性前提下，对器物进行吊装、支撑和搬运的整个过程。
hang 悬挂	When you hang an exhibition, you put paintings onto display in a gallery. 悬挂展品是将绘画布设在展厅中进行展示。
hanging 悬挂	Hanging is a method frequently used to store costumes by constructing supports more or less like mannequins on which the costumes are supported. 悬挂是一种经常通过构造支撑物来保存服装的方法。该支撑物类似服装人体模型。
hanging system 悬挂系统	A hanging system is a method of hanging a flat textile, such as a tapestry, on a wall. In textile conservation, a hook and loop fastener is mostly used . 悬挂系统是一种将扁平的纺织品（如挂毯）悬挂在墙上的方法。对于纺织品保护，最常使用的是钩环扣。
hazard 危害	A hazard is an identified cause of potential damage. 危害是导致潜在损坏的确定因素。
heritage management 遗产管理	Heritage management is the policies and practices which relate to preservation, documentation, interpretation and promotion of objects and sites of historic, environmental or scientific interest. 遗产管理是与器物和遗址的保存、记录、阐释和宣传相关的政策和做法。这些器物和遗址均具有历史、环境或科学研究意义。
holdings 馆藏	The holdings of an institution are its collections. 机构的馆藏是其收藏品。
Hostaphan®	Hostaphan is a film made of polyester. Hostaphan®（商标名）是由聚酯纤维制成的薄膜。
housekeeping 日常管理	Housekeeping involves the traditional methods for maintaining a house or collection by regular inspection, cleaning and protection. 日常管理涉及通过定期检查、清洁和养护来维护库房或藏品的传统方法。
housing 遮盖物	A housing is a protective enclosure which is used to preserve photographs. 遮盖物是用于保存照片的保护性遮盖物。

humidification 加湿	The humidification of an object or its environment is a treatment that adds water vapour. In organic materials and some inorganic materials such as clays, the added water expands the structure and acts as a plasticiser. These effects may increase the flexibility of components in the structure. In some cases, the water re-activates the original binding medium which has lost coherence and adhesion. Humidification is used as a pre-washing treatment for brittle textiles in order to reduce the shock of wetting. 加湿是对器物或其周围环境增加水蒸气的处理方法。在有机材料和某些无机材料（如粘土）中添加水，会使结构膨胀并起到增塑剂的作用。这可能会增加结构中组件的柔韧性。某些情况下，水会重新活化原来失去粘结力和附着力的粘结剂。加湿也被用作脆化纺织品的预洗处理方法，以减少润湿过程中对纺织品的冲击。
humidifier 加湿器	A humidifier is a piece of equipment that adds water vapour to an environment. 加湿器是一种将水蒸气添加到环境中的设备。
humidify 使湿润 / 加湿	When you humidify an object or its environment, you add water vapour. When you humidify a textile, you allow it to absorb a limited amount of water vapour without it coming into contact with liquid water. 给器物或其环境加湿，就是增加水蒸气含量。加湿纺织品时，就是在其不与液态水接触的情况下，使其吸收一定量的水蒸气。
humidistat 恒湿器	A humidistat is a sensor and switch which controls a humidifier or dehumidifier in order to achieve a specified humidity. 恒湿器是一种通过控制加湿或除湿来达到指定湿度的传感器及其开关。
humidity 湿度	Humidity is the amount of water vapour in a gas. See also relative and absolute humidity. 湿度是气体中水蒸气的量。另请参见相对和绝对湿度。
humidity buffer 湿度缓冲材料	A humidity buffer is any material that slows down the change of moisture content of the air in a sealed volume. In general these materials can contain large amounts of water without feeling moist. They absorb and desorb water easily. The buffer is used to reduce the effect on objects of external environmental changes. 湿度缓冲材料指能减缓封闭空间中空气水含量变化的材料。通常，这些材料可纳容大量的水但又不致潮湿感，容易吸水，也易于解吸。该材料用于减少外部环境变化对器物的影响。
humidity chamber 湿度箱	A humidity chamber is an enclosed space which maintains a specific humidity. It is used to maintain a constant level of water content in an object for treatment and test purposes. 湿度箱是保持特定湿度的封闭空间。它用于保持恒定的含水量，以便对器物进行保护处理和测试。
hygrometer 湿度计	An hygrometer is an instrument for measuring the water content (humidity) of air. 湿度计是一种用于测量空气中水含量（湿度）的仪器。

hygroscopic 吸湿	A hygroscopic material is a material that absorbs water without forming a solution. 吸湿性材料指吸收水分但不形成溶液的材料。
in situ 原位	An object which is in situ is still in its original position or where it has been deposited. 置于原位的器物指器物仍处于其原始位置或原来放置的位置。
Incralac® 	Incralac is the commercial name of an acrylic resin which contains the corrosion inhibitor benzotriazole and is used as a protective coating for metal Incralac®（商标名）是丙烯酸树脂的商品名，含有阻蚀剂苯并三唑，用作金属的保护涂层。
indemnity 赔偿	You provide an indemnity to someone when you promise to make good damage or loss to a particular object. This promise may be underwritten by a major institution (such a government) or by an insurance company, which usually imposes conditions on how the object should be cared for. 赔偿是由一方做出承诺，若造成指定器物损坏或损失，向另一方提供的赔偿金。该承诺可以由大型机构（如政府）或保险公司承保，这些机构通常对应如何保管该器物设定条件。
index 索引	An index is an inventory or list, usually alphabetical or under category sub-headings, of a collection, that can be used for data recording, retrieval or cross-reference. 索引是一个藏品的清单或列表，通常按字母顺序或在类别子标题下，可用于数据记录、检索或交叉引用。
infiltration 渗透	Infiltration of air is the uncontrolled leakage of air through cracks and small openings in buildings or storage units. 空气渗透是指空气通过建筑物或储藏室的裂缝和开口自然泄漏。
insect trap 昆虫诱捕器	An insect trap is a small container used to trap insects in order that the type and level of infestation can be assessed. The trap is commnoly made of cardboard with an adhesive surface for holding the insect and may include bait or other attractant such as a pheromone or a poison. 昆虫诱捕器是用于捕获昆虫的小容器，以便可以评估（昆虫）侵袭的类型和程度。诱捕器通常由硬纸板制成，并带有用于保持昆虫的粘性表面，同时可能装有诱饵或其它引诱物，例如信息素或毒药。
insulate 隔离 / 绝缘	When you insulate an object, you cover it with a solid or liquid material that makes it resistant against the flow of heat or electricity. 隔离或绝缘器物，就是采用固体或液体材料覆盖它，使其抵御热、电等因素的影响。
insurance 保险	When you arrange insurance for an object or service, a company agrees to make good a loss, for instance if the object is damaged or the service inadequate, by paying an agreed sum of money to the affected person. For this service you pay an insurance premium to the company. 为器物或服务投保，损失将由保险公司弥补。例如，如果器物受损或服务不周，保险公司将向受影响的人支付一笔约定的款项。此服务需要向保险公司支付保险费。

integrated conservation 综合保护	Integrated conservation brings together all the necessary conservation skills and specialisms to carry out a project. 综合保护是整合所有必要保护技术和专门知识，来执行一个保护项目。
integrated pest management 有害生物综合治理	Integrated pest management encompass the strategies adopted to prevent or control infestations of insects or rodents, including building design, maintenance of the internal and external building environment, inspection, prevention and eradication. 有害生物综合治理包括为预防或控制昆虫或啮齿类动物的侵扰而采取的策略，包括建筑物设计以及内部和外部建筑物环境的维护、检查、预防和灭杀。
intellectual property 知识产权	An author, artist or designer has intellectual property rights for work produced which are recognised by society and law. This applies to such instances as recognition of copyright. 作者、艺术家或设计师对由其制作并获得社会和法律认可的作品拥有知识产权。这适用于版权确认之类的情况。
interior climate 内部气候	The interior climate is the environmental conditions within a building. 内部气候是建筑物内的环境条件。
internal 内部的	An internal environment or influence is one which is experienced inside a building. 内部环境或内部影响指在建筑物内部的环境或其所受影响。
interpretation 阐释	The interpretation of an object or collection is the expression of its meaning conveyed to an audience through exhibition or recorded in documentation. 器物或藏品的阐释是通过展览或文字档案向观众传达其含义的表达方式。
intrinsic value 内在价值	The intrinsic value of an object or collection is one that arises from inherent attributes deemed of importance, such as spiritual, religious or social significance. It is not a monetary value. 器物或藏品的内在价值指源自被认为具有重要性的内在属性，如精神、宗教或社会意义，而非货币价值。
inventory 总登记帐	An inventory lists the objects in a collection or property, including relevant data such as description and location. 总登记帐列出了藏品或资产中的器物，包括相关数据，如具体描述和位置。
IPM 害虫综合治理	See integrated pest management. 见害虫综合治理。
keeper 藏品部门主管	A keeper is the curatorial member of a museum's staff who has responsibility for a specific collection including acquisition, documentation, preservation and interpretation. 藏品部门主管是博物馆负责特定藏品的收集、记录、保存和阐释的策展人员。

labelling 贴标签	Labelling an object is the process of applying an identifying mark, usually the accession number, either directly to the object or on a sheet material which is securely attached to the object. 为器物贴标签是将登记号直接粘贴到器物上或牢固地附着于器物片材上的过程。
laboratory 实验室	A laboratory is an area where scientific or conservation work is carried out. 实验室是进行科学研究或保护工作的地方。
legibility 易读性	The legibility of an object or image is the ease with which an observer can discern and understand the information revealed. 器物或图像的易读性指观察者辨别和理解其所显示信息的容易程度。
lender 出借方	A lender is an institution or individual who loans an object or collection, usually within a formal agreement. 出借方是通常在正式协议内借出器物或藏品的机构或个人。
LeParfait®jar	A LeParfait jar is a glass container used for storing fluid specimens. It has a glass top with rubber gasket which degrades and fails after 5 years LeParfait®jar（商标名）是一种玻璃容器，用于储存液体标本。其玻璃顶部带有橡胶密封垫，5年后会退化和失效。
level of conservation 保护程度	When carrying out a conservation treatment, you must decide on the level of conservation which is the degree of intervention proposed ranging, for instance, from investigative cleaning to complete restoration for exhibition. 进行保护处理时，必须确定保护程度，即拟干预的程度。例如，从因调查的需要对器物所做的清洁工作，到因展览的需要对器物所做的完整修复。
light 光	Light is electromagnetic radiation visible to the human eye, roughly 380-700 nm. 光是人眼可见的电磁辐射，波长大约为380-700纳米。
light fading 光退化 / 褪色	Light fading is the loss of density or colour change of chromogenic dyes due to exposure to light. 光褪色是由于暴露在光照下而导致发色染料的密度损失或颜色变化。
light sensitive 光敏感的	A light sensitive material or object is one that will be damaged by exposure to light. 光敏材料或器物是暴露于光照下会被损坏的材料或器物。
living object 实用器物 / 功能性器物	A living object is one in which the original materials are preserved or replaced when necessary to fulfil its original function, such as aesthetic or functional. 实用器物是必要时保留或替换原始材料以实现其原始功能（如美学或功能性）的器物。
loan 出借	A loan is an object or collection that is removed for a limited period under agreement from its normal custodian to another. 出借是器物或藏品的保管方，根据协议在特定时限将器物或藏品借给另一方。

loan agreement 出借协议	A loan agreement comprises terms and conditions determining the loan. 出借协议包括决定出借的条款和条件。
loan form 出借表格	A loan form is a document on which formal acceptance of the terms of a loan is signed by the borrower. 出借表格是借用方通过签署以确定正式接受出借条款的文件。
loan period 借用期	A loan period is the time for which a loan is agreed. 借用期是约定借用的时间。
location 位置	The location of an object is its exact position within an excavation, museum, storeroom or display. 器物的位置是其在发掘、博物馆、库房或陈列室内的确切位置。
loss (2) 损失 (2)	The loss of an object is its total destruction or unauthorised removal from a collection. 器物的损失是其被完全破坏或被以非正常注销程序从藏品中被移除。
maintenance 维护	The maintenance of a building or object is the combination of administrative and technical actions intended to retain it in a state in which it can perform a required function. 建筑物或器物的维护是行政措施和具体技术的结合，旨在维持建筑物或器物的正常功能。
manual 手册	A manual is a written document giving precise instructions for a procedure. 手册是对特定程序提供准确说明的书面文件。
mark (2) 藏品号	A mark is an identifying code applied to an object in a collection. 藏品号是藏品中应用于某器物的识别码。
mat 卡纸框	A mat is a flat support and covering frame into which an opening has been cut out. It is used in framing, mounting and/or storing a drawing, print or photograph which is visible and handled without being touched. The mounted object can be attached to the mat itself, stretched in its opening or hinged to the backboard. A mat can become an integral part of the mounted object for historical and/or ethical reasons. 卡纸框/开窗式夹裱框是由一个平面背衬板和中间预留窗口的盖板两部分组成。它用于保护或保存素描绘画作品、印刷品或照片。经这样处理的作品不会影响观赏，直接持拿时可避免接触作品本体。作品可以绷平在盖板开口内侧或与背衬板进行铰链固定（即合页方式）。考虑历史和/或文物保护原则的因素，卡纸框/开窗式夹裱框可被认为是这件作品不可分割的一部分。
measure 措施	A measure is a course of action taken in line with an agreed policy. 措施是根据商定制度采取的行动。
mechanical buffer 机械缓冲	A mechanical buffer is any material that absorbs and dissipates sudden shocks and so protect an object against mechanical damage. 机械缓冲指吸收和消除突然冲击以保护器物免受机械损坏的材料。

microclimate 小（微）气候	A microclimate provides an enclosed and controlled environment, usually designed to provide optimum conditions for storage or display of an object in a container or cabinet. 小（微）气候提供了一个封闭且受控的环境，其设计通常为柜架囊盒中的器物提供最佳的储藏或展示条件。
mobile rack 移动式货架	Mobile racking is racking which is capable of moving. 移动式货架是能够移动的货架。
molecular sieve 分子筛	A molecular sieve is synthetic zeolite that is highly porous and adsorbent, which are used as scavengers. 分子筛是具有高孔隙性和吸附性的合成沸石，可用作清除剂。
monitor 监测	You monitor a situation or object by carrying out regular checks on it. 监测是通过定期检查来监测某种情况或某个器物。
mount (1) 支架（1）	A mount is a support provided for an object. It is used in display or storage to make the object accessible whilst providing protection. 支架是为器物提供支撑的架子。它用于器物的展示或储藏中，旨在为器物提供保护的同时不妨碍其使用。
mount (4) 安装／固定／ 装镶／支护	When you mount an object, you attach it to a support for exhibition or storage purposes. 因库房保存或展厅展示的需要对器物进行安装、固定、装镶或支护。
movable 可移动的	A movable object is one which is not fixed in a specific situation. 可移动的器物指不固定在特定位置的器物。
museum object 博物馆器物	A museum object is one in which the original materials are preserved primarily as historical evidence. 博物馆器物指其原始材料主要作为历史证据而保存的物品。
natural environment 自然环境	The natural environment is an area free from non-man-made influences. See also built environment. 自然环境是未受到人为影响的地方。另见建成环境（本书建筑章）。
neglect 疏忽	Neglect is conscious or unconscious lack of care for an object, which frequently leads to deterioration. 疏忽是有意或无意地未对器物给予养护，这常常导致劣化。
nitrogen 氮	Nitrogen is a constituent of air which, when used pure, kills insects by anoxia. 氮是空气中的一种成分，单独对昆虫使用纯氮气可使其因缺氧而死。
nitrogen oxides 氮氧化物	Nitrogen oxides, NOx, is pollutant gas caused by combustion. 氮氧化物（NOx）是燃烧引起的污染气体。
number 编号	When you number a series of objects or parts, you assign an alphanumeric code to each, for example to assist in recording location of fragments during disassembly and assembly. 在对一系列器物或部件编号时，出于不同目的分别给予它们一个字母数字组合码，如装拆期间协助记录器物构件的位置。

object 器物	An object is an artefact which is considered to have historic, scientific or cultural significance. Examples are paintings, scientific specimens, fossils or pressed plants. 器物是被认为具有历史、科学或文化意义的人工制品。例如绘画、科学标本、化石或植物标本。
Occupational Exposure Limit 职业接触限值	An Occupational Exposure Limit (OEL) of a substance is the maximum concentration in air that can be breathed over a working week without harm. The term is used in the UK. 某种物质的职业接触限值（OEL）是指该物质在空气中的最大浓度，必须确保即使一个工作周内呼吸含有该浓度物质的空气也不会造成伤害。该术语通常在英国使用。
offgassing 挥发	Offgassing of vapours and gases is the evolution of substances from materials used in the construction of showcases or storage systems. 蒸气和气体挥发是因展柜或储藏空间在建造过程中使用材料所含物质发生的变化而造成的。
open air museum 露天博物馆	An open air museum is based wholly or partly on exhibits (such as buildings or industrial processes) sited in their original location or relocated to a specific site. 露天博物馆是展览全部或部分基于处于原址或已移至特定地点（如建筑物或工业过程）的博物馆。
original condition 原状	The original condition of an object was its state or appearance when it was first manufactured. 器物的原状是其首次制造时的状态或外观。
original object 真品	An original object is truly what it is purported to be, and recognised for its historic, artistic, cultural or scientific merit. 真品是描述详情与真实情况相符的物品，具有历史、艺术、文化或科学价值。
overshoe 鞋套	A overshoe is a temporary foot covering used when walking on sensitive floors. 鞋套是在易损地板上行走时使用的临时脚套。
owner 所有权人	An owner is the person or institution who has legal title to an object or collection. 所有权人是对器物或藏品具有合法所有权的个人或机构。
ozone 臭氧	Ozone, O_3, is pollutant gas caused by reactions between pollutants and nitrogen dioxide, especially under the influence of sunlight. 臭氧，即O_3，是污染物与二氧化氮反应，尤其是在阳光的影响下所产生的污染气体。
packaging 包装	The packaging of an object is the containers, coverings and padding used for protection during storage or transportation. The protection afforded may be against mechanical, chemical or environmental hazards. 器物的包装是保存或运输过程中出于保护目的而使用的容器、覆盖物和衬垫。所提供的保护可保证器物不受机械、化学或环境危害。

packing 填充物	Packing is material inserted into a void or around an object in order to reduce or restrict movement. 填充物是将材料插入空隙或器物周围以减少或限制其移动的材料。
perimeter protection 边界保护	Perimeter protection is the security measures, physical and electronic, which are introduced at the boundaries of a building or its estate. 边界保护是在建筑物周边或其地界处引入的物理或电子安全防护措施。
permanence 预期寿命	An obsolete term for life expectancy. 预期寿命, 现今该术语已废止。
passive conservation 被动性保护	See preventive conservation. 见预防性保护。
pest control 虫害防治	Pest control involves measures taken to control infestations of insects or rodents. 虫害防治是为控制昆虫或啮齿动物的侵扰而采取的措施。
pH value 酸碱度	pH is a logarithmic measure of the hydrogen ion concentration in aqueous solution, from 1 (strong acid), through 7 (neutral) to 14 (strong alkali) 酸碱度是水溶液中氢离子浓度指数, 从1（强酸）到7（中性）到14（强碱）。
Plastazote®	Plastazote is a porous polyethene sheet, used for packaging and cushioning. It is available in a number of densities and hardnesses Plastazote®（商标名）是一种多孔聚乙烯板, 用于包装和缓冲。有多种密度和硬度
plastic bubble wrap 塑料气泡包装材料	Plastic bubble wrap is a pre-formed packing material made by sealing pockets of air between two layers of clear plastic sheet. 塑料气泡包装材料是一种预制的包装材料, 它是通过密封两层透明塑料板之间的空气而制成的。
policy 制度	A policy is a statement, usually written, of the principles governing an area of activity. 制度是关于规范某个领域活动原则的说明, 通常为书面形式。
pollution 污染	Pollution is the combined pollutants in the environment, in the air, water or ground. 污染是指环境、空气、水分或地面中的混合污染物。
polyethene film 聚乙烯薄膜	A polyethene film is an extruded film of polyethylene (PE) made in different widths and thickness'. It is chemically stable, very flexible and transparent. It is also made in the form of tubing, sections of which can be heat sealed to form bags. Polyethylene film can have many uses, ranging from a temporary washable lining to packaging material. 聚乙烯薄膜是具有不同宽度和厚度的聚乙烯（PE）挤制膜。它具有化学稳定性, 柔软且透明。它也可以制成管状形式, 可以将其部分热封以制作成袋子。聚乙烯薄膜有多种用途, 如临时可清洗内衬、包装材料等。

polyethylene film 聚乙烯薄膜	See polyethene film. 见聚乙烯薄膜。
portfolio (1) 保存袋（1）	A portfolio is a case for storing works of art on paper or photographs. 用于保存纸质艺术品或照片的保存袋。
precondition 预置／预处理	A material is preconditioned by equilibrating it to a specific relative humidity. For example, silica gel is commonly preconditioned in order to control the RH in a micro-environment. 对某种材料的预处理是将其调整到特定的相对湿度。例如，对硅胶进行预处理以控制微环境中的相对湿度。
preventive conservation 预防性保护	Preventive conservation is planned change to the environment and surroundings of an object or building to remove or reduce the causes of neglect, deterioration or decay, through such strategies as improving environmental, storage, display and handling tec 预防性保护是指通过改善环境、保管、展示和处理技术等策略对器物或建筑物的环境和周围环境进行有计划的变更，以消除或减少造成其被疏忽，劣化或降解的成因。
priority 优先级	When a number of objects or activities are being considered for action, each one is given a priority which is the relative ranking for the implementation of the action. 当执行某项目涉及的多个器物或活动时，每个器物或活动都被赋予一个优先级。该优先级是执行项目的相对等级。
procedure 程序	A procedure is the established way of carrying out a process, which has usually been formalised in written form. 程序是执行过程的既定方法，通常已以书面形式正式化。程序是指执行某一过程的既定方式，通常以书面形式正式确定下来。
process 流程	A process is the set of stages undertaken during an identified activity. 流程是在确定的活动中实施的一系列阶段。
professional 专业的／专业人员	A professional activity is carried out under the oversight of a relevant regulator or recognised specialist body, which governs and disciplines the practitioners by externally agreed principles and codes of practice. The professional carrying out the activity will usually have at least graduate level education and a number of years of post-graduate vocational training in the specialism of the profession. 专业活动是在相关监管机构或获得认证专业机构的监督下实施的活动。该机构通过外部商定的原则和实践准则对从业人员进行监管。从事专业活动的人员通常至少接受过本科水平教育，并经过多年专业领域内的研究生职业培训。
protect 防护	You protect an object or building by installing physical barriers against vandalism, the environment, fire and similar hazards. 防护指通过安装物理屏障来保护器物或建筑物免遭人为破坏，环境伤害，火灾和类似危险。

protective glazing 防护玻璃	Protective glazing is the use of glass with specific properties in framing, display or the windows of a building to prevent damage from, for instance, light or vandalism. 防护玻璃是在边框、展示或建筑物的窗户中使用具有特定性能的玻璃，以防止其受到光线或人为的故意损害。
provenance 来源	The provenance of an object is its verifiable origin and history, including its geographical source and its passage through various ownerships. 器物的来源是其可验证的起源和历史，包括其地理来源信息和持有记录。
psychrometer 干湿计	A psychrometer is an instrument for assessing the humidity of the air by measuring the cooling effect when water evaporates. A whirling psychrometer is the standard method of providing an accurate RH measurement. 干湿计是通过测量水蒸发时的冷却效果来评估空气湿度的仪器。旋转干湿计是提供准确的相对湿度测量的标准方法。
public awareness 公众认知	The public awareness of an issue is the way the issue is perceived by a non-specialist audience. 对于事件的公共认知是指非专业观众对此事件的理解。
publication 出版	Publication is formal dissemination of information to the public in a permanent medium. 出版是通过永久媒介向公众正式发布信息。
quotation 报价单	A quotation for a task is a written statement of cost provided by a potential supplier in order to form the basis of a contract with a client. The quotation results from a calculation of costs for a quantity of work specified by the client. 报价单是潜在供应商提供的书面费用说明，以便构成与客户签订合同的基础。报价单是根据客户指定工作量的成本计算得出的。
receipt 交接单	A receipt is a formal written acknowledgement given by the recipient of an object or collection that has been transferred into the recipient's safekeeping. 交接单是收件人对已转移给其保管的器物或收藏品所作的正式书面确认。
recent history 藏品保存近况	The recent history of an object is any occurrence in its recent known lifetime which may affect its condition or status. 藏品保存近况是在其最近发生的可能影响其状况或状态的任何情况。
recommendation （藏品保存）建议	You provide a recommendation for an object by giving formal advice for future care such as environmental control, storage, or handling. （藏品保存）建议是关于藏品未来保管保存的正式意见，如环境控制、保存或操作步骤。
record 藏品档案	The record of an object is a document in which all relevant information about the object and its treatment is noted. 藏品档案指包含器物全部相关信息的文件，含其保护处理方式。

reference object 模拟样本/标本	A reference object is used to inform the restoration of an object when it has directly comparable features. 修复人员使用具有与某器物相类似性质的模拟样本/标本，来帮助其熟悉修复工作。
register 藏品编目	A register is a bound volume in which details related to accession are recorded. 藏品编目指藏品接收、登账相关详情的卷宗。
registrar 登记员/ 藏品账管理员	The registrar is a member of the museum staff who is responsible for documentation of its collection. 登记员/藏品账管理员是博物馆负责记录收藏事项的工作人员。
registration 登记入册	See accession. 见登记入册。
relative humidity 相对湿度	The relative humidity of a sample of air is the ratio of the vapour pressure of water vapour in the air sample (the absolute humidity) to the maximum possible water vapour pressure at the same temperature. Air of 0% RH contains no water and air of 100% is saturated. Organic objects suffer less humidity stress when RH changes as little as possible over time. 相对湿度是空气样本中，水蒸气的蒸气压力（绝对湿度）与相同温度下最大可能水蒸气压力之比。相对湿度为0%的空气不含水，相对湿度为100%的空气是饱和状态。一段时间内，相对湿度变化越小，有机质受到的湿度应压力越小。
renovate 翻新	You renovate a building or object when undertaking repairs and modifications for continued use at current standards of facilities and quality. 翻新建筑物或器物就是对其进行维修和修饰，以保障其设施和质量能按照当前标准被继续使用。
repellent 驱虫剂	An insect repellent is a chemical which vapourises into a space and discourages insects from entering the space. Many have been shown to have limited effect and to be toxic to humans. Examples are para-dichlorobenzene and naphthalene. 驱虫剂是一种可挥发的化学物质，通过挥发到某个空间来阻止昆虫进入。许多驱虫剂已被证明作用有限且对人有毒，如对二氯苯和萘。
replica 复制品	A replica of an object is a copy that matches as far as possible the appearance, original materials, production methods and even producer of the original. 器物的复制品指在外观、原始材料、生产方法甚至制作者都尽可能与原件一致的副本。
reproduction 仿制品	A reproduction of an object is a copy that is visually similar to the original, but may be physically very different. 器物的仿制品指在外观上与原件相似，但实物可能不尽相同的副本。

resources 资源	The resources for a specific project or use are the funds, equipment, facilities and staffing that can be drawn on. 特定项目或用途的资源指可以利用的资金，设备，设施和人员。
respond 响应 / 应对	You respond to a situation by carrying out actions informed by a conservation assessment. 响应指通过执行保护评估所提示的行动来应对特定情况。
restitution 归还 / 返还	The restitution of an object or collection is its return to the group for which it holds a specific significance. This may be an individual, a cultural or spiritual group or country of origin. 器物或藏品的返还指将其归还给对其具有特定意义的组织。该组织可以是个人、文化或精神组织或其来源国。
restoration studio 修复工作室	A restoration studio is the laboratory or workshop in which the conservation, usually of fine or decorative art material, is undertaken. 修复工作室指多为实验室或工作间，通常用于修复精美的装饰性艺术品。
restricted access 限制访问	Restricted access of people to an object, collection or space is the imposition of additional criteria for reasons of security or vulnerability. 人对器物、藏品或空间的限制访问是指出于安全或脆弱性而强加的额外标准。
RH 相对湿度	See relative humidity. 见相对湿度。
risk 风险	A risk is the probability that a known hazard will cause the identified harm in specified conditions within a specified time period. 风险是指已知危害将在指定时间段内和指定条件下，造成确定危害的可能性。
roller racking 辊式货架	See compactor. 见压土机。
rolling 卷起保存 （针对大幅平面文物）	Rolling large flat objects around a large cylinder is a method of storage that avoids folding and creasing. The method is particularly used for textiles. 采用大尺寸（直径）滚轴卷起大幅平面文物是一种避免折叠和折痕的保存方法。该方法常用于纺织品。
safe 保险间 / 保险柜	A safe is a room or cabinet that is physically strong to resist attack and theft of the contents. 保险箱指物理上坚固且可抵御攻击和盗窃的房间或柜子。
safeguarding 维护	You safeguard an object or collection by taking actions to prevent damage or theft. 维护指通过采取措施防止器物或藏品被损坏或盗窃。
safety regulations 安全法规	Safety regulations are rules laid down by government or an institution to ensure health and safety in the workplace. 安全法规是政府或机构为确保工作场所的健康和安全而制定的规则。

salvage operation 抢救操作	A salvage operation is carried out to recover objects from a potentially harmful environment or situation. 实施抢救操作是为了从潜在有害的环境或情况中对器物进行复原。
salvage plan 救助计划	A salvage plan is a plan that describes the steps to be undertaken after a disaster has occurred. It deals with the appropriate handling, packaging and/or storing of objects to minimise the risk of further damage. See also disaster plan. 救助计划是描述灾难发生后要采取的分步骤计划。它涉及对器物的适当处理，包装和/或存储，以最大程度地降低其进一步损坏的风险。另见灾害应急计划。
scavenger 清除剂	A scavenger is an adsorbant which is added to a package in order to remove harmful vapours or gases. Examples are Ageless for removing oxygen and zeolites for removing acetic acid. 清除剂是一种被添加到包装中以去除有害的蒸气或气体的吸附剂。例如脱氧剂 Ageless（爱持丽色）和去除乙酸的沸石。
scope 范围	The scope of an activity or responsibility is its extent, range or limit. 活动或责任的范围是其程度、幅度或限制。
security 安全 / 安防 / 安保	Security facilities and systems are installed to control access by people in order to prevent loss or damage to collections. 安装安防设施和系统是用于控制人员与藏品接触，以防止藏品丢失或损坏。
security officer 安保管理人员	A security officer is a person responsible for implementing security measures. 安保管理人员是负责实施安保措施的人员。
selection 选定的藏品清单	A selection of objects is a list of those chosen from a collection for a specific purpose, such as conservation, exhibition or publication. 选定的藏品清单是为特定目的（如保存，展览或出版）从藏品中选择的器物的列表。
separation 间隔分区	The separation of activities is the zoning of different functions that may have incompatible effects on the collection. 间隔分区指对可能会对藏品产生不兼容影响的不同功能进行的分区。
shatterproof glass 防碎安全玻璃	Shatterproof glass is made of a number of sheets of glass laminated with plastic sheet. It is used in display case construction to increase security and safety. 防碎安全玻璃由塑料内层将两片玻璃在一定温度和压力下粘贴而成。展柜中使用防碎安全玻璃以提高其安全性。
shelf life 保质期	The shelf life of a product is the period of time it can be stored in its original packaging while retaining its specified properties. 产品的保质期是指产品在原包装中能保持其特定性能的储存时间。
showcase 展柜	A showcase is a glazed cabinet for the display of objects. 展柜是用于展示器物的玻璃柜。

silica gel 硅胶	Silica gel is a highly porous form of silica that reversibly adsorbs up to forty percent of its weight in water. It has been used as a dessicant for objects requiring very dry conditions of storage. Conditioned silica gel has been equilibrated at a specific relative humidity in order to maintain a specified micro-climate as a buffering material. 硅胶是一种高度多孔的二氧化硅，能可逆地吸收多达自身重量40%的水分。它已被用作需要非常干燥存储条件器物的干燥剂。经过调节的硅胶可作为缓冲材料，用于稳定特定相对湿度。
sleeve 套筒	A sleeve is a protective tube, open at both ends, used for the storage of objects. Examples are calico sleeves for rolled textiles, and polyester sleeves used for photographic negatives. 套筒是两端开口的用于存放器物的保护管。例如用于卷筒纺织品的印花布套筒，及用于照相底片的聚酯套筒。
sponsorship 赞助 / 资助	Sponsorship for a specified use is resources provided by an external body which wishes to derive substantial benefit in public recognition from the transaction. 特定用途的赞助是由外部机构提供的资源，该机构希望从公众对该项业务的认可中获取实质收益。
stable burial environment 稳定的埋藏环境	A stable burial environment is one where the conditions surrounding an object in the ground do not change over time. 稳定的埋葬环境指埋葬在地下的器物周围状况不会随时间变化的环境。
stamp 印章	A stamp is a mark applied to the stretcher or canvas of a painting. It may be used to identify the manufacturer, maker, owner, dealer or conservator. 印章指施加到绘画框架或画布上的标记。它可以用来识别生产者、制造者、所有者、经销商或保管者。
standard 标准	A standard is an explicit minimum level or benchmark. The standard is set as a specific quality of an object or collection, its care, treatment or environment. 标准是经详细说明的最低级别或基准，如对器物或藏品的特质，其维护保养、修复处理或环境的特定要求。
state of preservation 保存状态	The state of preservation of an object is the extent of the survival of the original parts and its condition. 器物的保存状态是原始构件得以留存的程度及其状况。
storage 存储 / 保管 / 保存 / 库房	An object or collection in storage is one which is not on display or in any other active use and is being kept in a semi-permanent location. 存储是指器物或藏品在未被展示或用于其他任何用途之前，暂时保存在某地。
storage unit 存储单元	A storage unit is a discrete section of a collection held in a physical container. These units can be arranged in a hierarchy, for example: object container; packing unit, drawer, cabinet, compactor, store room, department, building. 存储单元是保存在物理容器中的藏品部件。这些部件可以按层次结构排列，例如，器物囊盒、包装单元、抽屉、展柜、密集柜、库房、部门、建筑物。

store 储藏	You store an object or collection when you put it in a safe place for future rather than present use. 储藏是将暂时不用的器物或藏品放置在安全的地方以备将来使用。
store room 储存室 / 库房	A store room is an enclosed space designated for the storage of objects. 储藏室是指定用于存储器物的封闭空间。
strong room 保险间 / 保险库	A strong room is a room that is resistant to physical attack. Such rooms are designed to achieve a particularly high degree of security to precious objects. 保险间/保险库指可抵抗物理攻击的房间。设计这样的房间是为了贵重器物能达到较高的安全性保护。
studio 工作室	See conservation laboratory. 见保护实验室。
sulfur dioxide 二氧化硫	Sulfur dioxide, SO_2, is pollutant gas caused by burning fossil fuels. 二氧化硫，即SO_2是燃烧化石燃料引起的污染气体。
sulfuryl fluoride 硫酰氟	See sulfur difluoride. 见二氟化硫。
surface deposition 表面沉积	Surface deposition is the reaction of a pollutant with a surface. The reaction may be with an object's surface or with other materials such as building materials or materials added deliberately to remove the pollutants. 表面沉积是污染物与表面的反应。该反应可能是因与器物表面或与其它材料（如建筑材料）或为去除污染物而特意添加材料而导致的。
surveillance 安防监控	Surveillance techniques use security personnel or close circuit television to monitor the well being of a collection. 安防监控技术指使用安保人员或闭路电视监控藏品完好与否的技术。
survey 调查	You carry out a survey when you examine, monitor and record in a systematic manner the condition of a building or a collection and its environment. 调查是以系统的方式检查、监测和记录建筑物或藏品及其保存环境。
technique 工艺	A technique is an accepted method used in carrying out a procedure. 工艺是通常用于执行某程序的方法。
tender 招标	A tender is a formal offer to carry out a project or consultancy, usually in writing, which describes the work to be undertaken and the charge to be made for the work. 招标是实施项目或咨询的正式要约（通常以书面形式）。招标应描述要进行的工作以及该工作涵盖的费用。
thermal cycling 热循环	Thermal cycling is the change in temperature of an object or building which can in turn cause dimensional changes. The change can be diurnal to annual. 热循环指可引起器物或建筑物尺寸变化的温度变化情况。尺寸变化的周期可为一周到一年。

threshold 阈值（临界值）	A threshold is a limit, or value, below which no reaction occurs. 阈值又叫临界值，是指一个效应能够产生的最低值或最高值。
title 所有权凭证	If you have title to an object or collection, you have the legal right to ownership. 拥有器物或藏品的所有权凭证，就拥有其合法所有权。
training 培训	The training of a person is the process of providing instruction and practice for the development of skills, both practical and intellectual, for carrying out a task. 人员培训是以促使受训人完成特定任务为目的，指导和实践相结合，以期促进受训人实践和知识技能的过程。
transit 运输	The transit of an object is its transportation from one location to another. 器物的运输是其从一个位置到另一位置的运输。
treatment report （保护修复） 处理报告	A treatment report is the documentation of the conservation treatment which an object has undergone, including details of all investigations undertaken, processes and materials used and the results obtained, together with samples and drawn and photographic records. 处理报告是对器物实施保护修复处理的记录文件，包括关于所有调查、处理步骤、使用的材料和获得结果的详细信息，以及取样、病害图和照片。
unprofessional 非专业的	An unprofessional action by a professional is one which in not in compliance with the standards of the profession, either explicitly stated or commonly accepted. 职业标准一般为明文规定或者被普遍认可的行为，而专业人士所做出的非专业行为是与职业标准不符的。
UV sleeve 紫外线套管	A UV sleeve is a plastic filter that is placed over fluorescent tubes in order to absorb the UV emissions. 紫外线套管是放置在荧光灯管上用于吸收紫外线的塑料滤光片。
value (2) 价值 (2)	The value of an object is worth that an individual or a society places on an object in comparison with other objects. 器物的价值指个人或社会所赋予其的相对其它器物的意义。
vapour barrier 防潮层	A vapour barrier is an impermeable material which prevents the movement of water vapour. This may be used in a building or in packaging. 防潮层是可防止水蒸气运动的不可渗透材料，可在建筑物或包装中使用。
ventilation 通风	Ventilation is the artificial or natural movement of air into, within and from a building or structure to improve comfort levels and remove unwanted levels of moisture vapour and airborne pollutants. 通风是指空气以人为或自然的方式在建筑物内外流动，以提高室内舒适度并去除多余的水蒸气和空气污染物。
Vikane 硫酰氟	See sulfur dioxide difluoride. 见二氧化硫二氟化物。

vitrine 玻璃橱窗式展柜	A vitrine is a display cabinet. 玻璃橱窗式展柜即展示柜。
water sprinkler 水喷淋器	A water sprinkler system is a method of fire control which releases piped water when sensors detect fire. See also dry pipe system. 水喷淋器系统是一种消防控制方法，其在传感器检测到火情时释放管道中的水。另见干管系统。
window mat 开窗式夹裱框	A window mat is an overlaying protective and/or decorative material with a cut-out to display the image. See also mat. 开窗式夹裱框是一种预留窗口以展现所保护作品的多层保护和/或装饰材料。另见卡纸框。
working object 工作对象（保护修 复中的器物）	A working object is one which is maintained, by remaking as necessary, to provide an aesthetic or informative purpose. 工作对象（保护修复中的器物）是指以提供美学或信息为目的，进行维护，甚至必要的翻新。
workshop 工作坊/讲习所	See conservation laboratory. 见保护实验室。
zoning (2) 分区 (2)	Zoning is the arrangement of objects or collections within a museum or similar institution based on their environmental needs. 分区是根据环境需求在博物馆或类似机构中对器物或藏品进行的布置。

03

绘 画
Painted Surfaces

abbozzo 草图	Abozzo is underpainting in monochrome used to indicate the general composition of a painting. 绘画单色底稿，用来确定构图。
academy board 油画板	An academy board is pasteboard or millboard which has been prepared as a substrate for painting and may have an applied texture. 被用作绘画底板的可能有纹路的厚纸板。
additive colour mixing 加色混合	Additive colour mixing is a retouching method in which the paint is mixed on a palette and applied in one application. 一种修整方法，颜料在调色板上混合并直接应用。
additives 添加剂	Additives are materials which are added to paint in order to modify its handling properties. 加入颜料中用来调节颜料的特性。
agate 玛瑙	Agate is a stone, composed of amorphous silica, used to make highly polished tools which are used for burnishing gold leaf during the water gilding process. 玛瑙是一种石材，成分是二氧化硅，曾被用于制作高度抛光的工具，用于在胶液贴金过程中研光金箔。
ageing crack 老化裂纹	An ageing crack in a painting is narrow and may run in a straight or slightly curved line through all the layers. The crack is caused by environmental conditions and internal and external stresses. 画作的老化裂纹很窄，沿着一条直线或略微弯曲的线贯穿所有涂层。裂纹是由环境条件和内外压力造成的。
alla prima 直接成画法	Alla prima is the technique of producing a painting in one session. 不等颜料干燥，持续在未干燥的画面上作画，一次完成的油画。
alligator crackle 鳄裂	Alligator crackle is a pattern of wide cracks in the upper paint or varnish layer, resembling alligator scales. It is produced by shrinkage in a rapidly drying upper layer lying on top of a slow drying under layer. This typically happens on picture varnish. 鳄裂是在颜料表层或光油层上出现的一种宽裂纹，类似鳄鱼鳞片。由于表层快速干燥收缩而底层还未干透所产生。这通常发生在绘画清漆层上。
alligatoring 鳄裂	See alligator crackle. 见鳄裂。
amvon 讲道坛	Amvon is an elevation before the iconostasis in an orthodox church. 东正教圣障前的讲道坛。
ancona 祭坛装饰品	An ancona is a panel or altarpiece. 指平板或祭坛装饰品。
animal black 骨炭黑	Animal black is made by burning bones in a reducing atmosphere. 在还原气氛下燃烧动物骨骼而制成的颜料。

applied brocade 仿织锦画法	Applied brocade is a polychrome painting technique used to imitate a brocaded and gilded textile using moulding to create relief. 一种用来模仿织锦和金线所织成织物的多色画法，用模具制作浮雕质感。
armenian bole 埃尔默尼让红土	See bole. 一种用于制作颜料的粉红色泥土，见贴金底灰。
arriccio 粗泥层	Arriccio is the preliminary plaster layer spread on masonry, which is left rough so that the final layer, intonaco, can adhere more easily. 涂抹在石上的第一层粗糙的灰泥层，能使最后一层的细泥层更好粘合。
asist 高光金	An asist is a golden highlight on icons made with gold leaf or imitation gold. It is found on the garments and hair of persons depicted in icons. 用金箔或贴金来提亮或作为画面高光，经常用于圣像的服装或头发上。
asphalt 沥青	Asphalt is a natural hydrocarbon mixture resulting from the evaporation of the volatiles in natural oil. Asphalt is now made as a by-product of oil refining. Asphalt can be used as a pigment in paint, and may often exhibit alligator crackle. 沥青是一种天然的碳氢化合物的混合物，是由天然石油中的挥发物蒸发后而形成。沥青现在是炼油的副产品。沥青可作为颜料，但易鳄裂。
auxiliary support 辅助支撑	An auxiliary support is a frame such as a strainer or stretcher to which a canvas painting support is attached. 一种附着画布的框架，如固定型和扩张型内框。
Azurite 蓝铜矿，石青	It is a natural blue pigment, it is a basic copper carbonate. 蓝铜矿是一种天然的蓝色颜料，成分是碱式碳酸铜。
back edge 背部边缘	A back edge is the edge of the frame which is furthest from the painting. 离画最远的框边。
backing (1) 背衬	Backing is a method used in painting conservation to protect the back of the painting on canvas from external mechanical stress and reduce atmospheric changes affecting the back of the painting. The material for backing can be for example an acid free cardboard or a sheet of rigid lightweight plastic and it is attached to the auxiliary support of the painting. 在绘画保护中使用的方法，用于保护画布上的绘画背面免受外部机械压力的影响，并减少会影响绘画背面的气体环境变化。例如，用做背衬的材料可以是无酸纸板或一块刚性轻质塑料，并附着在绘画的辅助支撑上。
balsa 热带美洲轻木	Balsa is a lightweight and porous wood from a South American tree, Ochroma lagopus. It is often used as a filler for missing areas of wood, for example, in panel paintings or polychrome sculpture. 一种轻而多孔的木材，产自南美洲一种名为轻木的树。它经常被用作填充物填补木材缺失的部分，例如用于板画或彩色雕塑中。

balsam 香脂	Balsam is a natural mixture of resins and ethereal oils as it is extruded from certain trees and shrubs. Examples are copaiva balsam and Venice turpentine. 树脂和醚油的天然混合物，从某些树木和灌木中挤出。例如科帕瓦香脂和威尼斯松节油。
basma 圣像画的金属覆层	A basma is a metal cover on an icon, mounted or collected from small pieces. It covers the borders and background of the icon but leaves figures fully exposed. 圣像画上的金属覆层，用小片安装。它覆盖了圣像画的边缘和背景，但使人物完全暴露在外。
batten 板条	A batten is a strip of wood attached across the back side of panel boards to reinforce the structure and prevent warping, for example on panel paintings and icons. 横穿面板背面的木条，用来加固结构和防止翘曲，例如应用于板画和圣像画上。
beard 石膏底料堆砌	A beard is a lip of gesso formed after the priming of the panel with an engaged frame. This lip can be visible on the paintings from which the frame has been removed . 石膏底料在面板涂底处理后在边缘形成的堆砌，是指在用边框对面板进行涂底处理后形成的石膏边缘，在移除边框的绘画上可以看到。
binding medium 胶结物质	See medium. 见媒介。
bitumen 沥青	See asphalt. 见沥青。
bitumen of judaea 沥青	See asphalt. 见沥青。
bleeding (2) 渗出	In a dried paint film, a bleeding colourant is one that diffuses and spreads away from the layer in which it is applied to other paint or varnish layers. 在干燥的漆膜中，着色剂渗出指它从其他油漆或清漆层中扩散和蔓延。
blister (2) 起疱、疱疹	A blister is a raised convex area of paint. It indicates a cleavage from the lower paint layer, ground layers or support. 绘画局部凸出。起疱现象意味着绘画正从较低的绘画层、底层或支撑层开裂。
blistering 泡状起甲	Bubbling deformation and detachment of the ground and/or paint and/or coating layer(s) leading to loss. 底色层，画层，表面涂层气泡变形导致脱落。
bloom 白雾状结晶	A bloom is a white film or particulate which forms on the surface of an object and obscures it. It is often caused by deterioration within the object. 在物体表面形成并使其模糊的白色薄膜或微粒。它通常是由物体内部劣化引起的。

Blue verditer 铜盐颜料	It is an artificial basic copper carbonate, which is similar in chemical composition to the mineral, azurite. This pale greenish blue pigment is little used today. 铜盐颜料是一种人造碱式碳酸铜，其化学成分与矿物石青相似。这种淡绿色的蓝色颜料现今已很少使用。
blush 白霜	Blush is the appearance of white that sometimes develops in varnish film almost immediately after application. It occurs only in humid weather and is caused by rapid evaporation of solvents, which produces cooling at the surface and which in turn causes condensation of moisture within the film. 白色外观，有时在涂刷后立即在漆膜上形成。白霜只形成于潮湿的天气中，是由溶剂的快速蒸发引起的，溶剂在表面产生冷却，进而导致薄膜内的水分凝结。
body (2) 不透明填料 (2)	The body in gouache is a white filler used to make the paint opaque. 水粉画中的"体"指白色的填充物，用来使绘画不透明。
body (3) 色料 (3)	The body in oil painting is the proportion of the pigment in the paint. 油画中的色料是指色素在颜料中的含量。
bole 贴金底灰	Bole is a white or coloured fine smooth clay applied to a substrate to prepare a uniform surface for gilding. Coloured bole is used as a ground for gold leaf and provides a smooth cushion and background colour to the gold. 白色或彩色的光滑粘土，用于在底层制备均匀的表面用来贴金。彩色粘土用作金箔基底，为金箔提供光滑的垫层和背景色。
Bologna chalk 博洛尼亚白垩	Bologna chalk is a very light and airy, repeatedly precipitated gypsum. 一种非常轻且透气，反复沉淀的石膏。
bolus 粘土填充剂	See bole. 见贴金底灰。
Bone black 骨黑	animal black, see also ivory black, carbon black, is made by charring animal bones in closed retorts. 动物黑，也见象牙黑、炭黑，骨灰是通过在密闭罐中将动物骨头炭化制成的黑色颜料。
bone glue 骨胶	Bone glue is impure gelatin prepared from bones. 骨胶是由骨头制备的不纯明胶。
box frame 盒型架	See cassetta frame. 见卡索莱画箱。
bozzetto 油画草图	Bozzetto is a rapid sketch in oil made as a study for a large painting. 油画草图，作为大型绘画的试画。
brand 标记	A brand is a mark burned into the back of panels, retables, wooden sculptures and altarpieces. It was applied as a mark of quality and controlled by the makers' guilds. 烙印在嵌板、祭坛装饰品、木雕和祭坛画背面的标记。被用作质量标志，并由制造商公会控制。

Brazil-wood 巴西木	Brazil-Wood is a natural red dye from the wood of Caesalpinia Braziliensis. 巴西木是来自巴西凯撒木材的天然红色染料。
breather 透气层	A breather is a strip of fabric with an open weave, used in vacuum-hot table treatment of paintings. The strip facilitates the air evacuation during the vacuum treatment. 一条织法稀松的织物，用于绘画的真空热台处理。在真空处理过程中，通气管有助于空气排出。
brushwork 笔触	Brushwork is the marks made by the brushes on the paint surface. The style of the brushwork is an expression of the painter and can aid in the identification of the maker. 画笔在颜料表面留下的痕迹。笔触的风格是画家的一种表现形式，有助于识别创作者。
buckle (1) 皱 (1)	Buckle is severe cockle of film due to uneven shrinkage. 由于不均匀收缩造成的薄膜严重皱折。
buckling (1) 屈曲、隆起	In a paint layer, buckling is a strong creasing caused by fatty oils such as poppy oil, which after an initial drying process may become soft again. Buckling may occur also if the paint layer contains non-drying components like spike oil, copaiba balsam oil or oil of cloves. 在漆层中，屈曲是由像罂粟油这样的脂肪油引起的一种严重的折痕，在最初的干燥过程后可能会再次变软。如果漆层含有非干燥成分，如穗花油、苦配巴香脂、丁香油，也可能发生屈曲。
bulge 膨胀变形	A bulge is an irregular distortion and swelling of a stretched fabric caused by uneven dimensional changes. 由于不均匀的尺寸变化引起的不规则变形和膨胀。
burlap 粗麻布	Burlap is a coarse canvas of plain weave. It is made from jute, flax or hemp. See also hessian. 粗麻布是一种粗糙的平纹画布。它是由黄麻、亚麻或大麻制成的。参见粗麻布。
burnisher 研磨器	A burnisher is an highly polished tool made of a hard material, for example agate. It is used to burnish gold leaf that has been applied onto a boled gesso ground. 研磨器是一种质地坚硬的高度抛光工具，例如玛瑙。用来打磨铺在石膏底板上的金箔。
butt joint 平接	A butt joint is a one between two planks of wood where the edges are brought together without interlocking overlaps. 指两块木板之间的接头，其边缘连接在一起，没有交错重叠。
butterfly key 蝴蝶榫	A butterfly key is a small butterfly shaped piece of wood set into and holding together two pieces of wood. A butterfly key can be used to join two planks in a panel and to secure a mitre joint on the rear side of frames. 一种蝶形的小木块，放置于两片木板内用于连接。蝴蝶榫可用于连接面板中的两片木板，并在框架后侧固定斜接接头。

Calcium Carbonate 碳酸钙	It is a white pigment and widely distributed over the world. 碳酸钙（CaCO₃）是一种白色颜料，在全球广泛分布。
canvas 画布	Canvas is a heavy closely woven cloth made with natural or synthetic materials. It is used as a painting support. 用天然或合成材料制成的重而密织的布料，被用作绘画支撑物。
canvas board 画板	A canvas board is a primed canvas stuck onto cardboard or pasteboard. 粘在硬纸板上的涂有底漆的画布。
canvas pliers 绷布钳	Canvas pliers is a tool used to stretch a canvas onto a stretcher or strainer. 一种工具，用于将画布拉伸到延伸器或拉紧装置上。
carmine 胭脂红	Carmine is the common name for the red animal dyes cochineal and kermes. 胭脂红是红色动物染料和胭脂虫的俗称。
cartellino 条幅状文字注记	Cartellino is a trompe l'oeil scroll or scarp of painted paper within a composition, used for an inscription or signature. From the italian word cartellino, meaning a small piece of paper. 在作品中画出的一个纸卷，用于题词或签名。来自意大利语 cartellino，意思是一小片纸
cartoon 卡通（草图）	A cartoon is a full-scale preliminary drawing for a painting. It is used for transferring a composition to the surface to be painted 卡通是一幅绘画作品的全尺寸草图，用来把定好结构的草图转移到正式画的表面。
casein paint 酪蛋白颜料	Casein paint is a water based paint with a casein medium that forms a matte surface. 酪蛋白颜料是水性颜料和酪蛋白介质组成的颜料。干后表面哑光。
cassetta frame 卡索莱画框	A cassetta frame is a frame used for paintings. It consists of a flat or slightly concave or convex frieze defined by distinct mouldings (Italy 16th-17th century). 16-17世纪盛行于意大利的画框。它由平整或稍微凹或凸的带状装饰组成，造型多样。
cassone 嫁妆箱	A cassone is an Italian marriage chest. In 15th century Italy it was customary to decorate these chests with inset panel paintings or 'cassone paintings'. 15世纪意大利的嫁妆箱。常见用镶板画或"箱柜画"装饰。
cast frame 铸造画框	A cast frame is a type of picture frame where the ornament is added to the wood by casting or pressing by hand from a mould. 一种画框，用手从模具中铸造或压入，将装饰物添加到木头上。
chalk 白垩	Chalk is a soft rock, composed of calcium carbonate, CaCO₃. See also whiting. 一种软岩，由碳酸钙（CaCO₃）组成。另见碳酸钙粉。

chalking 粉化	Chalking is the powdering away of pigment from a paint surface. It is caused by the disintegration or loss of the binding agent from the paint. 颜料表面形成粉末。粉化是由颜料中粘合剂的分解或损失引起的。
chamferred edge 斜切边	A chamferred edge is the sloped or bevelled edge of a wood panel that is fitted into the groove of its frame. 安装在框架凹槽中木板的倾斜或斜切边缘。
Charcoal black 碳黑	See also carbon black, the residue from the dry distillation of woods, is made by heating the wood in closed chambers of kilns.For pigment purposes, the charcoal is ground and well washed to remove potash. 另见炭黑，即木材干馏的残余物，是通过在密闭的窑炉中加热木材而制得的。出于着色的目的，将木炭磨碎并充分洗涤以除去含钾木灰。
chiaroscuro 明暗对比法	Chiaroscuro is a painting technique of modelling form by almost imperceptible gradations of light and dark. 一种绘画技巧，通过几乎不可察觉的明暗渐变来造型。
chromatic abstraction 色彩抽象	Chromatic abstraction is a technique for restoration of paintings. It is used to fill lacunae with a neutral abstract tonality without detracting from the legibility of the work. It is made by the cross hatching of four dominating or basic colours (yellow, red, blue or green, brown or black). 一种绘画修复技术。它用于在不损害作品的可识别性的情况下以中性的抽象色调填充脱落缺损的部分。用中性抽象色调来填补空白，而不减损画作的清晰程度。它是由四种主色或基本色（黄、红、蓝、绿、棕、黑）的交叉图案（影线）构成的。
chromatic selection 色彩选择	Chromatic selection is a technique for restoration of paintings by retouching a lacuna by applying paint in curved lines following the original brushstrokes. See also tratteggio. 一种绘画修复技术，沿着原始的笔触在曲线上涂上油漆，来修饰空白处。另见垂直影线。
Cinnabar 硫化汞，朱砂	See also Vermilion. 另见朱砂。
clavus 垂直条纹	See klav. 见垂直条纹。
cleaning window 清理窗口	See window. 见窗口。
clouding 白雾状结晶	See bloom. 见白障。
cochineal 胭脂虫红	Cochineal is a red dye, carminic acid, extracted from the cochineal insect, Coccus cacti. It is used to make crimson lake and replaced kermes in the 16th century as the primary red dye material. 一种红色染料，又称胭脂红酸，从胭脂虫中提取。胭脂虫红用于制造胭脂红，在16世纪取代了胭脂红，作为主要红色染料原料。

Cochineal 胭脂红	Cochineal is a natural organic dyestuff that is made from the dried bodies of the female insect, Coccus Cacti. 胭脂红是一种天然有机红色染料，由雌性胭脂虫昆虫干燥而制成。
cockling 起皱	Cockling is a wrinkle distortion without a crease which can occur in fabric. 起皱是织物可能发生的无折痕，却皱褶变形的现象。
cold lining 冷裱	Cold lining is a lining technique where solvents are used to activate the adhesive instead of heat. 一种裱褙技术，使用溶剂而不是加热来激活粘合剂。
colla -pasta 科拉面糊胶	Colla-pasta is a paste made from rye or wheat flour, glue and water. Many recipes exist with varying proportions and ingredients. It is used as an adhesive in the lining of paintings and was developed in Italy. 由黑麦或小麦粉、胶水和水制成的糊状物。许多配方的比例和成分各不相同。科拉面糊胶被用作绘画裱褙的粘合剂，这种方法在意大利得到发展。
colletta 兔皮胶	In Italy, colletta is a rabbit skin glue. It forms a low viscosity solution and is therefore not used for lining. Depending upon its proposed use, the formulation of the colletta can be adjusted and may have plasticisers added. colletta is used for adhering facings and/or for consolidation of paint and ground layers. It is also used to face wall paintings prior to transfer. 在意大利，colletta是一种兔皮胶。它形成的溶液粘度低，因此不用于裱褙。根据其用途，可调整兔皮胶的配方，并可添加增塑剂。兔皮胶用于粘附表面和/或加固油漆和基层。它也用于壁画揭取之前的画面加固。
compensation 填补	Compensation is a restoration of a painting which includes both filling and inpainting. 对画作的修复，包括填充和修补图像。
complete cleaning 完全清洁	Complete cleaning of a painted surface involves removing all yellowed varnish and restorations, without removing any part of the original painted surface. 着色表面的完全清洁包括去除所有发黄的清漆和修复物，而不移除原始涂漆表面的任何部分。
compo (1) 裱褙粘合剂	Compo is a glue based lining adhesive with potential additives like molasses, flour and Venice turpentine. See also pasta. 一种基于胶水的裱褙粘合剂，可能含有添加剂，如糖蜜、面粉和威尼斯松节油。另见面糊胶。
compo (2) 复合填充材料	Compo is a composite of filling material used in frame conservation. It can be pressed to make a moulded ornament. 一种用于框架保护的复合填充材料。可被压成模制的装饰品。
composition leaf 仿金箔	Composition leaf is a metal leaf made of bronze or brass. It is used to make an inexpensive substitute for gold leaf. See also Dutch metal. 仿金箔由青铜或黄铜制成，因价格便宜而用作金箔的替代品。参见荷兰金。

convection crackle 对流裂纹	A convection crackle is a type of crackle in a painting. Convection crackle is caused by the flow of moist air across the reverse of the painting. This results in local dimensional changes and crackle in areas exposed to the air flow. The crackle does not form in areas affected by barriers such as stretcher bars or keys. See also stretcher image. 对流裂纹是绘画中裂纹的一种。由于潮湿空气经过画的背面，导致接触气流的区域出现局部尺寸变化和裂纹。裂纹不会在受障碍物（如拉伸杆或榫）影响的区域形成。另见阅拉伸图像。
converter frame 转换器框架	A converter frame is an auxiliary unit which can be added to a hot table set-up. It provides a suction system to the existing system. 一种辅助装置，可添加到热台装置中。为现有系统提供吸入系统。
copaiba balsam 苦配巴香脂	Copaiba balsam is an oleo resin, derived from tropical trees. 一种油性树脂，从热带树木中获得。
copal 柯巴脂	A copal resin is a hard resin that is obtained both from living trees and in fossilised form. 一种硬树脂，既可以从活着的树中获得，也可以从化石中获得。
copper panel 铜面板	A copper panel is a metallic sheet used from about 17th century as a support for oil paintings especially in Northern Europe. 一种金属板，大约在17世纪就被用来支撑油画，尤其是在北欧应用广泛。
copper resinate 铜树脂酸盐	A copper resinate is a translucent green pigment based on verdigris or other copper salts. 一种半透明的绿色颜料，含有铜绿或其他铜盐。
Copper resinate 铜树脂酸盐	It is a green compound formed by dissolving copper acetate, verdigris, or other copper salt in Venice turpentine, balsam, or similar resinous solution. 铜树脂酸盐是一种绿色化合物，是通过将醋酸铜、铜绿或其他铜盐溶解在威尼斯松节油、香脂或类似的树脂溶液中而形成的。
corner block 角块	A corner block is a wooden block used to secure the mitre joint of a frame. It was also used to strengthen the outer and inner back frames during the 19th century. 用来固定框架斜接处的木块。在19世纪，它也被用来加固外部和内部的背框。
cracks 裂缝	Fissures that occur through any or all of the layers of the painting stratigraphy 穿过壁画结构中任何一层或所有层的裂隙。
cradle 格子支架	A cradle is a wooden structure attached to the back of a panel painting which strengthens it and prevents warping. 一种木质结构，附着在面板画的背面，用来加强面板并防止翘曲。
craquelure 龟裂	Craquelure is a pattern of fine cracks that forms on ageing in a paint layer or varnish on a painting or piece of furniture, due to differential movement of the coating and the substrate. 龟裂是由于涂层和基材的不同运动，在画作或家具的油漆层或清漆老化时形成的一种细微裂缝。

crater eruption & loss 火山口状鼓起与脱落	Bulges (from 0.5cm to 1cm in diameter) in the paint, ground and fine plaster layers leading to crater- shaped losses, containing small CaSO4 inclusions. 画层，底色层和细泥层中小范围起鼓（直径0.5至1厘米）导致火山口状的脱落，脱落部分留有硫酸钙硬核。
cross-stretcher 十字伸缩架	A cross-stretcher is a type of stretcher for paintings. They have stretcher bars from the centre of the sides and cross in the middle. 用于绘画的一种伸缩架。画框侧面的中心有伸缩杆，在中间交叉。
cusping 波浪状形变	Cusping is the wavy distortions in the weave at the edge of a canvas. It is caused by the canvas being stretched with cords in a strainer while being primed. 画布边缘的波浪状变形。这是由于画布在涂底漆时被拉紧装置中的绳索拉伸而引起的。
dabber 上漆垫	A dabber is a soft, absorbent wad usually covered with cloth, silk, leather or nylon net, used to apply paint or varnish. 一种柔软的、吸水性很强的絮状物，通常覆盖有布、丝绸、皮革或尼龙网，用于涂油漆或清漆。
dark fading 非光照褪色	Dark fading is a temperature dependant loss of density or color change of chromogenic dyes in the absence of light. 非光照褪色是指显色染料在没有光照的情况下，因温度而引起的密度损失或颜色变化。
dead colouring 灰色草图	Dead colouring is a historical technique of painting in which the composition is built up in grisaille before applying coloured paint. 历史上的一种绘画技巧，在使用彩色颜料之前，先用灰色颜料构图。
decoupage 剪纸装饰	Decoupage is a form of decoration in which pieces of paper are glued onto the frame moulding and then treated with successive layers of varnish. 一种装饰艺术形式，将剪纸粘在画板或框架上，然后用连续的清漆层处理。
Desco da Parto 出生托盘	Desco da Parto is a painted round or oval wood panel used in medieval and early Renaissance Italy to bring gifts to a woman who has just given birth. Today, they are framed and presented as panel easel paintings. Desco da Parto（带有精美图画的出生托盘）是在中世纪和文艺复兴早期的意大利用来给刚分娩的妇女带礼物的圆形或椭圆形涂色木板。如今它们被装裱起来，并作为板架绘画呈现。
dipper 颜料杯	A dipper is a small cup for paint medium or dilutent, made to be clipped onto the edge of a palette. It is usually made of metal and can be open or closed with a lid. 一个小杯子，用来盛放颜料溶剂或稀释液，可以夹在调色板的边缘上。通常由金属制成，盖子可以打开或关闭。
diptych 双联画	A diptych is a pair of painted panels hinged together. 一对用铰链连接在一起的画板。

disruption 酥碱	General term used to describe areas of usually salt-related deterioration where the painted plaster exhibits partial loss of cohesion within any or all of the layers. 酥碱是一种由盐造成的，壁画地仗层的一层或多层结构中，胶结力部分丧失的病害。
distressing 打磨做旧	Distressing is a method of simulating the patina of age on the frames by rubbing away some of the top layer of gilt or painted surface so that the base colour shows through. The distressing of a surface is deliberate damage often carried out fraudulantly. 通过磨去贴金或涂漆表面的顶层涂料使底色显现出来，用以模仿画框上的古旧铜色。通常是欺诈性的假意破坏。
double gilding 双层贴金	Double gilding is a water gilding process where a polished surface is covered with two layers of gold leaf. Usually double weight gold leaf is used to obtain a richer finish. 一种水贴金工艺，在抛光表面上覆盖两层金箔。通常使用双重量金箔来营造更丰富的饰面。
double lining 双层裱褙	Double lining is a conservation procedure where a second lining is adhered to the back of the first one. This may be required when a single lining has not provided sufficient strength for the painting. 一种保护性程序，第二层衬里附着在第一层衬里的背面。当单个衬里不能为画作提供足够的强度时，可能需要双层裱褙。
double weight gold 加厚金箔	Double weight gold is a type of gold leaf. It is usually of fine and regular gold, and is slightly thicker than single weight gold but not necessarily twice the thickness. 一种金箔，通常是由精致而规则的黄金制成，比单重量黄金稍厚，但不一定是其厚度的两倍。
dragging 拖抹 粉饰	Dragging is a painting technique for producing broken effects of colour by drawing a brush loaded with almost dry pigment over a still tacky undercoat. 一种绘画技术，通过在仍然具有粘性的底漆上涂抹几乎干了的颜料来产生破碎的色彩效果。
dragon's blood 血竭（龙血树脂）	Dragon's blood is a transparent red resin obtained from a number of Asian palms. It has been used as a colourant for varnishes, and for the decoration of gold. It is soluble in alcohol and is light sensitive. 一种透明的红色树脂，可从许多亚洲棕榈中提取。被用作清漆和黄金装饰的着色剂。可溶于酒精，对光敏感。
draping 悬垂褶皱	A draping is a fold or other 3-dimensional distortion in a fabric, usually caused by gravity. 织物的褶皱或其他三维变形，通常由重力引起。
draw 角波纹	A draw is distortion of a canvas found in the corners of a stretched painting. It appears in a form of radiating wrinkles or parallel wrinkles. 一幅被拉伸的画布边角处的变形。以放射状褶皱或平行褶皱的形式出现。

drying agent 催干剂	A drying agent is a substance which is added to an oil paint to enhance its drying properties. Drying agents usually catalyse the oxidative reactions which cause cross-linking. See also siccative. 添加到油漆中以增强其干燥性能的物质。干燥剂通常催化引起交联的氧化反应。另见干燥剂。
drying crack 干裂	A drying crack is found in a paint layer and occurs during drying. It is often curved and wide. 干裂见于颜料层，在干燥过程中出现。干裂通常弯曲且宽。
drying oil 干性油	A drying oil is an unsaturated plant oil which reacts with oxygen with crosslinking to produce a coherent film. Drying oils are frequently used as the binding agents for pigments in paint. Examples are linseed oil, walnut oil and poppy oil. See also oil 一种不饱和植物油，与氧气发生交联反应，生成一层连贯的薄膜。干性油常用作涂料中色素的粘合剂。例如亚麻籽油、核桃油和罂粟油。另见油
duck 不浸水画布	Duck is a strong untwilled linen or cotton fabric which can be used as a painting canvas or lining. Duck was given its name because it sheds water. 一种结实的非斜纹亚麻或棉织物，可用作画布或衬里。之所以得名"duck"，是因为它不浸水。
Dutch metal 荷兰金	Dutch metal is an imitation gold leaf. It comes in various shades and is most often made from copper-zinc alloys. Also called metal leaf, schlag leaf, composition leaf/gold and Dutch gold. It requires a finishing varnish to reduce tarnishing. 仿金箔。有各种不同的色调，通常是由铜锌合金制成的。也被称为金属箔，施拉格箔，复合箔/金和荷兰金。荷兰合金需要涂一层罩光清漆来减少变色。
Dutch method 荷兰裱褙法	Dutch method is a lining method using a wax or wax-resin adhesive. See also wax-resin lining. 一种使用蜡或蜡树脂粘合剂的裱褙方法。另见蜡树脂裱褙。
easel 画架	An easel is a freestanding structure used by artist to hold the painting support during the process of painting. 艺术家在绘画过程中用来支撑画作的独立结构。
easel painting 架上绘画	An easel painting is a painting on canvas, wood, metal or other portable support which has been executed on an easel. 在画架上安装画布、木头、金属或其他可移动的支撑物，进行绘画。
egg tempera 蛋彩画	Egg tempera is a paint using egg components, commonly the yolk, as the medium mixed with pigment. 用鸡蛋的成分（通常是蛋黄）作为混合颜料的媒介。
egg white varnish 蛋清清漆	The use of egg whites as a final varnish for paintings is documented by Cennino Cennini (end of the 14th century) and by Filippo Baldinucci (1681). See also glair. 使用蛋清作为绘画的最后一道亮漆是由切尼尼（14世纪末）和巴尔迪努奇（1681）记载的。另见蛋清。

Egyptian blue 埃及蓝	The inorganic blue colour most commonly found on wall painting of Egyptian, and it is an artificially made pigment. 埃及蓝是一种无机蓝色颜料（CaO·CuO·4SiO），最常见于埃及的壁画，它是人造颜料。
encaustic 蜡画	An encaustic painting is one which is created using pigments in a wax medium which is melted during application. 以蜡作为介质绘作的画，蜡介质在施涂过程中会熔化。
end 经线	An end is a single warp thread. 单根经线。
engaged frame 嵌板框架	An engaged frame is a type of frame for a panel picture which is formed out of the same panel or attached during the construction of the panel. It is covered with gesso at the same time as the panel. 一种用于嵌板图片的框架，由同一嵌板制成或在嵌板构造过程中附加，与嵌板同时被石膏覆盖。
entablature 檐部	The entablature of a picture frame consists of an architrave, frieze and cornice. It is based on the horizontal part of classical architecture. 画框的檐部由框缘、雕带和檐口组成。仿照古典建筑的水平部分。
exfoliation 酥碱起甲	Combined lifting of the paint layer, ground, and some fine plaster associated with the loss of cohesion of the plaster below the paint and ground layers. 画层，底色层和部分地仗起翘。
false crack 模拟裂纹	A false crack is a pattern resembling cracks which are painted onto or scratched into the surface of a painting. 一种类似裂缝的图案，被画在或刮到画的表面上。
faulting 微小破损	Faulting is the repair of small areas of breaks and tears while applying gold leaf. 在使用金箔时修复小面积的断裂和撕裂。
feathering (1) 羽化修饰	Feathering is a painting technique used in retouching to reduce the visibility of junction between the retouch and the original. It usually involves working the paint with a brush dampened with solvent. 一种用于修饰的绘画技术，可以减少修饰和原稿之间连接处的可见性。通常是用蘸有溶剂的刷子涂颜料。
feathering (2) 羽化处理	Feathering is the removal of edge threads of a strip of fabric in order to create a soft frayed edge. It is often used in strip lining and patches to prevent the edge of the patch forming a visible impression on the front of a painting. 去除一条织物的边线，以制成柔软的磨边。毛化通常用于条纹衬里和贴片，以防止补片的边缘在绘画正面形成可见的印痕。
fibreglass canvas 玻璃纤维画	See glass fibre canvas. 见玻璃纤维画。
fillet (1) 阶梯状画框	A fillet is a narrow flat step separating mouldings on a decorative picture frame. 将装饰性画框上的饰条分开的窄而平的台阶。

fish glue 鱼胶	Fish glue is impure gelatin prepared from fish heads, bones, and skins. 鱼胶是由鱼头，骨头和鱼皮制成的不纯明胶。
fixed interleaf 固定插页	See interleaf (1). 见中间层。
flaking 起甲	Fracturing and lifting of the ground and/or paint layer(s). 底色层，画层，表面涂层起翘并拌有破损。
flat 画框平条	a. The flat is a wide flat area or section between the inner and outer mouldings on a frame. b. A flat is an inset part of a frame bordering the painting. a. 框架上内外饰条之间的一个宽而平的区域或部分。b. 画框边缘的嵌入部分。
flattening of impasto 颜料压平	Flattening of impasto is the damage to a painting where the high points of the paint texture are pressed down. It occurs during lining where the painting has been placed face down on a rigid surface or when too much pressure is applied to softened paint layer during the lining in a vacuum envelope. Flattening is increased with the temperature to which the paint is raised and the pressure applied. 指对绘画造成的损害，其中绘画纹理的高点被压下。这种情况发生在裱褙时，颜料面朝下放置在坚硬的表面上，或在真空裱褙期间施加过大压力于变软的绘画层。随着绘画温度升高和施加压力，压平变多。
floating signature 后期涂写	A floating signature is a signature placed on the surface coating of a painting or on top of a layer which is not part of the original. 签署在绘画表面涂层上或不属于原作层上的签名。
fondo d'oro 金底	See gold ground. 见金底。
frame (1) 框架	A frame is a decorative structure around the edges of an image. It may be made of wood, metal or plastic. Its function can be: structural, for example, to control the movements and deformations of a painted wood panel; preservative, for example, to prevent knocking or abrasion; decorative, for example, to enhance the image. 围绕图像边缘的装饰性结构。框架可以由木头、金属或塑料制成。功能包括：结构性的，例如控制绘画木板的运动和变形；保护性的，例如，防止敲击或擦伤；装饰性的，例如，提升图像。
frame (2) 画框	A frame is a rectangular structure usually made of wooden bars onto which the edges of a canvas painting are attached. 画框是一种由木条制成的长方形结构，画布的边缘被附着在其上。
frayed edge 织物磨边	See feathering. 见羽化修饰。
French chalk 滑石粉	See whiting. 见碳酸钙粉。

fresco 湿壁画	A true fresco is a painting where pigments are applied to wet plaster and bond with it chemically as it dries. 湿壁画是在湿灰泥上涂上颜料，颜料在湿灰泥干燥过程中与它产生化学结合的画作。
frieze 平板	See flat. 见画框平条。
frottis 釉料	Frottis is the French term for glaze. 法语中对釉料的称呼。
garland 花边	See stress garland. 见压力花边。
garlic 大蒜	Garlic is a plant (Allium sativum) mentioned in various treatises for use as a surfactant or adhesive for gilding. In the sgraffito decoration technique a freshly cut bulb of garlic is used to rub the gilt surface before coating with tempera in order to improve adhesion of tempera to the surface. 一种植物，学名 Allium sativum，在许多论文中都提到大蒜可用作表面活性剂或贴金粘合剂。在刮擦贴金装饰技术中，在涂上蛋彩画之前，用刚切开的大蒜球刮擦贴金表面，以提高蛋彩画与表面的粘附性。
gathering (1) 收集整理	Gathering is the process of arranging folded sections in the right order prior to sewing and binding. 在缝制和装订之前将折叠的部分按正确的顺序排列。
gelatin 明胶	Derived from collagen, a protein found in animal skin and bone, animal protein substance having gel-forming properties. Gelatin is used extensively as an adhesive. 来源于存在于动物皮肤和骨骼中的胶原蛋白，具有凝胶形成特性，被大量用作胶结物质。
gesso (1) 石膏底	Gesso is a mixture of a white filler with a water soluble binding medium applied over a substrate as a ground for painting or gidling. In renaissance Italy, gesso was made with plaster of Paris and glue or casein. In Northern Europe, gesso has been made for many centuries from natural chalk. Gesso may now include materials like chalk, zinc oxide or other inert white filler. 一种白色填料与水溶性结合介质的混合物，应用于基底上，作为绘画或贴金的底层。在文艺复兴时期的意大利，石膏底是用巴黎石膏和胶水或酪蛋白制成的。在北欧，石膏底已经用白垩制作了许多世纪。石膏现在可能包括白垩、氧化锌或其他惰性白色填料等材料。
gesso grosso 粗石膏底	Gesso grosso is a layer of coarse, burnt gypsum powder mixed with glue and applied directly onto the painting support, usually made of wood. 煅烧过的粗糙石膏粉和胶水混合在一起，直接涂在绘画的木制支撑物上。

gesso sottile 细石膏底	Gesso sottile is a fine gypsum powder (formed by rehydrating burnt gypsum) mixed with glue and applied on top of the gesso grosso. 精细的石膏粉末（由煅烧石膏再水化而成）与胶水混合而成，涂在粗石膏上。
gilder's clay 贴金用粘土	See bole. 见贴金底灰。
gilder's whiting 贴金白粉	See whiting. 见碳酸钙粉。
gimatij 画中人物外衣	Gimatij is an outer garment of a person depicted in an icon. 圣像画中人物的外衣。
glair 蛋清	Glair is the white of egg that has been used as a size, glaze or varnish for paintings. 鸡蛋的蛋清，被用作绘画的浆料、釉料或清漆。
glass fibre canvas 玻璃纤维画	A glass fibre canvas is a canvas made with glass fibres. 用玻璃纤维制成的画布。
glaze (1) 釉、薄罩层	A glaze is a transparent or semi-transparent coating. It is applied over dried oil or tempera underpainting in order to modify the underlying colour. A coloured glaze can be used to make burnished silver look like gold. 一种透明或半透明的涂层。涂于干油或蛋彩画底色上，以改变基础颜色。彩釉可以使磨光的银看起来像黄金。
glue-paste lining 胶水糊裱褙	Glue-paste lining is a lining method for paintings using an adhesive of a solution of glue and flour in water with a plasticiser such as honey or Venice Turpentine. 一种绘画裱褙方法，使用含有胶水和面粉的水溶液及增塑剂（如蜂蜜或威尼斯松节油）作为粘合剂。
gold ground 金底	Gold ground is a medieval/early Renaissance painting technique in which tempera paint is applied to a wood panel previously covered with gold leaf, forming the background. 中世纪和文艺复兴早期的一种绘画技巧，将金箔覆盖在木板上形成背景，然后在上面绘制蛋彩画。
gouache 水粉	Gouache is an opaque gum-based paint applied to canvas or paper. It is applied less thinly than watercolour. Gouache is used in painting conservation for retouching to create coloured background to further layers of inpainting. 水粉是一种不透明的胶基涂料，涂在画布或纸张上。相比水彩，水粉画所用水粉较少。在绘画保护中，水粉用于修整画作的彩色背景，以对表面层以下层进行修复。
grafiya 雕刻圣像	Grafiya are the contours of a motif on an icon that are cut in the gesso ground using a sharp, thin tool, for example a needle. 用锋利、尖细的工具（例如针）在石膏基底上切割出来的圣像主题的轮廓。

Green earth, celadonite 绿土（青瓷土，灰绿土）	It has been used in European paintings since before classical times. 绿土是一种绿色颜料，成分是含铁、镁、铝、钾等元素的含水硅酸盐，从古典时代开始它就已经在欧洲绘画中使用。
grind 磨	You grind pigment powder with a medium in order to create a smooth fluid paint. Grinding can also be done without a medium. In this case, water can be used to create the pigment paste as a result of grinding. In this form, the ground pigment paste can be stored in a closed jar and when topped with water it can be used over a long period of time. 用一种介质研磨颜料粉，以制作顺滑的液体涂料。研磨也可以不用介质。在这种情况下，可以加水制作颜料膏。在此形式中，颜料膏可以储存在一个封闭的罐子中，当盖水时，可以长时间使用。
grinding slab 磨板	Grinding slab is a hard flat surface, usually made of stone or glass. It is used to grind pigment with or without a medium. 一种坚硬平坦的表面，通常由石头或玻璃制成。用于研磨颜料，可以使用介质。
grisaille (3) 纯灰色画	On canvas paintings, grisaille is a method of painting in gray tints to depict the relief in form. From the French word gris, meaning grey. 在油画作品中，纯灰色画是一种用灰色调来描绘浮雕的方法。来自法语单词gris，意思是灰色。
ground loss 粉层脱落	Loss of the ground and paint layers. 粉层和绘画层脱落。
guardapolvo 防尘罩	Guardapolvo is a protective canopy on an architectural frame that is part of an altarpiece. From the Spanish word guardapolvo, meaning dustguard). 建筑框架上的保护性遮篷，是祭坛画的一部分。来自西班牙语单词guardapolvo，意思是防尘罩。
gutter 订口	A gutter is the back margin on the inside of two facing pages in a book. 书中对开两页内侧的白边。
gypsum 硫酸钙（石膏）	white，$CaSO_4 \cdot 2H_2O$, Calcium Sulphate It is important among the raw materials that have been used in works of art, it is often associated with salt deposits, occurs widely over the world. 硫酸钙在艺术品中广泛使用的重要的白色颜料（$CaSO_4 \cdot 2H_2O$），它通常与盐分沉积有关。
Haemetite 赤铁矿	Haematite is a hard, compact, and nearly pure natural variety of anhydrous ferric oxide. 赤铁矿是一种坚硬，致密，几乎纯净的天然无水三氧化二铁，被用作红色颜料。
half-lap joint 半搭接	A half-lap joint is a joint between panels of wood where matching portions from opposite edges of the panels have been cut out so that they overlap one another. 指木板之间的接合处，从木板的相对边缘切出匹配的部分，使它们彼此重叠。

halo 圣光	A halo is a circle of painted light around the head of Christ, saints or angels. 围绕着基督、圣徒或天使头部的彩色光环。
hardboard 硬纸板	Hardboard is a sheet of compressed wood and thermosetting resin. It is used as a painting support and was first manufactured in 1926. 由压缩木材和热固性树脂制成的纸板。硬纸板被用作绘画支撑物,最早制造于1926年。
hatching 画影线	Hatching is the application of paint in long thin parallel brushstrokes. If the lines cross each other, the technique is cross-hatching. 用长而细的平行笔画作画。如果这些线互相交叉,即为交叉阴影。
hemp 麻	Hemp is a plant producing bast fibres used to produce for example, rope and textiles. It was frequently used in the making of painting canvases in Italy during the 17th and 18th centuries, but rarely used in Europe during the 19th and 20th centuries. 一种含有韧皮纤维的植物,用于制作绳索和纺织品。17世纪和18世纪,意大利经常用它来制作油画画布,但在19世纪和20世纪的欧洲很少使用。
hessian 粗麻布	Hessian is a strong coarse cloth made of jute or hemp, which is used in vacuum-hot table lining as breathers. See also burlap. 麻布是一种由黄麻或大麻制成的结实的粗布,用于真空热台裱褙中作为透气材料。另见粗麻布。
holiday 漏涂	When a coating is poorly applied, in small areas it may be too thin or completely absent. These areas are called holidays. 当涂层施涂不当时,在较小的区域颜料可能太薄或完全不存在。这些区域被称为漏涂。
hollow 凹形线	A hollow is a concave shaped curve on a decorative picture frame. 装饰性画框上的凹形曲线。
horugv 圣像旗帜	Horugv is a flag, made of cloth or metal onto which an icon is painted or fastened. It is attached to a pole to be carried in processions. 一种旗帜,由布或金属制成,上面画着或系着圣像。游行时它被固定在杆上。
hutch 祭坛画箱	A hutch is the case of an altarpiece. 装祭坛画的箱子。
hutch maker 家具木匠	A hutch maker is a medieval term for a cabinetmaker. 中世纪对家具木匠的称呼。
icon 圣像画	An icon is a religious painting executed in the Greek or Russian Orthodox tradition, usually on a wooden panel. Other supports can be textile or metal. 按照希腊或俄罗斯东正教传统进行的宗教绘画,通常画在木板上,也可画在织物或金属上。

imitative 模仿	See total retouching. 见全色。
impact crack 冲击裂纹	An impact crack is a type of crack on canvas paintings in the form of radiating circles, caused by a blow. 画布上由撞击引起的一种裂纹，呈放射状的圆形。
impasto 厚笔触	Impasto is paint applied in layers or strokes of widely varying thicknesses. 涂抹不同厚度的涂层或笔画上的颜料。
imprimatur 色底	An imprimatur is a thin wash or glaze painted onto the ground of a painting. It is used to modify the final colour effect of the painting. 在画的底层涂上一层薄薄的颜料或釉料。用来修改绘画作的最终色彩效果。
imprimeur 色底制作工匠	An imprimeur is a craftsman who applies grounds to canvases or panels. 将底层应用于画布或面板的工匠。
imprinting 压印	Imprinting is the damage occurred when any textured material (for example, a piece of glue, textured interlining material or lining canvas) underlying the painting canvas, imprints its texture onto the paint surface. This occurs while under pressure during a lining process. It frequently happens when the lining canvas is coarse relative to the painting support. 画布下面的有纹理的材料（例如一块胶粘剂、有纹理的衬布材料或衬里帆布）将其纹理印在颜料表面时发生的损坏。这发生在裱褙过程中施加压力时。它经常发生在衬布相对于绘画支撑粗糙的情况下。
Indigo 靛蓝	Indigo is a blue vegetable coloring matter which seems to have been used in the Far East very early for dyeing cloth and for painting. 靛蓝是一种蓝色的植物色素，在远东地区似乎很早就用于染布和绘画。
inpainting 补色、全色	Inpainting is retouching missing or damaged areas, for example in a painting or polychrome sculpture. 对缺失或损坏的区域进行修整，例如修补绘画或彩绘雕塑。
insect excreta 昆虫排泄物	Black, shiny expelled waste material of an insect. 昆虫黑色且带光泽排泄物。
insert (1) 嵌入	An insert is a piece of canvas cut to fit into the exact dimensions of a hole in a painted canvas. 切割一块画布，使其与画布上一个孔的精确尺寸相吻合。
insert (2) 滑动画框	See slip frame. 见滑架。
integral frame 整体框架	See engaged frame. 见嵌板框架。
intelaggio 连接布	Intelaggio is a cloth reinforcement over the structural join of a panel. 一种覆盖在面板结构连接处的筋布。

interim varnish 临时清漆	An interim varnish is highly diluted varnish applied to the painting surface before inpainting, in order to enhance the appearance of the original paint. 在图像修复之前在绘画表面涂上高度稀释的清漆，以改善原漆的外观。
interlayer cleavage 层间脱离	An interlayer cleavage is a structural problem in painting and polychrome sculpture resulting in the separation and flaking of paint layers. 绘画和彩绘雕塑中的结构问题，会导致漆层的分离和剥落。
interleaf (1) 中间层	An interleaf is a material inserted during the lining process between the original and the lining canvas. It is intended to give further support and rigidity and in some occasions to suppress weave interfearance between fabrics. A loose interleaf is sometimes inserted loosely between the original and the loose lining canvas. Fixed interleaf is where the interleaf is fixed onto the lining canvas. 在裱褙过程中插入原稿和画布衬里之间的一种材料。可以提供更好的支撑和硬度，并在某些情况下抑制织物之间的编织干扰。松散中间层有时松散地插入原稿和松散的衬布之间。固定中间层是将中间层固定在衬布上。
interlining 插页	See interleaf (1). 见中间层。
interstice 间隙	An interstice is a space or crevice between the threads of a canvas support. 画布支撑物的线之间的空间或缝隙。
intonaco 细泥层 / 灰泥	Intonaco is the surface onto which a fresco is painted by applying pigments whilst it is in a wet state. Intonaco is a fine plaster applied over the coarser ground, the arriccio. 细泥层是创作湿壁画时，在潮湿状态下用来涂颜料的表面。细泥层是一种精细的灰泥，涂抹在粗糙的底层上。
invisible retouch 隐形修整	An invisible retouch is one that is used where the primary intention is that the object should be viewed as a visual whole. The retouch should be detectable and easily reversed. 隐形修整的使用目的是让对象呈现为一个视觉整体。修整应该是可检测的，并且容易逆转的。
isolating varnish 隔离清漆	An isolating varnish is one that is applied to an original material surface which is to be retouched or filled. It provides a separation layer that can be identified during the reversal of the treatment. 涂在待修整或填充的原材料表面上的清漆。它提供了一个分离层，可以在反向处理期间识别出来。
Ivory black 象牙黑	It is made by charring waste cutting of ivory in closed vessels and then grinding, washing, and drying the black residue. 象牙黑是通过在封闭的容器中将象牙废料烧焦，然后研磨、洗涤和干燥黑色残留物而制成的。
japanning 涂漆	Japanning is a highly glossy black coating which imitated oriental lacquer. The coatings were made using a number of hard resins and drying oils. 一种高光泽的黑色涂料，仿照东方漆。由硬树脂和干油制成。

kaima 衣饰花边	Kaima is the decorative border of a garment of figures depicted in an icon. 圣像画中人物衣服的装饰性边缘。
kermes 硫养锑矿，虫胭脂， 胭脂虫红	It is one of the most ancient of the natural dyestuffs. It was derived from the dried bodies og the female insect, Coccus ilicis. 胭脂虫红是最古老的天然红色染料之一。它是从雌胭脂虫的干燥尸体中提取的。
key 榫	See wedge. 见楔。
klav 垂直条纹	Klav is a decoration on a himation. It is a depicted as a vertical stripe on the shoulder of Christ or of a saint. 长袍上的装饰。它被描绘成基督或圣徒肩膀上的垂直条纹。
kleima 独立小图	See kleimo. 见独立小图。
kleimo 独立小图	Kleimo is a small independent scene painted on the borders of an icon and around the central image. It is often tetragonal or rectangular in shape. Kleimo是一个独立的小场景，排列在圣像画中心图像周围的一个个独立小画面。它们通常是四方形或矩形的。它们所表现的或为该圣像中心主题的一个场景，或是对中心主题的解释。
lake pigment 色淀颜料	A lake pigment is a pigment that is made by reacting a dye with a particle substrate. 由染料与颗粒基质发生反应而成的颜料。
Lamp black 灯黑	It is nearly pure (99%), amorphous carbon which is collected in brick chambers from the condensed smoke of a luminous flame from burning mineral oil, tar, pitch or resin. 灯黑是几乎99%的无定形碳，是从砖室中燃烧矿物油、焦油、沥青或树脂发光火焰的冷凝烟中收集的。
lap joint 搭接	A lap joint is a corner joint in frames and stretchers where wood from one side overlaps the wood on the other side. 框架和延伸器中的一种角接接头，其中一侧的木材与另一侧的木材重叠。
layering 分层	Layering in a painting is multiple layers where some of the layers are transparent or semi-transparent glazes. 绘画中的分层是指多层，其中一些层是透明或半透明的釉料。
laying-in 效果图	Laying in is the first stage of defining the image of a painting, by drawing or painting the general effect of colour and form. 定义绘画形象的第一步，画出或涂出颜色和形式的大体效果。
Lead white 铅白（碱式碳酸铅）	white, basic lead carbonate. 白色颜料，碱式碳酸铅。

lean 哑光技法	A lean paint has a small amount of binding medium and may dry to a matte finish. 只混入少量的粘合媒介，干燥后形成粗糙表面。
lepidocrocite 纤铁矿	Lepidocrocite is an orange iron(III)oxy hydroxide mineral (γ-FeOOH) which is a common iron corrosion product and has been used as a pigment. 橘黄色的铁(III)氧氢氧化物矿物，一种常见的铁腐蚀产物，被用作颜料。
levkas 石膏底层	In an icon, levkas is a gesso ground, normally covering the entire surface. 在圣像画中，levkas是石膏底层，通常覆盖整个表面。
linen 亚麻	Linen is a fabric made from the fibre of the flax plant and used as a painting support. 用亚麻植物的纤维制成的织物，用作绘画的支撑物。
lining (1) 衬里	A lining is a piece of fabric attached to the back or inside of a textile object. It is used to protect the back of the object, to increase the object's strength, to cover construction details or to increase wearing comfort. 一块织物，附着在织物的背面或内部。用于保护织物背部，增加织物强度，覆盖结构细节或增加穿着舒适性。
lining (2) 裱褙	Lining is the process of adhering a fabric to the reverse side of a painting on canvas in order to support the original canvas. 将织物粘在画布反面以支撑原始画布。
lining canvas 画布衬里	Lining canvas is the canvas added in the lining process. 画布衬里是在裱褙过程中添加的画布。
linseed oil 亚麻油	Linseed oil is the most important of the vegetable drying oil, is obtained from the seeds of flax. 亚麻籽油得自亚麻籽，是最重要的蔬菜干性油。
Litharge 铅黄，黄丹 （一氧化铅）	see Massicot. 见铅黄。
loaded brush 沾满颜料的刷子	See impasto. 见厚笔触。
loose interleaf 松散插页	See interleaf (1). 见插页。
loose leaf 土红纸隔	Loose leaf is a type of gold leaf where each leaf is placed between sheets of paper in a book of gold leaf. The sheets of paper are treated with rouge, a red iron-containing clay, in order to prevent the leaf to be attached to the sheet. 一种金箔，每一页都放在一本金箔书的两张纸之间。为了防止金箔粘着在纸上，用土红（一种含铁的红色粘土）处理纸张。

loose lining 松托	A loose lining is a canvas which is not adhered to the original painting canvas but is stretched independently onto the stretcher under the original canvas. It acts as a protective barrier. 一种画布，它不粘在原始画布上，而是独立地拉伸到原始画布下的延伸器上。可起到保护屏障的作用。
luting 捻缝油灰	In painting conservation, luting is the filling of losses or cracks in the paint and ground layers. 在绘画保护中，捻缝油灰用于在颜料和底层上填充损失或裂缝。
Madder 茜草	Madder is a natural dyestuff from the root of the herbaceous perennial, Rubia tinctorium, which formerly was cultivated extensively in Europe and Asia Minor. 茜草红是从多年生草本植物染色茜草中提取的天然红色染料，该植物以前在欧洲和小亚细亚广泛种植。
maforij 圣母外衣	In icon paintings, maforij is the outer garment covering the head and shoulders of the Mother of God or a female saint. 在圣像画中，是圣母玛利亚或女圣徒盖着头和肩的外衣。
mahlstick 腕杖	A mahlstick is a painter's stick upon which he supports his hand while painting. One end is held by the painter while the other padded end rests on the canvas. 画家在作画时用来支撑手的棍子。一头被画家握住，另一头垫在画布上。
Malachite 孔雀石	Malachite is perhaps the oldest known bright green pigment. It is the natural basic copper carbonate, and is similar in chemical composition to the blue copper carbonate, azurite. 孔雀石也许是已知最古老的鲜绿色颜料。它是天然的碱式碳酸铜，化学成分类似于蓝色的碳酸铜（石青）。
mandorla 圣体光环	On a painting, a mandorla is an oval, almond-shaped light around Christ. 画中基督周围放射出来的椭圆形光圈。
marouflage 板托	Marouflage is the adhering of a canvas painting to a rigid support. 将布上油画转移粘贴到坚硬支撑物上的方法
masonite 纤维板	See hardboard. 见硬纸板。
massicot 铅黄	Massicot is a mineral which is a yellow lead oxide (PbO). 铅黄是一种矿物，是一种黄色的氧化铅 (PbO)
Massicot 铅黄，黄丹 （一氧化铅）	Both Massicot and litharge are names which have long been used for yellow monoxide of lead. Massicot 和 litharge 都是长期用于描述一氧化铅的名称，这是一种黄色颜料。
matte varnish 哑光清漆	A matte varnish is a varnish that has a non-glossy appearance.（self-explanatory） 一种外观无光泽的清漆。

Maya blue **玛雅蓝**	Maya blue is a name here provisionally given to a peculiar blue pigment which is found rather extensively on wall painting and painted objects from ancient Mayan sites in Central America. 玛雅蓝色是一种奇特的蓝色颜料，在中美洲古代玛雅遗址的壁画和彩绘物体上广泛发现。
mecca **表面金色涂层**	Mecca is a varnish used over silvered surfaces to give a gold colour. It has been in use since the Renaissance. Mecca 是一种涂在贴银表面上的清漆，使表面变成金色。这种方法从文艺复兴时期就开始使用了。
mechanical damage **机械损伤**	Physical harm inflicted on a painting which is either accidental or intentional. 无意或蓄意（如刻画涂写）所造成的物理损伤。
medium (1) **媒介 (1)**	The medium in which you produce a work of art is the technology used, such as watercolour paint on paper or cinematography. 媒介指制作艺术作品时所使用的技术，例如纸上的水彩颜料或电影摄影术。
medium (2) **媒介剂 (2)**	A medium is a binding agent which is mixed with pigment to produce paint. Examples are linseed oil and egg proteins. 媒介剂是一种粘接剂，和色素混合后用作颜料。例如亚麻籽油和蛋白。
megilp **调色油**	Megilp is a paint medium made by dissolving mastic resin in turpentine, with the addition of linseed oil. It has a gelatinous consistency. 调色油成胶状，是由松节油中溶解马来树脂，并加入亚麻籽油制成。
membrane **保护膜**	A membrane is the flexible cover sheet laid over a painting being treated on a suction table or vacuum hot table. Different materials are used, most often Melinex. 当画作在真空台上进行抽气时，覆盖在画表面上的保护膜，保护膜可以由不同材料制成，一般是 Melinex，一种聚酯膜。
millboard **硬纸板**	Millboard is a compressed pasteboard which is used as a painting support. 经过压缩和加固处理的硬纸板，用作画面的支撑物。
mineral oils **矿物油**	Mineral oils are hydrocarbons obtained in the distillation of petroleum. 矿物油是在石油蒸馏中获得的碳氢化合物。
mitre **阳角接角**	A mitre is a 45 degree angle cut in a piece of wood. 切成45度角的木材。
mitre joint **斜接**	A mitre joint joins two boards or corners of a frame with mitres, resulting in a 90 degree angle. 将两块切割成45度角的木板或画框木条，接合在一起形成90度角。
mixed media **混合媒介**	a. Mixed media is the technique of mixing together different binding media before adding pigments. b. Mixed media is the use of different binding media (for example, oil and tempera) for pigments in different areas of a painting. a.混合媒介是指在加入颜料之前，将不同的结合介质混合在一起的技术。b.混合介质是指在画作不同区域运用不同媒介(如油和蛋彩画)而完成的绘画作品。

moating 清漆褶皱	Moating is a small moat-like hollow on the paint surface created during the lining process. It is caused when a piece of material, lying between the paint surface and the pressure source, causes a high point while the surrounding textile becomes pressed down level with the rest of the surface. 在裱褶过程中在绘画表面形成的深沟似的凹陷。当一块材料位于油漆表面和压力源之间时，当周围的纺织品与表面的其余部分一起压平时，就会造成高点。
mordant (2) 媒染剂	A mordant is an oil- or water-based adhesive for attaching gold or silver leaf to a ground. 一种油基或水基粘合剂，用于将金箔或银箔附着在底层。
mordant gilding 粘合剂贴金	Mordant gilding uses a drying oil based adhesive in applying the gold leaf. The gilded surface cannot be polished as it might if water-gilded. 粘合剂贴金使用干燥的油基粘合剂来粘贴金箔。媒染剂贴金的表面不能像水贴金的表面一样抛光。
mosaic gold 彩金	Mosaic gold is artificial gold made of stannic sulphide appearing like bronze powder. It was formerly used for gilding purposes as a gold substitute. 由锡硫化物制成，呈青铜粉末状的人造金。以前被用作贴金的替代品。
moulding 造型（嵌条）	A moulding is a strip of plaster or a wood band running along the frame. It may be plain or decorated. 一条沿着框架的石膏条或木条。可以是素色的，也可以是装饰性的。
nap bond 即时粘接	A nap bond is the instanteous bond formed when a flat substrate coated with a tacky adhesive is brought against another surface. The adhesive is commonly activated to become pressure sensitive using heat or solvents. The adhesion only occurs where the surfaces are forced into contact. Nap bonds are commonly used to attach linings to canvas paintings. 涂有粘合剂的平板基板与另一表面接触时形成的瞬时粘合。通常使用加热或溶剂活化粘合剂使其压敏。粘附仅在表面被迫接触时发生。即时粘接通常用于将衬里粘接到画布上。
nap-bond method 点粘法	Nap-bond method is a lining technique for paintings where the adhesive is applied not to the whole area of the lining canvas but only in small spots. It can be achieved by using a screen or a net. 一种用于画作的裱褶技术，其中粘合剂不涂于整张衬里画布，而只用于小的点。它可以通过使用屏幕或网来实现。
neutral retouching 中性修整	Neutral retouching is a method of retouching painted surfaces where the area to be retouched is painted in a chosen neutral tone matching the surrounding area. Very often the neutral tone is called aqua sporca which is muddy-greyish in colour. Neutral retouching is best suited for three-dimentional objects like polychrome sculptures. 一种修整颜料表面的方法，其中要修整的区域用与周围区域相匹配的中性色调绘制。通常，中性色调被称为脏水色，一种泥灰色。中性修饰最适合三维对象，如彩色雕塑。
nimbus 光环	See halo. 见圣光环。

normal retouching 常规修整	Normal retouching is a method of retouching painted surfaces in which the area to be retouched is painted with dots or lines using a colour and form that makes the painted surface uniform from a normal viewing distance. 一种修整涂漆表面的方法，将要修整的区域涂上点或线，其颜色和形式使涂漆表面在正常观察距离内保持一致。
oak 橡木	Oak is the wood from the tree Quercus robur. This hard wood is heavy and fairly resistant to water. It was widely used for construction of buildings, ships, furniture and wood panel paintings in Northern Europe. 来自栎树的木材。这种硬木很重，而且相当耐水。在北欧，它被广泛用于建筑物、船只、家具和木板画。
Ochres 赭石（水合氧化铁）	An ochre is a natural earth which consists of silica and clay, and which owes its color to iron oxide in either the anhydrous or hydrous form。 赭石是由二氧化硅和粘土组成的天然土，其颜色归因于无水或含水形式的氧化铁，是黄色或红色颜料。
ogee S形曲线	An ogee is an S-shaped moulding on a frame. One half of the moulding is concave, the other convex shaped. 框架上的S形饰条。一半是凹的，另一半是凸的。
oil drying crack 干燥裂纹	See traction crackle. 见牵引力裂纹。
oil gilding 油性粘合剂贴金	See mordant gilding. 见粘合剂贴金。
oil ground 油底	An oil ground is a ground containing an inert filler such as chalk and lead white and a drying oil such as linseed oil. Pigments may also be added. 含有惰性填料（如白垩和铅白）和干燥油（如亚麻籽油）的底层。也可添加颜料。
oil mordant 油媒染剂	An oil mordant is a drying oil acting as an adhesive to stick gold leaf in thin linear designs onto a paint surface. 油媒染剂是干燥油的一种，它的作用是将金箔以细长的线状设计粘在颜料表面。
oil varnish 油清漆	An oil varnish is a mixture of a hard natural resin and drying oil, which often becomes difficult to dissolve. 坚硬的天然树脂和干燥油的混合物，通常很难溶解。
oklad 金属遮盖	An oklad is the metal cover on an icon, made of one piece. The oklad exposes the head, hands and feet of the person depicted in an icon. 圣像画的一整片金属遮罩。oklad露出了圣像画中人物的头、手和脚。
olifa 清漆	Olifa is the final varnish layer of an icon. It is usually made of boiled linseed oil with an addition of some resin. The varnish darkens with time. 圣像画的最后一层清漆。它通常是由煮沸的亚麻油加上一些树脂制成的。清漆日久会变暗。

omofor 主教衣服	In an icon, an omofor is a garment worn by bishops and placed over the sakkos. It is a sign of the episcopal office. 在圣像中，omofor是主教们穿的衣服，披在sakkos外。这是主教职位的标志。
omoforion 主教衣物	See omofor. 见主教衣服。
open work 镂空作品	Open work is a type of moulding of a frame carved with pierced, decorative ornaments. 一种用穿孔的装饰物雕刻的框架模子。
opush 彩色边缘线	In an icon, an opush is a line, painted in red, green or other colour along the edges. 在圣像画中，opush指沿边缘涂上红色、绿色或其他颜色的线。
orange peel 橘皮皱	Orange peel is a defect in surface coatings which have more or less pronouced depressions, resembling orange skin. This can occur in coatings that have been applied by spray. It may be caused by incorrect viscosity, too low a pressure, insufficient drying between applications or incompatible components in the coating material. 橘皮皱是表面涂层的一种缺陷，或多或少有内翻的凹陷，类似于橘子皮。橘皮皱出现在喷涂的涂层中。这可能是由于粘度不正确、压力过低、多次处理之间干燥不足或涂层材料中的成分不兼容造成的。
ormolu 铜锌锡合金	Ormolu is a copper alloy with zinc, and occasionally tin, that has a golden colour. It was widely used for decorative mounts and frequently gilt. 一种含锌的铜合金，偶尔还含有锡，呈金黄色。被广泛用于装饰底座，经常用于贴金。
ormolu varnish 贴金清漆	Ormolu varnish is a varnish used to protect gold leaf. 一种用来保护金箔的清漆。
Orpiment 雌黄	Orpiment was once widely used, but has now fallen into complete disuse because of its limited supply and because of its poisonous character. yellow, As_2S_3, arsenic sulphide, 雌黄，主要成分是三硫化二砷，曾经被广泛作为黄色颜料使用，但由于其供应有限和有毒的特性，现已不再使用。
over paint 过度补色	Over paint is a previous addition to a paint layer applied over original surface during its history of use or through inappropriate restoration. 在原表面使用过程中或通过不当修复而在原表面上添加的绘画层。
overcleaning 过度清理	Overcleaning is damage caused by the removal of the original surface or paint during the cleaning process. 过度清理是指在修复过程中因为过度清理导致原有画面或颜料被移除而带来的损伤。
ox gall 牛胆汁	Ox gall is the bile obtained from the gall bladder of oxen and used as a wetting agent. It is used to reduce surface tension in water based paints used for retouching. 牛的胆汁，作为润湿剂用来修复水性颜料作品，可减少表面张力。

paint loss 画层脱落	Loss of the paint layer reveaing the ground below. 画层脱落。
palette (1) 调色板	A palette is a flat piece of wood on which artists kept and mixed their paint. 扁平的木板，用于放置颜料和调色。
palette (2) 一系列颜料	The palette of an artist is the range of colours selected for his work. 艺术家为作品选择的一系列颜色。
palette knife 调色刀	A palette knife is a painter's tool for mixing or transferring paint on a palette. It can be used as a painting tool for applying paint on board or canvas. 画家用来混合或转移调色板上的颜料的工具。它可以作为一种绘画工具，用于在木板或画布上作画。
panel 板	A panel painting is one made on a rigid support, usually of wood. 板画是画在刚性支撑物（通常为木头）的画作。
parcel gilt 部分贴金	A surface is parcel gilt if only part of it has been covered with gold. 表面只有一部分被黄金覆盖。
Paris white 巴黎白	See whiting. 见碳酸钙粉。
partial cleaning 局部清洁	Partial cleaning of a varnished surface is the removal of some but not all of the discoloured varnish. This method may be chosen for a number of reasons, such as the need to retain evidence of the original varnish or the possibility of damage to the under paint layer. 清漆表面的局部清洁是指去除部分但不是全部变色的清漆。选择这种方法的原因有很多，例如需要保留原始清漆的证据或者绘画层下可能损害。
pasta 面糊胶	Pasta is a lining adhesive widely used in Italy. The pasta consists of flour paste, glue and Venice Turpentine and possibly other additives. Pasta contains more flour paste than glue-paste. 意大利广泛使用的一种衬里粘合剂。面糊胶由面粉糊、胶水、威尼斯松节油和其他添加剂组成。面糊胶中的面粉糊比胶水糊多。
paste glue 面糊胶	See pasta. 见面糊胶。
pastiglia 石膏装饰	Pastiglia is an ornamental decoration technique of raised patterns made from thick, liquid gesso. It is usually applied to frame or wooden panel. 一种由厚的液态石膏制成凸起图案的装饰技术。通常用于框架或木板。
pavimenteuse 正方形裂纹	Pavimenteuse is a type of ground common in Italy in the 17th century. It was made by spreading, with a knife, a thick paste ground into an open woven canvas. With age, a regular crackle pattern of tiny squares develops in the paint surface. 17世纪意大利常见的一种底层类型。用刀把厚厚的浆糊铺在一块镂空的编织画布上制成的。随着时间的推移，漆面上会形成规则的小正方形裂纹图案。

pavoloka 衬布	A pavoloka is a piece of cloth in an icon that is glued directly onto the panel and thus lies under the gesso layer. 衬布是直接粘贴在圣像画木质底板上的一层布料，衬布层位于石膏底的下方。
peach gum 桃胶	A reddish brown or yellowish brown gelatinous substance secreted from the bark of a peach tree. 桃树的树皮分泌出来的红褐色或黄褐色胶状物质。
pentimento 原笔画再现	Pentimento is a change made to a work of art during its execution by the artist. This may become visible as the index of refraction for the paint layers rises with time. Thus, more light can penetrate through the paint layers and the concealed drawing or painting can show through. 艺术家在创作过程中对艺术作品的一种改变。当油漆层的折射率随时间而增加时，原笔画显现出来。因此，更多的光线可以穿透油漆层，隐藏的绘画可以穿透而显现出来。
Pettenkofer method 佩滕科弗方法	The Pettenkofer method is a technique developed by Max von Pettenkofer in the 18th century to reform varnish layers by exposure to solvent vapours. 18世纪由马克斯·冯·佩滕科弗开发的一种技术，通过将清漆层暴露在溶剂蒸汽中来进行改造。
pietra paesina 褐黄色石灰岩	Pietra paesina is a brown-yellow limestone composed of calcite with ferric hydroxide deposits. It was used as a rigid painting support especially during the 17th century in Tuscany. 一种褐黄色石灰岩，由方解石和氢氧化铁沉积物组成。在17世纪托斯卡纳，它被用作一种坚固的绘画支撑物。
pigment alteration/ colorant fading 颜料变色	Alteration of mineral pigments or fading of organic colorants. 矿物颜料变色或有机染料褪色。
pigment ratio 颜料比例	In a paint, the pigment ratio is the proportion of pigment to its medium. The pigment ratio required to make a useable paint varies considerably according to the absorption properties of the pigment. 在画中，颜料比例是颜料与介质的比例。根据颜料的吸收特性，制作可用画作所需的颜料比例有很大不同。
pinpoint flaking 细微剥落	In a painting, pinpoint flaking is damage in very small areas of local loss. 在一幅画中，细微剥落是指在很小的局部区域内的损坏。
plain-sawed board 锯板	See tangential cut. 见弦切。
plaster detachment 空鼓	Lack of adhesion between the coarse plaster and the conglomerate 粗泥层与沙砾岩之间粘结力丧失。
pliers 绷布钳	See canvas pliers. 见绷布钳。
plug 插入	See insert. 见嵌入。

podlinnik 画家手册	Podlinnik is an icon painter's manual containing model drawings or recipies. 圣像画家的手册，包含模型图或配方。
podokladnye 有金属壳的圣像画	Podokladnye is a name for icons, covered with an oklad. It implies that those parts of an icon hidden under the oklad, may not be painted, or are painted in a poor and clumsy way. 圣像画的名字，上面覆盖着金属壳。这意味着隐藏在金属壳下的圣像画可能没有被绘制，或者是用一种糟糕而笨拙的方式绘制的。
podriznik 长下衣	A podriznik is the long lower garment of a priest depicted in an icon. 圣像中牧师的长下衣。
podstarinnaja 传统风格圣像画	Podstarinnaja are icons which are painted in a traditional style to simulate old icons. 一种传统风格的圣像画，用来模拟旧圣像。
podstarinnyia 传统风格圣像画	See podstarinnaja. 见传统风格圣像画。
pointillism 点彩派、点画法	Pointillism is a painting technique of using small dots of different colours of paint which can be seen as separate when viewed close to but which merge visually from a distance. This can be used as a retouching method. 使用不同颜色颜料的小点进行绘画，这些小点在近距离观察时可以被视为独立的，但从远处看，这些小点在视觉上是融合在一起的。点画法可以用作修饰方法。
pokrov 圣母肖像主题	In an icon, pokrov is an iconographical motif known as "The Protection of the Mother of God" and is based on one of the feasts dedicated to the Virgin. 在圣像画中，pokrov是一个肖像主题，被称为"保护上帝的母亲"，是基于一个献祭圣母的节日。
polia 圣像画的边界	Polia are the borders of an icon. 圣像画的边界。
poliment 填充剂	See bole. 见贴金底灰。
poliment 贴金用粘土	See bole. 见贴金底灰。
polyamide fabric 聚酰胺织物	A polyamide fabric is one that is made from nylon. 由尼龙制成的织物。
polycyclohexanone resin 聚环己酮树脂	A polycyclohexanone resin is a synthetic resin are made from cyclohexanone sometimes with methylcyclohexanone monomers. Examples are Laropal K and Ketone Resin N. The polymer was first patented by BASF in 1930. These resins have been used as picture varnishes as analogues of natural resins such as dammar. 由环己酮（有时与甲基环己酮单体合成）制成的树脂。例如Laropal K和Ketone Resin N。该聚合物于1930年首次获得巴斯夫专利。这些树脂被用作绘画清漆，作为天然树脂的类似物，如达玛树脂。

polyester fabrics 涤纶面料	Polyester fabrics are fabrics woven from poly(ethene terephthalate). The fibres were introduced in 1941. 由聚对苯二甲酸乙二醇酯编织而成的织物，于1941年被发明。
polyptych 多联画屏	A polyptych is an altarpiece made up of several panels. 由几个面板组成的祭坛画。
ponovlenie 改动证据	In the conservation of an icon, ponovlenie is the evidence of renovation or reconstruction on an icon. 在圣像画保护中，ponovlenie是对圣像画进行翻新或重构的证据。
pounce 撒印花粉	A pounce is a process used to produce an outline for drawing. A dark coloured, powdered material, such as charcoal, contained in a cloth bag, is knocked onto the surface of a sheet of paper which has had holes punched along the lines of definition. The powder goes through the holes leaving an outline on the underlying material which is usually plaster. For coloured grounds, whiting has been used. 用来画轮廓。将一种深色粉末状物质（如木炭）装在一个布袋里，撒在一张纸的表面上，这张纸上有沿着轮廓线打孔的孔。粉末穿过孔，在石膏基材上留下轮廓。对于彩色基底，使用白色粉末。
pounce bag 印花粉袋	A pounce bag is a small bag filled with gilder's whiting, used during oil gilding. Certain areas on the surface are pounced with whiting in order to distinguish the areas where the gilding is to be applied from the areas which should be left un-gilded. 装满了白垩粉的小袋子，用于油贴金。表面上的某些区域用白垩粉处理，以区分要贴金的区域和不贴金的区域。
pounced drawing 印花粉画	See pounce. 见撒印花粉。
predella 祭坛附饰画	The predella is a long horizontal structure made of wood panels supporting an altarpiece. It may have painted scenes on it. 一种长的水平结构，由支撑祭坛画的木板制成。上面可能画了一些场景。
press brocade 印锦	See applied brocade. 见仿织锦画法。
pre-stretching 预拉伸	Pre-stretching is a treatment, necessary when a painting's canvas has shrunk and must be stretched and flattened once again, to accommodate the original paint layer. In order to pre-stretch, you humidify the canvas and carefully enlarge the shrunken by stretching it. This is carried out as a separate procedure prior to, for example, the consolidation and lining procedures. 当油画的画布收缩时，需要预拉伸将其再次拉伸和压平，以适应原始的绘画层。为了进行预拉伸，湿润画布并仔细拉伸以扩大收缩的画布。这是在加固和裱褙处理之前，作为一个单独的处理步骤执行。
priming (1) 底漆	Priming is the application of a layer on top of the ground layer in order to give the ground a coloured surface. 底漆是在底层的表面施涂一层，以使底层具有彩色表面。

probela 提白	Probela is part of the traditional painting technique for producing an image by proceeding gradually from dark tones to light tones. The probela is a lighter layer painted on top of a layer of the same colour, but of a darker tone. Each lighter grade of the paint is prepared by adding a drop of white paint, called belila in icon painting. 提白是一种制作明暗调子渐变效果的传统绘画技法。提白是在较深的底色上用同色相的较浅颜色进行覆盖的画法。每提一个色阶时，会在颜料中加入一滴白色颜料，圣像画中称提白为"belila"。
protective backing 保护性支撑	See backing. 见背衬。
punching 冲孔	Punching is a method of decoration on surfaces which are gessoed and gilded. It is achieved with punching tools. 在涂有石膏和贴金的表面进行装饰。冲孔是用冲孔模来实现的。
punching tool 冲孔模	A punching tool is a metal tool with a decorative pattern at one end. The tool is used to impress this pattern onto a gilt gesso surface. 一端带有装饰图案的金属工具。用来把图案印在贴金石膏表面。
punctate loss 点状脱落	Rounded losses (less than 1mm in diameter) of the paint and ground layer. 画层和底色层直径小于1毫米的圆形脱落。
rabbet 槽口	See rebate. 见槽口。
radial cut 径向切	A radial cut is a method of converting a tree into timber in which the saw cut runs through the centre of the tree trunk. 一种将树木转化为木材的方法，锯痕穿过树干的中心。
Realgar 雄黄	Realgar is the natural orange-red sulphide of arsenic, and it is closely related chemically and associated with orpiment. 雄黄是砷的天然橙红色硫化物，在化学上与雌黄紧密相关。
rebate 槽口	A rebate is a groove cut along the inner edge of a frame into which the glass or the painting rests. 沿着框架的内边缘切出的一个凹槽，玻璃或画作放置于其中。
recutting 修磨	Recutting is a technique of preparing flat gessoed areas and to recreate the shape of mouldings for gilding. To smooth the flat hard gesso surface for painting and gilding, it is scraped with a stiff square edged cabinet scraper. 将石膏表面变平坦和重塑贴金模具的形状。为了使平整坚硬的石膏表面变得光滑，以便涂漆和贴金，用一个硬的方边木工刮刀将其刮平。
Red Lead 铅丹	The red tetroxide of lead, is made by heating litharge or white lead for some hours at about 480℃. 铅丹是一种红色颜料，主要成分是铅的红色四氧化物，可通过在约480℃下加热少量铅或白色铅几个小时而制得的。

reforming 重整	Reforming is used to assist the removal of a varnish which is difficult to remove with ordinary solvents or solvent mixtures or in cases where the removal of varnish with stronger solvents might affect the paint layers. The varnish is sprayed with a polar solvent or solvent mixture and left to stand, causing it to swell. The varnish is then removed with a weaker solvent. 用于帮助去除用普通溶剂或溶剂混合物难以去除的清漆，或在用更强溶剂去除清漆可能影响绘画层的情况下使用。将极性溶剂或溶剂混合物喷洒到清漆上，静置，致其溶胀，然后用较弱的溶剂去除清漆。
regilding 再贴金	Regilding is a restoration of surface where the areas originally gilt are covered with gold in whole or in part. 修复原来贴金区域的全部或部分覆盖金箔的表面。
relining 重托	Relining is a process where the painting which has been lined before is lined again. In this process the old lining support and lining adhesive are removed and the painting is lined on a new support with new adhesive. See also lining. 已经有衬里的画被重新加衬里。在此过程中，旧的衬里支撑物和衬里粘合剂将被去除，并在新支撑物上用新的粘合剂为画作加衬里。另见衬里。
repaint 重绘	Seeretouching (1). 见修整、润饰(1)。
repousse 冲压花	Repousse is decoration that is formed by punching and pressing into the gold leaf on a frame or wood panel. 冲压框架或木板上的金箔而形成的装饰。
retable 祭坛装饰	A retable is a painting or sculptural panel behind an altar. 在教堂祭坛后的绘画或雕塑。
retablum 祭坛装饰	See retable. 见祭坛装饰。
retarder 慢干剂	A retarder is a liquid mixed with a solvent in order to reduce its evaporation rate. 慢干剂是一种液体用来和溶剂混合以起到减缓蒸发的作用。
reticulation 网状裂纹	Reticulation is a defect of a paint or varnish layer where the upper layer adheres poorly to the layer below. As a result a net-like pattern of cracks occurs. 因颜料层或光油层之间附着差，而出现的网状纹路或裂纹。
retouching (1) 修整、润饰 (1)	Retouching of a surface is a restoration which simulates the colour, appearance, texture and finish of the original surface on an area of loss. See also invisible retouch. 一种修复手段，通过模仿原作的颜色，外观，纹理和最后处理以到达和原作破损的部位一样。另见隐形修整。

retouching (2) 上光 (2)	In French painting practice, retouching is the final painting stage when glazes are applied. 在法国绘画中，是指画一幅画最后的上光阶段。
retouching varnish 润饰清漆	A retouching varnish is a dilute varnish used to bring out the saturated colours of an oil painting before resuming retouching. 润饰清漆是被稀释后的清漆，用来在修复过程中暂时保护色层。
reverse section 反向部分	A reverse section is a frame which has its most prominent moulding closest to the picture. 一个框架，其最突出的模塑紧贴图画。
rigatino 水平影响	See tratteggio. 见垂直影线。
rigid support 刚性支撑物	A rigid support is a stiff inflexible support provided for an object whose flexing would cause damage. For example, wood or aluminium honeycomb panels can be used to support fragile canvas paintings. 刚性支撑物是为因弯曲会造成损伤的物体提供的坚硬支撑。例如，木材或铝蜂窝板可以用来支撑脆弱的布上油画。
riza 金属遮盖	See oklad. 见 oklad 金属遮盖。
roll 圆形框边	See fillet. 见阶梯状画框。
sailcloth 帆布	See duck. 见不浸水画布。
sakkos 主教穿的衣服	Sakkos is a garment worn by bishops depicted on icons. In the Byzantine period, a sakkos was not worn by bishops but was an imperial robe. 圣像画上的主教所穿的衣服。在拜占庭时期，sakkos 不是主教穿的衣服，而是皇帝穿的长袍。
sandwich layer 夹层	In a lining process of a painting, the sandwich layer is an additional support textile which is in direct contact with the back of the painting. It is often made of strong, finely woven, polyester textile. 在裱褙过程中，夹层是一种附加的支撑织物，它直接与画的背面接触。通常是由结实精细的涤纶织物制成的。
sankir 绿色	In an icon, sankir is the base colour in which the human body is painted. It is often used as a colour to paint shades. The colour is either olive green, dark green or greenish brown. 在圣像画中，sankir 是绘制人体的基础颜色。它常被用作画阴影。颜色为橄榄绿、深绿色或绿棕色。
scewings 金属片	Scewings are the waste pieces of metal leaf used in gilding which were not attached to the gilded surface. 用来贴金的废金属片，没有附着在贴金表面。

schlag leaf 仿金箔	See Dutch metal. 见荷兰金。
scrim 粗布	Scrim is a strong cotton or linen textile with an open weave. 松散强韧的棉、麻材质织物。
scumble 拟纹技法	Scumble is the uneven application of a thin layer of semi-opaque or opaque paint over a layer of a different colour in order to make a varied surface, for instance to simulate wood grain or marble. 在具有不同颜色的颜料上不均匀地涂上一层薄薄的半透明或不透明的颜料，以形成不同的表面，例如模拟木纹或大理石。
sealer 密封剂	A sealer is an undercoating used to seal a porous surface to reduce or prevent absorption. 一种底漆，用于密封多孔表面以减少或防止吸收。
seam 缝	A seam is the join between two pieces of textile. It is made by sewing two or more pieces of fabric together. 两件纺织品之间的接合处。由两块或两块以上的布料缝在一起形成的。
secco 干壁画	Secco is a type of wall painting on dried plaster. It is created by using a paint with a binding medium. 画在干灰泥上的壁画。通过使用颜料和结合介质绘制的。
secondary scalloping 二次扇形边	Secondary scalloping is a distortion in the canvas edges due to restretching. 画布边缘由于重新拉伸而造成的扭曲。
selective cleaning 选择性清洁	Selective cleaning is a treatment in which discoloured varnish is removed only from the light coloured areas of the painted surface, for example the areas of skin colour on a portrait. 只从涂漆表面的浅色区域（例如肖像上的肤色区域）去除变色清漆。
selvedge 织边	Selvedge is the border formed by the weft threads around the outermost warp thread. It prevents unravelling of the material. Its presence gives an indication of the size of the original canvas. 纬线围绕最外层经线形成的边缘。能防止材料散开。从织边可以看出原始画布的大小。
sfumato 渲染层次	In a painting, sfumato is a transition from light to dark so gradual as to be almost imperceptible. 在绘画中，渲染层次指颜色深浅的渐变过渡，这种过渡几乎让人难于觉察。
sgraffito (1) 刮涂（贴金表面）	Sgraffito is the technique of scratching a pattern in a paint layer on top of gilding, partly exposing the gilded surface underneath. It is most often used to create the effect of brocade textile patterns. 在贴金表面的漆层上刮出一个图案，露出部分贴金表面。它最常用于制造织锦图案的效果。

sgraffito (2) 刮涂（壁画表面）/ 五彩拉毛粉饰	Sgraffito is a mural painting technique where several coloured layers are put on top of each other and then the layers are scratched away to create a decoration. 一种壁画技法，将几层彩色的图层叠加在一起，然后将这些图层刮去，形成一种装饰。
shell gold 贝壳金	Shell gold is powdered gold originally made from leftover scraps of gold from the gilding process. They were kept and mixed in a shell. 最初由贴金过程中产生的碎金制成，成粉状，被放在贝壳中保存和混合。
shellac 虫胶	Shellac is the resinous secretion of the lac insect. 虫胶是紫胶虫的树脂状分泌物。
shponka 板条	A shponka is the slat (or pair of slats) on the reverse side of an icon, often horizontally wedged into the panel. 圣像画背面一个或成对的木板条，常见水平楔在画板上。
shrinkage crackle 收缩裂纹	See drying crack. 见干裂。
siccative 干燥剂	See drying agent. 见催干剂。
Sienna raw 黄土赭，生赭	Raw sienna is a special kind of yellow ochre. 生赭是一种特殊的黄色赭石。
Sienna, burnt 烧赭、熟赭	Burnt sienna is prepared by calcining raw sienna, in the process, the raw sienna undergoes a considerable change in hue and depth of color. 熟赭是通过煅烧生赭制备的。在煅烧过程中，生赭的色度和颜色的深浅都会发生较大变化。
sight edge 可视边缘	Sight edge is the edge of a picture frame closest to the picture. 最靠近图画的画框边缘。
silver gilding 贴银	See silvering. 贴银。
silver leaf 银箔	Silver leaf is thin leaves of silver used in silvering. After application, silver leaf is covered with a varnish to prevent tarnishing. 用来贴银的薄银片。贴银后在银箔上覆盖一层清漆，以防止失去光泽。
silvering 贴银	Silvering is the use of silver leaf in the same way as gold leaf in water gilding. It is possible to apply silver in a similar way as in mordant gilding but it is generally not used. 按金箔水贴金的方式使用银箔。可以用类似于粘合剂贴金的方法来贴银，但通常不使用。
sink in 下渗	Dark paints which sink in become increasingly transparent due to the painting medium being absorbed by ground. It causes changes in painting's colour balance. 由于颜料介质被底层吸收，下渗的深色颜料变得越来越透明。颜料下渗会改变绘画的色彩平衡。

sinking (2) 下渗	See sink in. 见下渗。
sinoper 赭石颜料	Sinoper is a red ochre pigment. 一种赭石红色颜料。
sinopia 赭石线画稿	Sinopia is the underdrawing for a fresco executed in sinoper. 用赭石颜料画的湿壁画的底图。
size (2) 浆底	Size is a thickened liquid to support water insoluble inks used for marbling. It is made by dissolving polysaccharides from Irish moss or gum tragacanth. 一种增稠的液体，可以支撑不溶于水的油墨，用于大理石花纹。浆底是通过溶解爱尔兰苔藓或黄檀胶中的多糖制成的。
size (3) 胶浆	Size is a solution of glue in water used in gilding. 贴金时使用的水胶溶液。
skin glue 皮胶	Skin glue is impure gelatin prepared from the skins of animals. 皮胶是从动物皮制备的不纯明胶。
skinning (1) 粉化起皮	Skinning is damage occurring as a loss of paint by chalking. 由于粉化使颜料损失造成的损坏。
skinning (2) 去皮	In painting conservation, skinning is the loss of paint during varnish removal. 在绘画保护中，去皮是指在去除清漆过程中绘画层的损失。
slate 板岩	Slate is a grey-black sedimentary metamorphic rock which ceaves readily to form thin plates. It was used as a support for oil paintings during the 16th and 17th centuries in Europe, especially Italy. 一种灰黑色的沉积变质岩，容易制成薄板。在16和17世纪的欧洲，尤其是意大利，板岩被用作油画的支撑物。
slice 木铲	A slice is a thin wooden tool where the edge of the blade runs at right angles to the axis of the handle. 一种薄的木制工具，刃的边缘与手柄的轴线成直角。
slip 扁条	A slip is a bevelled or flat strip fitted in the rebate section of the frame. 安装在框架的槽口部分的斜面或扁平条。
slip frame 滑架	A slip frame is the inner frame, inserted between the main frame and the picture in order to provide a decorative border. It is often covered with cloth. 内框，插入主框和图画之间，以提供装饰边框。它经常被布覆盖。
smalt 大青，蓝玻璃	Smalt was the earliest of cobalt pigments. It is artificial, in the nature of glass, a potash silicate strongly colored with cobalt oxide and reduced to a powder. 大青是最早的钴颜料。它是人造的，具有玻璃的性质，是用氧化钴强烈着色并还原成粉末的含钾硅酸盐。

soak-stain technique 浸染技术	Soak-stain technique is a method of painting which produces soft stains or blots of colour through the use of heavily diluted paint on unsized convas. 一种绘画方法，通过在未上浆的画布上使用大量稀释的颜料来产生柔和的色块或斑点。
spike oil 穗花油	Spike oil is an oil derived from the flowers of spike lavender. It is similar to turpentine but less volatile. It has been used as an solvent for soft resins and for making spirit varnish. When added to linseed oil in oil paints, it may cause buckling when the surface is warmed by sunlight. 一种从薰衣草花中提取的油。它与松节油相似，但不易挥发。穗花油曾被用作软树脂的溶剂和制造挥发清漆。当添加到油画用亚麻油中时，表面被阳光加热时，可能会导致（画作）屈曲。
spirit varnish 挥发清漆	A spirit varnish is a protective coating composed of a resin dissolved in an evaporating solvent, such as dammar in mineral spirit. 一种由溶解在蒸发溶剂中的树脂组成的保护性涂料，例如矿物油中的达玛脂。
spolvero 转印	Spolvero is a method of transferring a design to a surface by pouncing. 通过印花粉印图将图案转移到表面的方法。
staple 订书钉	A staple is a U-shaped piece of wire with pointed ends, used in painting conservation to fasten the canvas paintings to a strainer, stretcher or into a temporary working frame. See also rivet (1). U形的有尖头的金属丝，用于绘画保护，将油画固定在拉紧装置、延伸器或临时工作架上。另见铆钉（1）。
stippling (1) 戗彩 (1)	Stippling is small indentations on the surface of gilded gesso made with needles or other metal tools. 用针或其他金属工具，戗画是用针或其他金属工具制成的贴金石膏表面的小凹痕。
stippling (2) 点彩 (2)	Stippling is the application of paint in dabs or spots. 用小滴或小点涂颜料。
stippling brush 点彩刷	A stippling brush is a brush with coarse bristles which are cut straight across. It is used to produce gradation in colour when applying paint. In conservation it has been adapted for cleaning. 点彩刷刷毛粗糙，截面横切。用于在涂漆时产生颜色的渐变。在文物保护方面，它已经被改造成清洁用。
strainer 固定型内框	A strainer is an auxiliary support, usually made of wood on to which a painting on canvas is stretched. A strainer has joined corners which cannot be expanded. 一种辅助支撑物，通常由木头制成，画布在上面拉伸。拉紧装置连接了不能扩展的边角。
stress crackle 应力裂纹	See impact crack. 见冲击裂纹。

stress garland 压力花边	A stress garland is the distortion of the original canvas as regular scalloping of the threads at the perimeter. The peaks of the scallops indicate the canvas was originally tacked to the stretcher. 原始画布的变形，周围的线形成规则的螺纹扇形。扇形的尖峰表明画布最初是固定在延伸器上的。
stretcher 扩张型内框	A stretcher is an auxiliary support, usually made of wood on which paintings on canvas are stretched. They have expandable corners with keys/wedges causing the canvas to tighten. Stretchers have been used since the 18th century. 一种辅助支撑物，通常由木头制成，画布在上面伸展。有可扩展的角和楔子可使画布收紧。从18世纪起开始使用。
stretcher bar 扩张型内框的横杆	A stretcher bar is a piece of a stretcher, including any cross-bar. 扩张型内框的一部分，包括任何横杆。
stretcher crease 拉伸褶皱	Stretcher crease is the appearance on the paint surface of relatively uncracked paint overlying the stretcher bars. 覆盖在延伸器横杆上的相对未开裂的颜料表面的外观。
stretcher image 拉伸图像	A stretcher image is marks on the front of a canvas painting following the outline of the painting?s stretcher bars. It is caused by different tensions in canvas due to the environmental changes. The same marks can also be caused by the effect of a strainer. 画布正面随延伸器横杆的轮廓而拉伸。拉伸图像是由环境变化引起的画布张力不同造成的。同样的标记也可以由固定型内框的作用引起。
stretcher keys 拉伸器榫	See wedges. 见楔。
stretcher mark 拉伸标记	See stretcher image. 见拉伸图像。
strip lining 带衬	Strip lining is a treatment in which strips of frayed or feathered canvas are lined to the edges of a canvas painting and then used to attach the painting to its auxiliary support. 将磨损或羽状的画布条衬在画布的边缘，然后用来将油画附在其辅助支撑物上。
stripped state 剥离待修状态	A stripped state is a stage in the conservation process of a painting. The old retouches have been removed, filling has been completed but the inpainting has not yet started. 绘画保存过程中的一个阶段。旧的修整已被移除，填充已完成，但图像修复尚未开始。
structure absorbing material 结构吸收材料	Structure absorbing material is a soft foam used in vacuum table treatments of canvas paintings with seams. The material is placed under the painting and absorbs the impression of seams or any other irregularities on the back of the painting which otherwise would appear pronounced in the front side after the treatment. 一种软泡沫，用于真空吸附台处理有接缝的画布。该材料被放置在绘画下面，吸收绘画背面的接缝或任何其他不规则形状造成的压力，否则痕迹会在处理后明显地出现在正面。

suction converter frame 低压转换器框架	See converter frame. 见转换器框架。
suction table 低压台	See low pressure table. 见低压台。
support (3) 基底材	A support is the physical structure which holds or carries the ground or paint film of a painting. It can be a panel, a canvas, a wall or any flat surface on which painting can be made. 支撑或覆盖有画的底层或漆膜的物理结构。可以是一块面板、一张画布、一堵墙或任何一块可以用来作画的平面。
sverzatura 替换画框	Sverzatura is a method for flattening the wooden panel supports of paintings by cutting out parts of the original support and inserting new pieces or strips of wood. This method is no longer in use. 通过切除一部分原有支撑画框，用新木材代替的方法，曾被用于找平支撑画框，此方法已被废除。
swab 用棉签擦拭	You swab an object when you clean it using a liquid held in a soft cotton wool ball on a small stick. 用裹有棉球的小棍蘸取液体清洁物体。
synthetic canvas 合成材料画布	A synthetic canvas is canvas made from a synthetic material for example, polyester. 用合成材料织成的画布。例：聚酯纤维。
tabernacle frame 神龛框	A tabernacle frame is a picture frame with either gothic or classical architectural motifs, reminiscent of the recepticle for the consecrated Eurcharist. 神龛框是带有哥特式或古典建筑主题的画框，让人联想到神圣的欧洲艺术。
tack hole 钉孔	A tack hole is the hole in a canvas painting made by a tack. It is most often found on the turned down edges of a painting. 由于用图钉固定而在画布上造成的孔，经常出现在画框侧面。
tacking edge 固定边	The tacking edge is the edge of a canvas turned over on to the side of the stretcher or strainer and tacked. 用图钉把画布固定住的画框的侧面。
tacking margin 固定边	See tacking edge. 见固定边。
tangential cut 弦切	A tangential cut is a method of converting a tree into timber in which the saw cut is at right angles to the radius of the tree trunk. 弦切是指顺着树干主轴或木材纹理方向，垂直于树干断面半径的切割方法。
telnik 束腰军装外衣	Telnik is a type of late-antiquity military dress or short military tunic worn by soldiers depicted in an icon.Telnik 是古典时代晚期军装的一种或短宽军用束腰外衣。

tempera 蛋彩画	Tempera is a water-based paint that dries to a water resistant film. Egg proteins are used as the medium for egg tempera, but milk, various kinds of glue, gum, dandelion juice or the sap of the fig tree have also been used. 蛋彩是一种水性颜料，干燥后形成防水膜。蛋彩画的媒介一般是卵蛋白，但牛奶、各种胶水、树胶、蒲公英花汁或无花果树的汁液也曾被使用。
temporary stretcher 临时内框	A temporary stretcher is a temporary working frame which holds the painting in place during the conservation process. It can prevent the painting from shrinkage during drying after humidification and stretching. Expandable temporary stretchers are commercially available. 临时内框是一个临时的工作框，在修复过程中用来固定画面。可防止湿化、拉伸后的油画在干燥过程中收缩。市场上售卖可伸缩的临时内框。
tondo 圆形木版画	A tondo (pl. tondi) is a round, 15th century Tuscan panel painting. 15世纪圆形托斯卡纳木板油画。
tooth 糙面	Tooth refers to the quality of a roughened or absorbent surface which favours the application and adhesion of paint coatings. 指粗糙或易吸收的表面，有利于上色和颜料的附着。
total retouching 全色	Total retouching is a method of retouching where the retouched area is recognizable only when magnified. 一种修整方法，只有在放大时才能识别修饰区域。
traction crackle 牵引力裂纹	See alligator crackle and alligatoring. 见鳄裂和鳄纹。
transfer (1) 转移	The transfer of a painting is the removal of the paint layer from its original support and adhesion to a new support. For instance, paint is removed from a degraded wooden panel and reattached to new canvas, or a wall painting is removed with or or without some underlying plaster, from its original situation to another location. Transfer is usually undertaken because the painting is at risk. 绘画的转移是指将颜料层从原来的支撑物上移除，并粘附到新的支撑物上。例如，从退化的木板上移除颜料并将其重新附着到新画布上，或壁画带着或不带着底下的石膏层被从原来的位置转移到另一个位置。通常只在画作处于风险中时才会将绘画层转移。
transferred leaf 可转移金箔	A transferred leaf is a gold leaf which is attached to a rectangle of tissue paper slightly larger than the gold leaf. It is used mostly by amateur gilders or for work outdoors. 转印金箔附着在比金箔稍大一点的矩形薄纸上。它主要由业余贴金者用于户外工作。
transverse cut 横切	A transverse cut is a method of converting a tree into timber in which the saw cut is at right angles to the trunk axis of a tree. 横切是把树变成木材的一种方法，锯痕与树干的轴线垂直。

tratteggio 垂直影线	Tratteggio is a method of retouching where different colours are applied in fine, short, parallel and vertical brushstrokes, meant to recreate a aesthetic continuity from one border to another in a lacuna. 垂直影线是一种修复方法，在精细、短小、平行和垂直的笔触中应用不同的颜色，旨在在空白处重现从一个边界到另一个边界的美学连续性。
triptych 三联画	A triptych is an altarpiece made up of three panels, the two outer ones usually hinged so that they fold like doors in front of the main scene. 三联画是一种由三块板组成的祭坛画，左右外侧的两块通常用铰链连接起来，这样它们就像主场景前面的门一样可以折叠起来。
Tuchlein 薄纺画布	Tuchlein is a small thin cloth, painted with pigments in a water-based medium. It was used as a technique of early canvas paintings around the 14th and 15th centuries in the Netherlands and Germany. 薄纺画布是一种薄薄的布料，可以通过水性介质在它上面涂上颜料。大约在14世纪和15世纪的荷兰和德国，它被用作早期油画的一种技术。
Tung Oil or Chinese Wood Oil 桐油	Tung oil is obtained from the seeds of Aleurites cordata,A. fordii, and A. montana, contained in a nut. 桐油是从油桐树种子榨出的油。
turnover 侧边	On a painting, the turnover is the margin of the canvas which has been folded over the edge of a strainer or stretcher to which the canvas is fastened. 在一幅画上，侧边是画布的边缘，它被折叠在固定画布的拉紧装置或延伸器的边缘上。
Turpentine 松节油	Turpentine is a semi-liquid, natural exudates, containing terpenes associated with bodies of resinous charater, from pine trees. 松节油是一种半液体的天然分泌物，含有松树中与树脂质体相关的萜烯。
Ultramarine 群青	Genuine ultramarine blue pigment is from the semi-precious stone, lapis lazuli, which is a mixture of the blue mineral, lazurite, with calcspar, and iron pyrites. 真正的深蓝色颜料来自半宝石青金石，它是蓝色矿物，是天青石、钙石和黄铁矿的混合物。
Umber raw 生棕土	Raw umber is a brown earth pigment similar to the ochres and siennas but contains manganese dioxide as well as hydrous ferric oxide. 生棕土是一种黄棕色颜料，与赭石和熟赭相近，但是含有二氧化锰和含水三氧化二铁。
Umber, burnt 烧棕土	Burnt umber is made by roasting the raw earth at a dull red heat until the desired shade is obtained. 通过在无光的红色热量下烘烤生棕土，直到获得所需的阴影，即可制成烧棕土。

underbound paint 颜料过多	Underbound paint is paint containing little binding medium and is prone to powdering and falling. 含有少量胶结物质的颜料，颜料过多，胶结材料不足，造成颜料容易粉化、脱落。
underdrawing 草图	Underdrawing is the preliminary line drawing of the painting's composition often made directly onto the ground of a painting. 绘画构图的初步勾勒，通常直接画在底层上。
underpainting 底层色	The underpainting is the preliminary layer or layers of paint beneath the final coat of colour. 在最终一层颜色下面的一层或几层颜料。
underpinner 支撑	An underpinner is a machine used to join a picture frame by shooting metal wedges into the back of the mitre joint. 支撑是一种通过将金属楔片插入斜接接头背面来连接画框的装置。
unstable plaster detachment; prioritized detachment 严重空鼓	Detachment where the plaster has lost its overall cohesiveness and is often severely cracked and deformed. 空鼓部分的地仗丧失了整体的内聚力并伴有严重裂缝和变形。
vacuum envelope 真空密封外袋	In the lining of a painting, vacuum envelope is an airtight bag made of two plastic membranes sealed together. In use, two canvases with an adhesive between them are enclosed in the vacuum envelope from which the air is removed by a suction device. The atmospheric air pressure forces the two together. 在画作的衬里中，真空密封袋是由两个塑料薄膜密封在一起制成的密封袋。在使用中，粘在一起的两层画布被封闭于真空密封袋中，用抽吸装置将空气排出。大气压将这两层压在一起。
vacuum hot table 真空热桌	A vacuum hot table is a tool used in the conservation of paintings. It consists of an electrically heated plate and a vacuum pump. The air is withdrawn by breathers around the painting and directed out through ports in the table surface. It is used during the consolidation, lining and lamination of paintings. 真空热桌是一种用于绘画修复的工具，由一个电热板和一个真空泵组成。空气通过画作周围的呼吸器被抽离出去，并从桌子表面的孔中排出。
vehicle 媒介物	Vehicle The remaining liquid component excluding the pigment component in paint. See medium. 媒介物是涂料中除颜料成分外的剩余液体成分。见媒介。
Venice turpentine 威尼斯松节油	Venice turpentine is balsam obtained from the European Larch. It is often used as a plasticiser in pasta lining. In old receipes, Venice turpentine is mentioned as a varnish ingredient. 威尼斯松节油是从欧洲落叶松中提取的香脂。它经常被用作面糊胶里的增塑剂。在传统的配方中，威尼斯松节油被认为是一种清漆成分。

Verdigris 铜绿	Verdigris is specifically the normal acetate or one of the basic acetates of copper. It is also used to indicate copper carbonate or any of the other blue or green corrosion products which form on copper,brass,or bronze. 铜绿特别是普通醋酸盐或铜的碱式醋酸盐之一。它也用于指在铜、黄铜或青铜上形成的碳酸铜或任何其他蓝绿色腐蚀产物。
Vermilion 朱砂	Vermilion is red mercuric sulphide HgS. It is found in nature as the mineral. 朱砂是红色硫化汞HgS。在自然界中作为矿物质被发现。
Vine black 藤黑	Similar to charcoal, it is prepared by carbonizing vine twigs or vine wood. 藤黑是一种黑色颜料，与木炭类似，它是通过碳化藤树枝或藤木制成的。
vohrenye 赭素描	a. Vohrenye is the modelling of faces, hands and feet with different shades of colour in icon painting. b. Vohrenye is the colour which results from this modelling process. a. 赭素描是圣像画中为人物脸部、手部和足部铺设素描调子的步骤。 b.采用这种素描造型步骤完成的色层称之为赭素描。
wall painting transfer 壁画揭取	See transfer (1). 见转移。
walnut 胡桃木	Walnut is a wood from the tree belonging to the juglandaceae family and is hard and compact. It was frequently used for wood panel paintings in central and southern Europe, especially in France and Italy. 胡桃木，属胡桃科，质地硬且紧实。在中欧和南欧，特别是在法国和意大利，它经常被用做油画的底板。
water gilding 水溶粘接剂贴金箔法	Water gilding is a gilding technique where the gold leaf is applied onto a layer of gesso covered with a bole. The gold leaf is adhered with a water-based medium then polished. 水溶粘结剂贴金是一种贴金技术，将金箔涂在覆盖有贴金底灰的石膏层上。将金箔用水基介质粘合，然后抛光。
wax immersion method 蜡浸法	The wax immersion method is a conservation treatment of wooden panels or polychrome sculptures which are infested by insect pests. The wooden panels or sculptures are immersed in wax which penetrates into the support. 蜡浸法是一种对受虫害侵袭的木板或多色雕塑进行修复的方法。将木板或雕塑浸泡在蜡中，蜡液会渗透进支撑物中。
wax-resin lining 蜡树脂裱褙	Wax-resin lining is a technique of lining paintings using a mixture of beeswax and a resin, usually dammar, as the adhesive and where the adhesive totally penetrates the original structure. 蜡树脂裱褙采用蜂蜡和树脂（通常是达马脂）的混合物作为粘合剂，是将粘合剂完全渗透到原始结构中的一种裱画技术。
weave emphasis 织纹加强	Weave emphasis is the accentuation of the weave texture of a fabric on the paintings surface as a result of lining. The weave emphasis is caused by the forcing through of the texture onto the front side by the pressure against the flat rigid surface of the lining table. 织纹加强是由于裱褙而造成画作表面的织物纹理加强。织纹加强是纹理被裱褙台的扁平刚性表面压到绘画正面造成的。

weave interference 织纹干扰	In a lined canvas painting, weave interference is the accentuation of the yarns of the two superimposed textiles. The effect is most pronounced in a pair of textiles with similar weave, or of identical weaves slightly misaligned. The weave pattern is is transmitted through the ground into the painting surface . 在有衬里的画布绘画中，织纹干扰是两种叠加织物的纱线重叠。这种影响在一对织纹相似或相同的织物稍有错位时最为明显。编织图案通过基底层传到绘画表面。
weave texture loss 画布质感损失	Weave texture loss is damage where the whole surface becomes flatter as if painted on a finer canvas than originally. It may occur during the lining process of paintings. 画布质感损失是指整个表面变得更平坦，就像是在比原来更精细的画布上绘制的那样。它可能发生在绘画的裱褙过程中。
wedge 楔	A wedge is a flat piece of wood usually in a triangular shape fitted into the corner of a stretcher. When tapped, it forces the stretcher to open up at the corners, thus tightening the canvas. 楔是一块三角形的扁木，通常放置于油画框的四角内。安装楔后的油画框由于四角都被强迫撑开，因而更加稳固。
wet-in-wet 湿画法	Wet-in-wet is a painting technique where one paint is applied next to or on top of another whilethe first is still wet. 湿画法以一种用新颜料涂抹在还未干的颜料的旁边或覆盖在未干颜料层的技法。
white lead 铅白	It is the most important of all the lead pigments. It contains 70% of lead carbonate and 30% lead hydrate. 铅白是一种白色颜料，在所有含铅颜料中最为重要。它包含70%的碳酸铅和30%的水合铅。
whiting 碳酸钙粉	Whiting is finely ground calcium carbonate. 经过研磨成粉的碳酸钙。
window 窗口/小块清洁区域	A window is a small cleaned area of a painting from where the darkened varnish has been removed. 窗口是指一小部分已经清理完成的油画表面，原来由暗沉的上光油所覆盖。
woad 菘蓝 （植物靛青染料）	Woad is a blue dye very similar to indigo, which is obtained from the leaves of the woad plant, Isatis tinctoria. 菘蓝是一种与靛蓝非常相似的蓝色染料，它是从菘科植物菘蓝（板蓝根）的叶子中获得的。
working up 磨损	See grind. 见磨。

wrinkles 皱纹	Wrinkles are small scale undulations and folds caused by the swelling of an outer surface or the shrinkage of an inner support. This may occur due to the differential absorption of moisture which occurs in, for instance, skin and veneered wood, or due to the loss of material underlying a paint layer. 皱纹是由于吸水性不同所引起的外层胀大或内部支撑的收缩，从而产生的小面积波纹和折叠，常见于表皮和贴面木等，或由于绘画层下材料缺损。
wrinkling 起皱	Wrinkling is a small wave pattern in the paint layer caused by too much adhesive in the paint. 表现为颜料层上产生的细小波浪形纹路，由于颜料中添加过多的粘着剂所造成。

04

纸本、档案和书籍
Paper, Archives and Books

alkaline deterioration 碱性劣化	Alkaline deterioration of cellulose is damage caused by strong alkalis making the cellulose fibres swell and rupture. Alkaline conditions induce hydrolysis of the cellulose. Thus damaged cellulose often shows yellowing. 碱性劣化是由强碱引发的纤维素纤维的溶胀和断裂，碱性物质能诱发纤维素水解而泛黄。
alkaline reserve 碱贮 / 碱性缓冲物	An alkaline reserve is a substance, such as calcium carbonate, that reacts with acid contaminants. Alkaline reserves are added to paper during manufacture or precipitated in it during deacidification. 碱贮是预先加入纸张、能与酸性污染物发生中和反应的碱性物质。在造纸或脱酸过程中，通常会预先加入如碳酸钙之类的碱性缓冲物。
all rag paper 碎布优质纸	All rag paper is made from cotton-, linen-, and/or hemp rags or increasingly from cotton linters since rags are not often available. 碎布优质纸是由棉布、亚麻布和/或麻布等碎布料制成的纸。由于碎布不易得，多选用棉绒作为原料。
alum size 明矾胶	An alum size is an internal sizing in paper. During manufacture, aluminium sulphate (paper maker's alum) precipitates rosin on the cellulose fibres. The alum causes the paper to be acidic, thus hastening its deterioration. Alum sizing is responsible for the large amounts of books and papers having become extremely brittle (se brittle paper). Alum size was used in the paper manufacture between 1820 and 1960. It is sometimes used for cheap paper. 明矾胶是纸张自带的一种胶。在造纸过程中，硫酸铝（造纸明矾）会将松香沉淀在纤维素纤维上。明矾使纸张呈酸性并加速劣化。明矾胶是造成大量书籍和纸张变脆的主要原因（见脆性纸）。1820年至1960年期间，明矾胶有时会用于廉价纸的加工制作。
amorphous region 无定形区	An amorphous region in cellulose is a randomly organised region in the packing of cellulose chains. In the amorphous regions of cellulose, water can be present because the fibrils are not tightly packed. This gives the cellulose structure its suppleness. 纤维素中的无定形区是纤维素链随机排列的区域。在纤维素的无定形区域，由于原纤维并未紧密堆积，所以会有水分存在，使得纤维素的结构具有一定柔软性。
aqueous deacidification 水溶液除酸法	Aqueous deacidification is a chemical treatment used to neutralise unwanted acids present in an object by using an aqueous solution of a deacidification agent. 水溶液脱酸是一种化学处理方法，通过使用脱酸剂的水溶液来中和物体中不需要的酸。
back (1) 书背	a. The back of a book is the part of a book block where the sections are sewed, glued and/or stapled together. b. The back of a book is the material that covers the part of a book block where the sections are sewed, glued and/or stapled together. a.书背是书芯的一部分，通过缝制，粘合和/或装订在一起。b.书背是覆盖书芯部分的材料，通过缝制，粘合和/或装订与在一起。

back-board 背板	See board. 见板。
backbone 书背	See back (1b). 见书背。
beater 打浆机	A beater is a machine used to mechanically beat or macerate paper fibres to the required properties. Beating cuts the fibres to shorter lengths and causes them to fibrillate. It can be adjusted to vary the resulting paper properties. Main types of beater Main types of beater are pestle and mortar, stamper or hammer, Hollander, Jordan beater and disc refiner. 打浆机是一种纸张加工机器，通过浸染和敲打等机械作用切断纸张纤维使其长度缩短并发生原纤化作用，最终得到符合需求的纸浆。调整工作参数可以得到不同性能的纸浆。打浆机的主要类型有杵式打浆机、冲压或锤式打浆机、荷兰式打浆机、乔丹打浆机和盘式精炼机。
binding 装订	a. Binding is the hand or machine process of gathering and fastening together folded sheets of paper. These are then covered in a protective cover that can be decorated. b. A binding consists of folded sheets of paper which are gathered and fastened together such as a book, a volume or a tome. c. See book cover. a.装订是将折叠好的纸张汇集后，通过手动或机械方式固定在一起的过程。之后用起到保护作用的封皮对书进行装饰。b.装订由折叠的纸张组成，将其收集并固定成一本、一卷或一册书。c.见封皮。
bleeding (1) 晕色 (1)	Bleeding is damage whereby a pigment or dye present in a paint or ink, and applied to a material, dissolves partly and spreads to adjoining areas, creating a halo effect. The colourant may dissolve in a thermoplastic or solvent. 晕色是一种常见病害，是颜料或染料等着色物质溶解、扩散并沾染到相邻区域的现象。着色剂会溶解于热塑性塑料或溶剂中。
blind tooling 手工无色凹凸印	Blind tooling is the process of decorating and lettering a leather or cloth binding by using heated instruments such as rolls and fillets to impress patterns in the binding without the use of gold, metal foil or ink. 手工无色凹凸印是使用加热后的工具（如卷角和倒角）在皮革或布面封面上进行装饰和烫印的过程，全程无需使用金、金箔或墨水。
blotting paper 吸墨纸	Blotting paper is paper without sizing which is used to absorb water or ink from other materials. Usually it is made from cotton linters or chemical pulp that have low amounts of soluble contaminants so as not to affect the material dried with it. 吸墨纸是未经上浆的纸张，由棉绒或化学纸浆制成，用于从其他材料上吸水或吸墨。通常这些棉绒或化学纸浆中的可溶性污染物含量较少，不会与应用材料发生反应。
board 硬纸板	A board is a piece of cardboard or wood that provides stiffening to a book cover. The board is usually covered externally with leather or cloth and internally with the pastedown. Two boards are used in a book cover, one at the either side of the book block, while the back-board covers the last page of the book block. 硬纸板是一块硬纸板或木板，用作书籍的封皮可以使封面硬挺，通常外面用皮革或布料包装（覆盖），内部用环衬连接。书籍封皮通常使用两个硬纸板，形成封面和封底。

book block 书芯	A book block consists of the sewn sections, endpapers and flyleaves, excluding the covering. 书芯由缝合的部分、卷首及卷尾的空页和扉页（不包括封皮）组成。
book cover 封皮	A book cover is a protective, often decorated, outer cover to which the book block is secured with glue and/or thread. Book covers can be made from leather, vellum, paper and/or cloth. 书籍封皮是一种保护性、装饰性的外皮，多用皮革，牛皮纸，纸和/或布制成。书芯通过胶装和/或线装的形式固定到封皮上。
brittle paper 脆性纸	Brittle paper is paper of which the cellulose is degraded especially in the amorphous regions due to acid hydrolisis and/or oxidation. This can be caused by alum-rosin sizing, air pollution, production processes and material(s) in contact with and/or applied to the paper surface. 脆性纸是由于酸水解和/或氧化，纸张中的纤维素（尤其是无定形部分）被降解而脆化。催化原因可能为明矾松香胶、大气污染物或生产过程中与纸张表面材料产生反应所致。
brittleness (2) 脆化 (2)	Brittleness of paper is mostly the result of the degradation of the amorphous parts of the cellulose fibre resulting in a less flexibile structure. 纸张脆化是无定形状态下的纤维素纤维降解后，纸张的柔韧性能下降而变脆的现象。
buffer (3) 缓冲剂 (3)	A buffer is an alkaline reserve in paper, such as calcium carbonate, used to counteract acid deterioration. 缓冲剂是纸张中预先贮存的碱性物质，例如碳酸钙，用于抵消酸性物质对纸张的劣化。
carbon ink 碳素墨水	Carbon ink is ink made from finely ground carbon dispersed in a water/gum or water/glue mixture. The main types of carbon ink are Indian ink, Chinese ink and soot ink. 碳素墨水是将经过细致研磨的炭黑与水、胶相互混合而成的，碳素墨水的主要类型有印度墨水，中国墨水和烟灰墨水。
carboxymethylcellu-lose 羧甲基纤维素	See sodium carboxymethylcellulose 见羧甲基纤维素钠。
casing-in 装壳	Casing-in is the process of attaching a book block to a separately prepared cover. 装壳是将书芯装到单独制作的封面上的过程。
catch up stitch 缠针	See chain stitch. 见锁针。
chain line 帘线纹	Chain lines in laid paper are the lines which are spaced approximately 1 to 5 centimetres apart and run in a 90-degree angle to the longest side of an uncut sheet of paper. Chain lines, which are visible in transmitted light, are the result of the weft wires in the sieve causing a watermark. 直纹纸上的帘线纹是指间隔约1至5厘米，并垂直于未切纸张长边的隐形线，在透射光下可见。帘线纹是来自纸帘编线纹路的水印。

chain stitch 锁针	In bookbinding, a chain stitch is the linking stitch made at the head and tail of each section, forming a chain-like pattern. 在书籍装订中，锁针是在每一节的头尾形成链状图案的连接针。
chamfering 倒角	Chamfering is the process of bevelling or rounding the side-edges and/or corners of a heavy board by sandpapering or cutting. 倒角是通过砂纸打磨和／或切割，把厚板的边角和／或角削成斜角或圆角的过程。
chemical pulp 化学纸浆	Chemical pulp is a kind of paper pulp where lignin and hemi cellulose are dissolved chemically and washed away, in order to extract the cellulose from wood. It is made by boiling wood chips under pressure in aqueous solutions of chemicals. It can be made by boiling wood chips under pressure in aquepus solutions of chemicals. It can be made in acid 'sulphite' and alkaline 'sulphate' solutions with the latter yielding a strong pulp. It is often bleached to obtain a better colour. It is the pulp from which chemical pulp paper is made. 将木屑在加压条件下经化学溶液煮沸，其中的木质素和半纤维素被化学溶解并洗净，仅余下纤维素，即得化学纸浆。采用呈酸性的亚硫酸盐和呈碱性的硫酸盐制备而得的化学纸浆具有更好的机械强度，通过漂白可以获得更好的颜色。化学浆纸就是用化学纸浆制成的。
CMC 羧甲基纤维素钠	See sodium carboxymethylcellulose. 见羧甲基纤维素钠。
cockle 起皱	When paper cockles, it becomes deformed in one direction, with the deformation showing as waves or as a puckered surface. This is caused by extreme climatic changes or excessive heat. 纸张起皱通常表现为某个方向呈现波浪或褶皱之类的变形，多由极端的气候变化或高温所致。
collating (1) 装订	Collating is the process of arranging all the sections of a book in the right order. 装订是按照正确顺序排列书中所有章节的过程。
collating (2) 校勘 (2)	Collating is the process of checking if all the sections and pages of a book are present. 校勘是检查一本书所有章节和页面是否齐备的过程。
collating (3) 整理（文件或书）(3)	Collating is a bibliographer's description of the physical make-up of a book in a standardised formula. 整理是书目提要编纂者用标准化格式对一本书进行排版的过程。
copper green corrosion 铜绿腐蚀	Copper green corrosion of paper is damage caused by some copper compound pigments initiating deterioration reactions in cellulose where the copper acts as catalyst. Signs of this type of corrosion are a progressive brown/green discolouration on the verso of the colouring. The affected areas of paper become extremely brittle. 纸张的铜绿腐蚀是在含铜颜料中的铜的催化作用下，纸张纤维素发生劣化的现象。铜绿腐蚀的迹象常见于纸张背面，呈棕色或绿色。受影响的纸张区域发生严重脆化。

corrosion stain 腐蚀斑点	A corrosion stain on paper is a discolouration caused by the corrosion products of a metal present in, or in contact with, the paper. Corrosion products are often harmful to paper. 纸张上的腐蚀斑点是由与纸张与金属接触后而导致的腐蚀变色现象，这类腐蚀产物通常对纸张有害。
cotton linter 棉短绒	Cotton linter is a 1-3mm long cotton fibre left on the cotton seed after the raw cotton has been passed through the cotton ginny. This fibre is used to make very pure (for example, photographic) and durable papers since cotton consists of almost 100% cellulose. 棉短绒是原棉经轧花后留在棉籽上1-3毫米长的棉纤维。由于棉包含100%的纤维素纤维，因此可用于制造纯度极高的耐用纸张。（如摄影用）
crystalline region 结晶区	A crystalline region in cellulose is a highly organised area in the structure of cellulose fibrils. The molecules are in a parallel formation, bonded together by hydrogen bonds. In the crystalline regions of cellulose no water is present between the molecules. This arrangement gives the cellulose structure its stiffness. Crystalline regions make up approximately 70-80% of the cellulose. See also amorphous region. 纤维素中的结晶区是纤维素原纤维结构中高度组织化的区域。这些分子以一种平行的形式，由氢键连接在一起。在纤维素的结晶区，分子之间不存在水，使纤维素结构具有硬度。结晶区约占纤维素的70-80%。另见无定形区。
curl 起翘	When paper curls, one of its sides contracts or expands more than the other. This results in the warping and/or rolling up of the sheet. Paper sheets that are adhered on one edge cannot release this tension and are therefore more prone to this type of deformation. 当纸张的一侧比另一侧收缩或扩展更明显时，整张纸起翘和/或向上卷起。由于边缘处的应力难以释放，所以纸张边缘更容易出现这种类型的变形。
cutting plough 切书边刀	See plow 见切书边刀。
damp stain 水渍	A damp stain on paper is a diffuse stain caused by water. The water dissolves coloured deterioration products of the paper which migrate to the surface of the paper upon drying. 水渍是由水引发的扩散性污渍。纸张在劣化过程中会产生有色降解物，水使其溶解，待干燥后，有色降解物就迁移到纸张表面形成水渍。
damp stretching 潮湿拉伸	Damp stretching is a treatment which involves causing a sheet of paper, board or other hygroscopic material to swell by applying a small amount of water to it. Drying the object with its edges restrained by weight(s), clamps or adhered to a board with an adhesive or adhesive tape, prevents the object from shrinking back and renders it flat. Damp stretching can cause changes in format and, if done carelessly, can tear the object. 潮湿拉伸是一种处理方法，在纸、纸板或其他吸湿材料上喷洒少量水使其膨胀。之后，将材料边缘用重物压制、夹子固定或粘附在板上等方法进行干燥。湿润拉伸会造成材料变形，如果操作不当会将其撕裂。

dandy roll mark 水印	See watermark. 见水印。
deckle edge 毛边	The deckle edge is the outside edge of an uncut mould-made sheet of paper. Some fibres run between the deckle and the sieve resulting in an uneven, wavy and thinner edge. 毛边是未经切割的模制纸边缘。一些纤维在脱槽和筛网之间流动，导致边缘较薄且呈不均匀波浪状。
diethyl zinc 二乙基锌	Diethyl zinc is a volatile liquid that reacts with water or acids to deposit alkaline zinc salts. It is used in the vapour phase of paper deacidification. 二乙基锌是一种能与水或酸反应生成碱性锌盐的挥发性液体，常用于纸张的气相脱酸。
double cord sewing 双线缝纫	a. Double cord sewing is the technique of sewing the sections of a book to double raised cords, whereby the thread leaves and re-enters the section through the same hole. b. A double cord sewing is a book sewn with the double cord sewing technique. a.双线缝纫是将书的各部分用线绳通过同一孔穿进穿出，将书的各部分缝合在一起的书籍装帧技术。b.双线缝纫是用双线缝纫技术装帧的书。
double fold 双面折叠	A double fold is made by folding paper succesively in two directions. 双面折叠是将纸在两个方向上折叠的过程。
durable paper 耐久纸	See permanent paper. 见耐久纸。
egoutteur mark 水印	See watermark. 见水印。
endpaper 衬页	See pastedown. 见衬页。
ethoxymagnesium ethyl carbonate 乙氧基乙基碳酸镁	Ethoxy magnesium ethyl carbonate is an alkali that dissolves in organic solvents and is used for deacidification of paper. 乙氧基乙基碳酸镁是一种碱性物质，溶于有机溶剂中可用于纸张脱酸。
false band 假竹节	A false band is a strip of a flexible material such as leather or thin cardboard, glued to the inside of the back of a book cover or directly on the back of a book block to imitate raised cords. 假竹节是用皮革或薄硬纸板等柔韧材料制成的带子，粘在书皮下面或直接粘在书芯的书脊处，用以达到模仿竹节凸起的目的。
felt side 毛毡边	See feltmark. 见毡印。
feltmark 毡印	The feltmark on a sheet of paper is the impression of the felt on the upper side of the paper. In hand paper making, felts are used to couch the sheets from the sieve and to separate the sheets during pressing. On a paper machine, felts are used to carry the paper from the sieve. 毡印是毛毡在纸上留下的印记。在手工造纸过程中，毛毡被用来吸收纸张过筛后多余的水分，并在之后的压制过程中将纸张从纸帘上分开。

fillet (2) 倒角 (2)	A fillet is a bookbinding tool used for tooling a leather or cloth cover by impressing decorative features on it. This tool can be either a curved piece of brass fixed in a handle, or a brass wheel attached to a handle in such a way that it can turn. It can have various widths to make lines and can be engraved to make two or more lines, or ornaments. 倒角是一种装订工具，可在皮革或布料上压出装饰花纹。该工具可以是固定在手柄上的曲形黄铜片，也可以是装在手柄上可调节的黄铜轮，可以压制不同宽度的线条获得装饰效果。
flattening 压平	Flattening is the process of making a sheet of paper, board or other porous hygroscopic material flat. It involves relaxing the object with a small amount of moisture, followed by controlled drying. The material can dry under pressure in a press or under boards that are weighted down, under a stretched sheet of porous material, or strecthed along its edges. See also damp stretching. 压平是指将纸、纸板或其他多孔吸湿材料压制平整的过程，包括先用少量水分使材料浸湿伸展，然后控制干燥。这种材料可以在压力机的压力下干燥，在压着的木板下干燥，在拉伸的多孔材料下干燥，也可以沿着边缘拉伸。另见潮湿拉伸。
flour paste 糨糊	Flour paste is a more or less viscous adhesive made by pouring boiling water in a flour and water mixture, followed by stirring and normally without prolonged heating. Flour paste contains gluten. 糨糊是一种具有一定粘性的粘合剂，将沸水倒入面粉和水的混合物中，不断搅拌即得糨糊，通常不需要长时间加热。糨糊中含有面筋。
fly-leaf 折页	A fly-leaf is the part of a folded section of plain or decorated paper at either end of a book that is not pasted to the inside of the covering boards of the book. 折页是书的两端折叠起来的空白纸或装饰纸，它没有被粘贴到书的封面内侧。
foliation 标记页数	Foliation is the marking with numbers of the leaves of a book, usually on the recto side. If applied after the book was made or printed (for example, before a conservation treatment), usually both sides of the sheet are numbered (for example, 25r(ecto), 25v(erso)) 书籍的标记页数通常位于书的正面。如果在书本制作或印刷后进行页码标记（例如，修复前），那么纸张的两面通常都会编上号码。
fore-edge 前切口	The fore-edge of a book is the outer edge opposite and parallel to the back or spine of the book block. 书的前切口是与书脊或书脊相对平行的外边缘。
foxing 狐斑	Foxing is damage on paper which is visible as irregular reddish brown spots speckled over the paper surface. The spots are composed of fungal residue from the felts used in papermaking that discolour in humid conditions. 狐斑是散布于纸张表面的不规则红褐色斑点。这种斑点来自造纸毛毡中的真菌有色分泌物，在潮湿的条件下，斑点的颜色会发生变化。

French joint 法式宽书脊槽	In a book binding, a French joint is made by offsetting the board(s) a little from the backing joint of the book. The covering material is pressed in the resulting gully. A French joint allows thicker boards to hinge more freely with lesser strain to the joint. 在书籍装帧中，将纸板与书籍的背面接缝偏移出一个角度是法式宽书脊槽的制作方法，之后将封皮所用材料压到槽中。法式宽书脊槽使得较厚的木板能够更好地铰接，对木板的应力较小。
friction stretching 摩擦拉伸	See flattening. 见压平。
front-board 前板	See board. 见板。
gathering (2) 书帖组	A gathering consists of folded sections put together in one unit. 几个书帖被贴合在一起组成未缝的书芯称为书帖组。
gold tooling 烫金	See tooling. 见烫印。
groundwood paper 木质纸	Groundwood paper is made from groundwood pulp and contains all the components of wood such as lignin, hemi cellulose and other components. It is often alum/rosin sized and becomes darker in light because the lignin it contains is light sensitive. Because nothing is lost in the process of making it, groundwood paper is cheap. The lignin in the paper is thought to be responsible for the paper's short life span. 木质纸由磨木浆制成，包含木材中的所有成分如木质素，半纤维素和其他成分等。因为木质素对光敏感，在光照下纸张颜色会变暗。造纸过程中常会用到明矾或松香。因为在制作过程中没有损耗，所以木质纸价格便宜。纸张中的木质素被认为是导致纸张寿命短的原因。
groundwood pulp 磨木浆	Groundwood pulp is pulp made by grinding wood on end against a grindstone. It is the pulp from which groundwood paper is made. 磨木浆是指将木材在磨石上研磨而成的纸浆，是制作木质纸的原料。
half leather binding 半皮装	Half leather binding is a style of binding where only the back and corners of a book are covered with leather. 半皮装是一种装帧方式，只在书背和书角用皮革覆盖。
half vellum binding 半犊皮装	Half vellum binding is a style of binding where only the back and corners of a book are covered with vellum. 半犊皮装是一种装帧方式，只在书背和书角用犊皮覆盖。
hand-made paper 手工纸	Hand-made paper is paper made by dipping a mould and deckle into a vat containing an aqueous suspension of fibres . Hand-made paper sheets are made one by one. An uncut sheet of hand-made paper has four deckle edges and no distinctive grain direction. 手工纸是通过抄纸框在纸槽中抄取纸浆而得的纸张，每次只能制作出单张。未经切割的手工纸四周毛边，没有明显的纹理方向。

head 书头	a. The head of a book is the upper edge of the book. b. The head of a book is the uppermost part of a book block. c. The head of a book is the margin at the top of a page. d. The head of a book is where the headband is located at the top of the back of a book. a.指书的上边缘。b.指书芯的最上端。c.指书页上端的空白。d.指书背面顶部书头的位置。
headband 书头布	a. A headband is a reinforcement at the top and bottom of the back of a book that is sown onto the book block. It consists of threads wound and braided around a cord of any flexible material thus forming a band on top of the back. b. A headband is a woven reinforcement which is glued onto the top and bottom of the back of athe book block. a. 书头布是缝制在书芯上、位于书背顶部和底部的加固物。由多条线缠绕一根材质柔软的绳子编织而成，在书背顶部形成一条带子。b. 书头布是一种编织物，粘在书芯背面的顶部和底部，起到加固的作用。
headcap 书脊护舌	A headcap is the part of the back cover of a book that is turned in and shaped over the back at the head and tail of the book. It is made to protect the headband when the book is closed. 书脊护舌是书背面封皮的一部分，它顺着书头和书根的形状向内弯曲成形。书籍护舌可以在书合上后起到保护搭头布的作用。
hinge 合页	A hinge of a book is where the front- or back-board meet the back of the book and where the board can turn upon the book. See also joint. 合页指书槽位置起连接书心和封面板的粘贴物，纸或纱布等。一边贴在书脊边缘另一边贴在封板上。另见书槽。
Hollander beater 荷兰式打浆机	A Hollander beater is a machine for treating cellulose fibres. It employs a cylinder set perpendicular with parallel dull knives. The cylinder is mounted in an oblong shaped trough that is partly divided by a mid wall. The fibre suspension is moved round by the revolving cylinder. The fibres are cut or bruised between the knives and the foundation of the through. The Hollander beater was invented in Holland ing the 17th century. 荷兰式打浆机用于处理纤维素纤维，它的气（汽）缸同平行排列的钝刀垂直。气（汽）缸被安装在一个椭圆形的槽中，由中壁分隔。纤维悬浮液通过旋转气缸在打浆机中进行圆周转动，达到切割纤维的目的。荷兰式打浆机因17世纪在荷兰发明而得名。
hollow back 空心书背	A hollow back is the type of back that is not glued to the back of the book block. A book with a hollow back has an opening between the back covering and the book block when the book is opened. 空心书背是一种不粘在书芯背面的书背。书背中空的书在打开时，书背和书芯之间有一个开口。
illumination 彩图	In a manuscript or book, an illumination is decoration combining both illustration and ornament. An illumination is usually made by using gold and/or silver foil as well as paints. 在手稿或书籍中，彩图包括插图和其他装饰内容，通常有金箔、银箔、手绘等形式，具装饰性。

ink 墨水	Ink is a coloured liquid consisting of a pigment or dye in a suitable vehicle used for writing or printing. 墨水是一种含颜料或染料的有色液体，通过适当工具实现其书写或打印功能。
ink corrosion 墨水腐蚀	Ink corrosion of paper is damage caused by iron gall inks. The ink damages the paper in two ways, firstly, by acid hydrolysis due to sulphuric acid present in the ink and, secondly, by oxidation of the fibres caused by catalytic decomposition reactions that are triggered by soluble iron compounds available in the ink. The affected areas of paper become dark brown and lose their structure, which leads to the loss of the inked areas. 墨水腐蚀是由纸张上的铁胆墨水而引发的病害。墨水腐蚀有两种，一是由墨水中的硫酸导致纸张发生酸水解，二是由墨水中的可溶性铁化合物的催化作用下导致的纤维氧化。受影响的区域会变成棕褐色甚至失去原有的结构，从而导致缺失。
inner joint 内书槽	An inner joint is the inside of the hinge of a book and consists of endpapers. 内书槽是指位于合页内侧，由衬页组成的部分。
interleaf (2) 衬纸 (2)	An interleaf is a transparent or thin opaque blank sheet of paper placed between the pages of a book or between text and illustration, to prevent abrasion caused by the rubbing of the pages together. 衬纸是放置在书页之间或文字与图版之间的薄透型白纸，避免纸张摩擦而造成的磨损。
interleaved 插页的	An interleaved book is a book with blank leaves between printed or written pages to allow for making notes. 插页书是在印刷或书写的书页之间留有空白页，以便做笔记的书。
interleaving 插页	Interleaving is the act of inserting sheets of paper or plastic sheets between pages of a book or photographs for protective purposes. 插页是基于保护目的，在书的页面或照片间插入纸片或塑料片的方法。
joint (2) 书槽 (2)	The joint of a book is where the boards on either side of the book hinge. See also hinge. 书槽是书前后两边的板子合页的地方。另请参见合页。
joint (3) 书槽连接处 (3)	A joint in a book is a deformation of the outer sections of the book block over the boards. By rounding or backing the book block the sections are formed over the edges of the front- and back board. 书槽连接处是指书芯最外一贴的边缘盖住外封面板边缘的连接部位。通过起脊，书芯部分书帖向外延展，形成紧挨着前后封面板边缘的部分。
ketch stitch 双针	See chain stitch. 见锁针。
kettle stitch 穿线装订	See chain stitch. 见锁针。

laid line 竹丝纹	Laid lines in laid paper are the lines which are narrowly spaced and run parallel to the longest side of an uncut sheet of paper. Laid lines, which are visible in transmitted light, are the result of the warp wires in the sieve causing a watermark. 直纹纸上的竹丝纹是指与未裁切的纸最长边平行且间隔较窄的线。竹丝纹来自筛网经线产生的水印，透射光下可见。
leafcasting 纸浆修复	Leafcasting is a method of filling in losses or damages in paper by depositing cellulose fibres from suspensions in water. Leafcasting can also be used to strengthen vellum by using collagen fibres. 纸浆修复是一种从纸浆悬浮液中将纤维素纤维沉积出来，以填补纸张缺失或缺损的方法。此法还可以利用胶原纤维增强牛皮纸的强度。
leafcasting machine 纸浆补洞机	A leafcasting machine is an apparatus used to fill in losses in paper. The object to be treated is submerged in a suspension of fibres in water which, upon draining the water through the supporting screen, will settle in the missing parts. 纸浆补洞机是修补残缺纸张的机器，将待修补的纸张置于支撑网架上，浸没于纸浆中，利用负压抽吸作用，使得纸浆附着在纸张的缺失部分，达到修补的目的。
leather binding 皮革装	Leather binding is a style of binding where the cover of a book is made of leather or covered with leather. 皮革装是一种装帧方式，书的封面由皮革制成或用皮革覆盖。
lignin 木质素	Lignin is the substance in wood that cements the cells together. It is a highly aromatic, cross linked structure of high molecular weight. It is light sensitive and thought to increase the deterioration of groundwood pulp paper. In thermo-mechanical pulp,lignin is dispersed differently in the paper due to the higher temperatures and protects cellulose against oxidation. 木质素是木材中将细胞粘合在一起的一种物质，是具有交联结构的高分子酚聚合物。木质素对光非常敏感，被认为会导致木浆纸的劣化。在热机械浆中，由于温度较高，木质素在纸中的分散程度不同，可以保护纤维素不被氧化。
limp binding 软装	Limp binding is a style of binding where the covering material is very thin and flexible. Often thongs are used to secure the cover onto the book block. 软装是指一种书籍装帧样式，通常选用薄软的弹性材料作为封皮，借助皮带将封皮固定在书芯上。
line 托裱	You line a sheet of paper or piece of textile in order to strengthen it by adhering another sheet of paper or a suitable fabric to its back with an adhesive. 为了加固和保护艺术品，通常会用粘合剂将一张纸或合适的织物附到书画或纺织品背面，以增强其强度，这个过程被称为托裱。
lying press 压书脊机	A lying press is a tool that is used to press books or book blocks during several binding operations. It is used in a horizontal position. It can have a guide or groove on one side to accommodate for a plow. 压书脊机是在书籍装订过程中可多次使用的工具，主要用于对书芯或书籍进行压平处理，使用时水平放置，一端可安置一个用于安装槽刨的凹槽。

machine direction 丝缕方向	The machine direction of paper is the direction of the grain in machine-made paper. It results from the tendency of suspended fibres to orientate themselves in the direction of the movement of the sieve. 纸的丝缕方向是机器造纸过程中纸的纹理方向，其因纸张悬浮纤维倾筛网的运动方向所致。
machine-made paper 机制纸	Machine-made paper is paper made on a machine where the fibre suspension is poured on an endless sieve. Machine-made paper is produced on very large reels. It has a distinctive grain direction and no deckle edges. 机制纸是通过机器过滤纤维悬浮液而制成的纸和纸板。机制纸是在超大卷轴上生产而成，具有独特的纹理且不含毛边。
mechanical wood pulp 机械木浆	See groundwood pulp. 见木浆制纸浆。
methoxy magnesium methyl carbonate 甲氧基碳酸镁	Methoxy magnesium methyl carbonate is an alkaline material whose solution in organic solvents is used to deacidify paper. 甲氧基甲基碳酸镁是一种碱性材料，溶于有机溶剂中可用于纸张脱酸。
mould-made paper / imitation hand-made paper 仿手工纸	Mould-made paper is paper made on a machine where a stiff circular sieve revolves in a fibre suspension taking the fibres to form an endless length of paper. Mould-made paper can have two deckle edges and a grain direction. 仿手工纸由机器的圆形硬质筛网不断在纤维悬浮液中旋转，模拟人工抄纸而制成。与手工纸相比，仿手工纸的长度不限，只有两侧有毛边，纹理方向明显。
mount (2) 裱装 (2)	A mount is a card window used in framing, for instance, works of art on paper or textiles. 裱装是一种卡纸框架，用来装裱纸品艺术或纺织品艺术。
non-aqueous deacidification 无水脱酸	Non-aqueous deacidification is a chemical treatment used to neutralise unwanted acids present in an object by using a deacidification agent in a non-aqueous (usually organic) solvent. 无水脱酸是一种化学处理方法，在无水（通常为有机）溶剂中使用脱酸剂以中和某一物体中不需要的酸。
outer joint 外书槽	An outer joint is the outside of the hinge of a book and consists of the book covering. 外书槽是书合页的外部，由书的封面组成。
P.O.P. 道林纸	See printing-out paper. 见道林纸。
paper binding 纸装	A paper binding is a style of binding where the covers are made of paper, or covered with paper. 纸装是一种书籍装帧方式。书的封面是用纸制作，或用纸包裹。

paper splitting 贴折条	Paper splitting is the initial phase of a method used for strenghtening a sheet of paper. The paper is split mechanically in two layers which, in a later phase, are glued together again with a new sheet of paper in between. 贴折条是在纸张断折处贴上相匹配的纸条，再将它们粘合在一起，起到加固的作用。
parchment size 羊皮纸胶	Parchment size is a glue made by boiling parchment shavings in water, sometimes with the addition of acetic acid. Parchment size without acetic acid is used to size paper after wet treatment. With acetic acid, it is used to glue gold-beaters skin to parchment as a reinforcement to parchment. 羊皮纸胶是羊皮纸屑在沸水中煮制而得的胶水，可直接用于纸张上浆。加入醋酸，可用于粘贴金箔，对羊皮纸起到一定的加固作用。
pare 削薄/打薄	See paring. 见削薄/打薄。
pare down 削薄/打薄	See paring. 见削薄/打薄。
paring 削薄/打薄	In bookbinding, paring is the process of thinning leather, parchment or vellum on the flesh side and/or bevelling it on the edges. 削薄是书籍装订的一个步骤，即修剪书本内侧和/或边缘上的皮革、羊皮纸或牛皮纸使之变薄的过程。
paring knife 削薄刀	A paring knife is a tool that is used to pare down leather, parchment, vellum and paper. It has a flat underside and a bevelled cutting edge. 削薄刀是裁切皮革、羊皮纸、牛皮纸和纸张的工具，具有平直刀口和倾斜切刃。
paring machine 裁切机	A paring machine is a hand driven- or powered machine used for paring down thin materials such as leather, parchment and vellum. 裁切机是一种用于裁切皮革，羊皮纸和牛皮纸等材料的手动或电动机器。
pasteboard 硬纸板	A pasteboard is a board made by bonding several layers of paper together in order to achieve the required thickness and strength. 硬纸板是将几层纸粘合在一起，以获得所需的厚度和强度的纸板。
pastedown 衬页	A pastedown is the outer-most leaf of a folded section of plain or decorated paper, which is added to either end of a book block. The leaf is pasted to the inside of the back or front cover of the book. The other leaf of the section acts as fly-leaf. 书前后的空白纸一般为印刷页或装饰纸最外面的一页，是书芯任意一端的最后一页，同书的封底或封面内侧相连。书帖中的空白页被称作衬页。
permanent paper 耐久纸	Permanent paper is paper that is made according to the International Standard ISO 9706:1994 (Information and documentation--Paper for documents--Requirements for permanence). This type of paper has a buffer of calcium carbonate and is made of specific fibre types. The paper is identified by the infinity symbol in a circle. 耐久纸是根据国际标准ISO 9706：1994（信息和文档-文件使用纸张-耐久性要求）制造而成的纸，这种纸以碳酸钙作为缓冲液，由特定纤维制成。这种纸的标识是圆圈及其中的无穷大符号。

plough 切书边刀	A plow is a tool used for trimming down book blocks and boards. It is used on a lying press where it is guided by a ruler or groove. The knife cuts a few pages at a time on the back and forth movement of the plow over the lying press. 切书边刀是用来修剪书芯和纸板的工具。它用在由尺子或凹槽引导的压书机上。这种刀前后移动一次能在压书机上裁切数页纸。
pressmark 书架号码	See watermark. 见水印。
pulp 纸浆	Pulp is the cellulosic fibre mass from which paper is made. 纸浆是用来造纸的纤维素纤维。
quire 帖	See gathering (2). 见书帖组。
rag paper 布料纸	Rag paper is paper made from cotton linters, linen fibres, cotton-, linen-and/or hemp rags. 布料纸是由棉短绒、亚麻纤维、棉布、亚麻布和/或大麻布制成的纸。
raised cord 竹节	A raised cord is a string onto which the sections of a book are sewed. In a covered book, raised cords show as bands on the back of the book. 竹节是一种能把书帖部分缝在其上的绳子。在有封皮的书中，竹节以节状凸起连接的形式出现在书脊。
RC paper 树脂印相纸	See resin coated paper. 见树脂印相纸。
rebacking 重起脊	In book conservation, rebacking is a method of replacing the spine covering of a book without taking the book apart or recovering the boards. When parts of the old spine covering are still present they are usually placed in their original position on the 在书籍修复中，重起脊是在不拆散书本或影响纸板的情况下，替换书脊的方法。当旧书脊的书皮仍有部分存留时，一般还将它们保存在原来的位置上。
refiner 打浆机	A refiner is a beater in which paper pulp is processed. It consists of a closed housing containing a cone or discs set with knives which cut and bruise the cellulose fibre. In this way a fibre suspension can be pumped as slurry, thus enabling a continuous production process adapted to modern paper machines. 打浆机是一种纸张加工机器，封闭外壳内包含一个配备各类刀刃的圆锥或圆盘，用于切断纤维素纤维，形成悬浮液。通过泵送获得连续的纸浆，从而适应现代造纸机的连续生产过程。
regenerated cellulose 再生纤维素	Regenerated cellulose is the material from which the semi-synthetic fibres are made: rayon, viscose. The raw cellulose material is obtained from wood or cotton linters. 再生纤维素是制造半合成纤维的材料，如人造丝，粘胶纤维。纤维素原料可从木材或棉短绒中获得。

relaxation 醒纸	In paper conservation, relaxation is the process of easing stresses and deformations in a sheet of paper, board or other porous hygroscopic material by applying a small amount of moisture to it. This renders the material more supple and more able to adjus to physical conditions. See also flattening. 在纸张修复中，醒纸是指对纸张、纸板或其他多孔吸湿材料喷洒少量水，以缓解纸张张力和变形的方法，这样能使纸张更为柔顺，易于调整。另见压平。
resizing 重新上浆	In paper conservation, resizing is a treatment where a sizing material is applied to a piece of paper that has lost part or all of its original sizing. 在纸张保护中，重新上浆是一种将施胶材料应用于部分或全部失去原有施胶量的纸张上的处理方法。
rosin size 松香胶	See alum size. 见明矾浆料。
SCMC 羧甲基纤维素钠	See sodium carboxymethylcellulose. 见羧甲基纤维素钠。
section 书帖	A section of a book is made from a single written or printed sheet of paper. It can be folded up to four times, resulting in 4 to 32 pages. Sections are gathered to make a book or binding. See also gathering (2). 书帖是由一张写好的或印好的纸折叠而成，最多可以折叠四次，总共可以折叠成4到32页。收集起来的书帖可制成或装订成书。另见书帖组（2）。
sizing 施胶	Sizing is a treatment of a textile or paper which involves applying a size and allowing it to dry in order to make the material stiffer and its surface smoother or less porous. 施胶是对纺织品或纸张的一种处理方法，涂上胶水（浆料），待干燥后，材料会变得直挺，表面更为光滑，渗透性更低。
sodium carboxymeth-ylcellulose 羧甲基纤维素钠	Sodium carboxymethylcellulose (SCMC) is a cellulose ether consisting of the sodium salt of carboxymethylcellulose. It is a poly-electrolyte polymer. The white powder is water soluble, physiologically inert, and in solution susceptible to biodegradation. 羧甲基纤维素钠（SCMC）是由羧甲基纤维素钠盐组成的一种纤维素醚。它是一种聚合电解质聚合物。白色粉末溶于水，生理惰性，在溶液中容易生物降解。
spine 书脊	a. A spine is the covering of the back of the book. It often bears the title of the book and other marks. See also back (2) b. A spine is the back of the sown book block before covering. a.书脊是书的背部，通常有书名和其他标记。另见书背(2)。b.装上书皮之前，书芯的背部。
tail 书脚	a. A tail is the bottom edge of a book. b. A tail is the bottom margin of a page. a.书脚是书本的底部边缘。b.书脚指一页纸的页底空白。
tail-edge 书脚	See tail (1). 见书脚。

text block 文本块	A text block consists of the printed or written sections of a book excluding any additions made by the binder such as endpapers, fly-leaves and boards. 文本块是书中印刷或书写的部分，不包括装订过程中添加的扉页、衬页和纸板等。
thermo-mechanical pulp 热磨机械浆	Thermo-mechanical pulp is made by softening the structure of wood chips by heating them, followed by feeding the chips into refiners where the fibres are separated. The lignin is softened in this process and disperses in and around the cellulose fibres which it is though to protect against oxidation. Paper made from thermo-mechanical pulp is relatively inexpensive. 热磨机械浆是通过加热来软化木屑，之后将其送入精炼机进行纤维分离而得的纸浆。木质素在此过程中被软化并分散在纤维素纤维周围，可以起到一定的抗氧化作用。这种纸的价格相对低廉。
thong 书带	A thong is a narrow strip of vellum, alum-tawed skin or leather to which sections of a book are sewn. Thongs are then laced through the boards before covering or directly through vellum in limp bindings. 书带是用牛皮、矾鞣革或皮革制成的窄条，书的书帖部分都缝在上面。在装订制作封皮前，会将这条书带穿过纸板固定，或直接穿过软皮装帧的牛皮封面。
tide line 水迹	A tide line in paper is a highly pronounced discoloration caused by water. The water dissolves coloured deterioration products of the paper which, upon drying, migrate and concentrate onto the part of the stain where the water evaporates last. A tide line is often the edges of a damp stain. 水迹是由水分迁移而在纸张表面留下的明显变色现象。水溶解了纸张中的有色变质产物，干燥后，它们会迁移并集中到水最后蒸发的边缘处，形成水迹。
tide mark 潮痕	See tide line. 见潮痕。
tipping-in 粘插页	Tipping-in is the gluing of two pieces of paper together as if they were one folded sheet of paper. A narrow strip of adhesive is applied to the edge of one of the pieces, followed by pressing. Tipping-in is done to add an extra page to a section of a book. 粘插页是指将两张纸粘成一张折叠纸的过程。其中，人们需要在其中一张纸的边缘涂上粘合剂或粘上窄胶带，之后压制。同时，粘插页也是指将额外的页面添加到一本书的某个部分。
tooling 烫印	Tooling is the process of decorating and lettering a leather or cloth binding by using heated instruments such as rolls and fillets to impress patterns in the binding followed by applying gold leaf (gold tooling), metal foil or ink into the patterns. 烫印是使用加热的工具（如直角和圆角）在皮革或布料上烫压图案的过程，之后还可向图案上加金箔（烫金）、金属箔片或印墨，起到装饰效果。
true watermark 有效水印	See watermark. 见水印。

unbleached pulp 原色纸浆	Unbleached pulp is pulp that is not bleached. Unbleached pulps are used to make strong papers because the fibres are not deteriorated by bleaching. Due to their dark colour, they are not used to make fine papers . 原色纸浆是未经漂白的纸浆，因其纤维未经漂白变质，所制纸张具有较高强度。同时由于未经漂白，颜色较深，一般不用其制作高级纸张。
vellum 牛皮纸	Vellum is the limed, de-haired and pumiced skin of a calf or unborn calf that is stretched upon drying. It is considered to be the finest and most durable type of parchment. See also parchment. 牛皮纸是用小牛的皮或未出生小牛的皮，经干燥、拉伸、石灰处理、脱毛和打磨后的纸张，质量优异，经久耐用。另见羊皮纸。
vellum binding 犊皮装帧	Vellum binding is a style of binding where the cover is made of vellum or covered with vellum. 犊皮装帧是一种书籍的装帧方式，书的封面由犊皮制成或被犊皮覆盖。
verdigris corrosion 铜锈	See copper green corrosion. 见铜绿色的腐蚀。
waste paper 废纸	Waste paper is paper or board, used or recycled from production or processing, and intended for re-introduction into a manufacturing process as pulp. 废纸是从生产或加工过程中使用或回收的纸和纸板，可化作纸浆重新投入造纸流程。
waste sheet 保护纸	A waste sheet is a sheet of paper temporarily tipped in onto the outside of a completed book block in order to protect it during further binding. 保护纸是为保护书籍在装订过程中不受损、暂附于书芯外部的纸张。
water line 水线	See laid line. 见裁线。
watermark 水印	A watermark in paper is a distinguishing mark, visible in transmitted light, where the paper is thinner due to, either a sewn on thread laid out in a pattern on the sieve, or a mark pressed into the paper while it is still on the sieve of a paper machine. 水印是在透射光下可见的独特标记。因为纸张较薄，水印可能是筛网上用线缝出的图案留下的印记，或者是造纸机在过筛网时压在纸上的标记。
wire line 裁线	See laid line. 见裁线。
wire side 网面	The wire side of a piece of paper is the side that was in contact with the sieve while the paper was being made. It is the roughest side of the paper since it takes more or less the relief of the sieve. 网面是指纸在造纸过程中与筛网接触的一面。由于或多或少留有筛网的痕迹，因此网面是纸张最粗糙的一面。

wood free paper 无木纸	Wood free paper is paper which is made from chemical pulp. Because wood substances are lost in the process of making it, chemical pulp paper is relatively expensive. 无木纸是由化学纸浆制成的纸。用化学方法从木头中提取纸浆，需要去除木质成分，因此化学纸浆制成的纸价格相对昂贵。
wood free pulp 无木质纸浆	See chemical pulp. 见化学纸浆。
wove paper 布纹纸	Wove paper is paper made on a fine sieve leaving no distinguishing visible marks in the paper. 布纹纸是细筛网制成的纸，没有明显的纹路痕迹。

05

织 物
Textile

acid dye 酸性染料	An acid dye is a dye that, under slightly acid conditions, ionises and bonds to the amino groups of protein, nylon and acrylic fibres by salt linkages. The colouring materials are mostly sodium salts of organic acids. 酸性染料是一种在微酸性条件下能够离子化并与蛋白质、尼龙和丙烯酸纤维的氨基通过盐键进行结合的染料，其着色物质主要是有机酸钠盐。
adhered backing 粘合背衬	When you back a textile with an adhered backing, you use an adhesive to attach a backing of fabric or other material to the reverse of the textile. 从背后加固织物时，用粘合剂把织物或其他材料的背衬粘到织物的背面，即粘合背衬。
aniline dye 苯胺染料	An aniline dye is a basic dye made from aniline, which is derived from coal tar. The first aniline dye, mauveine (mauve colour), was made by William Perkins in 1856. 苯胺染料是从煤焦油中提取的苯胺制成的碱性染料。首个苯胺染料苯胺紫（淡紫色）是威廉·珀金斯于1856年制造的。
anthraquinone-type dyes 蒽醌类染料	An important class of dyes whose structure is based on anthraquinone. The resonance structure from the aromatic rings and the carbonyl groups provide the chromophore. The roots of dyer's madder which contain an impressive number of anthraquinone derivatives is the main source of red . 蒽醌类染料是以蒽醌结构为主的一类重要染料。来自芳香环和羰基的共振结构提供了发色团。茜草根含有大量蒽醌衍生物，是染红色的主要来源。
applied relief 仿妆花	See applied brocade. 见仿妆花。
asbestos fibre 石棉纤维	Asbestos fibres are natural mineral fibres composed of silicates. Asbestos has been made into textiles since ancient times. 石棉纤维是由硅酸盐组成的天然矿物纤维。石棉自古以来就被制成纺织品。
azo dyes 偶氮染料	An azo dye is a dye comprising diazonium salts. There are two groups of azo dyes based on application methods: one group can be applied as direct, acid, basic, mordant or reactive dyes. The other group is of an azo compound which requires an agent to bind it to the fibres. 偶氮染料是包含重氮盐的染料。基于应用方法可分为两类：一类是可以直接应用的染料，包括酸性、碱性染料，媒染剂和活性染料；另一类是偶氮化合物，需要与一种试剂将它与材料结合。
clothing 服装	Clothing are textiles and related items made to cover the human body. 服装指用来遮蔽身体的纺织品和相关物品。
back stitch 回针	An overlapping stitch made by starting next stitch at middle of preceding one. 回针是指缝完一针后，将针线返回，至前一针的中间再开始下一针的刺绣针法。

basic dye 碱性染料	A basic dye is a dye that, under slightly alkaline conditions, ionises and forms salt linkages with the carboxyl groups of protein and some synthetic fibres. The colourants can be chloride or oxalate salts. 碱性染料是一种在弱碱性条件下可以离子化并与蛋白质和一些合成纤维的羧基形成盐键的染料。着色剂可以是氯化物或草酸盐。
batik 蜡染	Batik is a resist dyeing technique applied to woven textiles using wax. The wax (the resist) is melted and then painted on the textile or printed on the textile with a copper block. It has been used since ancient times. See also resist printing. 蜡染是一种用蜡进行防染的技术，这里的蜡（防染剂）在熔化后描绘在纺织品上或用铜模印在纺织品上。这种技术由来已久。另见防染印花。
block out 平整	When you block out a textile, you apply weights to or pin it onto a supporting material of the same form as the textile. This is carried out to inhibit shrinkage, to correct distortion, and in general, to ensure that a wet or humidified textile dries in the desired form. See also pin out. 平整一件纺织品是给织物施加重量，或者把它固定在一个与其形状相同的支撑材料上。这样做是为了防止织物收缩，使织物经平纬直，防止变形，一般来说，保证湿或潮湿的纺织物以较好的状态晾干。另见平整。
block printing 模版印花	Block printing is a decorative technique using a wooden block in which a design is carved to apply a coloured design to a textile. When block printing a textile, you apply textile printing ink to the block which is then stamped onto the textile by hand a machine. For each colourant used in the design, a separate block is required. 模版印花是在木块上刻出图案、并将彩色图案印在纺织品上的一种装饰技术。模印时，可将将纺织品油墨涂在印版上，然后用手或机器按模版把图案印在纺织品上。不同颜色用不同模块染色。
braid 斜编组织	Two sets of silk yarns are braided lengthways. 以两组相互垂直的丝线沿与织物倾斜的角度进行编织。
brocade weave 妆花组织	Brocade weave is a weaving technique which involves the addition of one or more supplementary weft threads to a ground weave in order to create a decorative effect. The additional weft is restricted to the edges of the brocade woven pattern. 妆花是一种织造技术，在地部增加一根或多根纹纬形成地络组织而显花，但这些增加的纹纬仅限于在图案的边界内通经断纬织造。
buttonhole stitch 锁边针	The buttonhole stitch is used in embroidery and along the edges of blankets and buttonholes to prevent fraying. A buttonhole stitch begins at the edge of a fabric; the needle is then inserted close by and a distance above the edge as if to make a diagonal stitch. Instead, the needle is then passed under and above the inside of the diagonal and the thread is pulled down to form a mirror image of and L-shape. In textile conservation, it is used to secure raw or frayed edges on textiles. 锁边针迹沿着毛毯和扣眼的边缘，用于防止毛边。锁边针一般从织物边缘开始，然后把针插入离边很近和离边缘上方有一段距离的地方，就好像形成了一条对角线。而不是将针从对角线的内侧下方和上方穿过，然后将线拉下来，形成L形的镜像。相反，针从对角线的内侧下方和上方穿过，线被拉下，形成L形的镜像。在纺织品保护中，它被用来固定纺织品上的生边或磨损的边缘。

byssus silk *足丝纤维 / 海丝纤维*	Byssus silk is a collagen protein fibre which is obtained from a Mediterranean sea mollusc, Pinna nobilis. 从地中海软体动物耳廓扇贝中提取的一种胶原蛋白纤维。（中国文献中曾称"海羊毛"）
canvas work *帆布绣*	Canvas work is embroidery carried out on canvas. In this kind of embroidery, the canvas is completely covered by stitches. Canvas work is mostly used to decorate interior furnishings such as seat covers, cushions, or fire screens. 帆布绣是在帆布上完成的刺绣。在这种刺绣中，帆布上都被绣线覆盖。帆布绣主要用于装饰室内陈设，如椅套、靠垫或防火屏风。
chain stitch *锁针*	In bookbinding, a chain stitch is the linking stitch made at the head and tail of each section, forming a chain-like pattern. 锁针是一种在布料边缘由左往右穿绕，形成链式线迹的手缝刺绣针法。
chinese knot stitch *打籽绣*	Looping the embroidery thread around the needle while making a stitch is called knot stitch. 打籽绣是在刺绣过程中将线打结以形成特殊效果的针法。
chintz *印花棉布*	A chintz was originally a dyed textile which was imported to England from India in the 17th and 18th centuries. Since then, the term has been used to refer to all printed textiles that are coated with, for example, wax or resin and finished to have a sheen. 印花棉布最初是一种染色纺织品，在17和18世纪从印度进口到英国。此后这一术语一直被用来指表面涂有蜡或树脂、并经整理具有光泽的印花织物。
clamp-resist dyeing *夹缬*	Clamp-resist dyeing uses two symmetrically carved blocks to clamp the folded textile.When dyed, the symmetrical and repeated pattern of the block is obtained. 夹缬是用两块对称的雕版夹紧折叠的织物进行防染染色，染后夹板上的对称并连续的图案就会呈现。
coal-tar dye *煤焦油染料*	See synthetic dye. 见合成染料。
costume accessories *服装配件*	Costume accessories are items of clothing which are additional to the main items of clothing used to cover the body. They may be practical and decorative or only decorative. Some of the most common accessories are shoes, bags, belts, scarves, gloves and hats. 服装配件指除了用来遮盖身体的主要服装之外的服饰物品。其可能即实用又具装饰性，或只具装饰性。最常见的配件有鞋子、包、皮带、围巾、手套和帽子。
cotton *棉*	Cotton is a type of herbaceous plant whose fibers can be used to make yarns, fabrics, clothing. 棉是一种草本植物，其纤维可以用来制作纱线、面料及服装。

couching stitch 铺针	The couching stitch is a long stitch which is secured by applying small stitches at intervals across its length. It is an embroidery stitch which is used in textile conservation to attach weak and frayed areas of a textile onto a backing. 铺针是用短直针将较长的丝线固定住的针法。在纺织品文物修复中经常使用，用于固定文物及背衬织物。
damask weave 正反缎组织	Damask weave is a weaving technique in which a pattern is formed by the contrast between the front and the back of a satin weave. In this technique, the glossy warp-faced pattern on the front of the textile is exactly mirrored on the matt, weft-faced back. 正反缎组织是指在织物表面上以正反缎纹互为花地组织的单层提花织物，在这种技术中，位于正面光亮的经面缎纹花部和其背面较暗的纬面缎纹，刚好互为花地。
darning 织补	Darning is a technique used to repair damaged textiles. It involves the application of stitches across the affected area from two directions at right angles to each other, which correspond to the structure of the textile. In the case of a woven textile, the stitches follow the warp and weft. Where the two directions of stitches cross, they are woven together. 织补是一种修复受损纺织品的技术。织补从两个方向以直角穿过受影响区域进行缝线，与织物的结构相对应。在织造纺织品时，针脚是沿着经线和纬线走的。两个方向的针线交叉的地方，就会被织在一起。
diamond twill weave 菱形斜纹组织	Diamond twill weave is a variation on twill weave that is developed in diamond-shaped diagonals. Used rarely, canvas made using this weave can be found especially as a support in paintings, painted during the 17th century in Tuscany. 菱形斜纹组织也是斜纹组织的一种变化，发展成菱形的斜纹效果。这种组织的帆布在17世纪托斯卡纳的绘画作品中被用作支撑，虽然使用很少。
direct dyes 直接染料	Direct dyes are dyes which colour cellulose fibres, including viscose and rayon, by forming hydrogen secondary bonds with the hydroxyl side groups of these fibres. Many types will also dye protein fibres. Most direct dyes contain sulphonated azo compounds which are very similar to acid dyes. Direct dyes came into general use after 1884. 直接染料是通过与纤维素纤维的羟基侧基形成氢副键而使纤维素纤维（包括粘胶纤维和人造纤维）染色的染料。许多类型的直接染料也可以给蛋白质纤维染色。大多数直接染料含有磺化偶氮化合物，与酸性染料非常相似。直接染料在1884年后开始普遍使用。
discharge print 拔染印花	When you discharge print a textile, you first dye the textile and then print with a substance which removes the dye. See also printed textile. 拔染印花先给织物染色，然后用能除去染料的物质进行印花。另见印花纺织品。

disperse dye 分散染料	A disperse dye is a compound dispersed in water which dyes acetate, polyester, nylon and acrylic fibres. The colouring materials are azo compounds or anthraquinone derivatives. 分散染料是一种分散在水中的化合物，能对醋酸纤维、聚酯纤维、尼龙纤维和丙烯酸纤维进行染色。着色物质是偶氮化合物或蒽醌衍生物。
drugget 保护毯	A drugget is a protective sheet placed over a carpet in order to protect it from wear. Druggets are usually of good quality textiles. 保护毯是铺在地毯上以防地毯磨损的保护布。保护毯通常是质量很好的纺织品。
dry cleaning 干洗	Dry cleaning is a treatment for removing undesirable material from an object without using a liquid. 干洗是一种借助有机溶剂或者表面清洁，而不使用水来去除污染物的清洗方法。
dye (1) 染料 (1)	A dye is an organic molecule which can be fixed to fibres in order to colour textiles and other organic materials. A dye contains chromophore and auxochrome radicals. Modern synthetic dyes are preferred over natural dyes due to their superior light and wash fastness properties, consistent quality and convenience of use. 染料是一种有机分子，可以固定在纤维上，使纺织品和其他有机材料着色。染料含有发色团和助色团自由基。现代合成染料因其优越的耐光性和耐洗性、稳定的质量和使用的便利性，比天然染料更受青睐。
embroidery 刺绣	Embroidery is the technique of decorating a textile with a pattern of stitches. 刺绣是用针线绣出图案装饰纺织品的技术。
fabric (1) 织物	A fabric is cloth or other woven material used as a conservation material. 织物指用于保护修复的面料或梭织物。
felt 毡	A felt textile is a textile that is made from a dense mat of non-woven fibres. It is made by applying mechanical action, heat and chemicals to combed fibres in order to bind them together. The most commonly used fibre is wool. 毡是由致密的未经织造的纤维制成的纺织品。毡是通过对精梳纤维施加机械作用、加热和添加化学物质，使它们结合在一起而制成的。最常用的制毡纤维是羊毛。
fiber 纤维	A fibre is single unit of matter which is usually 100 times longer than it is thick. The average length of a fibre depends on the type, with most organic textile fibres varying in length from 15 to 150 millimetres. Most synthetic fibres can be made as long as desired. 纤维是一个单位的物质，通常它的长度是粗细的100倍以上。纤维的平均长度视乎种类而定，大部分有机纺织纤维的长度由15毫米至150毫米不等。大多数合成纤维可以根据需要制作长度。

filament 长丝	A filament is a very long or continuous fibre or bundle of fibres, whose length can range from meters (for example, silk) to kilometers (for example, synthetic fibres). In textile conservation, it is used as an almost invisible stitching thread. 长丝是指非常长或连续的纤维或纤维束，其长度从米（如蚕丝）到公里（如合成纤维）不等。在纺织品保护中，长丝被用作几乎隐形的缝合线。
flag 旗	A flag is a piece of textile attached along one edge to a staff or rope. Flags are designed to wave or hang in the air and are used as signals or distinctive symbols of a country. 旗是一边系在棍子或绳子上的织物。旗帜多用于在空中挥舞或悬挂，用作一个国家的象征或一种独特的标志。
flavonoid-type dyes 黄酮类染料	Flavonoids, which are produced by nearly all green plants, make up the largest group of yellow dyes. The most commonly used flavonoid-type dyes contain luteolin, quercetin and their glycosides. 黄酮几乎存在于所有绿色织物，构成了最大一类的黄色天然染料。最常用的黄酮类染料含有木犀草素，槲皮素以及它们的糖苷。
flax 亚麻	Flax is a plant (Linum usitatissimum) from which linen is made. 亚麻是用来制作亚麻织物的植物。
fray 毛边	When a woven textile frays, it unravels at the edges. 织物磨损时，边缘会散开，形成毛边。
fraying 产生毛边	Fraying is mechanical damage which occurs to a woven textile only when the woven structure has been cut, torn or abraded. 毛边是纺织品被裁剪、拉扯或磨损时才会发生的机械损伤。
fringe 流苏	A fringe is a decorative edge of a textile or an applied trimming, which is made of freely hanging threads. Fringes are found on oriental carpets and as trimmings for clothing, costume accessories and interior textiles. 织物的装饰性边缘，或是由自由悬挂的线头制成的装饰物。流苏常见于东方地毯，也可以用来装饰服装、服装配件和室内纺织品。
garment 服装	See clothing. 见服装。
gauze weave 绞纱组织	A gauze weave is a weaving technique with an open structure. This open structure is achieved by displacing warp threads so that some warp threads cross diagonally over the other warp threads between insertions of the weft. 绞纱组织因部分经线在与纬线交织过程中相互扭绞而形成透孔结构。
hem 缝边	A hem is a border formed by folding back a fabric and sewing down the edge. 缝边是将织物在布料折回并沿边缝合而成的边界。

hemp 大麻	Hemp is a plant producing bast fibre used to produce for example, rope and textiles. 大麻是一种含有韧皮纤维的植物，可用于制作绳索和纺织品。
herring bone weave 山形斜纹组织	Herring bone weave creates a zig-zag diagonal pattern as a variation of the twill weave. Canvas made with this weave was used as painting support especially in 15th and 16th century Venice. 山形斜纹组织是斜纹组织的变化，呈现锯齿形斜纹效果。用这种织法制成的帆布被用作绘画支撑物，尤其是在15世纪和16世纪的威尼斯。
herringbone stitch 鱼骨针	A herringbone stitch is an embroidery stitch which looks like a line of X s which overlap at the upper and lower points. It is made by applying a small horizontal stitch from right to left below and then taking the needle diagonally above to the right and to left. In textile conservation it is used to attach edges of conservation fabric or textile to a backing material. 鱼骨针是将绣线由左向右并上下回缝呈现交叉状的一种刺绣针法。它的制作方法是在下方从右到左施以小横针，然后在上方斜取针向右和向左。在纺织品修复中，用来固定纺织品文物与背衬材料。
humidification 回潮	The humidification of an object or its environment is a treatment that adds water vapour. In organic materials and some inorganic materials such as clays, the added water expands the structure and acts as a plasticiser. These effects may increase the flexibility of components in the structure. In some cases, the water re-activates the original binding medium which has lost coherence and adhesion. humidification is used as a pre-washing treatment for brittle textiles in order to reduce the shock of wetting. 藏品及其环境的回潮是通过增加水蒸汽的方式予以处理。水分子如同增塑剂，进入有机物和一些无机物质（如土壤）的内部，使物体柔韧性增加。在某些情况下，回潮可以使一些失去活性的粘合剂重新恢复作用。这种处理可以用于纺织品文物水洗前的预处理，从而缓解水洗对文物的冲击力。
ikat 绊	Ikat is a resist technique applied to the warp and/or weft threads of a textile before it is woven. Following a design, the threads are tightly bound with string or strips of fabric (the resist) so that dye cannot penetrate underneath. After dyeing, the bindings are removed; only exposed areas of the threads have been dyed. The design is revealed during the weaving process. 绊是一种对其经线或/和纬线事先进行扎染而进行织造的技术。根据预先设计好的纹样，在织布前将经丝或者纬丝分段扎紧后染色，以防止染料渗入。染色后，去掉捆绑物，只有线的外露部分被染色。在织造过程中，设计就会显现出来。
indigo 靛蓝	Indigo is a natural vat dye to produce a blue colour on textiles that is derived from plants from the genus Indigofera. Indigo has been in use since the ancient times. 靛蓝是一种天然还原染料，从靛蓝属植物中提取，可将纺织品染成蓝色。靛蓝使用历史悠久。

inorganic fibre 无机纤维	Inorganic fibres are obtained or made from minerals, metals or other inorganic materials, for example, asbestos, gold, silver and glass. 无机纤维由矿物、金属或其他无机材料制成，例如石棉、金、银和玻璃。
jute 黄麻	Jute is a fibre made from a plant of the Corchorus species which is used for making coarse fabrics. This is of poor quality, so is rarely used as a painting support. 黄麻是一种由黄麻属植物制成的纤维，用于制作粗糙的织物。质量较差，所以很少用作画布。
knot (1) 结	A knot is a loop that is has been pulled tight in the length of a thread or rope. 结就是在一根线或绳子上被拉紧的环。
lac 紫胶	lac is extracted from some species of Kerria, which are cultivated on various trees in South Asia. This insect dye has been used to dye textile fibers in red and purple since antiquity. 紫胶染料提取自南亚多种植物上养殖的紫胶虫。这种昆虫染料自古以来就被用以将纺织纤维染成红色和紫色。
lampas weave 特结锦	Lampas is a figured weave in which a pattern,composed of patterning wefts bound by an extra binding warp,is added to a foundation weave formed by a foundation warp and a foundation weft. The pattern wefts are bound by the extra binding warp forming a binding weave which could be either tabby or twill and is supplementary to the ground weave. 特结锦是一种提花组织，一般由地经和地纬织出地组织，由特结经固结显花纹纬，其地组织和接结组织可以是平纹、斜纹等各种规律，插入的纹纬可以是通梭也可以挖梭形式织入。
Lanaset® dyes 兰纳洒脱染料	Lanaset is a pre-metallized dye used to dye silk, wool and nylon conservation fabrics and threads. 兰纳洒脱染料（商标名）是一种金属络合物染料，用于为丝绸、羊毛、尼龙保护织物和线的染色。
laundering 洗熨	Laundering is the cleaning, starching and ironing of household textiles and clothing. 洗熨包括家用纺织品和衣物的清洗、上浆和熨烫。
lining (3) 加衬里	Lining is the process of applying a lining to a textile object. 加衬里就是为纺织品加上衬里的过程。
madder 茜草	Madder is a natural mordant dye to produce a red colour on textiles that is derived from plants from the order Rubiaceae. Madder has been in use since the ancient times. 茜草是一种天然的媒染剂染料，从茜草科植物中提取而来，可将纺织品染为红色。茜草使用历史悠久。
mannequin 模特 / 人体模型	A mannequin is a support for a garment made to fit and so reduce the chance of distortion. 人体模型用于支撑服装，以减少衣服变形的情况。

mercerisation 丝光	Mercerisation is a chemical treatment applied to cotton. Cotton fibres are treated with alkalis, causing permanent swelling and resulting in increased gloss, smoothness and strength of the fibres as well as improving their ability to absorb dyes. 丝光是一种应用于棉花的化学处理方法。棉纤维经碱液处理后，会产生永久性的膨胀，增加纤维的光泽、光滑度和强度，并提高其吸收染料的能力。
mercerised cotton 丝光棉	Mercerised cotton is cotton which has been treated by the mercerisation process. See also mercerisation. 经过丝光处理的棉花。另见丝光。
metal-complex dye 金属络合染料	See pre-metallized dye. 见金属络合染料。
mordant (1) 媒染剂 (1)	A mordant is a substance which reacts with a textile dye to form an insoluble colourant bound to the fibre. The mordant is usually a metal salt, of aluminium, iron, copper, titanium, boron, chromium or tin, which forms a lake pigment. Mordants are applied before, during or after dyeing. 媒染剂可与纺织染料反应生成不溶的着色剂，附着在纤维上。媒染剂通常是一种金属盐，由铝、铁、铜、钛、硼、铬或锡组成，形成色淀类颜料。媒染剂可以在染前、染中和染后进行使用。
mordant dye 媒染染料	A mordant dye is a dye of any type which is able to combine with a metallic oxide to bind the dye to the fibres. See also mordant (1). 媒染染料能与金属氧化物结合，从而使染料与纤维结合。另见媒染剂（1）。
natural dye 天然染料	Natural dyes are dyes which occur naturally. They can be derived from plants (for example, madder, indigo), some molluscs and insects (kermes, cochineal and lac). Natural dyes have been used since the ancient times. 天然染料是来自天然生成的染料，可来源于植物（例如茜草、靛蓝）、一些软体动物和昆虫（胭脂虫和紫胶虫）。天然染料自古以来就被使用。
natural fibers 天然纤维	Natural fibres are fibres obtained from naturally occurring organic and inorganic materials. 天然纤维是由天然的有机和无机物质制成的纤维。
netting 织网	Netting is the technique of making an open-worked textile in which the threads are joined at intervals by a knot or some kind of twining or weaving. A common example of this technique is the fishing net. 织网是一种在织物表面形成透孔的织造方式，线与线之间通过系结或者缠绕扭绞的方式编织在一起。最常见的例子就是渔网。
nylon mesh 尼龙筛	Nylon mesh is an open woven fabric made of heavy nylon mono-filament. In textile conservation, it is used during vacuum cleaning as a protective barrier between the vacuum cleaner and the textile. 尼龙筛是由粗尼龙单丝制成的透孔织物。在纺织品保护中，尼龙筛被用作真空吸尘器和纺织品之间的保护屏障。

nylon net 尼龙网	Nylon net is a lightweight, transparent, non-fraying, polyamide synthetic fabric. It is made with the machine-made bobbin lace technique. It is strong, elastic and easy to dye. In textile conservation, nylon net is used as a backing or overlay fabric. 尼龙网是一种轻质、透明、无磨损的聚酰胺合成纤维。尼龙网由机制梭结花边技术制成的。结实，有弹性，易于染色。在纺织品保护中，尼龙网被用作背衬或覆盖织物。
organic fibre 有机纤维	Organic fibres are fibres obtained from organisms. The fibre structure is based on organic polymers. Various plants, animals, insects and molluscs provide organic fibres. 有机纤维是从生物体中获得的纤维，其纤维结构基于有机聚合物。各种植物、动物、昆虫和软体动物都能产生有机纤维。
over-casting stitch 绕旁针	Stitch with equal distance and oblique stitch around the edge of the fabric. 绕旁针是指围绕布料边缘，等距离斜向绕缝的针法。
overlay 覆盖层	An overlay is a piece of transparent conservation fabric applied to the front of a textile. It is used to support weak and damaged areas. 覆盖层是透明的保护性织物，用于织物正面，以支撑残缺和糟朽的区域。
pad out 填充	When you pad out a three-dimensional textile object, you fill an empty volume in it with another material. This aims to prevent distortion of shape over time. It is applied to textiles which are subject to sagging or distorting under its own weight. 填充是在纺织品空缺处加入用另一种材料制作的立体填充物，以防止织物形状变化。适用于因自重较大而下垂或变形的纺织品。
patching 打补丁	Patching a textile is the supporting of a damaged or weak area by stitching or adhering a piece of fabric (a patch) onto it. 为织物打补丁是通过缝合或粘贴一块织物（补丁）来支撑受损或薄弱的区域。
pick 纬线	A pick is a single weft thread. 纬线是单根纬线。
pile weave 绒圈组织	A pile weave is a weaving technique in which supplementary threads extend beyond a ground fabric. Knotted carpets and velvets are examples of pile weaving. 绒圈组织其实是一种增加了高于底部绒线的织造技术。栽绒毯和天鹅绒都是绒圈组织的实例。
pin out 平整	See block out. 见平整。
pinna silk *足丝纤维 / 海丝纤维*	See byssus silk. 见足丝纤维。
plied yarn 合股线	See ply. 见合股。

ply 合股	When you ply yarns, you twist together two or more previously spun threads or yarns. The yarn which is created by twisting threads or yarns together is called a plied yarn. The direction of the plying twist is usually opposite to that of the individual threads or yarns. 把两根或两根以上已纺好的线或纱线再次捻合在一起，这种通过再加捻而合并在一起的纱线称为合股线。多根纱线合股加捻的方向往往与单根纱线的加捻方向相反。
plying twist 合股加捻	See ply. 见合股。
pre-metallized dye 金属络合染料	A pre-metallized dye is a synthetic mordant dye which contains a metal atom to bind the dye to the fibre. There are two types: 1:1 complexes applied in acidic dye solutions and 2:1 complexes which are applied in near neutral solutions. Pre-metallized dyes are used to dye wool, silk and nylon. 金属络合染料是一种合成媒染料，其中含有一个金属原子，用于将染料与纤维结合。金属络合染料有两种类型：用于酸性染料溶液的1:1混合物和用于近中性溶液的2:1混合物。金属络合染料被用于为羊毛，丝和尼龙染色。
printed textile 印花纺织品	A printed textile has had a design printed on it with textile printing ink applied with a printing tool. 印花纺织品是印有图案的纺织品，用织物印制专用油墨和印刷工具染成。
rail 横杆	A rail is a horizontal bar or rod used for hanging objects, for example, costumes or paintings. 横杆是用来悬挂服装或绘画等的横杆或横棒。
raw silk 生丝	Raw silk is silk filaments which have undergone the first stage of manufacture into threads or textiles. The silk filaments have been reeled off the cocoons of silk moths to form threads while their natural gum coating, known as sericin, has not yet been removed. 生丝是由蚕茧缫丝产生、可直接织用于制线或织绸的长丝。这样长丝从蚕茧中抽出，形成丝线，此时其天然包膜，即丝胶，尚未脱去。
reactive dye 活性染料	A reactive dye is a dye that forms covalent bonds with cellulose, protein and nylon fibres. The colouring materials are anthraquinones or phthalocyanines. Reactive dyes have been in use since 1953. 活性染料是一种与纤维素、蛋白质和尼龙纤维形成共价键的染料。染色材料为蒽醌类或酞菁类。活性染料自1953年开始使用。
resist print 防染印花	When you resist print a textile, you print the textile with a design using a resist substance (e.g. wax, clay, gum) which prevents dye binding to the fibres. After dyeing, the resist substance is washed out, revealing the undyed design. See also printed textile. 防染印花是先将防染剂（如蜡、粘土、胶等）印在设计好的图案上以防止在染色时染料上染纤维。染色后洗净防染剂，则露出原色图案。另见印花纺织品。

resist technique 防染技法	When you decorate an object using a resist technique, you apply a design to the material using a resist substance (for example, wax, clay, gum) which prevents colouring matter binding to the surface material. The resist substance is then washed off, revealing the uncoloured design. See also printed textile and resist printing. 防染技法是一种织物装饰技法，先在织物上印上防染剂（如蜡、粘土、胶等），以防止染料上染织物表面。再将防染剂洗净，便会露出原色部分图案。另见印花纺织品和防染印花。
rib weave 畦纹组织	A rib weave is a weaving technique which involves covering thick weft threads with thin warp ones, or vice versa. This technique produces textiles with strongly defined ridges on the surface. 畦纹组织与是一种织造技艺，用较细的经线与较粗的纬线交织，或相反。这种技术使织物形成强烈的畦纹。
roller printing 滚筒印花	Roller printing is a decorative technique involving rollers in which a design is engraved to apply a coloured design to a textile. The textile is passed between a pressure roller and a number of inked rollers, the number of which is decided by the number of colourants used in the design. 滚筒印花是一种纺织品印花技术，即在滚筒上雕刻图案，蘸取颜色后通过滚动的方式将图案印在纺织品上。纺织物在压辊和若干墨辊之间传递，墨辊的数量由设计中使用的着色剂数量决定。
running stitch 跑针	The running stitch is a variation of the traditional tacking stitch used to hold pieces of fabric temporarily together while the permanent construction stitching is done. In textile conservation, the running stitch is used to attach large areas of a backing to textiles and to achieve support over large areas. 跑针是传统针法的一种变化，用来将织物固定在一起，或是缝合破裂处。在纺织品保护中，这种针法因针迹较长，往往用来连接较大面积的文物与背衬织物。
sandwich 夹封	When you sandwich a textile, you apply both a backing and an overlay to it. This is used to provide support to very weak textiles. 夹封是在待保护的纺织品下方衬垫背衬织物，上方加封覆盖物，使其如同三明治一样被夹在两层现代织物中，这种方法可用来支撑非常脆弱的纺织品。
saponaria 肥皂草	Saponaria is a non-ionic detergent derived from the leaves of the plant Saponaria officinalis (common name: soapwort). It contains the active substance saponin which has the property of frothing with water. Saponaria was used to wash household textile goods and historical textiles before the advent of synthetic detergents. 肥皂草是一种非离子清洁剂，从植物皂角的叶子中提取。它含有活性物质皂苷，遇水起泡。在合成洗涤剂出现之前，皂草被用来洗涤家用纺织用品和历史悠久的纺织品。
saponin 皂苷	Saponins are steroid glycosides, that is molecules composed partly of steroids and partly of sugar moieties, derived from plants. They are used as surfactants and emulsifiers to aid washing, especially textiles. 皂苷是一种甾体苷，由部分甾体和部分糖组成的分子，来源于植物。皂苷被用作表面活性剂和乳化剂来帮助洗涤，尤其用于清洗纺织品。

satin weave 缎纹组织	Satin weave is a weaving technique in which each warp thread passes over at least four wefts before being bound by a weft thread. The result is a weave comprising long floating warp threads which produces a smooth, glossy effect. 缎纹组织是一种织造技术，每根经线在与一根纬线交织之前至少经过四根纬线，织物由长的浮线组成，因此产生平整、光滑的效果。
sea-silk 足丝纤维/海丝纤维	See byssus silk. 见足丝纤维。
selvages 幅边	Selvages are the two longitudinal edges of a piece of woven textile. 幅边是一件织物的两个纵向边缘。
silk 蚕丝	Silk is a protein fibre of fibroin produced by the larva of moths of various species. The most commonly used silk fibre is produced by the Bombyx mori moth under cultivated conditions. 蚕丝是由各种蛾类幼虫产生的丝素蛋白纤维。最常用的蚕丝纤维是由家蚕在培育条件下生产的。
silk crepeline 绉丝纱	Silk crepeline is a lightweight, transparent fabric woven in plain weave with fine silk filaments. In textile conservation, it is used as a backing and overlay fabric. 绉丝纱是一种平纹组织的丝织物，极为薄透。在纺织品保护修复中，绉丝纱可以被用作背衬织物或覆盖织物。
silk weighting 丝绸增重	Silk weighting is a finishing treatment that involves adding gums, sugar or mineral salts to the textile to replace the weight and stiffness lost by degumming the silk fibres. This treatment was sometimes also applied to rayon textiles. 丝绸增重是一种后整理处理，在织物上添加树胶、糖或无机盐，以补偿蚕丝纤维因脱胶而损失的重量和刚度。这种处理有时也适用于人造丝纺织品。
soak (2) 浸泡(2)	When you soak a textile, you immerse it in water or another solvent for a period of time. This results in saturation and swelling of the fibres, and can help in the dissolution and dispersion of the soiling. You soak a textile during wet or solvent cleaning to improve cleaning action. 浸泡是把纺织品浸在水或其他溶剂中一段时间。这会导致纤维饱和和膨胀，并有助于污垢的溶解和分散。
split (1) 裂缝	A split in a textile is a clean break of fibres along the warp or weft direction of a woven textile. 织物中的裂缝是指纤维沿着织物的经纬方向完全断裂。
stain removal 去污	Stain removal is the localised cleaning of stains on a textile using aqueous or solvent solutions. See also spotting. 去污是用水溶液或溶剂溶液对纺织品上的污渍进行局部清洁。另见预去污处理。

starching 上浆	Starching is a finishing and sizing treatment applied to cotton and linen textiles to stiffen them. It improves their appearance and handling properties and supports the structure of lace, ruffles and flounces. A starched textile is also more resistant to soiling and staining. The starch is dissolved in either boiling or cold water, depending on the recipe. The textile is dipped in the solution and allowed to dry. A starched textile can be ironed and polished to achieve a smooth and shiny finish. 上浆是对棉和亚麻织物进行的一种修整和上胶，以使它们变硬。上浆改善了织物的外观和操作性能，并支撑织物的蕾丝、褶边和荷叶边。经过上浆的纺织品也更耐脏、耐污。根据配方，将淀粉溶解在沸水或冷水中。将纺织品浸泡在溶液中并晾干。上浆纺织品可以通过熨烫和抛光来达到光滑和光泽的效果。
stencil 镂空版	A stencil is a sheet of paper, metal, plastic film or thin cardboard from which a pattern has been cut out. It is used for transferring the pattern to an underlying surface by applying paint through the cut out areas. See also stencilling. 镂空版可以用一张纸、金属、塑料薄膜或纸板刻出图案，通过在镂空区域刷印颜料来将图案转印到下层织物表面。另见镂空板印。
stencilling 镂空版印	Stencilling is a method of applying a design or lettering to an object. A stencil is laid on the object to be decorated. A colouring agent, such as paint, dye or graphic material, is applied through the cut out areas to the object beneath. Stencilling is widely used to apply repeated patterns in interior decoration. 镂空版印是将一个设计或字体应用于物体上的方法。在要装饰的物体上放置一个镂空版，将着色剂（如油漆、染料或图形材料）通过镂空区域涂在下面的物体上。镂空版印在室内装饰中广泛用于图案的重复印制。
stitched backing 背衬缝合	When you back a textile with a stitched backing, you use stitching to attach the backing to the reverse of the textile. 在织物背面加缝背衬材料，即用缝线将背衬材料与文物缝合在一起。
surface active agent 表面活性剂	See surfactant. 见表面活性剂。
surfactant 表面活性剂	A surfactant (term derived from surface active agent) is a substance which, when dissolved in a solvent, usually water, increases the wetting power of the solvent by reducing its surface tension. Surfactants increase the water's cleaning power by emulsify greasy soiling. 表面活性剂全称surface active agent，当溶解在溶剂（通常是水）中时，通过降低其表面张力来增加溶剂的润湿力。表面活性剂通过乳化提高水的清洁能力。
synthetic fibre 合成纤维	A synthetic fibre is an organic fibre that has been made by extruding and stretching a synthetic polymer. 合成纤维是通过挤压和拉伸合成的聚合物而制成的有机纤维。

tabby 平纹组织	See tabby weave. 见平纹组织。
tabby weave 平纹组织	Tabby weave is the most basic weaving technique. It is based on a weave unit of 2 warp and 2 weft threads. The odd and even warp threads alternate in position, so that when the odd warps pass over a weft, the even ends are under the same weft.When the even warps pass over a weft, the odd warps are under the same weft. This technique produces textiles with a regular, unpatterned surface. 平纹组织是最基本的组织结构。以2根经线和2根纬线组成一个基础的单位组织。奇数和偶数经线与纬线上下交织，这样当奇数经线经过纬线之上时，偶数经线则在同一根纬线之下。当偶数经线通过纬线时，奇数经线就在同一纬线下。这种技术可以产生表面均衡的素织物。
tapestry weave 缂毛组织	Tapestry weave is a weaving technique in which the weft threads cover the warp threads, producing a discontinuous weft-faced weave. The wefts do not pass from selvage to selvage, but are woven with the area of the warps that is required for a particular part of the design. 缂毛组织是一种织造技法，纬线并不是连续穿过经线直至幅边，而是"通经回纬"，到达原本设计的某个图案边缘后，该纬线折回，重新再换一根纬线用于显花。纬线不是从纱线到纱线的传递，而是以设计中某一特定部位所需的经线面积来织造。
tension frame 张力架	A tension frame is an adjustable mount to which a fabric or textile is attached. It is used to apply appropriate tension to the textile during drying, lining or backing. 张力架是一种可调节的支架，上面包裹有面料。它用于在干燥、裱褙或背面支撑过程中对织物施加适当的力。
Terylene® 涤纶	Terylene is a trade name for a fabric made from polyester 涤纶是一种聚酯织物的商标名。
tex 特克斯	Tex is the mass expressed in grams of the unit length of 1,000 metres of fibre, filament or yarn. 特克斯是指1000米纤维、长丝或纱线重量的克数。
textile 纺织品	A textile is an object manufactured by binding threads or yarns together. Some common binding techniques are interlacing (including weaving), knotting and knitting. In textile conservation, the term usually refers to a historical textile. See also fabric. 纺织品是用线或纱织造出的物品。一些常见的织布技艺有交织（包括梭织）、打结和针织。在纺织品保护中，这个词通常指纺织品文物。另见面料。
textile print 纺织品印花	See printed textile. 见印花纺织品。

textile printing ink 纺织印花油墨	Textile printing ink is a dispersion of pigments or dyes in a paste. It is used to print coloured patterns on a fabric and can be applied by brush or various printing techniques. In textile conservation, it is used to prepare backing fabrics when the reconstruction of a pattern or texture is desirable. 纺织印花油墨是指将颜料或染料与胶黏剂融合，用于在纺织品上印刷彩色图案，可以用刷子或各种印刷技术加以实施。在纺织品保护中，当背衬织物需要印制与文物相似的图案时，可用此方法获得。
texture magnification 结构放大	See weave emphasis. 见织纹强化。
thread 线	Thread is a fine, hard, continuous bundle of overlapping fibres brought together by spinning. The amount of twist applied to the fibres is medium to hard. It is used in textile conservation for stitching techniques and machine sewing. 线是一种细密、坚硬、连续的纤维束，通过加捻纺纱结合在一起，捻度由中等到强。在纺织品保护中，线可以用于手缝或机缝。
thread count 织物密度	A thread count is the number of threads found in one centimetre of a woven material. A separate count is given for the warp and weft threads. 织物密度是在长度为一厘米的纺织材料中发现的线数。经纱和纬纱单独计数。
tie dyeing 扎染	Tie dyeing is a resist technique which pinches a portion of fabric and ties it tightly with a waxed thread or rubber bands. When the fabric is dyed, various pattern is formed and revealed after the ties removed. 扎染是一种防染技术，先捏取一部分织物然后用蜡线或橡皮筋扎紧，再将织物染色并拆除打结，织物就会形成不同的图案。
triacetate 三醋酸纤维	Triacetate is a shortened name for cellulose triacetate. The degree of polymerisation of about 225 is greater than acetate. Triacetate has been made into fibres since 1950. 三醋酸纤维是 cellulose triacetate 的简称，其聚合度大约为 225，大于醋酸盐，三醋酸自 1950 年被制成纤维。
tussah silk 柞蚕丝	Tussah silk is a brown, wild silk fibre that is produced by the Antheraea mylitta moth in India. It is coarser and stiffer than cultivated silk. Tussah silk is the most commonly used wild silk fibre. 柞蚕丝是一种棕色的野生蚕丝纤维，由印度的天蚕蚕丝制成，比家蚕丝粗而硬。柞蚕丝是最常用的野生蚕丝纤维。
twill weave 斜纹组织	Twill weave is a basic weaving technique based on a weave unit of three or more warp threads and three or more weft threads. Each warp thread passes over two or more adjacent wefts and under the next one or more. The result is a satin-like surface with a faint diagonal pattern. Twill fabric was used as painting canvas in the 18th and 19th centuries. 斜纹组织也是一种基础组织，一个单位组织里包括三根或三根以上的经线和纬线，每一经线连续压在两根或两根以上的纬线之上，并在一根纬线之下，最后在光面上形成斜纹效果。斜纹织物在 18 世纪和 19 世纪被用作画布。

twist 加捻	Twist is the result of turning or spinning a thread around its axis. The direction of the twist is given by the letter "S" or "Z" : the diagonal direction of the spun thread corresponds to the diagonal bar of each letter. Threads without a twist are called twistless or untwisted. 加捻是将纱线通过绕轴转动或旋转形成有捻度的纱线的过程。可以根据加捻方向分为"S"捻或"Z"捻：线缠绕方向的对角线对应着字母的对角线。未加捻的线称为无捻线。
twistless 无捻	A yarn without twist is described as twistless or untwisted. The letter "I" is used to indicate the lack of twist. See also twist. 无捻是指纱线没有经过扭转处理。字母"I"用来表示未加捻。另见加捻。
unpick 拆除缝线	When you unpick a textile or part of a textile, you sever or remove stitches from it. This is done to remove previous repairs, linings and backings or to gain access to the inside of a multi-layered textile object. 拆除一件或者一部分纺织品时，需要将其线迹剪断并去除，以便于取出不需要的内衬，或将纺织品部分打开进行修复。
untwisted 无捻	See twistless. 见无捻。
upholstery 软装	Upholstery refers to all the textile and related components added to the basic frame of seating furniture. These components include webbing, springs, tacks, fillings, covers and trimmings. Upholstery is applied to furniture in order to increase sitting comfort. 软装是在椅座类家具的基本框架上，增加的所有纺织品和相关部件，包括织带、弹簧、大头钉、填充物、毯子和饰件。家具上使用软装会增加椅座的舒适度。
vat dye 还原染料	A vat dye is a non-water-soluble dye with few auxochromic groups in the molecule. During the dyeing process, the dye is made water soluble by alkaline reduction (leuco form) and can then diffuse into the fibres. The textile is removed from the dye bath to to expose it to the oxygen in the air which oxidises the leuco form back to the non-water-soluble form. Vat dyes include indigo, anthraquinones and phthalocyanines. 还原染料是一种不溶于水的染料，分子中含有少量的助色团。在染色过程中，染料通过碱还原（无色形式）溶于水，然后扩散到纤维中。将纺织品移出染浴，暴露在空气中无色形态的染料被氧化回不溶于水的形态。还原染料包括靛青、蒽醌和酞菁染料。
Velcro® 维可牢 / 魔术贴	See hook and loop fastener. 见钩环扣。（一种尼龙搭扣的商标名称，即魔术贴。）
velvet weave 起绒组织	Velvet weave is a pile weaving technique that is made by placing rods under warps during weaving. The rods form loops which may be left as loops or cut to form tufts. The tufted surface has a luxurious, fur like appearance. There are many varieties of velvet weave techniques. 起绒组织也是一种绒圈组织，通过绒经之下织入起绒杆得到高于地部的绒圈，绒圈可以保留或经割绒后成为绒毛。外观豪华，类似皮毛。起绒组织技术种类很多。

warp (1) 经 (1)	In a textile, the warp is the threads that form the direction of the weaving process and run parallel to the selvages. The warp threads pass alternatively over and under the weft threads. See also weft. 在纺织品中，经线是与织造过程方向相同并与布边平行的线。经线与纬线上下交替穿行。另见纬线。
water cleaning 水洗	Water is used as the cleaning solvent to remove the pollutants accumulated on the surface of the fabric and the interior of the fiber. 水洗是以水为清洗溶剂，去除累积在织物表面及纤维内部污染物地清洁方式。
weave 组织	Weave is the system of interlaced warp and weft threads in a woven textile. 组织是梭织物中经线和纬线进行交织的系统或规律。
weaving 织造	Weaving is the technique of making a textile by interlacing units of a warp and weft at right angles to each other in a specific order. 织造将经线和纬线按一定的顺序以直角交织而成织物的技术。
weft 纬线	The weft threads of a woven textile pass through the warp threads and run at right angles to the selvages. See also warp. 梭织物的纬线穿过经线，与布边成直角。另见经线。
wild silk 野蚕丝	Wild silk is silk obtained from the cocoons of silk moths living in a wild state or in semi-domesticity. 野蚕丝是生活在野外或者半家养环境中生活的蚕吐出的丝。
wool 羊毛	The wool fibre sheared from animals (such as sheep) and twisted into yarn for weaving. 羊毛是从动物身上（如绵羊）剪下的纤维，加捻成线用于纺织。
yarn 纱线	A yarn is a thick, soft, continuous bundle of overlapping fibres which have been brought together by spinning. Wool, silk, hair and acrylic fibres and mixtures of these fibres are commonly in yarn form. Yarns are used for knitting, weaving and embroidery. 纱线是通过纺纱而聚集在一起的一束连续且又厚又软的纤维。羊毛、丝绸、毛发和丙烯酸纤维以及这些纤维的混合物通常可以制成纱线。纱线可用于编织、织造和刺绣。

06

视听
Audio-visual

audio 音频	Audio is the recording and playback of a physical representation of sound. 音频是对声音物理表现的记录和回放。
accidental erasure 意外擦除	Accidental erasure refers to the complete or partial removal of magnetic information on audio and video tapes caused by unsuspected magnetic fields, especially in storage. See also stray magnetic fields. 意外擦除是指由于意外的磁场（尤其是在存储中）完全或部分去除音频和视频磁带上的磁性信息。另见杂散磁场。
acetate disc 醋酸纤维唱片	See instantaneous disc. 见瞬时盘。
acetate tape 醋酸胶带	Acetate tape is an early form of magnetic audio tape made of cellulose triacetate or diacaetate. It is usually brown in colour and unstable. It snaps easily, attracts mould growth, and distorts into a u-shaped section. It was popular with broadcasters and film companies. 醋酸胶带是一种由三醋酸纤维素或双乙酸纤维素制成的磁性音频带的早期形式，通常为棕色，不稳定。它容易折断，引发霉菌生长，并变形为U形截面。广播和电影公司经常使用。
Adaptive Transform Acoustic Coding 自适应变换声编码	Adaptive Transform Acoustic Coding is an audio data compression system used on Minidisc. It works by using psychoacoustic principles to mask unwanted sounds produced by the action of the compression system. 自适应变换声编码是迷你光碟上使用的音频数据压缩系统。它通过使用心理声学原理来掩盖压缩系统动作所产生的不需要的声音。
ageing of film 胶片的老化	Ageing of film is a breakdown of polymer chains in cellulose nitrate or cellulose acetate. It is accompanied by the release of plasticisers and nitrogen oxides or acetic acid and leads to brittleness, shrinkage deformation, or even complete deterioration.In airtight containers with acetate film, the released acetic acid can act as a catalyst leading to an autocatalytic reaction. See also vinegar syndrome. 胶片的老化是硝酸纤维素或醋酸纤维素中聚合物链的分解，它伴随着增塑剂和氮氧化物或乙酸的释放，导致胶片脆性，收缩变形，甚至完全变质。在有醋酸膜的密闭容器中，释放的醋酸可作为催化剂导致自催化反应。另见 醋酸综合症。
album 相册	An album is a bound volume with blank pages for the insertion of, for instance, photographs or paper ephemera. 相册是装订成册的空白页，用来插入照片或蜉蝣纸品。
albumen 蛋白	Albumen is the white of egg which contains water and a number of proteins. It was used as the binder in the image layer in albumen paper and albumen negatives. 蛋白是含有水和许多蛋白质的蛋清。它被用作相册纸和相册底片图像层的粘合剂。
albumen paper 蛋白相纸	Albumen paper is silver chloride printing-out paper, using albumen as the binder in the image layer. 蛋白相纸是氯化银印相纸，用蛋白作为图像层的粘合剂。

albumen print 蛋白印相法	An albumen print is a print on albumen paper. 蛋白印相法是在蛋白相纸上完成印相的方法。
ambrotype 玻璃干版照相 / 安布罗摄影法	An ambrotype is a collodion positive on glass, which is backed with dark paper, cloth velvet or paint. Ambrotypes are usually framed or cased. 制作玻璃干版照片是将火胶棉正片置于玻璃上，然后在其背面涂黑，或装裱时置于黑纸或天鹅绒上。玻璃干版照相通常需要装裱。
ampex quadruplex 安培四工磁带	Ampex quadruplex is an early video recording tape format using 2 inch wide magnetic tape held on 12 inch diameter spools. 安培四工磁带是一种早期的视频录制磁带格式，使用2英寸宽的磁带缠绕在12英寸直径的卷轴上。
analogue recording 模拟记录	An analogue recording of sound or vision is a physical representation whose amplitude is in direct proportion to the intensity (such as the audio frequency of sound) as captured on gramophone records or on magnetic tapes. 声音或视觉的模拟记录是一种物理表现形式，其振幅与在留声机记录或磁带上捕获的强度（例如声音的音频频率）成正比。
anamorphic 变形宽银幕	An anamorphic cinematographic image is an image which is laterally compressed by an anamorphic lens. 变形宽银幕图像是由变形宽银幕镜头横向压缩形成的图像。
anamorphic lens 变形镜头	An anamorphic lens is an optical system with different lateral and horizontal magnifications. 变形镜头是具有不同的侧向和横向放大倍数的光学体系。
antihalation coating 防光晕涂层	An antihalation coating is a dark layer which is placed under a silver halide negative emulsion or on the verso of a film. It is used to prevent exposure to light reflection off the film or glass support. Antihalation coatings usually discolour during processing. 防光晕涂层是置于卤化银负乳剂下或胶片表面的一层暗色涂层。用来防止光线从胶片或玻璃支撑物上反射出来。防光晕涂层在这一过程中通常会变色。
archive (3) 存档 (3)	An audio or video archive is a collection of historic recordings intended to survive into perpetuity. 音频或视频存档是旨在永久保存的历史记录的集合。
archive (4) 归档 (4)	In the broadcast and record industry, an archive is a collection of recorded audio and/or video material regarded as a commercially exploitable resource without necessarily having regard to long-term retention for historical purposes. 在广播和录制行业中，归档是被视为商业可开发资源的录制音频和/或视频材料的集合，不必考虑出于历史目的而长期保留。
aristotype paper 珂罗酊氯化银印相纸	Aristotype paper is a silver gelatine printing-out paper. 珂罗酊氯化银印相纸是一种银胶状印相纸。

artefact (2) 伪影 (2)	An artefact is a unwanted warbling background sound heard on replaying a digital audio recording that has been manipulated in a computer. It is caused by the excessive removal of information from the digital signal in an attempt to remove unwanted hiss, and noise from a recording. 伪影是回放计算机中已处理过的数字音频录音时，听到的不需要且令人不快的背景声音。它是由于过度去除数字信号中的信息而造成的，如试图去除的嘶嘶声，以及录音中的噪音。
asphaltum 沥青	Asphaltum is a bituminous resin. In J. N. Niepce's heliochrome process, asphaltum was used as a light-sensitive substance. It was also used as a dark varnish component in ambrotypes and tintypes and as etching resist in the photogravure process. 沥青是指沥青树脂。在 J. N. Niepce 的天然色照片处理中，以沥青铬作为感光物质。它也被用作暗版和彩色版的深色清漆成分，并且在照相凹版印相过程中用作抗蚀剂。
ATRAC 自适应变换声编码	See Adaptive Transform Acoustic Coding. 见自适应转换声学编码。
audio noise 音频噪声	See noise (1). 见噪声。
audio tape 录音磁带	See tape. 见带。
autochrome plate 彩色底片板	An autochrome plate is a direct positive colour screen plate (transparency) which were invented and marketed by the French Lumiere brothers. 彩色底片板是直接正色屏幕板（透明度），由法国卢米埃尔兄弟发明和推广的。
azimuth 方位	The azimuth setting is the correct vertical alignment of the playback or recording head gap on an analogue tape machine. It is particularly important when copying analogue recordings to match the azimuth playback setting on the replay machine to the azimuth recording setting on the tape to ensure fidelity. 方位设置是模拟磁带机上播放或记录磁头间隙的正确垂直对齐。复制模拟录音时，将重放机上的方位角重放设置与磁带上的方位角记录设置相匹配，对于确保其保真度尤为重要。
baking 烘焙	Baking is a technique to recover the audio and video signals of tapes affected by extreme hydrolysis of the binder layer. The tapes are gently heated in an oven for a pre-determined temperature and time. The drying of the binder lasts long enough to allow copying to take place. 烘焙是一种恢复受粘合剂层受到极端水解影响的磁带音频和视频信号的技术。将磁带在烤箱中缓慢地加热到预定的温度和时间，粘合剂得以干燥，以供复制磁带内容。

baryta layer 氧化钡层	A baryta layer is a thin coating of barium sulphate and gelatine, which is placed between paper support and emulsion. It is used with most gelatine and collodion P.O.P.s and silver gelatine D.O.P.s to provide a smooth, bright white substrate, and to prevent yellowing of the paper. 氧化钡层是一层硫酸钡和明胶的薄层，放置在纸载体和乳液之间。它与大多数明胶和胶棉印相纸和银色明胶显相纸一起使用，以提供光滑明亮的白色基片，并防止纸张变黄。
baryta paper 氧化钡纸	Baryta paper is photographic paper with a baryta layer between paper support and emulsion. 氧化钡纸是在相纸载体和乳剂之间有一层钡层的相纸。
batch number 批号	Batch numbers indicate the production batch of a photographic material. 批号表示照相材料的生产批次。
berliner 柏林唱片	A berliner is an early flat disc recording of various diameters introduced by Emile Berliner (1851-1929). 柏林唱片是由 Emile Berliner（1851-1929）推出的各种直径的早期平板唱片。
Betacam SP 广播级 SP	Betacam SP is an analogue professional video format often used for archival copying. 广播级 SP 是一种模拟专业视频格式，通常用于存档复制。
Betamax Betamax	Betamax is a video tape format which was once the main rival to VHS. Although technically superior, it is now largely a redundant system. It was extensively used for video recording and early digital sound recording. Betamax 是一种录像带格式，曾经是 VHS 的主要竞争对手。尽管在技术上有优势，但现在基本上是冗余系统。它被广泛用于视频录音和早期数字声音记录。
bichromate 重铬酸盐	An older term for dichromate. 重铬酸盐的一个旧的术语。
bleach (1) 漂白 (1)	In photochemical bleaching, metallic silver is converted into silver halide. 在光化学漂白中，金属银被转化成卤化银。
bleach (3) 漂白 (3)	When you bleach discoloured black and white photographic paper on fibre base, you reduce or eliminate the unwanted colour. The bleaching is achieved by applying strong UV and humidity and/or oxidising or reducing agents. 漂白纤维基上的变色黑白相纸可以减少或消除不需要的颜色。漂白是通过施加强紫外线和湿度和/或氧化剂或还原剂来实现的。
blocking 阻塞	Blocking is the sticking together of adjacent layers in a tape pack. 阻塞是将胶带包装中的相邻层粘在一起。
blow-up 放大	A blow-up is the enlargement of an image. 放大是图像的放大。
blue print 蓝图晒印法	See cyanotype. 见蓝晒法。

bromide paper 溴化银相纸/感光纸	See silver bromide gelatin paper. 见溴化银明胶纸。
bromoil print 溴化油印相	A bromoil print is a photographic image which is created by applying oil paint to a swollen gelatin relief. The gelatin relief was formed by photochemical bleaching a silverbromide gelatin print. 溴化油印相是通过在膨胀的明胶凸印上用油性涂料生成的摄影图像。明胶凸印是由光化学漂白溴化银色明胶印相形成的。
bromoil transfer 溴化油转印	A bromoil transfer is a paper print which has received the ink from a freshly made bromoil print in a hand printing press. 溴化油转印是在手印机上从新制成的溴化油油墨中接收油墨的纸印。
buckling (2) 屈曲 (2)	In fabric supports and paper, buckling occurs in the form of waves or bulges. 在织物支架和纸张中，屈曲以波浪或凸起的形式出现。
bulk erase 批量擦除	You can bulk erase tapes of all kinds, audio and video, by passing them through a bulk erasure unit, essentially a powerful electromagnet. The tapes can then be re-used. 通过大容量擦除器（本质上是功能强大的电磁体）可批量擦除各种类型的磁带，包括音频和视频。这些磁带可以重复使用。
burn-in (1) 局部曝光	In photography, burn-in is a partial density increase by selective light exposure. 在摄影中，局部曝光是通过选择性曝光形成的局部密度的增加。
burn-in (2) 烧机	In cinematography, burn-in is the production of white titles on already exposed film. 在电影摄影中，烧机是在已曝光的胶片上刻上白色标题。
CA 醋酸纤维素	See cellulose acetate. 见醋酸纤维素。
calotype 碘化银纸照相法	A calotype is a salted paper print from a paper negative, made by using the W.H.F. Talbot method. 碘化银纸照相法是用塔尔博特的技术，用相纸负片印制盐纸照片。
capstan 绞盘	A capstan is a thin driving spindle attached to the motor of an audio tape recorder in order to provide a constant drive speed. The tape passes between the capstan and a circular rubber-coated horizontal wheel known as the pinch-roller or pinch-wheel. 绞盘是一根细的驱动轴，它连接到录音机的电动机上，以提供稳定的驱动速度。磁带在绞盘和一个圆形的涂有橡胶的水平轮之间穿过，该水平轮称为压轴或压轮。
capstan crease 绞盘折痕	Capstan crease is a vertical crease on the tape which can affect playback. This occurs when the tape drive mechanism of a tape recorder is left accidentally in play mode during periods of inactivity with the tape caught between the thin capstan spindle and rubber pinch-wheel. 绞盘折痕是磁带上会影响播放的垂直折痕，当磁带被夹在薄的主导轴之间，处于非活动状态，磁带录音机的磁带驱动装置意外地处于播放模式时，磁带被夹在薄薄的转轴和橡胶夹轮之间时，就会发生这种情况。

carbon print 碳纸晒印 / 碳素印相	A carbon print consists of a pigmented gelatin relief on a support, usually paper. The pigmented, dichromated, and exposed gelatin was first transferred to a new support. The relief of hardened gelatin, which was created by the tanning action of light, was then created by washing off all unhardened gelatin in warm water. 碳纸晒印是在支撑物（通常为纸）上的着色明胶凸印。暴露于空气中的着色重铬盐酸明胶将最先转移到新的支撑物上。光的鞣制作用会将明胶凸印硬化，然后在温水中冲洗掉未硬化的明胶。
carbon transfer 碳转印	See carbon print. 见碳纸晒印。
carbro print 碳溴印相	A carbro print consists of a pigmented gelatin relief on a support, usually paper. The relief was created by photochemical bleaching a silver gelatin bromide print while in contact with a pigmented gelatine layer. This hardened the pigmented gelatine proportionally to the amount of image silver. After transferring the pigmented gelatin onto a new support, the resulting relief of tanned gelatin is developed in warm water. It is almost impossibel to distinguish visually between a carbon print and a carbro print. 碳溴印相是由在一个支撑物（通常是纸）上的着色明胶凸印组成。凸印是通过光化学漂白银色明胶溴化印相同时与一个着色明胶层相接触而生成的。这使着色明胶变硬，与图像银的量成比例。将色素明胶转移到新的载体上后，鞣制的明胶在温水中显影。仅凭肉眼很难分辨碳素印相和碳溴印相。
carrier 载体	A carrier is a physical object that stores stored audio and/or video information for replay. Examples are gramophone record, CD or video tape. 载体是存储音频和/或视频信息以供回放的物理对象，例如唱片、光盘或录像带。
carte de visite 肖像名片	The carte de visite image size (about 5,5 x 8,5 cm) was introduced by Eugene Disderi in 1854. It has been very successful for commercial portraiture and collectable image series. 肖像名片（大小约 5.5 × 8.5 厘米）由尤金·迪斯德里于 1854 年首创，指贴有本人肖像的名片。作为商业肖像画和可收藏的图像系列，肖像名片风靡一时。
cased photograph 裱框照片	Cased photographs are photographs whose housing is an essential aesthetic, functional or protective part of the object. See also daguerreotype and ambrotype. 裱框照片的包装遵循物体的基本美学，对照片具有功能性或保护性作用。另见银版照相法和玻璃干版照相法。
cassette 盒式磁带	A cassette, correctly known as Compact Cassette, consists of a plastic outer shell containing a narrow magnetic tape. The usual binder for the tape usually contains ferric oxide magnetic material. Because of the recording and playback speed, other formulations have been used to improve sound quality. Although one of the most successful audio products ever made, it is easily damaged unless handled and stored correctly. 盒式磁带，准确地说是卡式录音带，由一个装有窄磁带的塑料外壳组成。磁带的常用粘合剂通常含有氧化铁磁性材料。由于录音和播放速度的原因，已经使用其他配方来提高音质。虽然是有史以来最成功的音频产品之一，但应妥善保管和使用，否则很容易损坏。

cast and credits 演职员表	Cast and credits is the list of people and companies involved in the production of a movie, which is displayed at the end or at the beginning of the film. 演职员表是参与电影制作的人和公司的名单，显示在影片的结尾或开头。
CD 光盘	See compact disc. 见光盘。
CD-R 可写光盘	See compact disc - recordable. 见可刻录光盘。
CD-ROM 只读光盘存储器	See compact disc - Read Only Memory. 见只读光盘-只读存储器。
CD-RW 读写光盘存储器	See compact disc - read/write. 见可读写光盘。
celluloid 电影胶片	Celluloid is clear plastic made of cellulose nitrate and camphor as plasticiser. Until the 1940's it was used as a film base and for making objects. 电影胶片是由硝酸纤维素和作为增塑剂的莰酮制成的透明塑料薄膜。直到20世纪40年代，它一直作为胶片片基用于制作对象。
cellulose acetate 醋酸纤维素	Cellulose acetate (CA) is a thermoplastic polymer made by reacting cellulose with acetic anhydride. Two main types are made, cellulose diacetate and cellulose triacetate. Cellulose acetate is used to make coatings, fibres and films with added plasticisers.When deteriorating, cellulose acetate releases acetic acid fumes, loses plasticiser and shrinks. This is an auto-catalytic process described as vinegar syndrome. 醋酸纤维素是一种热塑性聚合物，由纤维素和醋酸酐反应而成。主要有两种类型，二醋酸纤维素和三醋酸纤维素。醋酸纤维素用于制造涂料、纤维和添加增塑剂的薄膜。醋酸纤维素劣化时，会释放醋酸烟雾，失去塑化剂并收缩。这是一个自动催化过程，被称为醋酸综合症。
cellulose diacetate 二醋酸纤维素	See cellulose acetate. 见醋酸纤维素。
cellulose nitrate 硝酸纤维素	Cellulose nitrate is clear plastic made of cellulose esterified with nitric acid. It is highly flammable, especially during decomposition due to ageing when it evolves nitrogen oxides. At a very advanced state of decomposition and in a closed container, self-ignition is possible. It was widely used as: a coating medium, for making objects, and a film support both in still photography and cinematography until its replacement by cellulose acetate during the 1940's - 1950's. It is widely used in conservation as an adhesive for ceramics and as a lacquer, principally for metals. Commercial adhesives where the main solid constituent is cellulose nitrate include H.M.G., UHU Hart, Durofix and Duco cement. 硝酸纤维素是由硝酸酯化的纤维素制成的透明塑料。它是高度易燃的，特别是在分解过程中，由于老化而产生氮氧化物。在分解的高级状态下，处于封闭的容器中可能会自燃。在20世纪40-50年代被醋酸纤维素取代之前，它被广泛用作：制作物体的涂层介质，摄影和电影摄影胶片的片基。修复工作中，它被广泛用作陶瓷的粘合剂和金属表面的清漆。主要固体成分为硝酸纤维素的商业粘合剂包括H.M.G., UHU Hart, Durofix和Duco水泥。

cellulose triacetate 三醋酸纤维素	See cellulose acetate. 见醋酸纤维素。
channelling 通道	Channelling is a linear delamination pattern due to base deterioration. 通道是由于基底退化，而形成线性分层模式。
chinagraph 瓷器描笔	A chinagraph pencil is a wax-based crayon used by broadcasters to mark the surface of gramophone records to indicate required areas for broadcasting. The marks made in this way are difficult to remove and damage the surface area of discs, especially instantaneous discs. 瓷器描笔是蜡基蜡笔，广播员用它来标记留声机录音的表面，以指示需要广播的区域。用这种方法做的标记很难去除和损坏光盘的表面区域，尤其是 瞬间盘。
chroma noise 色度噪声	In the reproduction of the video image, chroma noise is the movement of the signal identifying the colour, especially reds, from their true location within the image. 在视频图像的再现中，色度噪声是信号的移动，该信号从其在图像中的真实位置识别出颜色，尤其是红色。
chrome cassette 铬磁带	A chrome cassette tape has a magnetic binder of chromium dioxide powder which provides superior performance over ferric oxide. It is extensively used in cassette duplication, as well as in some video tapes. 铬盒式磁带具有二氧化铬粉末的磁性粘合剂，其提供了优于氧化铁的性能。它广泛用于盒式磁带及某些录像带的复制。
chromogenic colour print 彩色印相	A chromogenic colour print is the most widely used photographic colour material. The colours are formed during the processing of the print by the reaction of developer oxidation products with colourless colour couplers. See also c-print. 彩色印相是应用最广泛的彩色照相法。颜色是在印相过程中，显影剂氧化产物与无色成色剂反应而形成的。另见 c 印相。
cibachrome 冲洗显影 / 西巴克罗姆印相法	See ilfochrome. 见伊尔福相纸。
cinching 磁带松折	Cinching is the wrinkling and folding over of tape inside a tape pack or reel of audio and tapes. Cinching is often caused by poor handling or faulty equipment. 磁带松折是指磁带盒或录音带和磁带中的磁带起皱和折叠，它通常是由于操作不当或设备故障引起的。
cine centre reels 电影中心卷	Cine centre reels are audio tape reels with a notched 8mm diameter centre hole. 电影中心卷是带有 8 毫米凹口中心孔的磁带卷轴。
CN 硝化纤维素	See cellulose nitrate. 见硝酸纤维素。

coercivity 矫顽力	Coercivity is the strength of the magnetic field required to erase a tape either during recording or in storage. The higher the coercivity, the greater force is required to erase or remove a programme. Audio tapes are easier to erase than video tapes. Typically values are: audio reel to reel and cassettes 350-450 Oersteds; Chrome cassettes 750 Oersteds; U-matic 750 Oersteds; VHS 750 Oersteds; DAT 1440; Hi-8 1500 Oersteds; Beta SP 1700. Partial erasure can take place at levels well below these figures. 矫顽力是在记录或存储过程中擦除磁带所需的磁场强度。矫顽力越高，擦除或删除程序所需的力就越大。录音带比录像带更容易擦除。典型的数值是：音频卷到卷和磁带 350-450 Oersteds；铬合金磁带 750 Oersteds；U-matic 750 Oersteds；VHS 750 Oersteds；DAT 1440；Hi-8 1500 Oersteds；Beta SP 1700。部分擦除可以在远低于这些数字的水平上进行。
collodion paper 火胶棉纸	Collodion paper is silver chloride printing-out paper with collodion as image layer. 胶棉纸是以胶棉为图像层的氯化银印相纸。
collodion positive 火胶棉正片	A collodion positive is a direct positive photograph, which is made with the wet collodion process. Underexposed negatives are made to look like positives by either coating the emulsion onto a dark support, or backing the glass plate with a dark material. 火胶棉正片是用湿胶棉工艺制作的直接正片。曝光不足的底片可以通过将感光乳剂涂在深色片基上或将玻璃板背部涂黑的方法，使其看起来像正片。
collodion process 胶印工艺	See wet collodion process. 见棉胶湿片工艺。
colloidal silver 胶态微粒银	Colloidal silver consists of very small metallic silver particles. It is the image forming substance in silver chloride printing-out paper. It is also formed during the deterioration of aged silver gelatin developing out-prints, causing the image to turn ellow-brown and fade or to show mirroring. It has also been used as a component of yellow filter layers in early as well as low-speed contemporary colour negative films. 胶态微粒银是由很小的金属银微粒组成的。它是在氯化银印相照片中纸中的成像物质。它也是在老化的银色明胶劣化过程中形成的，导致照片中图像变成黄褐色并褪色或显示镜像。在早期低速当代彩色负片中，它还被用作黄色滤光片的组成部分。
colloidal silver deposit 胶体银沉积	Colloidal silver deposit is a form of silver image deterioration, showing colloidal silver as reflective, bluish-metallic sheen in high density areas. 胶体银沉积是一种银图像退化的形式，在高密度区域，胶体银呈蓝色金属光泽。
collotype 珂罗版	Collotype is a high-quality, photomechanical printing process. The image is printed from inked gelatin glass plates. The gelatin has been hardened proportionally to the image densities and humidified. It then repels or accepts greasy ink depending on humidified content. 珂罗版是一种高质量的照相机械印刷工艺。图像是用涂布明胶感光液的玻璃板印制而成。感光膜产生不同程度的硬化反应，用水对其进行处理以显影。水分保持情况决定其对于油墨的吸收情况。（版面胶层吸水过多，则难于吸收大量油墨。）

colour screen plate 彩色丝网印版	A colour screen plate is a positive transparency in natural colours, in which a fine, regular or random dot or line screen of additive primary colours are used for colour rendition. 彩色丝网印版是通过精细的常规（或随机）点状线条状三色交替滤镜来显现正透明的自然彩色。
colour shift 色差	A colour shift is an unwanted change of the colour of the imaging substance. 色差是成像物质颜色的意外变化。
compact cassette 小型盒式磁带	See cassette. 见盒式磁带。
compact disc 光盘	An audio compact disc (CD) is a high-density digital storage medium holding up to 74 minutes of stereo audio on a 120mm diameter flat polycarbonate disc with a reflective layer. It is replayed using laser technology. See also Optical Disc Technology. 音频光盘(CD)是一种高密度数字存储介质，在一个直径为120毫米的带有反射层的平坦聚碳酸酯光盘上，可以存储高达74分钟的立体声音频。采用激光技术重播。另见光盘技术。
compact disc - Read Only Memory 光盘－只读存储器	A compact disc - Read Only Memory (CD-ROM) use the same technology as an audio CD but contains data such as computer programmes, databases, encyclopaedias or dictionaries. See also Optical Disc Technology. 光盘-只读存储器（CD-ROM）使用与音频CD相同的技术，但包含诸如计算机程序、数据库、百科全书或词典之类的数据。另请参见光盘技术。
compact disc - read/write 可读写光盘	A compact disc –read/write (CD-RW) is similar to a compact disc – recordable except that the discs can be re-recorded. See also Optical Disc Technology. 可读写光盘（CD-RW）与可刻录光盘相似，不同之处在于可以重新刻录光盘，另见光盘技术。
compact disc - recordable 可刻录光盘	A compact disc –recordable (CD-R) has the same format as a compact disc but on which the user can record data. In contrast with an audio CD, a CD-R has a reflective layer covered by a dye layer. The information is recorded in the dye layer which is altered by the recording laser, so preventing reflection from the reflection layer beneath. The discs can only be recorded once. They are used for storing audio, images (e.g. Kodak Photo CD), and computer data. They can be susceptible to light damage and should be stored in darkness. See also Optical Disc Technology. 可刻录光盘（CD-R）与光盘具有相同的格式，但用户可以在其上记录数据。与音频CD相比，可刻录光盘（CD-R）的反射层被染料层覆盖，信息被记录在染料层中，而染料层会被记录激光改变，因此可以防止下面反射层的反射。光盘只能刻录一次。它们用于存储音频、图像（如柯达照片光盘）和计算机数据。它们很容易受到光线的影响，应保存在暗处。另见光盘技术。

control track 控制磁道	On a video tape, a control track is a linear track laid down independently of the image information, in order to provide synchronisation during recording, editing and playback. 在录像带上，控制磁道是独立于图像信息放置的线性磁道，以便在记录、编辑和播放期间能够同步。
copy negative 复印底片	A copy negative results from rephotographing a photographic print with negative film. 复印底片来自对底片的影印片进行的再次拍摄。
c-print 显色印相	A c-print is a chromogenic colour print. C印相是一种显色印相。
cross talk 串扰	Cross talk is unwanted reproduction of an audio signal from an adjacent magnetic track. 串扰是来自相邻磁道的音频信号发生不期望的影响。
cut 剪辑切换	A cut is the change from one film scene to the next. See also rough cut and fine cut. 剪辑切换是指从一个电影场景到下一个场景进行的切换。另见粗剪和细剪。
cyanotype 蓝晒法	A cyanotype is a blue image on paper or occasionally on canvas, printed-out from iron salt compounds, and intensified and fixed in water. It was used as tracing process for technical drawings or cheap printing process for photographic negatives. It was also available, but not widely used, as direct positive process. 蓝晒法是在纸上或偶尔在画布上呈现的蓝色图像，由铁盐化合物印制并在水中加厚和定影。它用于照片底片的技术性绘制或成本较低的印制流程。它也可以直接制作正像照片，但没有被广泛使用。
cylinder recording 圆筒录音	A cylinder recording is an format for recording audio information. The physical representation of the audio is initially cut directly into the surface of a cylinder made of wax or tin foil. A recording was made using an inverted megaphone or recording horn that vibrated a membrane causing a stylus to vibrate and cut into the rotating cylinder. Invented by Thomas Edison in 1877, they are amongst the earliest recording media. They are particularly prone to damage through incorrect handling and storage. Later cylinders were mass produced using celluloid instead of wax. 圆筒录音是用于记录音频信息的格式。音频的物理表示形现首先被直接切入由蜡或锡箔制成的圆柱体的表面，录音是使用一个倒置的扩音器或录音喇叭，振动薄膜，使测针振动并切入旋转的圆筒。1877年由托马斯-爱迪生发明，是最早的录音媒体之一。它们特别容易因不正确的操作和储存而损坏。后来的圆筒是用赛璐珞代替蜡大量生产的。
D.O.P. 显相纸	See developing-out paper. 见显相纸。

daguerreotype 银版照相法	A daguerreotype is a photograph on a polished silver plate. The plate has to be kept sealed in cases or frames in order to be protected from corrosion. This first successful photographic process was invented by J. L. M. Daguerre and made public in 1839. 银版照相法是使用抛光后银版的摄影法。为了防止腐蚀，银版必须密封装框。这种照相法很成功，是由达盖尔发明并于1839年发布的。
DAT 数字音频磁带	See Digital Audio Tape. 见数字音频磁带。
dataplay 数码播放器	Dataplay is a coin-size optical disc data storage system. It is used to store audio and other digital data for use in WAP phones, and hand-held computers. 数码播放器是硬币大小的光盘数据存储系统，它用于存储音频和其他数字数据，以供WAP电话和手持计算机使用。
DCC 袖珍数字磁带	See Digital Compact Cassette. 见袖珍数字磁带。
degaussing 消磁	Degaussing is the complete erasure of magnetic tape media using a mains operated machine known as a bulk eraser. The machine produces a magnetic field stronger than the coercivity of the material being erased. Following erasure tapes can be reused for recording. 消磁是使用被称为大容量擦除器的电动机器完全擦除磁带介质，机器产生的磁场比被擦除材料的矫顽力强。随后，擦除磁带可以重新用于录制。
demagnetising 消磁	Tape heads, guides and other metal parts on both audio and video equipment need demagnetising periodically to remove stray cumulative magnetism that can affect tapes. 音频和视频设备上的磁带头、导轨和其他金属部件需要定期消磁，以消除可能影响磁带的累积的杂散磁。
demagnetising tool 消磁工具	A demagnetising tool is small hand-held device powered by electricity, used to induce a strong alternating current with a local magnetic field via a solid probe. The magnetic field is induced close to magnetised parts of tape machines such as tape heads. 消磁工具是一种小型的手持设备，由电力驱动，用于通过固体探头在局部磁场中感应出强交流电。磁场是在磁带机器的磁化部分附近感应产生的，例如磁头。
developing-out paper 显相纸	Developing-out paper is the paper that has to be developed in order for the exposed, latent image, to become visible. 显相纸是通过冲洗是潜影曝光可见的纸张。
dichroic fog 二向色雾	In photographic materials, dichroic fog is sheen on black and white transparent materials caused by contaminated processing chemicals. It looks greenish in reflected and reddish in transmitted light. 在照相材料中，二向色雾是由于受到污染的加工化学品在黑白透明材料上造成的。它在反射光中呈绿色，在透射光中呈红色。

dichromate **重铬酸盐**	Dichromates are chromic salts (like ammonium or potassium dichromate) which are used in a variety of photographic processes to sensitize polymers for the ultraviolet and blue part of the spectrum. It enables light to influence the polymers' solubility in water or to reduce the chromated polymers' swelling capability. In combination with acids dichromates are also used in photographic bleaching baths. 重铬酸盐是一种铬盐（如铵或重铬酸钾），用于各种摄影过程，使聚合物在光谱的紫外和蓝色部分敏化。它使光线能够影响聚合物在水中的溶解度或降低铬酸盐化聚合物的溶胀能力。与重铬酸盐结合使用的酸也可用于照相漂白促进浴。
digital audio data compression **数字音频数据压缩**	Digital audio data compression is the alteration of digital data to reduce its storage size without apparent loss of sound quality. Commercially important standards for compression include: MP3, used to transmit audio on the Internet and store audio on CD-Rs; and ATRAC, used on Minidiscs. 数字音频数据压缩是指在不明显损失音质的情况下，对数字数据进行修改，以减小其存储容量。商业上重要的压缩标准包括：MP3，用于在互联网上传输音频并将音频存储在用于在互联网上传输音频，并将音频存储在CD-R上；以及用于小型磁盘的ATRAC。
Digital Audio Tape **数字音频磁带**	Digital audio tape (DAT) is an audio format using a small tape to record and replay sound at high-quality as digital information. It is also used to back up computer information. 数字音频磁带（DAT）是一种音频格式，使用小磁带以高质量的数字信息形式录音和回放声音，它还用于备份计算机信息。
Digital Compact Cassette **袖珍数字磁带**	Digital Compact Cassette (DCC) is a digital audio system using the Compact Cassette dimensions with improved tape. 袖珍数字磁带（DCC）是一种数字音频系统，使用带改进磁带的袖珍磁带尺寸。
digital image **数字图像**	A digital image is an image whose information is described in a binary numeric system. 数字图像是其信息在二进制数值系统中描述的图像。
digital image processing **数字图像处理**	Digital image processing is the alteration of digital image data by applied math. 数字图像处理是应用数学对数字图像数据进行修改。
digital imaging **数码影像**	Digital imaging is the capture, processing, storage and display of digital image information. 数码影像是数字图像信息的捕获、处理、存储和显示。
digital recording **数字记录**	Digital recording is an electronic system in which audio or video information is received and converted from an analogue signal into a series of coded pulses that can be recorded in a physical form on a carrier then converted back into sound or vision on replay. There are significant technical reasons for using digital in preference to analogue, for example, clearer sound, better picture quality, and preservation of quality in subsequent copies. 数字记录是一种电子系统，该系统中，接收音频或视频信息并将其从模拟信号转换为一系列编码脉冲，这些脉冲可以以物理形式记录在载体上，然后转换回声音或视觉信号。使用数字技术比使用模拟技术有重要的技术原因，例如，更清晰的声音，更好的图像质量，以及在随后的副本中保存质量。

Digital Versatile Disc 数字多功能光盘	A digital versatile disc (DVD) is physically similar to a compact disc, but is multilayered and capable of reproducing video images, data and still images, especially movies. The original name was Digital Video Disc. See also Optical Disc Technology. 数字多功能光盘（DVD）在物理上类似于光盘，但它是多层的，能够再现视频图像、数据和静态图像，尤其是电影。最初的名字是数字视频光盘，另见光盘技术。
Digital Video Disc 数字视频光盘	See Digital Versatile Disc. 见数字多功能光盘。
dissolve (1) 使消失\ 叠化（1）	When a film scene or slide image dissolves, it switches to the next scene or image by time-overlapping projection. 当一个电影场景或图像消失时，它通过叠化画面切换到下一个场景或图像。
drop out 丢失	Drop out is the momentary loss of audio or video signal from magnetic tape. 丢失是磁带上音频或视频信号的瞬时丢失。
duplicate negative 复制底片 / 翻拍负片	A duplicate negative is created by photographing or contact copying an original photographic negative with subsequent reversal development or by exposing onto direct positive film. If regular development and negative material is used, an interpositive has to be made first. 复制底片是通过拍摄或接触复印原始底片，并随后反转显影或曝光在直接正片上而产生的。如果使用常规显影和底片材料，需要先完成原版正片的制作。
duplicate positive 复制正片	See duplicate negative. 见复制底片。
durium disc 杜力姆树脂碟	A durium disc is a single-sided coated flexible record, brown in colour, made around 1930 and given away free from bookstalls and in magazines. 杜力姆树脂碟是一种单面涂布的棕色软唱片，制作于1930年左右，通过书摊发放和杂志赠品的形式免费赠送。
DVD	See Digital Versatile disc. 见数字多功能光盘。
dye (2) 染色（2）	A dye is a print made in the dye transfer process. 染色是在染印工艺中产生的印相。
dye diffusion 染料扩散	In a dye diffusion process, added materials change the solubility of dyes and allow them to move into an image layer. 在染料扩散过程中，添加的材料改变了染料的溶解度，并使其移动到图像层中。
dye imbibition 染料吸收	In a dye imbibition process, a polymer relief is dyed proportionally to its thickness. 在染料吸收过程中，聚合物凸印是按其厚度成比例染色的。
dye transfer 染料转移	In a dye transfer process, a dyed polymer relief transfers its colour to a receiver material. 在染料转移过程中，染色聚合物凸印将其颜色转移到接收材料上。

edge mark 边缘标记	Edge marks are written or graphic manufacturer's codes, which are exposed outside the image area of roll film and indicate the film type. 边缘标记是制造商代码文字或图形，暴露在胶卷的成像区域外，表明了胶片类型。
editing 编辑	Editing is the process of re-arranging sections of a recorded audio or video programme either by splicing or copying. 编辑是通过剪接或复制来重新编排录制的音频或视频节目的过程。
ektachrome ektachrome	Ektachrome, originally a Kodak brand name, is used as a general term for colour transparencies larger than 35mm. 最初是柯达的一个品牌，它是大于35mm的彩色透明胶片的通用术语。
emulsion (2) 乳剂 (2)	In photography, an emulsion is the suspension of silver halide crystals in a polymer (usually gelatine). It forms the image layer. 在摄影中，乳剂是卤化银晶体在聚合物（通常是明胶）中的悬浮液。它形成了图像层。
emulsion transfer 乳剂转移	Emulsion transfer is the separation of an emulsion from its original support and its mounting on a new one. 乳剂转移是将乳剂从原来的支撑物上分离出来，并将其放在新的支撑物上。·
encased photograph 裱框照片	See cased photograph. 见裱框照片。
equalisation 均衡	Equalisation (EQ) is the use of an electronic filter system to compensate for loss or change of frequency response and other distortions introduced during recording or playback of audio material. A simple example would be a bass or treble control on a radio. 均衡（EQ）是使用电子滤波系统来补偿音频材料录制或回放过程中产生的频率响应和其他失真的损失或变化。一个简单的例子就是收音机上的低音或高音控制。
Estar ® Estar ®	Estar is a Kodak brand name for polyester (Polyethylenetherephthalate, PET). Estar是柯达旗下聚酯版（聚对苯二甲酸乙二醇酯）的品牌。
exfoliation (2) 剥落 (2)	In audio tapes, exfoliation is the loss of some or all of the entire binder layer, especially with poorly stored acetate audio tapes. 在录音带中，剥落是整个粘合剂层的部分或全部损失，尤其是在醋酸纤维录音带存储不佳的情况下会发生。
exfoliation (3) 剥落 (3)	In instantaneous discs, exfoliation is the flaking of the surface layer (cellulose nitrate or acetate) from the supporting platen of the discs. This damage is irreversible and often caused by the contraction of the layer due to hydrolytic action. 在瞬时磁盘中，剥落是指从磁盘的支撑压板的表面层（硝酸纤维素或乙酸纤维素）剥落。这种损坏是不可逆的，通常是由于水解作用导致的涂层收缩所致。

fast forward 快进	Fast forward is the process of electrically winding audio or video tape from the beginning of the programme or reel to the desired point on the tape. 快进是将音频或录像带从节目开始或卷轴的开头，缠绕到磁带上所需点的过程。
ferric oxide 三氧化二铁	Ferric oxide is the commonest magnetic material which is mixed with a binder to form the coating on audio cassettes and tapes. 三氧化二铁是最常见的磁性材料，它与粘合剂混合形成录音带和磁带上的涂层。
ferrotype 铁板照相	An older term for tintype. 是锡版照相法的旧术语。
ferrotyping 铁板照相	Ferrotyping is the process of glazing a photographic print by drying it in contact with a glossy surface. 铁板照相是将照片去湿并与有光泽表面接触的过程。
fibre base paper 纤维原纸	Fibre base paper is photographic paper which often has a baryta layer between paper support and emulsion. See also resin coated paper (RC paper). 纤维原纸是一种照相纸，通常在纸张支撑物和乳剂之间有一层钡层。另见树脂涂层纸（RC纸）。
film, 35mm 35毫米胶片	A 35mm film is a perforated photographic film with a width of 35mm. Originally a standard gauge for movie film, it has been the preferred film size for press and amateur photographers since the late 1920's. 35mm胶片是一种宽度为35mm的穿孔摄影胶片。最初是电影胶片的标准尺寸，自20世纪20年代末以来，它一直是新闻界和业余摄影师的首选胶片尺寸。
fine cut 精剪片	A fine cut is the final version of a motion picture film. 精剪片是动作电影的最终版本。
fixing 定影	Fixing is the process of making a photograph permanent by removing the light-sensitive, unreduced, silver from the emulsion. 定影是将感光的、未还原的银从乳剂中除去，使照片长久保新的处理。
fixing bath 定影液	See fixing. 见定影。
flare 耀斑	A flare is a non-image forming, scattered light within an optical system. 耀斑是光学系统中的非成像散射光。
focal length 焦距	Focal length is the distance from the centre of the lens to the focal plane. 焦距是从透镜中心到焦平面的距离。
focal plane 焦平面	Focal plane is the location within a camera where a sharp image is formed. 焦平面是相机内形成清晰图像的位置。
format 格式	The format of a sound or video carrier (magnetic tape, CD, DVD, LP etc.) is a standard set of specifications that together describe its size, style, form and technical characteristics for recording and playback. 声音或视频载体（磁带，CD，DVD，LP等）的格式是一组标准的规范，这些规范一起描述了其大小、样式、形式和录制和播放的技术特征。

FPM 帧/分钟	FPM stands for feet per minute and describes the cinema film transport speed in the U.S.A. and U.K. 帧/分钟代表每分钟的帧数，在美国和英国用来描述电影胶片的传输速度。
FPS 帧/秒	FPS stands for frames per second and describes the film transport speed. FPS代表每秒帧数，描述胶片传输速度。
frame (3) 帧 (3)	A frame is a single image of a roll of movie film. 帧是一卷电影胶片中的单个图像。
frame line 帧线	A frame line is the space between two images on movie film. It is visible during projection if the image is not centred correctly in front of the machine's projection window. 帧线是电影胶片中两个图像之间的间隔。如果图像在机器投影窗前没有正确居中，则在投影过程中可见。
frequency response 频率响应	The frequency response (FR) of an audio format is its capability to record and replay a specified range of frequencies and harmonics accurately. For example, Minidiscs reproduce frequencies from 5Hz to 20kHz, covering the frequencies needed for music. 频率响应（FR）是其准确记录和重放指定范围的频率和谐波的能力，例如，小型磁盘可再现5Hz至20kHz的频率，覆盖了音乐所需的频率。
Fresson print 弗雷松印相	A Fresson print is a direct carbon print (wash-off relief), monochrome or four-colour, made by a proprietary, unpublished process by the Fresson Co., France. 弗雷松印相是由法国弗雷松采用未发表的专有工艺制作的单色或四色的直接碳素印相法（水洗式凸版印相）。
gauge 宽度	Gauge is the width of (cinematographic) film material. 宽度是（电影）胶片材料的宽度。
gelatin relief 明胶相片	See carbon print. 见碳纸晒印。
generational loss 累积损耗	Generational loss is the addition of noise and distortion when copying either audio or video from an analogue source to another analogue source. This loss accumulates each time the signal is copied. 累积损耗是将音频或视频从模拟源复制到另一个模拟源时噪声和失真的增加，每次复制信号时，此损耗就会累积。
glitch (1) 故障 (1)	In video playback, a glitch is a form of low frequency interference appearing as a narrow horizontal bar moving vertically through the picture. 在视频回放中，故障是低频干扰的一种形式，表现为垂直穿过图像的窄水平条。
glitch (2) 故障 (2)	In audio playback of digital material, a glitch is an audible click caused by electrical interference, mis-match of digital signal to sound card, or faulty recorded material such as a surface damaged CD. 在数字资料的音频回放中，故障是由于电干扰、数字信号与声卡的不匹配或记录的资料有缺陷（例如表面损坏的CD）引起的咔嗒声。

gradation 渐变	Gradation refers to the contrast rendition of photographic materials. 渐变是指摄影材料表现出的对比度。
grading 调试	Grading is the technique of controlling and adjusting the overall density and colour balance of a film print. 调试是控制和调整胶卷印相的整体密度和色彩平衡的技术。
graininess 颗粒状	Graininess is the random microstructure of a image, which is visible under high magnification and determined by the size of the image forming particles. 颗粒状是图像的随机微观构造，在高倍数放大镜下可见，由形成图像的粒子大小决定。
gramophone 留声机	A gramophone is a generic name for any equipment capable of replaying grooved flat disc audio recordings. The Gram-o-phone was invented by Emile Berliner (1851-1929) to play such recordings. 留声机是任何能够播放带凹槽的平板唱片设备的总称。留声机是埃米尔·柏林（Emile Berliner，1851-1929年）发明的，用于播放此类录音。
grey value 灰度值	Grey value is the local density of a black and white photograph. 灰度值是黑白照片的局部密度。
gum dichromate print 重铬酸胶印刷	A gum dichromate print is a pigment image on paper. It was formed by contact-printing a negative onto dichromate-sensitised, pigmented gum Arabic. The light crosslinks the gum proportionally to the negative's density, thus reducing its solubility in water. The visible image is formed by washing-out the uncrosslinked polymer. 重铬酸胶印刷是纸张上的颜料图像。它是通过在感光重铬酸盐着色阿拉伯树胶上接触性印制底片而成。光照使阿拉伯胶与底片的密度按比例交联，从而降低阿拉伯胶的水溶性。通过洗出未交联的聚合物形成可见图像。
guncotton 火棉	Guncotton is cellulose nitrate early in the manufacturing process. It incorporates a relatively large proportion of nitrate and is therefore relatively unstable. 早期制造过程中，火棉是硝酸纤维素。它含有相当大比例的硝酸盐，相对不稳定。
half-track 半轨录音	Half-track recording is an audio recording format in which approximately half the width of the tape is used at a time. There is a slight physical gap between the tracks to avoid cross talk. 半轨录音是一种音频记录格式，其中一次使用大约磁带宽度的一半。磁道之间有一点物理间隙，以避免串扰。
helical scan 螺旋扫描	Helical scan is the system used in video and DAT recorders where the signal is added to the tape in a series of short discrete tracks at an angle to the tape edge. This is achieved by passing the tape round a rotating drum containing record/replay heads. 螺旋扫描是在视频和DAT录制机中使用的系统，在与磁带边缘成一定角度的一系列短离散轨道中，将信号添加到磁带上，这可以通过使磁带绕过包含记录/重放磁头的旋转鼓而实现。

Hi-8 Hi-8	Hi-8 (pronounced high eight) is a high-quality video cassette format used in amateur portable video cameras. Hi-8（发音为高-8）是一种用于业余便携式摄像机的高质量录像带格式。
holograph 全息照相	A holograph is a light interference based recording of a three-dimensional image. 全息照相是一种基于光干扰原理的三维图像记录。
hydrolysis (2) 水解 (2)	In audio and video tapes, hydrolysis is a chemical reaction that incorporates water from the atmosphere causing the binder of the tape to become sticky and unplayable. See also sticky tape syndrome. 在音频和视频磁带中，水解是一种化学反应，它吸收了来自大气中的水，从而导致磁带的粘合剂变得有粘性且无法播放。另见磁带综合症。
hypo 定影剂	Hypo is a colloquial abbreviation for sodium thiosulphate which reacts with silver ions. See also fixing. 定影剂是与银离子反应的硫代硫酸钠的缩写的术语。另见定影。
ilfochrome ® 伊尔福相纸	Ilfochrome (a.k.a. Cibachrome) is an Ilford brand name for a direct positive colour paper using the silver dye bleach process. Ilfochrome（又名Cibachrome）是伊尔福公司旗下使用银色染料漂白工艺的直接正片彩色纸的品牌名称。
image layer 图像层	An image layer is the combination of a polymer binder (such as albumen, collodion, starch or gelatin) and the image forming substance (for example, image silver pigment or dye). 图像层是聚合物粘合剂（例如蛋白、胶棉、淀粉或明胶）和图像形成物质（例如，图像银颜料或染料）的组合。
image processing 图像处理	See digital image processing. 见数字图像处理。
image silver 图像银	Image silver is the image forming silver which is present in the image layer after processing. 图像银是经过处理后存在于图像层中形成图像的银。
image substance 图像物质	An image substance is the image forming matter which is present in the image layer after processing. 图像物质是在处理之后存在于图像层中形成图像的物质。
instant photograph 即时照片	An instant photograph is a silver or dye diffusion-based, direct-positive photograph, which is developed immediately after image capture. 即时照片是基于银或染料扩散原理的直接正向照片，它是在图像捕获后立即显影的。
instantaneous disc 瞬时盘	An instantaneous disc is a round flat platen - usually of aluminium although glass, and other materials were also used - covered with a coating of cellulose nitrate or acetate. The discs were made in the 1930's. The soft surface allowed instant recording using a special disc-cutting lathe. The soft coating is unstable and can shrink and exfoliate making the recording unplayable. 瞬时盘是圆形平板，通常为铝制，虽然也使用玻璃和其他材料，但表面覆盖有硝酸纤维素或醋酸纤维素涂层。光盘是在1930年代制造的，柔软的表面允许使用特殊的光盘切割车床进行即时录音。软涂层不稳定，可能会收缩和脱落，导致录音无法播放。

internegative 中间底片	An internegative is a duplicate (colour) negative , especially one prepared from a reversal camera original or print. 中间底片是复印的（彩色）底片，可由反拍相机原片或印相片制成。
interpositive 中间正片	In cinematography, an interpositive is any positive element used as an intermediate stage, that is not the final print. 在电影摄影中，中间正片是用在中间阶段的正片，不是最后出来的相片。
intertitle 中间字幕	Intertitles are text still images cut between film scenes in silent movies. 中间字幕是无声电影中电影场景之间的静止图像上的文字。
iso-chromatic 等色乳剂	An iso-chromatic emulsion is sensitive to the full visible spectrum, but less to the red than to the blue and green part. See also ortho-chromatic and pan-chromatic. 等色乳剂对完全可见光谱敏感，但对红色不如对蓝色和绿色部分敏感。另见正交色和泛色。
lacquer damage 漆膜损坏	Lacquer damage is accidental perforation or scratching of the microscopically thin coating on the label side of a CD and similar optical disc media, thus exposing the vulnerable reflective layer beneath. Lacquer damage can be caused during manufacture, using acid-based printing inks, careless handling, or poor storage. The deterioration of the underlying reflective layer can seriously interfere with the ability of the laser to retrieve complete digital information held on the disc, rendering the disc unplayable. 漆膜损坏是CD和类似光盘介质的标签面上的微观薄涂层的意外穿孔或刮擦，从而暴露出下方脆弱的反射层。漆面的损坏可能是在制造过程中造成的，使用酸基印刷油墨，不小心处理或储存不当。底层反射层的损坏会严重干扰激光检索光盘上完整数字信息的能力，使光盘无法播放。
lantern slide 幻灯片	A lantern slide is a transparent image, usually on or between glass, which is projected with a magic lantern. 幻灯片是一种透明的图像，通常在玻璃上或玻璃之间，用早期幻灯放映机放映。
laser disc 激光唱片	A laser disc (LD) is a 30cm flat glass or polycarbonate disc read by laser. There are two main types: CLV – Constant Linear Velocity, capable of holding up to 2 hours of movie film (60 minutes per side) and CAV – Constant Analogue Velocity which allows random access frame by frame holding up to 54,000 still images. An LD is easily damaged, some types being affected by light. 激光唱片（LD）是通过激光读取的30厘米的平板玻璃或聚碳酸酯光盘。主要有两种类型：CLV –恒定线速度，可容纳多达2个小时的电影胶片（每面60分钟），以及CAV - 恒定模拟速度，可随机逐帧访问，最多可保存54,000张静态图像。LD很容易损坏，有些类型的LD会受到光线的影响。

latent image 潜影	A latent image is the invisible change in a silver halide crystal, which is caused by light and made visible in development. 潜影是卤化银晶体中不可见的变化，它是由光引起的，在显影过程中可见。
layer (2) 圈 (2)	A layer is a single revolution winding of magnetic tape in a tape pack. 圈是磁带组中磁带的单圈缠绕。
LD 激光光盘	See laser disc. 激光光盘。
lenticular screen film 透镜状屏幕胶片	A lenticular screen film uses tiny embossed lenses on a black and white film and a filter with stripes of additive primary colours in the lens during image capture and projection. The film lenses focus the filtered image onto the emulsion according to the object's colour intensity. The colour image is formed during projection. The technique was used for colour transparencies and cinema film. 透镜状屏幕胶片在黑白胶片上使用小型凸印透镜，并且在图像捕捉和放映时，使用镜头中带有加法三原色条纹的滤光器。胶片透镜根据物体的颜色强度将过滤后的图像聚焦到乳剂上。彩色图像在投影期间形成。该技术用于彩色透明胶片和电影胶片。
line film 硬性胶片	See lith film. 见特硬胶片。
lip sync 唇同步	Lip sync is the exact correspondence between picture and sound recording. 唇同步是图片和录音之间的准确对应关系。
lith film 特硬胶片	Lith film is a high-contrast film material which achieves very high density in special development. 特硬胶片是一种高对比度的薄膜材料，在特殊的显影过程中可以实现非常高的密度。
longitudinal damage 纵向损坏	Longitudinal damage on audio and video tape are scratches and other striations along the length of a magnetic tape caused by the presence of dirt and other debris on equipment rollers and guides. In video, it can result in a black line on the image. 音频和视频磁带的纵向损坏是由于设备滚轮和导轨上的灰尘和其他碎屑导致的沿磁带长度的划痕和其他条纹。在视频中，它可能导致图像上出现黑线。
long-playing record 密纹唱片	See microgroove disc. 见密纹唱片。
low chroma level 低色度水平	Low chroma level is weak colour saturation in a video image. 低色度水平是视频图像中较弱的色彩饱和度。
LP 密纹	See microgroove disc. 见密纹唱片。

magnetic particle 磁粉	A magnetic particle is a finely ground pigment that can be readily magnetised and hold this state until remagnetised. Magnetic particles are the information carrier on a magnetic medium such as audio and video tape. Typical materials used for these particles are ferric oxide, chromium dioxide and ferric metal. 磁粉是一种细粉状颜料，它很容易被磁化并保持这种状态直到被再次磁化。磁粉是诸如录音带和录像带之类的磁性介质上的信息载体。这些颗粒的典型材料是氧化铁、二氧化铬和金属铁。
magnetic tape 磁带	Magnetic tape consists of a long narrow ribbon of support material usually plastic (early types were on paper) carrying a thin coating of magnetic material capable of being recorded and replayed. 磁带由长而窄的支撑材料组成，通常是塑料（早期类型是在纸上），上面带有一层薄薄的磁性材料涂层，可以记录和重放。
magnetic tape deformation 磁带变形	Magnetic tape deformation is a physical distortion of audio or video magnetic tape which is not rewound to the beginning after playing. After a long period of storage, the tape, which is still under slight longitudinal tension and under the influence of gravity, assumes a u-shape section. This distortion can prevent intimate contact between tape heads and tape resulting in poor reproduction of sound or image. 磁带变形是音频或视频磁带的物理变形，在播放后不会重绕到开始。磁带经过长期存放后，由于磁带仍处于轻微的纵向张力下，在重力的影响下，磁带的断面呈U型。这种变形会使磁带头和磁带之间无法紧密接触，导致声音或图像的再现效果不佳。
magneto-optical technology 磁光技术	Magneto-optical technology is a system for recording and re-playing digital data, usually audio, using a specially coated disc. In order to record, a laser heats the surface of the coating at the point of focus on a disc during recording. The surface material thus becomes paramagnetic, and its reflectivity is then altered using a magnetic field. During replay, reflected polarised light from the disc produces an 'on' or 'off' signal – that is a digital code. 磁光技术是一种记录和重放数字数据（通常为音频）的系统，使用特殊涂层的磁盘。为了记录，在记录过程中，激光在光盘上聚焦点加热涂层的表面。因此，表面材料变成顺磁，然后利用磁场改变其反射率。在重放过程中，光盘反射的偏振光会产生一个"开"或"关"的信号，即数字代码。
masking (1) 掩蔽 (1)	In the production and processing of photographic material, masking is the density correction of single or multiple image layers. It is used to improve colour and contrast rendition and can be achieved by material-integrated masking layers or by combination with masking films. 在感光材料的生产和加工中，掩蔽是对单个或多个图像层的密度校正。它用于改善颜色和对比度的呈现，可以通过材料集成掩蔽层或通过组合来实现。
masking (2) 掩蔽 (2)	In image capturing or rendition, masking is a black frame which is used to crop the image. 在图像捕获或呈现中，掩蔽是用于裁剪图像的黑色边框。

matt backing 亚光背衬	Matt backing is an anti-static coating applied to the back of audio and video tapes to ensure smooth winding at speed. 亚光背衬是一种防静电涂层，涂施于音频和视频磁带的背面，以确保快速平滑地缠绕。
metal evaporated tape 金属蒸镀带	Metal evaporated tape (ME) is a recording tape which has a microscopically thin layer of metal evaporated directly on to the substrate under a vacuum. 金属蒸镀带（ME）是一种记录带，在真空下直接将微细的金属薄层蒸发到衬底上。
metal particle 金属粒子	A metal particle tape is a coating of metal particles in a binder. The tapes are used in both audio and video recording. The metal particles often treated to prevent degradation caused by playback damage and subsequent atmospheric corrosion. 金属粒子磁带是粘合剂中金属粒子的涂层。磁带既用于音频录制，也用于视频录制。应经常对金属颗粒进行处理，以防止由于回放损坏和随后的大气腐蚀而导致的降解。
microgroove disc 密纹唱片	A microgroove disc is audio disc usually made from polyvinyl chloride (PVC). They are capable high quality reproduction in stereo, but susceptible to damage from scratches, and from warping caused by excessive heat. 密纹唱片是通常由聚氯乙烯（PVC）制成的音频光盘，它们能够以立体声方式进行高质量复制，但容易因刮擦和过热导致变形损害。
minidisc 小型磁盘	A minidisc is a high-density digital storage format for audio recording launched in 1990, holding 140MB capacity or 72 minutes stereo. Smaller than a compact disc, it is housed in a protective polycarbonate case. The system uses magneto-optical technology and allows, in the record/playback consumer form, 106 re-writes before becoming unrecordable. 小型磁盘是 1990 年推出的用于录音的高密度数字存储格式，容量为 140MB 或 72 分钟立体声。它比光盘小，装在保护性的聚碳酸酯盒中。该系统采用磁光技术，可刻录和播放的磁盘，可被刻录106次。
mono 单声道的	See monophonic sound. 见单声道声音。
monophonic sound 单声道声音	Monophonic sound, commonly called mono, is electronically or mechanically reproduced sound replayed to the listener without stereophonic information. 单声道声音通常称为单声道，是电子或机械复制的声音，在没有立体声信息的情况下重播给听众。
mordant (3) 媒染剂 (3)	A mordant is a metal salt (silverhexacyanoferrate) used to apply and fix basic dyes to polymers. In photography, the conversion of metallic image silver into silverhexacyanoferrate is used to replace the silver with a dye. 媒染剂是一种金属盐（铁氰化银），用于在聚合物上应用和定影的碱性染料。在摄影技术中，将金属图像银转换为铁氰化银的方法常使用染料来置换银。
mounting board 安装板	A mounting board is a flat material to which a photograph is fixed. 安装板是一种使照片定影的扁平材料。

M-PEG (1) M-PEG（1）	M-PEG is a set of digital video compression standards. An example is M-PEG audio layer 3, abbreviated to MP3. See also Digital Audio Data Compression. M-PEG是一组数字视频压缩标准，一个示例是M-PEG音频层3，缩写为MP3。另见数字音频数据压缩。
M-PEG (2) 动态图像专家组	M-PEG is an acronym for Moving Picture Experts Group. M-PEG是动态图像专家组的缩写，一种流行的视频文件格式。
multitrack 多声道	Multitrack or multi-tracking is a system of recording and playing back parallel tracks on magnetic tape, for example on 16 tracks. Each track is capable of being recorded and played back independently as required. Its principle advantage is in allowing greater flexibility in recording music and in the post-production and mastering of recordings. 多声道是在磁带上（例如16条磁道）上记录和播放平行磁道的系统。每个磁道都可以根据需要独立记录和播放。它的主要优势在于可以更灵活地进行音乐录音和录音的后期制作和母带制作。
multi-tracking 多轨	See multitrack. 见多声道。
NAB reel NAB卷轴	A NAB reel (pronounced nab) is a 10 ½ inch aluminium reel characterised by a large centre hole meeting the US National Association of Broadcasters standard. NAB卷轴（发音为nab）是10½英寸铝卷，其特点是中心孔大，符合美国广播协会的标准。
noise (1) 噪音 (1)	Audio noise is unwanted sound (such as hiss) derived from equipment electronics, magnetic tape, or turntables. 音频噪音是源自设备电子、磁带或转盘的不需要的声音（例如嘶嘶声）。
noise (2) 噪点 (2)	Video noise is unwanted signal interference during recording or playback characterised by picture disturbance, excessive graininess and interference with colour content. 视频噪点是录制或播放过程中的不利的信号干扰，其特征是图像干扰，过多的颗粒感和对色彩成分的干扰。
noise reduction 降噪	Noise reduction is an electronic method of reducing unwanted playback hiss in audio and video systems to acceptable levels. Various proprietary standards are available, for instance by Dolby Laboratories. 降噪是一种将音频和视频系统中不必要的回放嘶嘶声，降低到可接受水平的电子方法。有各种专有标准，例如杜比实验室的标准。
notch code 刻痕代码	Notch codes are cutouts at the upper right edge of a sheet film, which indicate the emulsion side and film type. 刻痕代码是在胶片右上边缘的切口，它表示乳剂面和胶片类型。
oil print 油印	An oil print is a pigment print, created by dabbing or rolling oil paint onto a swollen gelatin relief on paper. The relief was formed by contact exposure of dichromate sensitised gelatin under a negative, followed by washing in water. 油印是颜料印相，通过在纸上的膨胀的明胶凸印上涂抹或滚动油漆而生成。凸印是在底片下接触重铬酸盐感光明胶，然后用水冲洗。

oil transfer 油转印	An oil transfer is a paper print which has received the ink from a freshly made oil print in a hand printing press. 油转印是一种在手工压印机中新制成的油印中获得墨汁的纸质印相。
optical density 光密度	Optical density is the measure of darkness of a photographic material. It is calculated from the logarithm of opacity. 光密度是照相材料暗度的大小。它是对不透明度取对数计算出来的。
optical disc technology 光盘技术	Optical disc technology (ODT) is a format for a high density digital storage medium consisting of pits or marks etched or indented into the surface of a polycarbonate or glass, flat circular disc. The marks or pits represent retrievable digital data that can be read using appropriate laser reproduction equipment, the light being reflected from the disc's reflective layer (usually aluminium) into the playback equipment. ODT includes magneto-optical systems such as Minidisc. 光盘技术（ODT）是一种高密度数字存储介质的格式，该介质由刻蚀或压入聚碳酸酯或玻璃扁平圆盘表面的凹坑或标记组成。这些标记或凹坑代表可检索的数字数据，可以用适当的激光复制设备读取，光从光盘的反射层(通常是铝)反射到播放设备中。ODT包括磁光系统，如微型光盘。
optical sound 光学声音	An optical sound is a sound which is recorded and played by modulating a light beam. 光学声音是通过调制光束记录并播放的声音。
ortho-chromatic 正色乳剂	An ortho-chromatic emulsion is an emulsion which is sensitive to the blue and green part of the spectrum. See also iso-chromatic and pan-chromatic. 正色乳剂是对光谱中的蓝色和绿色部分敏感的乳液。另见等色乳剂和泛色度学。
out of focus 失去对焦	An image that is out of focus is blurred due to wrong distance between lens and photographic material. 由于镜头和摄影材料之间的距离不正确，失去对焦的图像会变得模糊。
overexposure 过度曝光	Overexposure occurs when the amount of light to which a photographic material is exposed has exceeded the maximum amount of light for which this material is designed. 当感光材料的曝光量超过该材料设计的最大光量时，就会发生过度曝光。
oxide shedding 氧化脱落	Oxide shedding is the loss of magnetic oxide from audio tape during recording and replay. The oxide builds up on tape heads necessitating cleaning of the affected parts. 氧化脱落是录音和重放期间录音带中的磁性氧化物损失。氧化物堆积在磁带头上，需要清洁受影响的零件。
palladium print 钯印相	A palladium print is a photograph with palladium as image forming substance. See also platinum print. 钯印相是以钯为成像物质的照片。另见白金印相。

pan-chromatic 全色的	A pan-chromatic emulsion is equally sensitive to all parts of the visible spectrum. See also iso-chromatic and ortho-chromatic. 全色乳剂对可见光谱的所有部分都同样敏感。另见等色的和正色的。
pannotype 铁板照相版	A pannotype is a collodion positive transferred to dark leather or waxed cloth. 铁板照相版是转移到深色皮革或蜡布上的火棉正片。
paper tape 纸带	Paper tape is an early form of quarter inch wide reel to reel magnetic audio tape. It consists of a thick flexible paper ribbon coated with magnetic oxide on one side. It tears easily on fast forward or rewind on a tape machine, and is prone to mould growth when incorrectly stored. Exfoliation of oxide onto tape heads and tape machine guide rollers is common. see also oxide shedding. 纸带是四分之一英寸宽的卷到卷磁性音频磁带的早期形式。它由厚的柔性纸带组成，在其一侧涂有磁性氧化物。在磁带机上快进或倒带时容易撕裂，存放不当容易发霉。氧化物脱落到磁带头和磁带机导辊上是很常见的。另见氧化物脱落。
perforation 穿孔	Perforations are the holes at the edge of a film for the sprockets of the transport mechanism. 穿孔是薄膜边缘的孔，用于输送机械装置中的链轮。
photocollage 光胶卷	A photocollage is an image created by gluing together (parts of) photographs. 光胶卷是将照片的全部或部分粘在一起而形成的图像。
photogram 黑影照片	A photogram is a photograph created on paper or film without a camera. 黑影照片是在没有照相机的情况下在纸或胶片上生成的照片。
photographic process 摄影过程	Photographic process is the method of recording, saving or displaying a photographic image. 摄影过程是记录、保存或显示照片图像的方法。
photogravure 照相凹版	A photogravure is a photomechanical print from an aquatint grained copper plate. The image information has been etched into the plate through a carbon print. 照相凹版是来自于浅绿色磨砂铜板的照相制版。图像信息已通过碳素印相蚀刻在印版上。
photomontage 蒙太奇照片	A photomontage is created by exposing different or composed negatives to photographic paper. 蒙太奇照片是把不同的或合成的底片暴露在相纸上而制成的。
picture roll 图片滚动	Picture roll is the uncontrolled up or down movement of a video image on a screen. 图片滚动是视频图像在屏幕上不受控制的向上或向下移动。
pigment print 颜料印相	Pigment prints are photographs with pigments as image forming substance. 颜料印相是以颜料为成像物质的照片。

pinch-roller 压紧辊	A pinch-roller is a rubber-coated horizontal roller situated in close proximity to the capstan spindle used in audio recorders. 压紧辊是一种涂有橡胶的卧式辊，其位置紧靠录音机中使用的绞盘主轴。
platinum print 铂印相	A platinum print is a photograph with platinum as image forming substance. It is manufactured as developing-out and printing-out paper, using light sensitive iron(III) salts and platinum salts. 铂印相是以铂为成像物质的照片。通过使用光敏铁（III）盐和铂盐可将其制成显相纸和印相纸。
playback damage 回放损坏	Playback damage is deterioration of audio or visual information on a carrier caused during replaying. Examples are, scratches on LPs and shoe-stringing of audio tape. Damage is caused by a variety of factors including careless handling, burns from cigarette ash, lack of equipment maintenance, excessive heat, dirt on tape heads and guide paths or incorrect tension. It is the main threat to the long-term survival of audio and video materials. 回放损坏是指在播放过程中导致载体上的音频或视频信息变差，例如，LP 上的刮擦和录音带的绞带。造成损坏的原因有很多，包括操作不慎、烟灰烫伤、设备缺乏维护、温度过高、磁带头和导引道上的污垢或磁带卷地过紧或过松。这是对音频和视频材料长期保存的主要威胁。
Polaroid® 宝丽来	See instant photograph and dye diffusion process. 见即时照片和染料扩散。
preservation (2) 视听保存 (2)	Preservation is the retention of audio and/or video information content for posterity, irrespective of the carrier. 保存是指为后代保留音频和/或视频信息内容，而不考虑载体。
preserver 保护器	A preserver is a decorative edge protection made of embossed brass foil for the paper sealing of cased photographs. It is mainly used with American or English daguerreotypes or ambrotypes. 保护器是装饰性的边缘保护装置，由压纹铜箔制成，用于裱框照片中的纸制密封。它主要在美国或英国的银版照相法或玻璃干版照相法中使用。
primary support 主要支撑物	A primary support is the carrier of an image layer. 主要支撑物是图像层的载体。
print (1) 印相 (1)	In a still photograph, a print is a copy of a negative or transparency viewed by reflection. 在静止照片中，印相是通过反射可见图像的复印底片或正片。
print (2) 印相 (2)	In cinematography, a print is a film copy of another film. 在电影摄影中，印相是另一个胶片的拷贝。
printing-out paper 印相纸	Printing-out paper is paper on which an image is formed in contact with a negative during exposure to sunlight. It is not developed but just fixed and eventually toned. 印相纸是感光过程中，与底片接触形成图像的纸。它不是显影，而只是定影并且最终调色。

print-through 复印效应	Print-through is the transfer of magnetic information from adjacent layers in a reel of tape, resulting in an audible but lower level repetition of sound. The condition is exacerbated by too high a recording level, heat, and thin tapes. 复印效应是指磁带卷中相邻层的磁信息传递，从而产生声音可听但低级重复。过高的录音电平、热量和薄磁带会加剧这种情况。
projection speed 放映速度	Projection speed is the frame rate per second at which a movie film is projected. 放映速度是电影放映时每秒的帧速率。
PVC tape PVC 磁带	PVC tape (polyvinyl chloride) is magnetic audio tape made with a plasticised PVC substrate, popular with broadcasters because of its increased strength compared with acetate tape. PVC胶带（聚氯乙烯）是一种由增塑的PVC基材制成的音频磁带，由于它比醋酸纤维磁带的强度更高，因此在广播行业中颇受欢迎。
quarter track 四声迹	Quarter track is an audio reel-to-reel format on a quarter inch wide tape in which it is possible at the end of the first side to turn the reel over and continue. At the end of the second side, track three is selected and the process continues until there are four parallel tracks on the tape. 四声迹是在四分之一英寸宽的磁带上的音频卷到卷格式。其中可以在第一面的末端翻转盘并继续，在第二面的末尾选择声迹三，此后继续延续直到磁带上有四个平行声迹。
radiation damage 辐射损伤	See solarisation. 见过度曝光。
rain 雨幕	Rain is the vertical scratching of a movie film, which is caused by dirt or malfunction of the projector. 雨幕是由于灰尘或放映机故障引起的，对胶片的垂直划伤。
recording 录音	a. A recording is a physical representation of sound or vision preserved on a playback carrier such as a gramophone record, CD or magnetic tape. b. Recording is the act of creating the physical representation of sound or vision on playback carrier. a. 录音是保留在回放载体（如留声机唱片，CD或磁带）上的声音或视觉的物理表现。b. 录制是在播放载体上创建声音或视觉的物理表现行为。
reel to reel 卷到卷／带盘驱动	A reel to reel recording is one made using audio tape contained on open reels, rather than in cassettes or cartridges. 卷到卷录音是使用包含在敞开的卷中，而不是卡式磁带或盒式磁带中的录音带制作。
reflective layer 反光层	The reflective layer in a CD or Minidisc is a mirror-like surface from which the laser beam is bounced back. The reflective layer is modified in order to store digital information for reading. The reflective layer is usually made of aluminium, although silver and gold are also used. CD或小型磁盒中的反光层是一个类似镜子的表面，激光束会从该表面反射回来，修改反光层以便存储用于读取的数字信息。反光层通常由铝制成，同时也会使用金银。

reprint 重印	A reprint is a print from the original negative, made long after (usually more than 5 years) the date of the image capture or out of its original context. 重印是从原始底片上印相而成的，是在拍摄日期之后很久（通常超过5年）或脱离原始环境制作的。
resin coated paper 树脂涂布纸	Resin coated paper is paper which has a white polyethylene layer (containing titanium dioxide) between paper support and emulsion and a clear polyethylene layer on the back. It allows for much shorter processing times than fibre base paper. 树脂涂布纸是在纸托和乳液之间有一层白色聚乙烯层（含二氧化钛），背面有一层透明的聚乙烯层的纸。它的处理时间比纤维原纸短很多。
resolution 分辨率	The resolution of an imaging method is the smallest detail that it can record. 成像方法的分辨率是它可以记录的最小细节。
restoration (2) 视听修复 (2)	Restoration is the enhancement, often undertaken electronically or digitally, of an audio or video recording towards its supposed original state or performance. It applies primarily to the audio and video content rather than the restoration of the physical carrier. 修复是对音频或视频录制品进行的增强，通常以电子或数字方式进行，使其恢复到原来的状态或性能。它主要适用于音频和视频内容，而不是物理恢复。
reversal development 反转显影	Reversal development is the process of turning a negative material into a direct positive material. 反转显影是把底片材料变成直接正片材料的过程。
rewinding 倒带	Rewinding is the process of returning to the beginning of a recorded programme or beginning of an audio or video tape. 倒带是返回到已录制节目的开头或音频或录像带开头的过程。
roll film 胶卷	A roll film is a non-perforated photographic film with a width of 60 mm and a length of 120 or 220 mm. 胶卷胶片是一种宽度为60毫米、长度为120或220毫米的无穿孔摄影胶片。
rough cut 粗剪	A rough cut is the roughly assembled version of a film. 粗剪是胶片的大致拼接版。
safety film 安全胶片	A safety film is a cellulose acetate or polyester-based film with reduced flammability. 安全胶片是指可燃性降低的醋酸纤维素或聚酯基薄膜。
salted paper 盐渍纸	Salted paper is printing-out paper with an image of colloidal silver embedded in the paper surface. It is created by treating a sheet of paper in a (sodium-) chloride and silver nitrate solution and contact printing with a negative. 盐渍纸是胶态银的图像嵌入纸张表面的印相纸。它是通过在氯化钠和硝酸银溶液中处理一张纸，然后用底片接触印相而成的。

screech and squeal 尖叫声（磁带）	Screech and squeal are properties of recording tapes that have dried out and need re-lubrication. It can result in the oxide being deposited on tape heads and guides. Re-lubrication is not a long-term solution and the tapes should be copied as soon as possible. 尖叫声是已经变干并需要重新润滑的录音带的特性。重新润滑可能会导致氧化物沉积在磁头和导板上，不是长久的解决方案，应尽快复制磁带。
screen plate or film 筛板或薄膜	See colour screen plate or film. 见彩色丝网印板。
secondary support 辅助支撑物	A secondary support is the mounting material used to stabilise or present a photograph. 辅助支撑物是用来稳定或呈现照片的安装材料。
sheet film 单张胶卷	A sheet film is a single sheet of photographic film material. Standard sizes are or were 6x9 cm, 9x12 cm, 4x5", 13x18 cm, 5x7", 18x24 cm, 8x10". 单张胶卷是一张照相胶片材料。标准尺寸目前仍然包括：6x9 cm, 9x12 cm, 4x5", 13x18 cm, 5x7", 18x24 cm 和 8x10"。
shellac disc 虫胶唱片	A shellac disc is a coarse grooved audio recording on a disc whose surface is made from moulded shellac. The shellac compound can include fillers of clay, limestone, and carbon black. The discs were designed to be rotated at or around 78 revolutions per minute, so were frequently called 78s. 虫胶唱片是一种粗纹有凹槽的录音唱片，它的表面是由模压的虫胶制成的。虫胶化合物可以包括填料、石灰石和炭黑的填充剂。转虫胶唱片。唱片的设计转速为每分钟78转左右，所以常被称为78转虫胶唱片。
shoe-string 绞带	A shoe-string is an excessively stretched polyester audio or video tape forming a long round narrow shape. This damage to the tape is often caused by a sudden stop during rewinding, or trapping of tape in an audio cassette, especially on poorly maintained equipment. 绞带是过度拉伸的聚酯音频或视频带形成一条细长的圆形。磁带的这种损坏通常是由于倒带过程中突然停止或磁带被卡在录音带中引起的，特别是在维护不善的设备上。
shrinkage (2) 收缩 (2)	Shrinkage is dimensional loss of cellulose nitrate or acetate film base, which is caused by material decomposition due to ageing. 收缩是硝酸纤维素或醋酸纤维薄膜基片尺寸的损失，是由于材料老化而引起的。
signal 信号	A signal is a fluctuating electrical current carrying audio, video or digital information. 信号是承载音频，视频或数字信息的波动电流。
signal processing 信号处理	Signal processing is the electronic modification of audio or video information to remove unwanted noise or to create special effects such as reverberation. 信号处理是对音频或视频信息进行电子修改，以消除不必要的噪声或产生诸如混响之类的特殊效果。

silver bromide gelatin paper 溴化银明胶纸	Silver bromide gelatin paper is a kind of developing-out paper with mostly neutral-black image tone due to silver bromide as light sensitive component. 溴化银明胶纸是一种显相纸，由于溴化银是感光成分，其图像色调大多为中性黑色。
silver dye bleach print 银染料漂白印花	In a silver dye bleach print, non-image-forming azo dyes are destroyed by oxidating agents in the developer to form direct-positive color images. 在银染料漂白印花中，非成像偶氮染料被显影剂中的氧化剂破坏，形成直接的正色图像。
silver gelatin P.O.P. 银明胶P.O.P.	Silver gelatin P.O.P. is silver gelatin printing-out paper. 银色明胶 P.O.P. 是指银色明胶印相纸。
silver gelatin paper 银明胶纸	Silver gelatin paper is any developing-out or printing-out paper based on silver as image forming substance and gelatin as image binder. 银色明胶纸是以银为成像物质，明胶为图像粘合剂的显相纸或印相纸。
silver halide 卤化银	Silver halides are light-sensitive components of silver and halides (like silver bromide, silver chloride and silver iodide). They are used in most photographic materials. 卤化银是银和卤化物（如溴化银、氯化银和碘化银）的光敏成分。它们用于大多数的摄影材料中。
silver mirroring 银镜反应	See colloidal silver deposit. 见胶体银沉积。
slide 幻灯片 / 正片	See transparency. 见正片。
snow 雪花点	Snow is random noise interference on a TV screen or severe sparkle on film. 雪花点是电视屏幕上的随机噪音干扰或电影中的剧烈闪光。
soft focus 柔焦	An image in soft focus has been deliberately blurred by lens design, filters or light-scattering objects in front of or behind the lens. 柔焦中的图像通过镜头设计、滤光片或镜头前后的散射物体而刻意变得模糊。
solarisation (1) 过度曝光 (1)	In photography, solarisation is a decrease in density due to strong overexposure. A pseudo solarisation effect (Sabatier effect) can be achieved by shortly exposing photographic material to light during development. 在摄影中，过度曝光是由于过分强烈的曝光而导致的密度降低。通过在显影过程中将感光材料短时间暴露在光下，可以实现假过度曝光效果（萨巴蒂迪亚效应）。
sparkle 麻点	Sparkles are images of dust on film prints. 麻点是影片洗印过程中灰尘的影像。
splice 拼接头	A splice is a joint between two parts of a recording on cinema or an audio recording, made by using either pressure sensitive adhesive tape or adhesive. The adhesive used in ordinary domestic tape quickly deteriorates causing the joint to fail. The adhesive can contaminate adjacent layers in the tape pack causing them to stick to one another on playback. 拼接头是使用压敏胶带或粘合剂将电影院现场录音或录音带的两段之间接合的连接处。普通家用胶带所用的粘合剂会迅速变质而导致接头无法粘合。粘合剂会污染磁带包中的相邻层，导致它们在重放时相互粘连。

sputtering 溅射	Sputtering is the application of the magneto-optical layer on to a polycarbonate surface used in Minidiscs by applying the liquid as droplets. 溅射是通过将液体以液滴形式，施加到微型光盘使用的聚碳酸酯表面上的磁光层。
stereo 立体	See stereophonic sound. 见立体声。
stereophonic sound 立体声	Stereophonic sound is reproduced sound which appear spatially placed simulating how the human ear would have heard the original sound. For example, the sound output simulates the layout of a band with instruments to the left and right, and singer in centre. In practice most stereo is contrived using multitrack and other methods of playback. There are many variations on stereophonic reproduction, some employing multi-speaker arrangements situated around the listener. 立体声是在空间模拟人耳听到原始声音时再现的声音，例如，声音输出模拟一个乐队的布局，乐器在左、右，歌手在中间。在实践中，大多数立体声都是利用多轨和其他重放方法来实现的。立体声重现的方式有很多方式，有些采用在听众周围安排多个扬声器的方法。
sticky shed syndrome 粘接剂脱落综合症	See sticky tape syndrome. 见胶带综合症。
sticky tape syndrome 胶带综合症	Sticky tape syndrome is a hydrolytic chemical reaction in the binder of audio and video tapes which react with water from the atmosphere causing the binder of the tape to become sticky and unplayable. The audio and video may be retrieved by baking. 胶带综合症是音频和视频磁带黏结剂中的一种水解化学反应，它与大气中的水发生反应，导致磁带黏结剂变得粘稠且无法播放。音频和视频可以通过烘干来恢复。
still 剧照	A still is a photograph taken before, during or after shooting a film scene, for documentation or advertising purposes. 剧照是在拍摄电影之前、期间或之后拍摄的照片，用于记录或广告。
stray magnetic field 杂散磁场	A stray magnetic field is a unwanted magnetic field capable of erasing or partially erasing magnetic signals on audio and video tape. Sources of stray magnetic fields include dynamic loudspeakers and microphones, headphones, magnetic key fobs, fridge magnets etc. Steel shelving can also possess magnetic fields strong enough to erase audio tape – video tapes being less at risk because of their higher coercivity. 杂散磁场是一种有害的磁场，能够擦除或部分擦除音频和视频磁带上的磁信号。杂散磁场的来源包括动态扬声器和麦克风、耳机、磁性钥匙扣、冰箱磁铁等。钢架也可以拥有强大的磁场，足以擦除录音带--录像带的风险较小，因为其矫顽力较高。

stylus 手写笔	A stylus is usually a specially shaped semi-precious stone designed to run in the continuous groove of a gramophone record or cylinder. The stylus conveys the lateral and vertical movement to the electronics of the record deck. Early forms of stylus and the weight applied to it in order to prevent damage to the recording surface, as well as ensuring good technical transfer of the information. 手写笔通常是一种特殊形状的半宝石，设计目的是用于留声机唱片或圆筒的连续凹槽中的延伸。手写笔将横向和纵向运动传递到记录台的电子设备。早期形式的测针和施加在它身上的重量，以防止损坏记录表面，以及确保信息的良好技术传输。
substrate (2) 衬底 (2)	In an audio and/or video recording, the substrate is a structural support onto which thin coatings of carrier material are deposited. For example, polyester foil is the substrate of a video tape and the polycarbonate disc is the substrate of a compact disc. 在音频和/或视频记录中，衬底是结构支撑物，载体材料的薄涂层沉积在该载体上，例如，聚酯箔是录像带的衬底，而聚碳酸酯光盘是小型磁盘的衬底。
subtitle 字幕	Subtitles are the printed dialogue (translated in foreign films) which appears at the bottom of the screen. 字幕是显示在屏幕底部打印出来的对话文字（通常在国外电影中出现，是翻译后的文字）。
sulfiding 硫化物沉淀	See colloidal silver deposit. 见胶体银沉积。
support (5) 支撑	See also primary support and secondary support. 见主要支撑物和辅助支撑物。
S-VHS S-VHS	S-VHS stands for Super Video Home System which is a video format for domestic hand-held video cameras offering higher quality than conventional VHS video tape. S-VHS即"超级视频家庭系统"，这是一种用于家用手持摄像机的视频格式，提供了比传统的VHS录像带更高的质量。
swarf 木屑	Swarf is the filaments of cellulose nitrate or acetate produced by disc cutting machines cutting into the soft surface of instantaneous discs. 木屑是由圆盘切割机切割成瞬时圆盘的柔软表面后，产生的硝酸纤维素或醋酸纤维素的细丝。
synchronisation 同步	Synchronisation is the process of aligning any separate sound track with a picture image. 同步是将任何单独的音轨与图片图像对准的过程。
tail-out 脱尾	Reel to reel audio tapes are said to be tail-out when played to the end of the tape and not rewound. The advantages of this procedure include a reduction in print through and tension in the tape pack. 卷到卷录音带播放到录音带的末端时，被称作是尾脱而非倒带。此过程的优点包括减少透录和避免磁带回卷时过紧。

talbotype 卡罗法	See calotype. 见碘化银相纸。
tape (2) 磁带（2）	Audio and video tape, used to record and replay audio and video images, consists of a long thin ribbon available in various widths. It is made of a flexible sheet coated with a binder incorporating magnetic particles. Various materials have been used to make tape substrate including paper, cellulose acetate, and polyester. A wide variety of magnetic particles have been used including ferric oxide and chromium dioxide. Tape is often housed in a plastic cassette to prevent physical damage. 音频和视频磁带，用于记录和重放音频和视频图像，由一条不同宽度细长的带子组成。它由涂有粘合剂加磁粉的柔性板制成。已经使用了各种材料来制作胶带基材，包括纸、醋酸纤维素和聚酯。磁性颗粒的种类繁多，包括氧化铁和二氧化铬。磁带通常装在塑料盒中，以防止物理损坏。
tape pack 磁带包	The tape pack is magnetic recording tape wound uniformly round a common point such as the centre of a reel. 磁带包是均匀地围绕公共点（例如卷轴中心）缠绕的录音磁带。
technicolor 彩色印片法	Technicolor is a dye imbibition process which is used to produce presentation copies of a movie film. 彩色印片法是一种染料吸取过程，用于制作电影胶片的演示拷贝。
tinting 着色	Tinting is the overall colouring of an image layer or image support by incorporation of a dye. 着色是通过掺入染料使图像层或图像支撑体整体着色。
tintype 锡版照相法	A tintype is a collodion positive on black metal. 锡版照相法是在黑色金属上实施的玻璃板照相法。
tonal value 色调值	Tonal value is the local density of a photograph, including its colour. 色调值是照片（包括其颜色）的局部密度。
toning 调色	Toning is the conversion of metallic image silver into different silver compounds or its replacement by other metals or dyes. In most cases, image stability increases rather than diminishes. 调色是将金属图像银转换成不同的含银化合物或通过使用其他金属或染料生成其替代物。大多数情况下，图像稳定性会增加而不是降低。
transfer (2) 转印	See bromoil transfer and oil transfer. 见溴化油转印和油转印。
transparency 正片	A transparency is a translucent image on film or glass for projection. It is usually larger than 35mm. See also slide. 正片是胶片或玻璃上用于投影的半透明图像。通常大于35mm。另见幻灯片/正片。

trapezoidal error 梯形误差	A trapezoidal error is an unwanted change in the angle of a helical scan video track on a magnetic video tape. One of the commonest reasons this occurs is incorrect tensioning and positioning of the tape guide assemblies in the video machine. Trapezoidal error frequently results in damage to one edge of the video tape as the tape leaves the cassette at an incorrect angle, or is returned to its cassette at the wrong angle thus catching on the guides of the cassette. Although usually a video phenomenon, it can also occur in DAT recordings rendering them unplayable. 梯形误差是录像磁带上螺旋扫描视频轨道角度的不必要的变化。发生这种情况的最常见原因之一是录像机中的导带组件收紧和定位不正确。梯形误差经常导致录像带的一个边缘受损，因为磁带以错误的角度离开磁带盒，或者以错误的角度返回磁带盒，从而卡在磁带盒的导向上。虽然通常是一种录像现象，但它也可能发生在DAT录音中，使其无法播放。
U-matic U-matic 系统	U-matic is a semi-professional video tape format. U-matic是一种半专业的录像带格式。
underexposure 曝光不足	Underexposure occurs when the amount of light to which a photographic material is exposed has not reached the minimum amount of light for which a photographic material is designed. Underexposure leads to reduced information. 曝光不足是指感光材料的曝光量没有达到感光材料设计的最小光量。曝光不足会导致信息减少。
unsensitised 非感光的	An unsensitised emulsion is an emulsion which is sensitive only to the ultraviolet and blue light. 非感光乳剂是一种只对紫外线和蓝光敏感的乳剂。
VHS 家用视频系统	VHS is a domestic video tape format in a cassette case housing half inch wide video tape. VHS is an acronym of Video Home System. See also S-VHS. VHS是一种家用录像带格式，位于带半英寸宽录像带的盒式磁带盒中。VHS是Video Home System（家用视频系统）的缩写。另请参阅S-VHS。
VHS-C VHS-C	VHS-C is a physically a smaller form of VHS for use in camcorders. It can be replayed in domestic VHS machines using an adapter to make the casing fit, the tape width being the same as VHS. VHS-C在物理上是一种较小的VHS形式，可用于便携式摄像机。可使用适配器使其适合在家用录像机中重放，磁带宽度与VHS相同。
VHS-Compact 家用录像光盘	See VHS-C. 见家用录像光盘。
video 视频	Video is the recording and playback of a physical representation of something seen. 视频是对所见事物的物理表现的记录和回放。
Video Home System 家用视频系统	See VHS. 见家用视频系统。

video noise 视频噪声	See noise (2). 见噪声。
video tape 录像带	See tape . 见磁带。
Video-8 Video-8	Video-8 is a video cassette system used in amateur portable video cameras. Video-8是便携式摄像机中业余爱好者使用的盒式录像带系统。
viewing copy 影片副本	A viewing copy is the final film version as it is shown in a movie theatre. 影片副本是供电影院播放的电影最终版本。
viewing table 胶片观片器	A viewing table is a monitor-equipped viewing device for movie film. 胶片观片器是配有监视器的察看电影胶片的设备。
vinegar syndrome 醋酸综合症	Vinegar syndrome is the release of acetic acid during the decomposition of cellulose acetate materials. 醋酸综合症是乙酸纤维素材料分解过程中释放的乙酸导致的病害现象。
vintage print 复古印相	A vintage print is an original print, made by or authorised by the photographer in the close context and/or time proximity (usually less than 5 years) to the date of image capture. 复古印相是指由摄影师在距离拍摄日期较近的环境和/或时间范围内（通常不超过5年）制作或授权制作的原始印相。
virage 变色	A virage is the colouring of the image silver by dye absorption. 变色是通过吸收染料使银影像染色。
wet collodion process 棉胶湿片工艺	In the wet collodion process glass plates, hand-coated with a suspension of silver halides in collodion, are used to create in-camera negatives or collodion positives. The plates have to be exposed and processed while still wet. 在棉胶湿片工艺中，手工涂上胶棉中的卤化银悬浮液的玻璃板可用于制作相机底片或胶棉正片。胶棉板必须在湿润的情况下曝光和处理。
wire recording 钢丝录音	A wire recording is a spool of thin round or flat steel wire on to which a magnetic signal is recorded on a special recorder. Invented by Valdemar Poulsen who used 'strung out piano wire and an electromagnet attached connected to a microphone'. The record were commercially introduced in 1899 and extensively used as dictation machines, telephone answering machines, and exhibition announcements. The US Army used them extensively as field recorders. 钢丝录音是一卷薄的圆形或扁平钢丝的线轴，在其上将磁信号记录在特殊的录音机上。由瓦尔德玛·波尔森（Valdemar Poulsen）发明，他使用了"一串钢琴线和连接到麦克风的电磁铁"。录音机于1899年开始商业化，并被广泛用作听写机、电话应答机和展览公告。美国陆军将其作为野战录音机广泛使用。

wow and flutter 抖晃度	Wow and flutter are momentary variations in audio playback speed due to mechanical inadequacies in the recording and replay equipment resulting in audible changes in pitch. Wow refers to lower frequencies and flutter to higher audible frequencies. 抖晃度是音频回放速度的瞬时变化，这是由于录制和回放设备中的机械不足导致音高变化所致。哇声指较低的频率，而颤振则是较高的可听频率。
wrinkled emulsion layer 起皱乳液层	A wrinkled emulsion layer is the result of shrinkage of a support due to the ageing of film, often accompanied by delamination of the emulsion from the support. 起皱乳液层是由于薄膜老化导致支撑物收缩的结果，通常伴随着乳液从支架上剥离。

07

金 属
Metals

alpaka 镍白铜 / 德国银	Alpaka is a cupronickel alloy with about 55-65% copper, 7-30% nickel and the remainder zinc. 镍白铜是一种铜镍合金，含约55-65%的铜，7-30%的镍，其余为锌。
annealing (2) 退火 (2)	Annealing is the process of heating a metal to a temperature where its structure recrystallises, in order to remove work hardening and brittleness. For metals such as copper, silver or gold typical annealing temperatures are 600℃. 退火是将金属加热到一定温度使其再结晶，以消除加工硬化和脆性的处理过程。对于诸如铜、银或金等金属，典型的退火温度为600℃。
argentite 辉银矿	The mineral Argentite (silver sulphide Ag_2S) is one of the most common silver ores. 辉银矿（硫化银 Ag_2S）是最常见的银矿之一。
brazing 硬（钎）焊	Brazing is a soldering technique which uses a molten copper-zinc alloy (brass) to join two pieces of metal. 硬（钎）焊是使用熔融的铜锌合金（黄铜）将两块金属结合在一起的焊接技术。
carburizing 渗碳	Carburizing of iron is carried out by heating the metal in close contact with charcoal. Some carbon diffuses into the surface of the iron and generates a surface layer of hardenable steel on a wrought iron object (for example, a knife blade). 渗碳是通过加热与木炭紧密接触的金属来实现的，碳将扩散到铁的表面，并在熟铁器物（例如刀刃）上生成硬化的钢表层。
cathode 阴极	The cathode is the negative (reducing) electrode in an electrolytic or galvanic cell. Reduction usually occurs at the cathode, due to a gain of electrons. 阴极是电解质或原电池中的负（还原）电极。由于获得电子，还原反应通常发生在阴极。
cupellation 灰吹法	Cupellation is the traditional refining technique for silver by extracting silver ore or impure silver with molten lead in a crucible. 灰吹法是通过熔融的铅在坩埚中提纯银矿石或含杂质银的传统技术。
cyaniding of gold 氰化法	Cyaniding is the extraction of gold from crushed rocks with a concentrated cyanide solution which dissolves gold as a cyano complex. 氰化法是利用浓氰化物溶液将粉碎矿石中的金溶解成氰基络合物而提取金的方法。
damascening 叠钢 / 花纹钢	Damascening is a metalworking technique particularly for the manufacture of sword blades. Multiple layers of iron and steel with different carbon contents are forged together in patterns. The product combines the hardness of carbon steel with the toughness of wrought iron. 叠钢 / 花纹钢是一种特别是用于刀剑制造的金属加工技术。此技术将不同含碳量的多层钢铁锻造成各种图案，其产品兼具碳钢的硬度和铁的韧性。

electrode 电极	An electrode is a conductor through which an electric current enters (-, cathode) or leaves (+, anode) a medium. 电极是一种导体，电流通过导体输入（－，阴极）或导入（＋，阳极）介质。
finishing (2) 精加工 (2)	Finishing is the final process in metal manufacture, such as polishing and planishing. 精加工是金属制造中的最后一道工序，例如抛光和锤光。
galvanic 电的 / 电化的	Galvanic processes are electrochemical reactions and are named after the Italian 18th century physicist L. A. Galvani. 电化过程即电化学反应，以意大利18世纪物理学家L. A. Galvani的名字命名。
galvanic cell 原电池	A galvanic cell consists of a positive electrode (anode) attached by a conductor to a negative electrode (cathode). Both electrodes are in contact with an electrolyte which closes the electric circuit. 原电池由通过导体连接到负极（阴极）的正极（阳极）组成，两个电极均与电解液接触，形成一个闭合的电路。
metal 金属	A metal is a material which is crystalline when solid, opaque, ductile, malleable and good conductor of heat and electricity. See also metal object. 金属是一种固态时结晶的材料，不透明，有韧性，可塑性好，是热和电的良好导体，另见金属物体。
silver sulfide 硫化银	Silver sulfide (Ag_2S) is a common black corrosion product on silver. It was used for niello inlay. 硫化银（Ag_2S）是银上常见的黑色腐蚀产物，它用于乌银镶嵌物。
striking 压印	Striking is the normal technique to impress a design on a coin or medal by hitting a blank with a die engraved with a negative image. 压印是通过将坯料置于刻有负像的模具中敲击，将设计图案压在硬币或奖章上的常规技术。
weep 泪珠状腐蚀	An object is weeping when small droplets of liquid are produced at its surface as a result of deterioration. Examples are weeping iron during active corrosion and weeping plastics by the exudation of plasticisers. 器物劣化时在表面产生的泪滴状腐蚀产物。例如，铁器在腐蚀过程中及塑料在失去增塑剂后都会产生泪滴状腐蚀产物。
wrought bronze 熟铜（可锻青铜）	Wrought bronze is a malleable copper-tin alloy which is hammered into shape hot or cold with frequent annealing. These alloys do not contain more than a small amount of lead which would render them brittle. 熟铜是一种有延展性的铜锡合金，经过频繁的退火处理后，可冷热加工成形。这些合金只能含有很少量的铅，否则就会变脆。
archaeometallurgy 冶金考古	Archaeometallurgy investigates the prehistoric and historic practice of mining, metal smelting, refining, and the manufacture of metal objects. 冶金考古研究史前和历史时期人类的采矿、冶炼、精炼和金属器物制作活动。

electrode potential 电极电位	The electrode potential is the voltage of an electrode in an electrochemical cell measured against a reference electrode. 电极电位是相对于参考电极测得的电化学电池中的电极的电压。
counter electrode 对电极	The counter electrode is an auxiliary electrode in a galvanic cell used for the quantitative determination of corrosion properties of materials. It serves to carry the electric current created by the investigation. 对电极是原电池中的辅助电极，用于定量确定材料的腐蚀性能，它用于维持研究中产生的电流。
wet-grit blasting 湿喷砂	Wet-grit blasting is an abrasive and often destructive surface cleaning technique using grit and water to remove deposits from wall and other surfaces. The water reduces the amount of dust produced by the process. 湿喷砂是一种通常是破坏性的表面磨蚀清洁技术，使用砂砾和水去除墙壁和其他表面上的沉积物，水能减少该过程产生的粉尘。
anodic inhibitor 阳极钝化剂	An anodic inhibitor is an oxidising agent such as chromate which causes anodic protection (passivation) of a metal surface. 阳极钝化剂是一种对金属表面进行阳极保护（钝化）的氧化剂，例如，铬酸盐。
barrier coating 封护（涂）层	A barrier coating is a protective layer applied to a metal surface to prevent contact with harmful agents such as water and oxygen, and so inhibit corrosion. 封护（涂）层是施加于金属表面以防止其与有害物质（如水和氧气）接触，从而抑制腐蚀。
cathodic inhibitor 阴极缓蚀剂	A cathodic inhibitor is a corrosion protection agent such as a zinc salt or polyphosphate which reduce corrosion rates by forming deposits on the cathode. 阴极缓蚀剂是一种腐蚀保护剂，如锌盐或聚磷酸盐，通过在阴极上形成沉积物来降低腐蚀速率。
lute 密封胶泥	Lute is a soft adhesive material of varying composition that hardens over time. It is used for a wide range of applications, one of which is fixing and sealing window glass in the frame. 密封胶泥是一种柔软的粘性材料，成分多种多样，随着时间的推移会硬化。它有着广泛的用途，其中之一是将窗玻璃固定和密封在窗框中。
pickle 酸洗液	A pickle is a corrosive solution, usually an acid, which is used after annealing to remove oxides from the surface of a metal object. 酸洗液是一种腐蚀性溶液，通常是一种酸，在退火后用来去除金属物体表面的氧化物。
prime coat 底漆	The prime coat is the first layer in a protective or decorative coating. In the case of metals, it includes a corrosion inhibitor. In a paint system, it acts as a base to which further layers will adhere. 底漆是保护性或装饰性涂层的第一层。对于金属而言也起到缓蚀剂的作用。在漆层系统中，它是外层油漆附着的基础。

rivet (2) 铆钉 (2)	A rivet is a small metal peg passing through holes in metal pieces then hammered flat at both ends in order to join the pieces of metal permanently. 铆钉是一种在金属片上穿孔的小金属钉，两端用锤平后可将金属组件永久连接。
wash primer 蚀刻底漆	A wash primer is the first paint coat for metals and which provides corrosion protection. 蚀刻底漆是金属的第一道漆层，可提供防腐保护。
stainless steel 不锈钢	Stainless steel is an alloy of iron with chromium and other metals. A number of grades have been specified for different applications. 不锈钢是铁与铬和其他金属的合金，根据用途的不同分为多种等级。
Jenolite gel® 杰诺莱特凝胶®	Jenolite gel is a commercial rust remover in which the main active constituent is phosphoric acid. Jenolite has been used for the removal of rust stains on ceramic, glass and stone objects. The use of phosphoric acid has been shown to etch glass and is thought to form insoluble calcium phosphate salts in earthenware bodies. 杰诺莱特凝胶（商标名）是一种以磷酸为主要活性成分的工业除锈剂，用于去除陶瓷、玻璃和石材上的锈迹。现已证明使用磷酸能蚀刻玻璃，可以在陶器体内形成不溶性磷酸钙盐。
peen 锤顶	The peen of a hammer is the end of the hammer head. 锤子的锤顶指锤头的末端。
akaganeite 四方纤铁矿	Akaganeite is an iron(III) oxyhydroxide mineral (γ-FeOOH). It is a common iron corrosion product which forms only when high concentrations of chlorides are present. 四方纤铁矿是一种铁（III）氧氢氧化物矿物（γ-FeOOH）。它是一种常见的铁腐蚀产物，只有在高氯情况下形成。
atacamite 氯铜矿	Atacamite is a copper hydroxy chloride [$Cu_2(OH)_3Cl$] which is formed during bronze disease. It is a common constituent of green patina on copper. 氯铜矿是一种羟基氯化铜 [$Cu_2(OH)_3Cl$]，在发生青铜病时形成。氯铜矿是铜表面锈蚀的常见成分。
bimetallic corrosion 电偶腐蚀 （双金属腐蚀）	Bimetallic corrosion is galvanic corrosion occurring when two different metals are in contact with one another. 电偶腐蚀是当两种不同的金属相互接触时发生的电化学腐蚀。
brochantite 水胆矾	Brochantite ia a copper hydroxy sulphate [$Cu_4(SO_4)(OH)_6$] which is a typical constituent of green patina on copper in urban environments. 水胆矾是一种羟基硫酸铜 [$Cu_4(SO_4)(OH)_6$]，是城市环境中铜锈蚀的典型组成部分。
bronze disease 青铜病	Bronze disease is a disease that affects copper alloy objects and manifests itself under the surface of these objects in the form of voluminous pustules containing pale green powder. It is the result of the reaction of water with copper (I) chloride to form hydrated copper (II) chloride. 青铜病是一种侵蚀铜合金器物的病害，它在器物表面下以含淡绿色粉末的大量疱状物形式存在。它是水与氯化亚铜反应生成的二水合氯化铜。

cathodic corrosion 阴极腐蚀	Cathodic corrosion is a kind of corrosion that is accelerated by alkaline conditions at the cathode. It occurs especially in aluminum, zinc and lead. 阴极腐蚀是一种由于阴极碱性条件而加速的腐蚀，尤其在铝，锌和铅上最为常见。
catholyte 阴极电解液	In a galvanic cell the electrolyte surrounding the cathode is sometimes called catholyte. 在原电池中阴极周围的电解液有时被称为阴极电解液。
caustic cracking 碱腐蚀开裂	Caustic cracking is stress corrosion cracking caused by alkaline solutions concentrated in crevices. 碱腐蚀开裂是指在缝隙中富集碱性溶液引起的应力腐蚀开裂。
cavitation corrosion 空蚀 （穴蚀、空泡腐蚀）	Cavitation corrosion is a form of erosion-corrosion which manifests itself as roughened pits on the surface of a metal. 空蚀是冲蚀腐蚀的一种形式，表现为在金属表面产生粗糙的凹坑。
chalkonatronite 蓝铜钠石 （羟碳铜镍矿）	Chalkonatronite is a water soluble sodium copper carbonate $[Na_2Cu(CO_3)_2 \cdot 3(H_2O)]$ which is occasionally found as a copper corrosion product in arid climates (Egypt). 蓝铜钠石是一种水溶性的铜钠碳酸盐 $[Na_2Cu(CO_3)_2 \cdot 3(H_2O)]$，偶见于干旱条件下的铜腐蚀产物（埃及）。
concentration cell 浓差电池	A concentration cell is a galvanic cell driven by a difference in the available concentration of a reaction partner between anodic and cathodic areas, leading to localized corrosion. This occurs for example in crevices where the reactant is consumed faster by the corrosion reaction than it can be replenished by diffusion. 浓差电池是一个由阳极和阴极区域之间反应对活度差驱动的原电池，它会导致局部腐蚀。例如，腐蚀发生在缝隙处，在此处反应物腐蚀反应消耗的速度快于通过扩散补充的速度。
concentration polarization 浓差极化	Concentration polarization is polarization in a galvanic cell caused by ion concentration changes at the electrodes because of the ongoing electrochemical reaction in the cell. 浓差极化是因为电池中正在进行的电化学反应造成电极处离子浓度变化，从而引起的原电池中的极化。
corrosion fatigue 疲劳腐蚀	Corrosion fatigue of a metal is the formation of cracks or failure due to the effect of cyclical stresses in a corrosive environment. 金属的疲劳腐蚀是由于在腐蚀环境中循环应力的影响而形成的裂纹或破坏。
crevice corrosion 缝隙腐蚀	Crevice corrosion is the result of the formation of a concentration cell in a crevice, for instance through small differences in water retention. 缝隙腐蚀是缝隙中浓差电池形成的结果，例如通过保水量的微小差异。
dealloying 去合金化（腐蚀）/ 选择性腐蚀	Dealloying is a corrosion phenomenon where one component of an alloy is leached selectively, for example dezincification in the corrosion of brass. 去合金化是一种腐蚀现象，在此过程中，合金的一种成分被选择性地浸出，例如，黄铜腐蚀中的脱锌作用。

denickelification 脱镍	Denickelification is corrosion of copper-nickel alloys resulting from nickel being leached selectively from the alloy. Copper-nickel alloys generally display very good corrosion resistance. 脱镍是由于镍被选择性地从合金中浸出而导致的铜镍合金的腐蚀，铜镍合金通常显示出非常好的耐腐蚀性。
depolarization 去极化	Depolarization is the removal of hydrogen formed on the anode as part of a corrosion reaction. Hydrogen acts as a barrier and slows down further corrosion through polarization of the electrode. 去极化是将阳极上形成的氢作为腐蚀反应的一部分除去，氢起着屏障的作用，并通过电极的极化减缓进一步的腐蚀。
destannification 脱锡	Destannification would be the loss of tin from an alloy, which does not happen because tin forms insoluble oxide hydrates particularly on corroding low tin bronzes (single phase copper-tin alloys). 脱锡会造成合金中锡腐蚀流失。特别是在低锡青铜（单相铜锡合金）腐蚀时不会发生脱锡，因为锡会形成难溶的碱式氧化物，阻止其流失。
dezincification 脱锌	Dezincification is a common corrosion phenomenon of brasses (copper-zinc alloys). Zinc as the less noble partner is leached selectively from the alloy. 脱锌是黄铜（铜锌合金）的常见腐蚀现象，从合金中选择性地浸出惰性较弱的锌。
differential aeration cell 氧浓差电池	A differential aeration cell is a galvanic cell driven by a difference in the available concentration of oxygen between anodic and cathodic areas, leading to localized corrosion. This occurs for example in crevices where oxygen is faster consumed by the corrosion reaction than it can be replenished by diffusion. 氧浓差电池是由阳极和阴极区域之间的氧气活度差驱动的原电池，它会导致局部腐蚀。例如，在缝隙中氧气反应消耗的速度快于通过扩散补充的速度。
diffusion limited current 扩散抑制电流	If the current in a galvanic cell is diffusion limited the overall rate of the electrochemical reaction is determined by the rate at which the concentration of one of the reaction partners on the electrode surface is replenished by diffusion towards the electrode. 如果原电池中的电流受到扩散限制，则电化学反应的总速率取决于该电极表面上反应对之一的浓度可否由扩散得到补充的速率。
electrochemical cell 电化学电池	An electrochemical cell consists of a positive electrode (anode) attached to a negative electrode (cathode). Both electrodes are in contact with an electrolyte which closes the circuit. 电化学电池由与负极（阴极）相连的正极（阳极）组成，两个电极都与闭合电路的电解质接触。
erosion-corrosion 冲刷腐蚀	Erosion-corrosion of metal is a deterioration reaction that is accelerated by erosion caused by, for instance, fast flowing solutions carrying an abrasive which damages a protective film. 金属的冲刷腐蚀是一种劣化反应，该反应可由冲刷侵蚀而加快。例如，快速流动的液体会裹挟磨料从而损坏金属的保护膜。

filiform corrosion 丝状腐蚀	Filiform corrosion on metals manifests itself in a characteristic linear pattern. It is caused by differential aeration underneath a lacquer or other protective coating. 金属上的丝状腐蚀表现为典型的线性模式。这是由漆或其他保护性涂层下面的不均匀透气引起的。
fretting corrosion 微动 / 微振腐蚀	Fretting corrosion of metal is deterioration caused by repetitive slip at the interface between two surfaces. 金属的微动腐蚀是由金属两个表面之间的界面重复滑动引起的劣化。
galvanic corrosion 电化学腐蚀	Galvanic corrosion is a kind of corrosion that results from an electrolytic cell set up either between two different metals or a metal and a non-metallic conductor, such as carbon. The more reactive metal oxidises. 电化学腐蚀是一种腐蚀现象，是由于在两种不同金属或金属与非金属导体（例如碳）之间建立的原电池而引起的，活性越强的金属越易氧化。
hydrogen embrittlement 氢脆	Hydrogen embrittlement is the weakening of metal because of internal evolution of hydrogen gas. At high temperatures such as during welding or plasma treatment, iron and steel may absorb atomic hydrogen which is released on cooling and builds up high pressures in pores and defects inside the metal. 氢脆是由于内部产生氢气而导致的金属的弱化。在高温下（例如在焊接或等离子处理期间），钢铁可能吸收冷却时释放出的原子氢，并积累较高的氢气压。
hydrogen overvoltage 氢超电压	Hydrogen overvoltage is the extra voltage required to overcome the barrier caused by the accumulation of hydrogen in an galvanic cell. Electrochemical corrosion of a metal with the formation of hydrogen requires a voltage higher than the equilibrium potential of the galvanic cell because of an accumulation of hydrogen on the cathode which acts as a barrier and slows down the reaction. 氢过电压是为了克服由原电池中氢积累引起的势垒所需的额外电压，形成氢的金属的电化学腐蚀需要高于平衡电位的电压。这是因为氢在阴极上积聚减慢了反应速度。
immunity 免蚀性	Immunity denotes the ability of a metal to resist corrosion as a result of thermodynamic stability. 免蚀性表示金属由于热力学稳定性而获得的抗腐蚀能力。
intercrystalline corrosion 晶间腐蚀	Intercrystalline corrosion occurs where a corrosion cell forms in a metal between the unstable, high energy area at the grain or crystal boundary and the lower energy area at its centre. 晶间腐蚀发生于晶粒或晶体边界的不稳定高能区和晶粒中心的低能区之间所形成的腐蚀电池区域。
localized corrosion 局部腐蚀	Localized corrosion is corrosion progressing in small areas of a metal surface at a much faster rate than over the rest of the surface. Examples are crevice corrosion or pitting corrosion. 局部腐蚀是指金属表面发生的小面积腐蚀，其速度比表面上剩余部分快得多，例如，缝隙腐蚀或点蚀。

magnetite **磁铁矿**	Magnetite is the black iron (III) oxide mineral (Fe_3O_4) which is a common iron corrosion product. 磁铁矿是黑色氧化铁矿物 (III) (Fe_3O_4)，是一种常见的铁腐蚀产物。
metal dusting **金属尘化**	Metal dusting is a form of high temperature corrosion which produces dust-like corrosion products and occasionally pitting of susceptible metal surfaces. 金属尘化是高温腐蚀的一种形式，会产生粉尘状腐蚀产物，偶尔会在敏感的金属表面产生点蚀。
nantokite **铜盐**	The grey copper (I) chloride nantokite (CuCl) is an important intermediate in the rapid corrosion of copper alloys in the presence of chlorides. See also bronze disease. 在氯化物存在的情况下，氯化亚铜(CuCl) 是铜合金快速腐蚀的重要介质，另见青铜病。
overvoltage **过电压**	An overvoltage is an extra potential applied in a galvanic cell in order to maintain the electrochemical reaction. The galvanic cell is not in equilibrium due to electrode polarisation. 过电压是原电池中为维持电化学反应而施加的额外电势。原电池由于电极极化而处于非平衡态。
paratacamite **副氯铜矿**	Paratacamite is a copper hydroxy mineral [$Cu_2(OH)_3Cl$] which is a typical constituent of green patina on copper. Its crystal structure is different from Atacamite. 副氯铜矿是一种铜羟基矿物 [$Cu_2(OH)_3Cl$] ，是铜表面的铜绿的典型成分，其晶体结构与氯铜矿不同。
passive **钝化**	A metal in its passive state carries an inert surface layer as a result of anodic corrosion protection. 由于阳极腐蚀保护，处于钝化状态的金属带有惰性表面层。
polarization **极化**	Polarization is a surface reaction which occurs when a current is applied in a galvanic cell. It reduces the voltage between anode and cathode and slows down the electrochemical reaction. An overvoltage in addition to the standard potential difference must be applied to maintain the reaction. 极化是在原电池中施加电流时发生的表面反应。它降低了阳极和阴极之间的电位差并减慢了电化学反应。除标准电势差外，还需施加过电压以维持反应。
redeposited metal **再沉积金属**	During corrosion, a redeposited metal is one that has been precipitated out of solution onto an object. Metals such as copper or silver with a high standard potential are often deposited on surrounding base metal objects when dissolved ions come into contact with a less noble metal such as iron. 在腐蚀过程中，再沉积金属是从溶液中沉淀到物体上的一种金属。当溶解的离子与金属接触时，具有高标准电极电势的金属（例如铜或银）通常沉积在周围的贱金属物体上。
redox blemish **氧化还原缺陷**	Redox blemishes are small circular spots of colloidal silver deposit of orange-reddish colour in microfilm and RC paper caused by image silver deterioration. 氧化还原缺陷是由于影像银的变质而产生的银胶体沉积缩微胶卷和RC纸上形成的橘红色小圆斑。

redox potential 氧化还原电位	The redox potential is the electrical potential which describes the reducing or oxidising character of an electrochemical reaction partner. 氧化还原电位是描述电化学反应配体还原或氧化特性的电位。
rust 铁锈	Rust is a mixture of hydrated iron oxides. It is an orange/red corrosion product found on ferrous metals. 铁锈是水合氧化铁的混合物，它是黑色金属上的橙色/红色腐蚀产物。
scale 氧化皮 / 锻鳞	A scale is a small, thin, flat piece of iron oxides which is detached from the metal surface during the forging process. 氧化皮是在锻造过程中从金属表面脱落的一小块薄而扁平的氧化铁。
silver chloride 氯化银	Silver chloride (AgCl) is a white insoluble light-sensitive silver corrosion product which forms on silver in the presence of chlorides. 氯化银（AgCl）是一种白色的不可溶光敏性银腐蚀产物，在氯化物存在的情况下形成于银表面。
standard electrode potential 标准电极电势	The standard electrode potential of a metal is the voltage, the electrode potential, which reduces metal ions to their metallic state under standard conditions relative to a standard hydrogen reference electrode. 金属的标准电极电势是指相对于标准氢参比电极，在标准条件下将金属离子还原到金属状态的电压，即电极电势。
surface corrosion 表面腐蚀	Surface corrosion denotes the chemical deterioration of a metal only on its surface. 表面腐蚀是指仅发生于金属表面的化学腐蚀。
tarnish 暗锈	Tarnish on a metal surface is a thin film of corrosion products which causes discolouration. 暗锈是指导致金属表面变色的腐蚀薄层。
tenorite 黑铜矿	Black cupric oxide tenorite (CuO) is a mineral formed in equilibrium with red cuprite (Cu_2O) as a copper corrosion product in the absence of chlorides. 黑铜矿（CuO）是一种在无氯化物情况下与红铜矿（Cu_2O）相平衡形成的矿物。
tin pest 锡疫	Tin pest is the transformation reaction of the metallic structure of tin to its non-metallic modification, below 13℃. However, the reaction is too slow to be significant. Non-metallic spots on tin objects are almost always tin corrosion products, not non-metallic elemental tin. 锡疫是在13℃以下锡的金属结构向非金属改性的转化反应，但反应太慢而不显著。锡器上的非金属斑点几乎都是锡的腐蚀产物。
vivianite 蓝铁矿	Vivianite is an iron (II) phosphate mineral [$Fe_3(PO_4)_2 \cdot 8H_2O$] which may form as a corrosion product on archaeological iron if the surrounding soil is rich in phospates. 蓝铁矿是一种铁(II)磷酸盐矿物 [$Fe_3(PO_4)_2 \cdot 8H_2O$]，如果周围土壤富含磷酸盐，可能会在考古铁器上形成腐蚀产物。

surface enrichment 表面富集	Surface enrichment is a metal corrosion phenomenon affecting, for example, gold-silver or silver-copper alloys. It refers to the preferential dissolution of one alloying element which increases the concentration of another (usually the more noble component) on the surface. 表面富集是影响诸如金银或银铜合金的一种金属腐蚀现象。它指一种合金元素的优先溶解，这增加了另一种合金元素（通常为更贵重的成分）的浓度。
electrolyte 电解液	An electrolyte is a solution closing the electric circuit between anode and cathode in an electrochemical cell. 电解液是封闭电化学电池中阳极和阴极之间电路的溶液。
aluminium bronze 铝青铜	Aluminium bronzes are alloys composed of minimum 70% copper and a usual content of 14% aluminium. In addition to aluminium, the alloys contain iron, nickel, manganese or silicon but no zinc. 铝青铜通常是由不少于70%的铜和14%的铝组成的合金。除铝以外，这种合金还含有铁、镍、锰或硅，但不含锌。
argentarium 铅锡器	Argentarium is the latin name of an alloy of tin and lead. Due to its silver-gray colour it was used by the Romans as protective and decorative thin layer on the surface mostly of copper alloy objects. Argentarium 是锡铅合金的拉丁名称。由于呈银灰色，它被罗马人主要用作铜合金物体表面的保护和装饰薄层。
base metal 基体金属	Base metal is the major part of an alloy. 基体金属是合金的主要部分。
bell metal 响铜	Bell metal is a brass alloy composed of copper and 15 - 40% tin and small amounts of zinc, lead or iron. 响铜是一种黄铜合金，由铜和15 - 40%的锡以及少量的锌、铅或铁组成。
Britannia metal 不列颠合金	Britannia metal is a silver-coloured alloy of 80-90 % tin with antimony, copper, lead and / or zinc. The metal was first developed in the late 18th century. 不列颠合金是一种银色合金，含80-90%的锡，以及锑、铜、铅和/或锌。这种金属最早是在18世纪末研发的。
cast bronze 铸造青铜	Cast bronzes are copper-tin alloys which were melted and cast into moulds. They usually contain lead to lower the melting point and improve casting properties. 铸造青铜器是铜锡合金，可将其熔化后铸造成模具。通常含有铅，以降低熔点和改善铸造性能。
cast iron 铸铁	Cast iron is iron with more than 2.11%carbon which is hard and brittle and can only be cast, not forged. 铸铁是含碳量超过2.11%的铁碳合金。铸铁性硬且脆，只能铸造，不能锻造。
Champleve enamel 錾胎珐琅	Champleve is an enamelling technique where enamel is introduced into troughs or cells, moulded in or cut out of the metal base. 錾胎珐琅是一种搪瓷技术，将珐琅质引入槽或小室中，在金属基底上模制或切割而成。

Cloisonne enamel 景泰蓝	Cloisonne is an enamelling technique where enamel is introduced into areas defined by metal strips or wires soldered in place on the underlying metal. 景泰蓝是一种搪瓷技术，将搪瓷引入金属条或金属丝限定的区域，金属条或金属丝焊接在底层金属上的适当位置。
ferrous metal 钢铁	A ferrous metal is an alloy composed mostly of iron, such as wrought iron and steel. 钢铁是一种主要由铁组成的合金，如熟铁和钢。
nickel silver 镍银	Nickel silver is a common silver coloured alloy of copper with typically 20-30 % nickel. 镍银是一种常见的银色的铜合金，通常含有20-30%的镍。
non-ferrous metal 有色金属	A non-ferrous metal is a metal other than iron and steel. Copper and its alloys, and the precious metals are examples of non-ferrous metals. 有色金属是除钢铁以外的金属，例如，铜及其合金和贵金属都是有色金属。
paktong 白铜	Paktong is a silver coloured alloy of copper, (42-58%), nickel, (9-13) %, and zinc, (33- 46%). It was used in China many centuries before it became known to western civilizations. 白铜是一种银色的合金，铜含量为42-58%，镍含量为9-13%，锌含量为33-46%。在西方人认识它之前，它已经在中国被使用了许多世纪。
pewter 镴	Pewter is an alloy between tin (80-90%) and lead (20-10%) which has recently been replaced by antimony. 镴是锡（80-90%）和铅（20-10%）的合金，铅最近已被锑替代。
precious metals 贵金属	Precious metals are relatively expensive metals like gold, platinum or silver with a high electrochemical standard potential. 贵金属是相对昂贵的金属，如金、铂或银，具有较高的电化学标准电位。
steel 钢	Steel is an alloy of iron with typically 0.02-2.11 % carbon, which can be hardened. It may contain additional alloying elements such as chromium, nickel, manganese, silicon or phosphorus. 钢是一种含碳量一般为0.02-2.11%的可硬化的铁合金，可能也含有其他的合金元素，如铬、镍、锰、硅或磷。
wrought iron 熟铁	Wrought iron is iron with less than 0.02 % carbon, which cannot be hardened. 熟铁是含碳量低于0.02%的铁，不可硬化。
blowholes 砂眼	Blowholes are small cavities on cast metal objects generated by gases which form when the molten metal comes into contact with moisture in the casting mould. 砂眼是铸造金属物体上的小空腔，当熔化的金属与浇铸模具中的水分接触时形成的气体产生这类空腔。
casting-on 后铸	Casting-on is a joining technique for metalwork. One piece is part of the casting mould, another is permanently attached by pouring molten metal into the mould. 后铸是金属制品的一种连接技术。一块是铸造模具的一部分，另一块是通过向模具中浇注熔融金属而永久连接在一起的。

chaplets 芯撑	Chaplets are metal pins which hold the core in position within a mould for metal casting. 芯撑是一种金属销，它将型芯固定在金属铸造模具中的适当位置。
chasing 錾刻	Chasing is a decorative technique for metalwork in which lines are incised with a pointed tool. In contrast to engraving, no material is removed. 錾刻是一种金属制品的装饰技术，用尖头的工具刻画线条。与雕刻相反，该工艺不会去除原材料。
chills 凝固核	Chills are metal plates inserted in a casting mould for metals to accelerate cooling and solidification. 凝固核是放入铸造模具中的金属片，用来加速金属的冷却和凝固。
dendrite 枝晶	Dendrites are characteristic tree-shaped features in the structure of cast metals. 枝晶是铸造金属结构中的典型树枝形特征。
electroplating 电镀	Electroplating is the deposition of a thin metal layer from a metal salt solution on the cathode of an electrolytic cell. Often used for gold, chrome or nickel plating. 电镀是从金属盐溶液中在电解槽的阴极上沉积一层薄金属层，常用于镀金、镀铬或镀镍。
electrotyping 电铸	Electrotyping is a technique to make identical copies of sheet metal objects. A negative cast taken from the object and coated with a conductive layer is used as a cathode in a galvanic cell and electroplated with a thick layer of a suitable metal which forms an exact positive copy of the original. 电铸是一种将金属板复制成相同的物体的技术。从物体上取下涂有导电层的阴模铸件用作原电池的阴极，并在其上镀上一层厚的合适的金属，该金属层可复制与原形完全一致的正片拷贝。
embossing 压花	Embossing is a decorative technique for sheet metal in which a raised pattern is impressed from the back with punches. 压花是一种从背面用冲头压印形成凸起图案的装饰技术。
filigree 细金	Filigree is a decorative metalworking technique which uses complex ornaments of thin wire, either soldered on a support or freestanding. 细金是一种使用细金属丝制作装饰部件的金属加工技术，可将装饰物焊接在支架上，也可以是独立装饰。
honey gilding 蜂蜜贴金 / 泥金法	Honey gilding is fire gilding using honey as a medium. 蜂蜜贴金是以蜂蜜为媒介的火法表面施金技术。
martensite 马氏体	Martensite is a very hard and brittle microstructure which is formed when red-hot steel is quenched in a hardening process. 马氏体是高温加热的钢在淬火过程中形成的一种非常硬而脆的组织。
metal object 金属器	In archaeology, a metal object is one that was made of metal, but which may now be composed of largely corrosion products. 在考古学中，金属器是指金属制成的器物，但现在可能主要由腐蚀产物组成。

niello 乌银	Niello consists of black sulphides of silver, copper and lead which were used as decorative inlay on metalwork. 乌银由银、铜和铅的黑色硫化物组成，用于金属制品上的镶嵌装。
noble patina 漆古	Noble patina is a thin and stable corrosion layer which protects underlying metal against further corrosion. 漆古是薄而稳定的腐蚀层，可保护底层金属免遭进一步腐蚀。
original surface 原始表面	The original surface of an archaeological metal object, defined by toolmarks and / or original surface decoration, is the identified layer of corrosion products formed during its working life, which has subsequently become encapsulated in corrosion products during further degradation of the object. 考古金属物体的原始表面由工具标记和/或原始表面装饰确定，是在其使用寿命期间形成的已识别的腐蚀产物层，该腐蚀产物随后被封入腐蚀产物中。
outdoor bronze sculptures 户外青铜雕塑	Outdoor bronze sculptures are works of art made of a copper alloy which are permanently placed in an outside location. 户外青铜雕塑是由铜合金制成的艺术品，永久放置在户外。
sand casting 砂型铸造	Sand casting is a metal casting technique which uses moulds made of dried sand. 砂型铸造是使用干砂模具的金属铸造技术。
slag 炉渣	Slag is a waste product from the smelting of a metal based on silica reacted with a number of fluxes. 炉渣是金属冶炼过程产生的废弃物，由二氧化硅与各种助溶剂反应形成。
plating （金属）覆层	Plating is the application of a thin metal coating for corrosion protection or aesthetic purposes. The application can be achieved physically, chemically or by electroplating. Common plating metals are gold, silver, tin, zinc, chrome or nickel. （金属）覆层是为了防腐蚀或美观的目的而施加的金属薄层。施加镀层可以通过物理、化学或电镀的方式来实现。常见的电镀金属有金、银、锡、锌、铬或镍。
azurite 蓝铜矿	Azurite is a copper hydroxy carbonate mineral $[Cu_3(OH)_2(CO_3)_2]$ which has been used as a blue painting pigment since antiquity. 蓝铜矿是一种铜羟基碳酸盐矿物 $[Cu_3(OH)_2(CO_3)_2]$，自古以来就被用作蓝色绘画颜料。
fine gold 纯金	Fine gold is pure gold of 24 carats. 纯金是24开的金。
cerussite 白铅矿	Cerussite is a white lead carbonate mineral $(PbCO_3)$ which is a typical lead corrosion product. It is also a component of the painting pigment lead white. 白铅矿是一种白色的碳酸铅矿物（$PbCO_3$），是典型的铅腐蚀产物，它也是绘画颜料铅白的组成部分。
tremolierungen 浮雕纹饰	Tremolierungen is a relief design made with a metal gouge. 浮雕纹饰是一种用金属凿槽制作的浮雕设计。

burnish 打磨	When you burnish a surface, you rub it using a hard tool. This makes the high points flow into the low points and produces a polish. 用一个硬的工具摩擦打磨一个表面时，可使高点流入低点，从而产生抛光效果。
chiselling 凿刻	Chiselling is a stone- or woodworking technique which uses a tool with a straight cutting edge driven by a hammer. 凿刻是一种通过使用由锤子驱动的直刃工具来实施的石工或木工技术。
carat 开（K）	The purity, or fineness, of gold is measured in carats (ct). Pure gold is 24ct, while 22ct gold is an alloy in which there are 22 parts of gold and 2 parts of other metals. 开是衡量黄金纯度或精度的单位，纯金是24开，而22开是一种合金，其中有22份的金和2份其它金属。
marcassite 白铁矿	The mineral marcassite is an iron sulphide FeS_2 which has the same composition as pyrite but with a different crystalline structure. 白铁矿是铁的硫化矿物（FeS_2），与黄铁矿成分相同但晶体结构不同。
malachite 孔雀石	Malachite is a copper hydroxy carbonate $[Cu_2(OH)_2CO_3]$ which is a typical constituent of green patina on copper. It was also used as a green pigment in paintings. 孔雀石是铜的碱式碳酸盐 $[Cu_2(OH)_2CO_3]$，是铜表面锈层的典型成分，也可用于绘画中的绿色颜料。
metal fibre 金属丝	Metal fibres are inorganic fibres that are made from metals such as gold, silver and copper alloys. They have been in use since the ancient times. 金属丝是由金、银和铜合金等金属制成的无机丝线，自古一直被使用。
alkaline sulphite treatment 碱性亚硫酸盐处理	Alkaline sulphite treatment is a method for the stabilization of archaeological iron with high chloride concentrations. 碱性亚硫酸盐处理是一种使高氯含量考古出土铁器稳定化的方法。
anodic protection 阳极保护	Anodic protection is the protection from corrosion of some metals such stainless steel through the formation of a thin inert oxide layer (passivation). This can be achieved by contact with an oxidising electrolyte or a noble metal which acts as a cathode. 阳极保护是通过形成惰性氧化薄层（钝化）以阻止金属（如不锈钢）腐蚀的方法，可经接触氧化性电解液或作为阴极的贵金属来实现。
cathodic protection 阴极保护	Cathodic protection is protection from corrosion of metal through a conductive connection with a less noble metal which is more readily oxidised (sacrificial anode). A common example is zinc plating on iron. 阴极保护是指通过与更容易氧化的惰性较弱的金属（牺牲阳极）的导电连接来保护金属免受腐蚀，常见的例子是在铁上镀锌。
cold stitching 冷缝合	Cold stitching is a method of joining cracked cast iron objects. A line of holes is drilled along the crack into which stainless steel dowels are adhered. 冷缝合是连接开裂铸铁器物的一种方法。其做法是沿着裂缝钻出排孔并通过锈钢销钉固定。

electrochemical reduction 电化学还原	Electrochemical reduction is the conversion of metal salts (corrosion products) into the metallic state by connecting them to the cathode. 电化学还原是通过将金属盐（腐蚀产物）连接到阴极将其转化为金属的方法。
electrochemical treatment 电化学处理	Electrochemical treatment is the deliberate oxidation or reduction of a metal object used for the removal of corrosion products. 电化学处理是有意识地对金属物体进行氧化或还原处理，以去除腐蚀产物的方法。
electrolysis 电解	Electrolysis is an electric process in which a voltage is applied to oxidise and reduce materials. Oxidation takes place at the positive electrode (anode), reduction at the negative electrode (cathode). 电解是通过施加电压以使材料发生氧化和还原反应的电过程。氧化反应发生在正极(阳极)，还原反应发生在负极(阴极)。
electrolytic cleaning 电解清洗	Corrosion products and other surface matter can be removed from a metal by electrolytic cleaning. The metal is placed in an electrolyte solution and made one electrode of an electrolytic cell, with the resulting current causing reduction and loss of adhesion of the corrosion products. 通过电解清洗可将腐蚀产物和其他表面物质从金属上去除。其方法是将金属置于电解质溶液中，制成电解池的一个电极，由此产生的电流导致粘附力的减少和损失。
electron beam welding 电子束焊接	Electron beam welding is a technique for the joining of two metals on a microscopic scale through localised heating to their melting point with an electron beam. 电子束焊接是通过电子束将金属局部加热至熔点，以连接两件金属的微形焊接方法。
hydrogen plasma treatment 氢等离子体处理 / 氢等离子体还原	Hydrogen plasma treatment is a stabilization technique for corroded metals, especially iron, through partial reduction of corrosion products with a gas plasma. 氢等离子体处理是一种通过用气相等离子体部分还原腐蚀产物来稳定腐蚀金属（特别是铁）的技术。
lost-wax casting 失蜡铸造	Lost wax casting is a metal casting technique in which a mould is prepared by covering a wax model with clay. The wax is removed by heating after which the empty mould is filled with molten metal. 失蜡铸造是一种金属铸造技术，通过用粘土覆盖蜡模型，以制备模具。通过加热去除蜡，然后用熔融金属填充空模具。
passivation 钝化	On some metals such as aluminium and chromium, passivation is the protection from further oxidation by a thin dense oxide layer on the surface which preserves their metallic appearance. Passivation makes these metals very corrosion resistant even though they are not in a state of chemical equilibrium. 在铝和铬等一些金属上，钝化是通过在表面上形成薄而致密的氧化层阻止进一步氧化，从而保护其金属外观。钝化使这些金属即使不处于化学平衡状态，也具有很强的耐腐蚀性。

planishing 锤光	Planishing is the process of making a metal (or other material) level and smooth by rolling or hammering with a polished metal surface. 锤光是通过轧制或锤击使金属（或其他材料）获得平整光亮表面的过程。
repatinate 作锈	You repatinate a metal surface by creating a new artificial patina by the use of heat, oxygen, water or other chemical reaction. 作锈是通过加热、氧化、浸泡或其它化学反应以在金属器表面形成新的锈层。
sinking (1) 冲形 (1)	Sinking is a technique for the forming of sheet metal by hammering into a depression from the inside of the piece. 冲形是通过从内部将金属片捶打冲入凹模的成型方法。
soldering 钎焊	Soldering is a technique for the joining of metals through application of a molten metal below the melting point of the joined metal. Soft soldering uses tin-lead solder, hard soldering uses brass (brazing) or silver-copper alloys. 钎焊是熔融低熔点金属（低于被焊接件）实现金属连接的工艺，软钎焊使用锡铅焊料，硬焊使用黄铜（硬焊）或银铜合金。
strip 锈层剥离	When you strip a metal object, you remove all the corrosion products from the surface by chemical or mechanical means. This may result in loss of surface detail and even the whole object if little or none of the original metal survives. 锈层剥离是通过化学或机械手段去除表面上所有腐蚀产物的处理过程。若原始金属残余较少或完全锈蚀，这一操作可能会导致表面花纹甚至整个物体的损失。
welding 焊接	Welding is a technique for joining of metals by heating and fusing them. This may be achieved by melting with a gas flame or a strong electric current, or heating and hammering at a forge. 人焊接是通过加热熔化被连接金属来接合的技术，可通过气焰或强电流加热，或在锻造时通过加热和锤击来实现。

08

陶瓷、玻璃和石制品
Ceramics, Glass and Stone

acid etching 酸蚀刻（酸腐蚀）	Acid etching is a decoration technique whereby a glass surface is partly removed by hydrofluoric acid. The glass surface is covered with an acid resistant wax through which the design is scratched, after which the acid is applied. 酸蚀刻（酸腐蚀）是一种玻璃装饰技术，该技术通过氢氟酸对玻璃表面的腐蚀形成纹饰。先将玻璃表面覆盖耐酸蜡，然后将图案部分的蜡刮去暴露于氢氟酸中形成纹饰。
acid gilding 酸烫金	Acid gilding is a decoration technique used on porcelain surfaces. A decoration is etched into the surface of the porcelain with acid. After the application of gold leaf and polishing, a contrast is seen between the shiny unetched surface and the mat etched surface. This technique was introduced in England by the Minton factory in 1873. 酸烫金是一种用于瓷器表面的装饰技术。先用酸将纹饰蚀刻到瓷器的表面。涂上金叶并抛光后，可以看到未蚀刻的光泽表面与蚀刻后亚光表面之间所形成的对比。该工艺在1873年于英国首次出现。
acidic rocks 酸性岩石	Acidic rocks are igneous rocks with a high quartz content.酸性岩石是石英含量高的火成岩。
air twists 气泡扭曲	Air twists are spiral veins of air formed by blowing air bubbles in stems of glass drinking vessels and ornamental objects. 气泡扭曲是指通过向玻璃器皿或装饰物的胎体中（通常是高脚杯的茎部）吹入气泡，形成螺旋状的装饰。
alabaster 雪花石膏	Alabaster is a rock, composed of a massive usually translucent form of gypsum, $CaSO_4.2H_2O$. Alabaster was used for sculptures and as a substrate for oil paintings during the 16th - 17th centuries in Italy. 雪花石膏是一种岩石，由大块通常半透明的石膏组成（$CaSO_4.2H_2O$）。在16-17世纪的意大利，雪花石膏被用于雕塑和作为油画的底子。
alignment 配补	Alignment is the process of positioning component pieces during reconstruction, for instance when sherds of a broken ceramic are reconstructed. 配补是陶瓷碎片粘接过程中对组成部分进行定位的过程，比如，瓷片的拼接。
alkali glass 碱玻璃	Alkali glass is a glass material, made using alkali salts, usually soda or potash. See also soda glass and potash glass. 碱玻璃是一种使用碱金属盐（通常为苏打或钾盐）制成的玻璃材料。另见苏打玻璃和钾盐玻璃。
Aloplast® Aloplast®	Aloplast is a modelling material used to model missing areas in glass objects prior to the making of moulds. Alplast是一种在模型制作前，用于对玻璃物体中缺失区域进行建模的建模材料。（商标名）
amethyst 紫水晶	Amethyst is a precious stone which is a purple variety of quartz (S_iO_2) coloured by traces of manganese. 紫水晶是一种宝石，它是一种紫色的石英（S_iO_2），因所含锰元素而呈紫色。

amine resin 胺基树脂	An amine resin is a thermosetting polymer that is made from amine containing monomer such as urea or melamine reacted typically with formaldehyde. The material is usually applied as an oligomer which is further reacted in situ. Amine resins were used as consolidants. They are now used for restoration of ceramic coatings. 胺基树脂是由通常与甲醛反应的含胺单体（例如尿素或三聚氰胺）制成的热固性聚合物。该材料通常以低聚物形式使用，并在原位进一步反应。胺树脂被用作固结剂，现在用于陶瓷涂料的修复。
anhydrite 硬石膏	Anhydrite is totally dehydrated calcium sulphate, $CaSO_4$, used in the gesso grosso layer of Italian panel paintings. It is prepared by heating gypsum to drive off the water. 硬石膏是一种完全无水的硫酸钙，$CaSO_4$，用于意大利板画的石膏底料。它是通过加热石膏去水而制成的。
annealing (1) 退火 (1)	Annealing is the process of subjecting glass to heat and subsequently cooling it slowly in order to remove internal stresses and to toughen the glass. 退火指先对玻璃加热、后让其缓慢冷却，以去除内应力的方式来增强玻璃的强度。
annealing point 退火点	The annealing point is the temperature at which the stress in melted glass is substantially relieved in a few minutes during the process of annealing. At this point the viscosity of the melted glass reaches $5x10^{12}$ Nsm^{-2}. 退火点指熔化的玻璃内大部分内应力在退火过程中数分钟内被移除时的温度。达到退火点时，熔化玻璃的粘度达到 $5x10^{12}$ Nsm^{-2}。
at-the-fire 再次加热	At-the-fire is the process of reheating a blown glass object at the oven during manufacture. It permits further blowing to enlarge the object, to alter its shape or to enable its manipulation with tools. 再次加热指玻璃器皿吹制过程中，对冷却的玻璃料再次加热的过程。再次加热可以通过使用工具对物品进行进一步吹制，以改变其形状或实现对其的其它操作。
at-the-flame 火焰加热法 （灯工工艺）	At-the-flame is the technique of shaping glassware from rods and tubes of readily fusible glass, by heating and thus softening them to be manipulated. Originally an oil lamp was used, later a gas burner. 火焰加热法（灯工工艺）是一种用易熔性玻璃棒或玻璃管制作玻璃器皿的技术，通过加热使其软化以便于操作。最初加热工具用的是油灯，后来改为煤气灯。
at-the-lamp 灯工工艺	See at-the-flame. 见火焰加热法。
backmatching corrosion 对称腐蚀	Backmatching corrosion is the pitting on the outside of stained glass, corresponding exactly in form and extent to the enamel decoration on the inside of the glass. Its occurrence is due to the corrosion of a porous paint layer on the outside of the glass exactly behind the enamelled layer. 对称腐蚀是彩绘玻璃外表面出现的点蚀，其形式和程度完全对应于玻璃内部的珐琅装饰。因玻璃外部的多孔涂料层被腐蚀而导致的。

backpainting 背面彩绘	Backpainting is painting on the back of glass which is to be viewed from the front. 背面彩绘是在玻璃背面绘制纹饰的方法。人们从正面观看纹饰。
ball clay 球粘土	Ball clay is a fine textured clay which contains a high amount of organic matter and is very plastic when wet. 球粘土是一种质地细密的粘土，含有大量的有机质，潮湿时可塑性极强。
barilla 巴里拉	Barilla is a small marsh dwelling plant (Salsola sp.) that was traditionally an important source of soda used in glass making in the area. It grows in the Mediterranean region. 巴里拉是一种生长于地中海地区的小型沼泽植物。传统上，它是一种制作苏打的重要原料。当地用苏打制作玻璃。
Bassetaille enamel 浅浮雕珐琅	Bassetaille is an enamelling technique where a low relief in metal is covered with enamel to produce differences in depth and colour. 浅浮雕珐琅是一种上釉技术，在金属的浅浮雕上覆盖珐琅，以产生深度和颜色的差异。
batch 料	A batch is the aggregate of the various ingredients weighed out and mixed ready to be placed into the melting pot and fused in the process of making glass. 料是称量、混合好、准备在制作玻璃过程中放入熔炉熔化的各种成分的集合。
battledore 整形工具	A battledore is a glass making tool in the form of a square wooden paddle with a projecting handle. It is primarily used to smooth the bottom of glasses and other objects. 整形工具指带突出把手且外形为方形木制的玻璃制作工具。主要用于玻璃及其它物体底部的平滑处理。
beaded lead 珠铅	Beaded lead is a modern leading used in the making of stained glass. It has a beaded profile in the form of a lip along each rim of the lead. 珠铅是现代用于制造彩色玻璃的铅补丁，在铅条边缘呈现出珠状轮廓。
biscuit porcelain 素烧胚	Biscuit porcelain is a high fired porcelain body which has not been glazed and has a matte surface. 素烧胚是高温烧结的未上釉陶瓷胎体，其表面因未上釉而显得粗糙。
bisque 素瓷	See biscuit porcelain. 见素烧胚。
blow pipe 吹管	A blow-pipe is a metal tube which is longer than 1m. It is used by glass-blowers to gather portions of glass from the furnace and blow it into a desired shape. It was first used in the 1st century B.C. by Roman glass makers. 吹管指长度超过1米的金属管。玻璃吹制工匠使用吹管从炉中挑取适量熔融玻璃并将玻璃吹制成想要的造型。吹管的使用历史可追溯至公元前1世纪的罗马玻璃工匠。

body (1) 胎体	The body of a ceramic is the fired clay which makes up the substance of the ceramic. It is determined by the original clay type, its firing temperature and subsequent properties such as porosity and hardness. 陶瓷的胎体指构成陶瓷物质的煅烧粘土。烧成温度以及随后的性质（如孔隙率和硬度）是由原始粘土类型决定的。
bone china 骨质瓷	Bone china is a high fired white clay with calcined bone which is a filler and flux. 骨质瓷是向高温煅烧的白粘土中加入骨粉的瓷器。骨粉充当填料和助熔剂。
broad glass 板状玻璃	See cylinder glass. 见圆柱型法（得到的片状）玻璃。
bull's eye pane 牛眼窗玻璃	See crown glass. 见皇冠法（得到的片状）玻璃。
burnt clay 红烧土	Burnt clay is clay which has been heated to temperatures above 500℃. The heating drives out physically and chemically bound water, and the silicates undergo an irreversible change to become ceramic. 红烧土是已经加热至500℃以上的粘土。通过加热，会使黏土中的水（以物理和化学方式结合于其中）蒸发。部分硅酸盐在烧制过程中，已转变为陶瓷。
cage cup 笼形杯	A cage cup is a glass cup in the form of a footless, ovoid beaker about 12 cm high. The cup bears a cold-cut pattern that stands out from the cup as an open network or cage. Most of the pattern is completely undercut so that it stands free from the main vessel (the cup) being held to it by a small number of glass rods. There is often a Greek or Roman inscription in raised letters below the mouth. It is also known by its Latin name, diatreta. 笼形杯是一种约12厘米高的无足卵形玻璃杯。杯子上有着冷加工成型的镂空笼形纹样。大部分图案完全悬浮于杯体之外，只有数个支点连接杯体与浮雕图案。笼型杯口沿下常见希腊或罗马字符雕刻。因其拉丁名字"diatreta"（玻璃磨花桶形杯）而闻名。
calcareous sandstone 钙质砂岩	Calcareous sandstone is a sedimentary rock which consists of quartz grains cemented with carbonates. 钙质砂岩是由石英颗粒与碳酸盐胶结而成的沉积岩。
cameo glass 套料雕刻玻璃	A cameo glass is an object formed from glass with two different layers of colour, usually opaque white on coloured glass. The outer layer is carved on a wheel to leave a decorative white relief on a coloured background. The technique was known to the ancient Egyptians and Romans as well as the Chinese in the 18th century. It was revived in Bohemia, France and England in the 19th century. 套料雕刻玻璃是指由两层不同颜色的玻璃（通常将有颜色的玻璃覆盖在不透明的白色玻璃上）制成的玻璃器皿。用车轮雕刻（玉器琢刻）的方法形成图案，与底层的白色背景形成鲜明对比。该技术见于古埃及、罗马的玻璃制品，以及18世纪的中国清代玻璃器。19世纪时，波西米亚，法国和英国的玻璃工业中再次复兴了该工艺。

cane 条状玻璃料	a. A cane is a long rod of coloured glass used to make or decorate glass objects. Canes are made by bundling together slender rods of coloured glass which are then heated and drawn out to the required diameter. Inlays are then sliced from the bar, each retaining an identical design. This technique is used to make Millefiori or mosaic glass. b. A cane is a stick of glass made into the stems of certain types of drinking glasses. Often a white or coloured glass thread or air bubble was incorporated into a colourless glass rod and then drawn and twisted to create a vertical pattern. a. 条状玻璃料是一根长条形的有色玻璃棒，用于制造或装饰玻璃器物。条状玻璃料是通过将细长的彩色玻璃棒捆扎在一起、加热并拉至所需的直径而制成。冷却后切割成片，每个都有着相同的纹样。这种工艺被用来制作千花玻璃或者马赛克玻璃。b. 条状玻璃料被制成某些类型玻璃高脚杯的茎部。通常是将白色、彩色玻璃条或气泡添加进入无色玻璃的主体中，然后拉伸、扭曲形成垂直图案。
cased glass 套料玻璃	See cameo glass. 见套料雕刻玻璃。
chalcedony 玉髓	Chalcedony is a precious stone which is a coloured cryptocrystalline variety of quartz (S_iO_2). 玉髓是一种宝石，是彩色隐晶质石英的变种（S_iO_2）。
chamotte 火泥	Chamotte is burnt clay. Potters use it in small portions as non plastic additive to raw clay while preparing the clay for pottery. 火泥是烧制过的粘土。陶工在准备陶土时，会少量使用它作为生粘土的非塑性添加剂。
china clay 瓷土	See Kaolin. 参见高岭土。
China glaze® 瓷漆（胶）	China glaze is a butylated amino-formaldehyde, modified by the addition of an alkyd. It is used as a retouching medium on glazed ceramics. In tests it has been shown to yellow badly over time. China glaze® 牌瓷漆（胶）是一种丁胺基甲醛，经醇酸改性而成，用作涂釉陶瓷的补釉材料；试验发现其将随着时间的推移而严重发黄。（商标名）
cold colour 冷色	Cold colour is a pigmented synthetic medium for retouching glass or ceramic, which does not need heating to cure the medium. See also cold painting. 冷色是一种用于修饰玻璃或陶瓷的着色合成介质，使用时无需烧制。另见冷涂饰。
cold painting 冷涂饰	Cold painting is the application of varnishes or oil paint to glass or ceramic objects without firing. It is applied to the back of the surface to be viewed and protected by a layer of varnish or metal foil or by another sheet of glass. It has often worn off antique pieces. 冷涂饰是无需烧制将清漆或油性涂料施用于玻璃或陶瓷器物的方法。它常被涂在器物的内壁。所使用的清漆、金属箔或玻璃层对器物起到保护作用。通常文物上的冷涂饰层均已老化脱落。

copper ruby glass 铜红玻璃	Copper ruby glass is a red coloured window glass. Its colouring agent is copper. The colour was often so intense the glass appeared black. It was produced predominantly from the 12th to the 14th century. 铜红玻璃是一种红色的窗户玻璃。使用铜作为着色剂，通常颜色浓烈，以致有时看上去呈现黑色（因厚度关系）。主要产于12至14世纪。
core-forming 内核成型技术 （砂芯法）	Core forming is an early glass-making technique where narrow necked vessels are formed round a core of mud or straw on a rod. The core is dipped into molten glass or trails of glass are wound around the core. 内核成型技术（砂芯法）是一种早期的玻璃成型技术，用于制作细颈玻璃器皿。将泥芯置于一小木棒之上，然后将泥芯伸入熔融玻璃中包裹泥芯，待退火冷却后挖去泥芯，形成空腔。
crackled glass 裂纹玻璃	See ice glass. 见冰裂纹玻璃。
crisselling 泛碱	See crizzling. 见泛碱。
cristallo 威尼斯水晶玻璃	Cristallo is a type of soda glass developed in Venice, perhaps as early as the fifteenth century. It was made with sea plant ashes or natron and had a pale-yellow, straw-like or grey colour. By the use of manganese as a decolourising agent, the glass was made colourless and thus resembled rock crystal. 威尼斯水晶玻璃是威尼斯生产的一种苏打玻璃，最早或可追溯至15世纪。它是用海洋植物灰或泡碱作为助熔剂而制成，呈淡黄色，稻草色或灰色。使用锰作为脱色剂而制成的无色威尼斯水晶玻璃外观接近天然水晶矿石。
cristobalite 方石英	Cristobalite is a mineral which is a high-temperature modification of silicon dioxide (SiO_2). 方石英是一种矿物，是二氧化硅（SiO_2）的高温变体。
crizzled glass 泛碱玻璃	Crizzled glass is glass that, due to the deterioration process known as crizzling, has a hazy appearance caused by a network of fine internal cracks. See also sick glass and weeping glass. 泛碱玻璃是因玻璃劣化，产生内部网状裂隙最终导致玻璃表面呈现云雾状。另见病态玻璃和"出汗玻璃"。
crizzling 泛碱	Crizzling is a stage of glass deterioration which manifests itself as a network of fine internal cracks giving the glass a hazy appearance. Crizzling is a sign of instability in the glass. See also sick glass and weeping glass. 泛碱是玻璃呈现出网状的内部细裂纹而导致其呈现雾状外观的的劣化现象。泛碱是玻璃不稳定的一个标志。另见病态玻璃和"出汗玻璃"。

crown glass 皇冠法（得到的片状）玻璃	Crown glass is a type of flat glass that is made by blowing a bubble of glass, transferring it from the blow-pipe to a rod, cutting it open and then rapidly rotating it with repeated heating. Due to centrifugal force, the glass spreads into a large flat disk up to 1.2 meters in diameter. The rod is broken off, the glass annealed, and the disk cut into rectangular pieces. The pane in the middle has a rough knob where the rod had been attached. This knob is known as the bull's eye pane. This fabrication process is also known as Normandy mode. 皇冠法是一种制作平板玻璃的工艺：先吹出玻璃泡、然后将玻璃泡从吹管转移至实心金属棒上，张开玻璃泡后快速旋转，使软化状态下的玻璃在离心力的作用下摊平成一张较大的直径约1.2米的圆盘。然后将玻璃从金属棒上取下，进行玻璃退火。最后将圆形平板玻璃切成若干长方形玻璃片。原先进行金属棒转接的地方会留下一个凸起，该凸起被称为"牛眼"。皇冠法的生产工序也被称为"诺曼底"模式。
crusting 结皮	Crusting is a type of glass deterioration whereby a calcite-rich weathering crust develops on the surface of the glass (usually window glass). The hydroxides produced by the attack of water on susceptible glass are converted into carbonates by CO_2 in the air. 结皮是玻璃（通常为窗玻璃）形成富含方解石风化壳的一类玻璃劣化现象，是水对易感玻璃的侵蚀产生的氢氧化物被空气中的二氧化碳转化为碳酸盐的过程。
cullet 碎玻璃	Cullet is clean broken glass from glass objects discarded during manufacture. It is melted together with fresh ingredients of a new batch. 碎玻璃是指制造过程中丢弃的干净碎玻璃。它常与新的原料混合在一起形成新的料。
cutline 切割线	In the production of stained glass, the cutline is the tracing of the pattern of the leads onto the glass surface before cutting. The pattern is traced from a master drawing or 'cartoon'. 生产彩色镶嵌玻璃时，切割线指得是在切割前将图案描绘到玻璃表面上的描摹。原始的设计图案被描摹和转移。
cylinder glass 圆柱型法（得到的片状）玻璃	Cylinder glass is flat glass made as early as 1100 by blowing a large bubble and swinging it on the blow pipe to form a long bottle. After cutting off both ends, the resulting cylinder, which could be up to 1,5 meters in length, was cut lengthways with sheers. It was then reheated and flattened or allowed to sink flat. Cylinder glass has straight ripples on the surface and is less glossy than crown glass. 圆柱型法（得到的片状）玻璃的历史可追溯至公元12世纪制作的平板玻璃，它是将玻璃料吹制成一个大玻璃泡，并将玻璃泡拉伸成一个圆柱体。切断两端后，将长度最长可达1.5米的玻璃圆柱体刨开而形成平板状玻璃。圆柱型法得到的片状玻璃表面通常有水波涟漪似的纹样，而且通常比皇冠法（得到的片状）玻璃的表面粗糙些。
dechlorination 脱氯	See desalination. 见脱盐处理。

decrepitation 爆裂作用	Decrepitation is the breaking up of minerals when exposed to heat, frequently accompanied by a crackling noise. 爆裂作用是指矿物质在受热时会破碎，经常伴随有爆裂声。
delftware 代尔夫特陶器	Delftware is a blue and white tin-glazed earthenware produced in Holland. 代尔夫特陶器是荷兰生产的蓝白色的锡釉陶器。
desalinate 脱盐处理	When you desalinate a porous object, you wash out the contaminating soluble salts using numerous changes of fresh water. 对多孔材料进行脱盐处理是使用清水多次清洗物体，以析出造成污染的可溶性盐。
desalination 脱盐处理	Desalination is the removal of soluble salts, especially chlorides, from archaeological finds. 脱盐处理指从考古发掘品中去除可溶性盐，特别是氯化物的保护处理工序。
Desmodur N75® Desmodur N75®	Desmodur is a toxic monomer, hexamethylene diisocyanate, which was used with an acrylic oligomer in creating a polyurethane coating on stained glass. The coating has been shown to trap corrosion products at the interface with the glass surface, due to its permeability. Desmodur是一种有毒单体，即六亚甲基二异氰酸酯，其与丙烯酸低聚物一起用于在彩色玻璃上形成聚氨酯涂层。由于其渗透性，已表明该涂层会在与玻璃表面的界面处截留腐蚀物。（商标名）
development of fossils 化石采掘	The development of fossils is the uncovering of fossil material by removal of the stone matrix in which the fossil is embedded. The matrix may be only partially removed. 化石采掘是通过移除化石中所嵌各种石头的方式，来开采化石材料。嵌入石头或只能部分移除。
devitrification 脱玻作用	Devitrification is the conversion of glass into a crystalline substance by heating it to just below its liquification temperature. The glass forms a definite crystal compound and has an opaque appearance. 脱玻作用是通过将玻璃加热到刚好低于其液化温度，将其转化为晶体，此时玻璃从无定形态转化成晶体，并呈不透明状。
diamond-point engraving 金刚钻刻花	Diamond-point engraving is a technique of decorating glass by engraving, using a diamond point to scratch the surface. 金刚钻刻花是一种通过雕刻来装饰玻璃的技术，纹饰是通过金刚钻笔的尖端刻划玻璃形成的。
diatreta 笼形杯	See cage cup. 见笼形杯。
dichroic 二向色晶体	A dichroic crystal or solution can transmit and reflect different wavelengths of the incident light. 二向色晶体或溶液可以透射和反射入射光的不同波长。
diseased glass 病态玻璃	See sick glass. 见病态玻璃。

dry run 预粘接	A dry run is the process of taping together sherds of a fragmented ceramic to ascertain sticking order prior to edge joining. 预粘接工序，是陶瓷碎片修复过程中，在连接碎片边缘之前，将碎片用胶带粘在一起，以确定粘接顺序的过程。
dry stick 干粘接	When you dry stick ceramic or glass sherds, you tape or tack the sherds. This reconstruction is carried out prior to the introduction of a low viscosity adhesive into the joins by capillary action. 干粘接工序，是在陶瓷或玻璃碎片修复过程中，先用胶带粘或选点固定碎片。利用此方法拼接器物，是为了其后在碎片间注入低粘度粘接剂。
dulling 昏暗	Dulling is the simplest type of glass deterioration of the surface. The glass loses its original clarity and transparency and becomes translucent. 昏暗是玻璃表面劣化的常见类型。玻璃失去了原有的清晰度和透明度，变成半透明状。
earthenware 陶器	Earthenware is a soft, low fired 800-1200℃, porous ceramic body of variable colour, with or without a glaze. 陶器是一种质地相对较软，800-1200℃低温烧制的的多孔陶瓷体，颜色多样，可上釉或不上。
edge joining 边缘粘接法	Edge joining of fragments is carried out by applying a viscous adhesive to the break-edge of one fragment and pushing its mating fragment into place. The sherds are joined in sequence and one at a time after the adhesive has set. 边缘粘接是通过对其中一个碎片断裂边缘涂施粘接剂，并将与其配对的另一个碎片推摁至相应位置来实现的。碎片粘接按序完成，前一个粘接剂固化后再进粘接下一个。
Egyptian Blue 埃及蓝	Egyptian Blue is a blue pigment. It is a crystalline compound containing 45 - 65% of the mineral copper calcium tetrasilicate. To produce the distinctive blue colour, silica is usually present in excess. Egyptian blue may be ground and used as a pigment or moulded into objects and fired. 埃及蓝是一种蓝色颜料。它是一种结晶化合物，含有45-65%的矿物四硅酸铜钙。为了产生独特的蓝色，通常在配方中加入过量二氧化硅。埃及蓝磨碎后可用作颜料，或将整块镶嵌于器物上。
Egyptian faience 埃及釉砂（费昂斯）	Egyptian faience is a blue glassy material which has been fired into a substrate. 埃及釉砂（费昂斯）是一种部分烧结的蓝色玻璃状材料。
enamel 珐琅	Enamel is a glasslike opaque or semi-transparent coating on metallic surfaces, usually copper or gold. In porcelain and glass, enamel is a low temperature melting glass coloured with metal oxides and applied to glassware and porcelain as surface decoration by low temperature firing in a muffle oven. 珐琅是金属表面（通常是铜或金）上的玻璃状不透明或半透明涂层。在瓷器和玻璃中，珐琅是一种用金属氧化物着色的低温玻璃，常作为表面装饰用于玻璃器和瓷器上。

enamelling 金属胎画珐琅	Enamelling is a decoration technique where powdered glass or frit is fused to a metal base, usually copper or gold. 金属胎画珐琅是一种装饰技术，该技术将粉末状玻璃料实施到金属胎体上，通常为铜或金。
etching 蚀刻	Etching involves treating metals or glass with corrosive chemicals (usually acids) to obtain a matte or coloured surface for decorative or analytical purposes (metallography). 蚀刻即用腐蚀性化学物质（通常为酸）来处理金属或玻璃，以获得用于装饰或分析用的磨砂或有色表面（金相学）。
faience 费昂斯	Faience is a tin glazed earthenware, in particular one that is produced in Italy, France, Germany or Scandinavia. 费昂斯是一种锡釉陶器，主要生产于意大利，法国，德国或斯堪的纳维亚半岛。
feather-type cracking 羽毛型开裂	Feather-type cracking is a glaze fault resulting in matt areas in the glaze. It is caused by a deposit of calcium sulphate during the firing process. 羽毛型开裂是釉料中亚光区域出现的釉断层。这是由于烧制过程中硫酸钙的沉积而引起的。
feldspars 长石	Feldspars are potassium-, sodium- or calcium aluminium silicate minerals ($KAlSi_3O_8$, $NaAlSi_3O_8$, $CaAl_2Si_2O_8$), or mixed forms of the three. 长石是钾、钠或钙铝硅酸盐矿物 ($KAlSi_3O_8$, $NaAlSi_3O_8$, $CaAl_2Si_2O_8$)，或三者的混合形式。
fettling 补炉	Fettling is a step in the manufacturing of terracotta ornaments after removal of the dried clay from the mould prior to firing. It involves cleaning and smoothing the clay surface. 补炉是生产陶器装饰品过程中的一个步骤，该步骤处于烧制之前和从模具中除去干燥的粘土之后。它涉及清洁和平滑处理黏土表面。
fire finishing 火抛光	Fire finishing is the brilliant surface condition given to glass by heating it in the mouth of the furnace, the so-called glory hole, after the making of the object. This process removes imperfections and the dull surface sometimes produced by the mould. 火抛光是指在器物制成后，通过在炉口（即所谓的再次加热孔）中加热以使其表面呈现光亮状态。该过程消除了瑕疵，并消除了有时因模具而产生的钝化表面。
fire polishing 火抛光	See fire finishing. 见火抛光。
fired colour 釉上彩／火烧颜色	a. A fired colour is an overglaze enamel which has been fired on in the kiln during the process of manufacture. b. A fired colour is a retouching medium which needs stoving to cure it. a.釉上彩指施于瓷釉之上后，通过入窑烧制而使其固定的陶瓷玻璃上彩工艺。b.火烧颜色是一种需要烘干才能定型的修饰色料。

firing 烧制	Firing an air-dried clay object involves heating the object in a kiln until the sintering point. This treatment is used particularly to stabilise clay cuneiform tablets which cannot be treated in an alternative manner. 烧制风干的粘土器物是将物体放在窑中加热至烧结点。该处理方式特别用于稳定无法用其它方式处理的楔形粘土片。
flash 接胎痕	A flash is a raised line left on the surface of an object, such as ceramic or metal, made in a multi-piece mould. The flash is formed where surplus material escapes through the gaps between sections of the mould. 接胎痕是模制成型的陶瓷或金属接胎时在器物表面上留下的凸痕。毛边形成是因材料从模具的间隙逸出。
flat lead 扁平铅补丁	Flat lead is modern leading with a flat profile, used in the making of stained glass. See also mending leads. 扁平铅补丁是具有扁平轮廓的现代铅补丁，用于制造彩色玻璃。另见铅补丁。
floating 碎片沫	A floating sherd of a fragmented ceramic does not join to any existing sherds. During a reconstruction, it may have to be placed in an area of fill based on its profile and decoration. 陶瓷碎片拼接修复过程中，某个变形或损伤的碎片不能与其他碎片匹配粘接在一起，其称为碎片沫。器物复原出现该情况时，可视该瓷器外形及装饰情况，将碎片沫所在部位用其他材料填充。
flux 助熔剂	A flux is a substance mixed with other materials to promote fusion (notably metal, glass, and ceramic materials). In the case of glass, glazes or vitrifiable bodies such as porcelain, fluxes are added to lower the fusion point during firing as well as to promote fusion. Fluxes for ceramics or glass are generally alkaline oxides which interact with glass-forming silica in the production of glass or the glazing process. Common fluxes are borax, potash, soda and ash. 助熔剂是与其他材料（特别是金属，玻璃和陶瓷材料）混合以促进熔化的物质。对于玻璃，釉料或可玻璃化的物体（如瓷器），通过添加助熔剂以降低烧制过程中的熔化点以促进烧结。陶瓷和玻璃材料中常用的助熔剂多为碱金属氧化物，它们在烧结过程中促进氧化硅的熔融。常见助熔剂有硼砂，钾盐，苏打及草木灰。
forest glass 森林玻璃	See potash glass. 见钾玻璃。
frit 玻璃炉料	Frit is the granular product of the first stage of ancient glass- or glaze-making. The raw materials are heated to around 850℃ to produce solid-state reactions between them. When cool, the frit is ground to produce a homogeneous material. 玻璃炉料是古代玻璃或釉料制造第一阶段的颗粒状半成品。原料被加热到850℃左右，原料之间的固态反应使之形成玻璃炉料。冷却以后将玻璃炉料研磨以产生均匀的材料（以备再次冶炼）。
fritting 加玻璃料	Fritting is the addition of frit to a clay body or glaze in order to increase stability or improve the working properties of glaze material. See also flux. 加玻璃料作业指向粘土或釉料中添加玻璃料以达到增强釉料稳定性，或改善其工作性能的操作。另见助熔剂。

frosting (1) 结霜 (1)	Frosting is a network of small cracks on the surface of a glass object due to weathering. This should not be confused with crizzling. 结霜是由于风化作用在玻璃物体表面形成的网状微小裂痕。不应将其与泛碱现象混淆。
frosting (2) 结霜 (2)	Frosting is a decorative effect on glass where the surface is made opaque or matte by the use of hydrofluoric acid. 结霜是一种玻璃表面装饰效果，通过使用氢氟酸使其表面变得不透明或哑光。
Fynebond® Fynebond®	Fynebond is a two-part epoxy resin using the bisphenol A, epichlorohydrin epoxy. It is used as an adhesive and fill-material in porcelain and glass conservation. Fynebond是使用双酚A，环氧氯丙烷环氧树脂的两部分环氧树脂。其在陶瓷和玻璃保护中用作粘接剂和填充材料。
gather 挑料	A gather is a blob of molten glass attached to the end of the blow-pipe, preparatory to forming a glass object. 挑料（得到的待吹制玻璃料）指的是用吹管从窑炉中挑起的一团熔融玻璃，以待吹制成型。
ghosting 重影	Ghosting on a ceramic sherd is the staining of a porous body along a break edge due to the unintended absorption of, for example, dirt or low viscosity adhesives. 陶瓷碎片上的重影是指由于沾染污垢或低粘度粘接剂等，导致多孔胎体沿断裂边缘而发生的污染。
glass cutting 玻璃切割	Glass cutting is the process of cutting glass to make facets, groves, and depressions by grinding, using rotating disks of various materials, sizes and shapes. This technique has been used since before the Roman period. 玻璃切割是指使用各种不同材料、尺寸和形状的旋转圆盘，通过研磨方式将玻璃切割并制作成小面、凹槽和凹陷的过程。该项技术的应用早于罗马时代。
glass melt 玻璃熔液	See glass melting. 见玻璃熔融。
glass melting 玻璃熔融	Glass melting is the preparation of melted glass by melting down fragments of cullet and frit. 玻璃熔融指通过高温加热碎玻璃和玻璃料的方式制备熔融状态的液体玻璃。
glass paste 玻璃浆	See pâte-de-verre. 见碎玻璃融合技术。
glaze (4) 釉 (4)	You glaze a ceramic by applying a vitreous coating. 为陶瓷上釉是为其涂上一层玻璃质釉层。
glaze fit 釉适性	The fit of a glaze to a ceramic body is the extent to which properties such as expansion and contraction are matched. Where the match is poor, the glaze will crackle and may lift. 釉适性指釉料与陶瓷毛胚合适与否，取决于膨胀和收缩等性能方面的匹配度。匹配度差时，釉料会开裂，甚至会出现翘起的现象。

glaze pooling 积釉	Glaze pooling is a manufacturing fault whereby excess glaze collects in undercuts and crevices. 积釉指釉料因制造缺陷而聚集于咬边和缝隙中的现象。
glory hole 加热口（或炉）	A glory hole is a hole in the side of a glass furnace. It is used for reheating already molten glass that is in the process of being fashioned or decorated. It is also used for the fire-finishing of objects that have been mould-blown and which have imperfections. 加热口（古时）指位于玻璃窑炉侧面的孔。该孔用于对处于成型或装饰过程中已熔化的玻璃重新加热。同时，其还被用于对模具吹后存在缺陷的物体进行火抛光处理。（现代的加热炉为独立炉）
gloss (2) 光泽 (2)	On an unglazed ceramic, such as Samian ware, gloss is a mineral surface coating that has a high sheen. 在未上釉的陶瓷（如萨满瓷器）上，光泽由一层高亮度矿物涂层形成的。
goethite 针铁矿	Goethite is a red, brown or yellow iron(III)oxy hydroxide mineral (α-FeOOH) which is a common iron corrosion product. It is also used as a pigment. 针铁矿是红色，棕色或黄色的氢氧化铁矿物（α-FeOOH），是常见的铁腐蚀产物。同时，它也用作颜料。
gold sandwich glass 金箔夹层玻璃	Gold sandwich glass is a decorative technique in which a design in gold leaf is incorporated between two glass vessels which fit precisely together. 金箔夹层玻璃是将设计好的金叶置入精准契合的两个玻璃容器的一项装饰技术。
granite 花岗岩	Granite is an igneous rock made of the minerals feldspar, quartz and mica. 花岗岩是一种由长石、石英和云母组成的火成岩。
grisaille (1) 浮雕彩色玻璃 (1)	Grisaille is a clear glass, ornamented in muted colours, with delicate patterns and leaded into decorative designs. 浮雕彩色玻璃是一种用柔和色调装饰的透明玻璃，具有精美的图案，嵌有装饰设计。
grisaille (2) 纯灰颜料 (2)	Grisaille is a brown coloured paint made with iron oxide and fused onto the surface of painted glass to define details. 纯灰颜料是一种由氧化铁制成的棕色颜料，用于彩绘玻璃表面上用以描绘细节。
grozing 压花	Grozing is a technique used to shape flat glass, usually window glass. The edges of the glass are chipped away with pliers or a hooked grozing iron in order to shape it in a precise manner. 压花是一种整形平板玻璃的技术，通常整形对象为窗玻璃。（将不平整的）玻璃边缘用钳子工具齐整或钩状烙铁进行精确的齐整。
gypsum 石膏	Gypsum is a white mineral, calcium sulfate dihydrate, which is a major component of alabaster and ground into powder. Gypsum is roasted to make plaster of Paris and anhydrite. 石膏是一种白色矿物，硫酸钙二水合物，是雪花石膏的主要成分，可磨成粉末。石膏经烘烤后制成熟石膏和硬石膏。

haematinum 血色玻璃	Haematinum is a red coating applied prior to burnishing on ceramics in order create a gloss surface. 血色玻璃是一种红色玻璃质涂层，提前涂在陶瓷表面，抛光后产生光泽效果。
haematite 赤铁矿	Haematite is a hard iron oxide mineral, Fe_2O_2. It is used to make tools for polishing gold. Haematite is used in a paint for stained glass windows in order to achieve the colour of carnations. 赤铁矿是一种坚硬的氧化铁矿物，化学式为Fe_2O_2，常用于制造工具或抛光黄金。赤铁矿被用于建筑用彩色镶嵌玻璃彩绘颜料中，以获得淡红色。
heel ball 黑蜡	Heel ball is a black wax composition used to make rubbings of glass panels on thin paper in the process of painted glass restoration. 黑蜡是彩绘玻璃修复过程中，用于在薄纸上制作玻璃面板拓片的黑色的蜡。
high fired 高温煅烧	A high fired ceramic is one that is heated to a high temperature producing a dense, hard and non-porous body. Examples are porcelain and stoneware. 高温煅烧陶瓷是加热到高温产生致密、坚硬且无孔的陶瓷胎体。瓷器和石器都是经过高温煅烧的。
HXTAL Nyl-1 HXTAL Nyl-1	Hxtal is an epoxy resin system made of diglycidyl ether of bisphenol A and triethylene diamine. Hxtal是由双酚A和三亚乙基二胺的二缩水甘油醚制成的环氧树脂体系。
ice glass 冰裂纹玻璃	Ice glass is a type of decorative glassware that has a rough irregular outer surface resembling cracked glass. The effect was produced by sudden cooling during production or melting glass splinters onto the surface. It was first produced in Venice in the 16th century. 冰裂纹玻璃是一种装饰玻璃器皿，其外表面粗糙不规则，类似于破裂的玻璃。这种效果是通过在生产过程中突然冷却或将玻璃碎片熔化到表面上而产生。最初诞生于16世纪的威尼斯。
intaglio 阴刻	Intaglio is a style of decoration on glass created by engraving or cutting. The hollowed out areas appear to the eye to be raised decoration. Such decoration was carried out by wheel engraving in medieval Rome, but especially in Silesia and Germany in the 17th century. 阴刻是通过在玻璃进行雕刻或切割创造装饰纹样的工艺。被挖空的区域看起来像是凸起的装饰。这种装饰在中世纪的罗马是通过车轮雕刻设备完成的，这种技术在17世纪的西里西亚和德国尤为流行。
intaglio engraving 阴纹雕刻	See wheel-engraving. 见车轮雕刻
isothermal glazing 等温上釉	Isothermal glazing is a system of protecting externally exposed painted glass windows. An external protective glazing is ventilated to the interior of the building in order to equalise as far as possible the temperature on both sides of the painted glass. 等温上釉是一种保护暴露在室外的彩色玻璃窗的系统。通过对建筑内侧上一层等温釉的方式，以便尽可能平衡彩绘玻璃两侧的温度。

jet 煤精	Jet is black fossilized bitaminous resin. It is very dense and therefore easily carved and can be polished. It was used as a semi-precious stone in jewellery. 煤精是黑色的沥青树脂化石，它非常致密，因此非常容易雕刻和抛光，它被用作珠宝中的次级宝石。
kaolin 高岭土	Kaolin is a fine, white china clay. The word is a corruption of the Chinese Kao-ling, meaning mountain. Kaolin is used to make porcelain and china, and as a filler or in grounds on paintings. 高岭土是一种精细的白色粘土。因其来自于中国景德镇高岭而得名。高岭土用于制作陶瓷、被用作填充剂或绘画的打底。
kiln 窑	A kiln is the oven used for firing ceramics. 窑指用于烧制陶瓷的炉子。
knop 球形装饰	A knop is a decorative knob. In glass objects it specifically refers to a component, usually spherical or oblate, of the stem of a drinking glass. 球形装饰是一种装饰性名称。在玻璃器物中，专指一个部件，通常是玻璃高脚杯的茎部装饰，通常是球形或扁球形。
lampworking 灯工玻璃	See at-the-flame. 见火焰加热（灯工玻璃）。
larmes de verre 玻璃泪滴	See Rupert's drops. 见鲁珀特水滴。
lead 铅	See beaded lead and mending leads. 见珠铅和铅补丁。
leading-up 铅条组合	Leading-up is the act of assembling pieces of glass for window panels with lead strips. 铅组合指将用于建筑的片状玻璃板与铅条进行集合组装的工序。
lechatelierite 焦石英	Lechatelierite is a naturally fused silica glass sometimes formed in desert areas by lightening striking a large mass of quartz sand. Irregular tubes (fulgurites) of crude silica are formed, sometimes of considerable length. 焦石英是一种天然熔融的石英玻璃，在沙漠中焦石英有时会形成于被雷击中的大块石英砂上的，这样形成的焦石英具有不规则的粗二氧化硅管（石英）形态，有时长度相当长。
lock out 失位	A ceramic sherd is locked out when it cannot be fitted into position because adjacent sherds do not leave enough room for proper adjustment. 失位是在陶瓷器拼接修复过程中，由于操作不当，造成周围其他碎片匹配粘接不当，致使某个碎片没有足够空间粘接回原位。
low fired 低温煅烧	A low fired ceramic is one that is heated to a relatively low temperature producing a soft and porous body such as earthenware. 低温煅烧陶瓷是一种加热到较低温度的陶瓷，其陶瓷胎体相对较软且多孔，如陶器。
majolica 西班牙锡釉陶	Majolica is a tin glazed earthenware produced in Spain. Majolica是产于西班牙的锡釉陶器。

manganese 锰	Manganese (Mn) is a metal used in the form of manganese oxide to colour glass and decorate ceramics. When used in glass, it gives a pale red or pink colour. When used to decorate ceramics, it yields a colour from purple to rich brown, depending on the the glaze and intensity. manganese oxide was also used as a decolourizing agent in the production of glass. 锰（Mn）是一种以氧化锰形式用于对陶瓷进行着色和装饰的金属。其用于玻璃时，会使玻璃呈淡红色或粉红色。而用于装饰陶瓷时，在不同的瓷釉上，它会产生从紫色到深棕色等各种颜色。锰的氧化物也被用作玻璃生产中的脱色剂。
marble 大理石	Marble is a metamorphic rock made of calcium carbonate ($CaCO_3$), often used for sculptures and in architectural applications. 大理石是一种由碳酸钙($CaCO_3$)组成的变质岩，通常用于雕塑和建筑。
marl 泥灰岩	Marl is a natural clay containing iron oxide and a high proportion of calcium compounds. Marls are used as potting clays for low-fired earthenware and brick clays. 泥灰岩是一种天然粘土，含有氧化铁及高比例的钙化合物。其常被用作低温煅烧陶器的陶土。
marver 滚料板 （吹制玻璃工作台面）	A marver is a flat surface, originally of stone or marble, later of iron, on which the gather of molten glass on the end of the blow-pipe is rolled into a cylindrical or globular mass. The process is known as marvering. 滚料板（吹制玻璃工作台面）最初是一个用石或大理石制成，后改用铁制成的平坦工作台面。在此工作台面上，玻璃吹制工匠往往将吹管末端的熔融玻璃塑造成圆柱形或球形。这一过程称为滚料。
marvering 滚料	See marver. 见滚料板（吹制玻璃工作台面）。
melamine resin 三聚氰胺树脂	A melamine resin is an oligomer that is crosslinked with formaldehyde to form a rigid thermosetting polymer. Melamine resins have been used as coatings in restoring ceramics. 三聚氰胺树脂是与甲醛交联以形成刚性热固性聚合物的低聚物。三聚氰胺树脂是已被用作修复陶瓷的涂料。
mending leads 铅补丁	Mending leads were used in the traditional way of repairing breaks in pieces of glass. A thin 'string' strip of lead was fixed between the glass edges. In order to accommodate the leads, the edges of the glass had to be chipped away or grozed. 铅补丁是传统的玻璃裂缝修复方式。一根细铅补丁被固定于玻璃边缘之间。为了安置铅补丁，必须切除玻璃的边缘或用烙铁修整铅补丁（压花）。
mica 云母	Mica is a group of silicate minerals with a two-dimensional layer structure. 云母是一组具有二维层状结构的硅酸盐矿物。
milky weathering 乳状风化	Milky weathering is the first stage in a form of deterioration of buried glass. Patches or streaks, usually opaque white, appear on the surface, gradually eating more deeply into the walls of the vessel. Later stages are known as enamel-like weathering. 乳状风化是出土玻璃器劣化的第一阶段。玻璃表面通常会出现不透明的白色斑点或条纹，并逐渐深入到玻璃壁中。后期则被称为珐琅状风化。

millefiori "千花"工艺	Millefiori is a style of decorating glass with slices of coloured canes embedded in molten glass, usually in flower like designs. This technique was first known to have been used in Alexandria in the 1st century B.C. The term derives from glass of this sort produced in Venice in the 16th century. Literally translated it means 'thousand flowers'. "千花"工艺是一种将带有纹样的（通常是花）条状玻璃料切成薄片后通过融合这些玻璃片形成装饰的风格，该工艺最早见于公元前一世纪的埃及。Millefiori这个词来源于16世纪威尼斯生产的此类玻璃器，意为"千朵花"。
mineral 矿物	A mineral is a naturally occuring material of defined chemical composition and crystalline form. Mineral names are sometimes used to describe man-made materials with the same properties. 矿物是一种天然存在、具有确定的化学成分和晶体形态的物质。矿物名称有时用于描述具有相同性质的人造材料。
mineral fibre 矿物纤维	A mineral fibre is an inorganic fibre made from minerals usually silicates. Asbestos is the name given to a group of naturally occurring crystalline fibres such as chrysotile $H_4Mg_3Si_2O_9$. 矿物纤维是由矿物（通常是硅酸盐）制成的无机纤维，石棉是一组天然晶体纤维的名称，如温石棉（$H_4Mg_3Si_2O_9$）。
minium 铅丹	Minium is the name for red lead, a red pigment used since antiquity and raw material for making lead glass. 铅丹是红色铅的名称，红色铅是自古以来就使用的红色颜料，是制造铅玻璃的原料。
mirror painting 镜面玻璃画	See backpainting. 见背面涂漆。
montmorillonite 蒙脱土	Montmorillonite is an important group of clay minerals (hydrated aluminium silicates) with a platelet structure which can accommodate varying amounts of water. 蒙脱土是一组重要的粘土矿物（水合硅酸铝），具有片状结构，含水量各不相同。
mosaic glass 马赛克玻璃	Mosaic glass is a term applied to glass objects formed or decorated with many small adjacent pieces of coloured glass, usually slices from long canes. The pieces of glass are placed in a double mould and reheated until the edges of the slices fuse together. See also millefiori. 马赛克玻璃是将很多小的彩色玻璃片融合在一起形成的玻璃物件，小的玻璃片一般切取自长条状玻璃料。将玻璃片置入模具中（上），经二次加热使其融合产生造型。另见"千花"工艺。
muff 筒	A muff is the cylinder of glass made during the production of cylinder glass. 筒指的是在制作圆柱形玻璃过程中形成的玻璃圆柱。
muff glass 筒状玻璃	See cylinder glass. 见圆柱型（方法得到的片状）玻璃。

muffle kiln 马弗炉	A muffle kiln is a small kiln used for low-temperature re-firing of ceramic and glass objects, notably in the process of applying enamel colours and fired gilding. It is used for temperatures from 700 - 900℃. 马弗炉是用于陶瓷和玻璃物体低温再煅烧的小型窑，特别是在施加珐琅彩和烫金的过程中。使用温度在700-900℃之间。
network modifier 陶瓷基体改性剂	A network modifier is a material used in glass and glazes to modify the basic silica structure in order to lower its working and melting temperatures. 陶瓷基体改性剂是一种通过改变二氧化硅基本结构降低其工作和熔融温度的材料。
Norman slab 诺曼平板	A Norman slab is a type of flat glass produced by blowing glass into a square mould producing an oblong bottle shape. The square is then cut so that each side becomes a small, flat piece of glass. 诺曼平板是一种平板玻璃。先将玻璃料吹入长方体模具以形成长方体玻璃泡，然后将长方体玻璃泡的四面切割下来形成小型的平板玻璃。
Normandy mode 诺曼底模式	Normandy mode is the name of the process by which crown glass is made. 诺曼底模式指的是皇冠法玻璃工艺的制作过程。
obsidian 黑曜石	Obsidian is a volcanic material and the earliest from of natural glass used by man. It is usually black or very dark in colour. It has been found in the near east and Mexico and was much used for flaked tools of a similar form to flint tools. 黑曜石是一种火山物质，是人类最早使用的天然玻璃。它通常是黑色或其他深色。近东和墨西哥都有发现，被广泛用于类似于燧石的片状工具。
on-glaze colour 釉中彩	On ceramics, on-glaze colour is a design applied over the main glaze which may or may not be fired on. 陶瓷中，釉中彩是施用在底釉上的装饰材料和技法，上釉之前底釉可经素烧或不素烧。
opacifier 乳浊剂	An opacifier is a material that produces opacity in an otherwise translucent material such as a glaze, glass or varnish. 乳浊剂是在半透明的材料（如釉料，玻璃或清漆）中产生不透明性的材料。
opalising agents 乳浊介质	Opalising agents are materials used to produce opacity in glass. In the Roman period, calcium antimonate was used. By 500AD tin oxide was in use. In the 18th century this was replaced by calcium fluoride or lead arsenate. 乳浊介质是用于制作不透明玻璃的媒介。罗马时期使用锑酸钙为乳浊介质。公元500年前后，氧化锡被普遍用作乳浊介质。18世纪氟化钙和砷酸铅成为主要的乳浊介质。
opus sectile 马赛克玻璃制作中的一个环节名称	An opus sectile is a mosaic panel made of pieces of glass which are not fused together, but embedded in mortar. opus sectile指的是尚未进行高温融合的，尚嵌于砂浆中的，由玻璃片组合而成的马赛克板。

oxblood 牛血红	See sang de boeuf. 见铜红釉。
p̂ate-de-verre 碎玻璃融合技术	P̂ate-de-verre is a material used to produce moulded glass. It is made by grinding glass to a powder, adding a fluxing medium so that it will melt readily, and then colouring it. It is put in a mould and fused by firing. The process was first used in ancient Egypt and was revived in France in the 19th century. 碎玻璃融合技术是一种利用模具成型玻璃的方法。将玻璃研磨成粉末，添加助熔剂使其易于熔化，然后再进行着色，它的烧制过程是在模具中完成的。该工艺最初见于古代埃及玻璃生产，19世纪的法国复兴了该工艺。
petroglyph 岩石壁画	A petroglyph is a rock-carving or inscription. 岩石壁画是在岩石上进行雕刻或题刻。
pinhole 针孔	A pinhole is a fault in a glaze or glass produced during manufacture through release of gasses and manifested as tiny, raised holes. 针孔是在制造过程中，因气体的挥发导致在釉料或玻璃中产生的缺陷，表现为微小的凸起孔。
plique a jour 金属网嵌珐琅	Plique a jour is an enamelling technique where enamel is applied to open metal network (without a metal base) so that light can shine through. 金属网嵌珐琅是一种珐琅镶嵌技术，将珐琅镶嵌在开放的金属网（非金属胎）上，以便光线可以穿透。
porcelain 瓷	Porcelain is a fine textured vitrified ceramic body, fired to above 1260℃. 瓷是一种具有玻璃质地的陶瓷胎体，烧制温度需在1260℃以上。
potash glass 钾玻璃	Potash glass is glass in which the alkali constituent is potash (potassium carbonate). Potash serves as a flux to reduce the fusion point of silica when making glass. Potash for glassmaking was obtained in early Germany and Bohemia by burning beechwood and oak and in France by burning fern and bracken. 钾玻璃是由钾盐（碳酸钾）作为助熔剂制成的玻璃。钾盐作为助熔剂可减低二氧化硅的熔点。在德国和波西米亚，制造玻璃的钾盐是通过燃烧山毛榉木或橡木获得的，在法国钾盐通过燃烧蕨类植物获得。
Prince Rupert's drops 鲁珀特王子之泪	See Rupert's drops. 见鲁珀特水滴。
prunt 贴花装饰	A prunt is a blob of glass applied to a glass object as decoration and/or to provide a better grip on the object if there is no handle. 贴花装饰是一种施加于玻璃器物上用以装饰的玻璃点状物，若器物没有手柄，则此点状贴花便于人们抓握。
purple-of–cassius 金锡紫	Purple-of-cassius is a pigment of crimson purple colour that was sometimes used to colour glass. The pigment was prepared by precipitating a gold solution by means of chloride of tin to produce colloidal gold. This was then added to the batch. 金锡紫是一种深红色的颜料，有时用于玻璃着色。该颜料是通过用锡氯化物将金溶液中的金，以胶体形式沉积出来而制成的。然后将金锡紫加入到料中使玻璃呈色。

pyrite 黄铁矿	Pyrite is an iron sulphide mineral [FeS$_2$] which is an important iron ore. It occurs as a corrosion product, especially on waterlogged iron. 黄铁矿是一种重要的铁矿石，硫化铁矿物[FeS$_2$]。它以腐蚀产物的形式出现，特别是在浸水的铁上。
pyrite disease 黄铁矿病害	Pyrite disease is the oxidation of pyrite inclusions in stone to sulphur-based acids which attack carbonates also present in the stone. Pyrite disease is a major cause of damage to palaeontological specimens. 黄铁矿病害是石头中夹杂的黄铁矿被氧化为硫基酸，从而腐蚀石头中的碳酸盐。黄铁矿病害是破坏古生物学标本的主要因素。
quarry 采石场	A quarry is an open source for the extraction of building stone. 采石场是用于开采建筑石材的露天资源。
quartz 石英	Quartz is a mineral which is a modification of silicon dioxide (SiO$_2$). It is common in rocks and gemstones. 石英是二氧化硅的改性矿物（ SiO$_2$ ），它在岩石和宝石中很常见。
ramped fill 倾斜填充	A ramped fill is a fill applied along a mis-aligned bond so that the flll runs from the surface of one side of the lacuna to the surface on the other side. It is angled to produce a more uniform profile and prevent the defect detracting from the final appearance. 倾斜填充指沿着未对齐的粘接线进行的填充，以便填充物从空隙一侧的表面过渡至其另一面。倾斜的目的在于以下两个方面：一方面，保持外型顺畅；另一方面，阻止缺陷偏离最终的器表。
releading 重打铅补丁	Releading is the replacement of lost or weak leading on stained glass panels. 彩色镶嵌玻璃的修复过程中，替换遗失或薄弱处铅补丁的过程。
relief engraving 浮雕	See wheel engraving. 见车轮雕刻。
revetment 铺面 / 护墙	See opus sectile. 见马赛克玻璃制作中的一个环节名称。
rib mark 旋痕	A rib mark is a groove and ridge produced on a ceramic when a wooden or metal tool (rib) is used to smooth the clay during the process of throwing on a wheel. 旋痕是陶瓷坯件在利坯过程中，用金属或木质工具在旋转的轮车上修整坯件时，留下的凹槽和脊线。
rivet (1) 铆钉 (1)	A rivet is a mechanical method of joining ceramic sherds, using a metal wire or strip which spans the break between two sherds. The wires are secured with adhesive into holes or slot cut into the sherds. Because of the damage caused to the original mater, this method is no longer employed. 铆钉是一种使用金属丝或金属条横跨两个陶瓷碎片将其连接的机械方法。金属丝用粘接剂固定于陶瓷碎片的洞中或槽中。由于会对本体造成损害，此方法已不再使用。
rock crystal 水晶	Rock crystal is natural quartz which is pure silica. It is usually colourless and transparent or translucent. 水晶是天然石英，是纯二氧化硅。通常呈无色透明或半透明状。
running crack 流动裂纹	A running crack is a crack in a ceramic that gradually opens from an intact portion. 流动裂纹是指陶瓷中从完整部分逐渐产生的开裂。

Rupert's drops 鲁珀特水滴	Rupert's drops are tadpole shaped hollow glass objects about 50mm long with a bulbous end tapering to a thin curved tail. They were made by dropping a small blob of fully molten glass into cold water and leaving it until it cooled. They are not affected by a blow to the bulbous end, but if the tail is broken or the surface scratched, the piece explodes loudly into a fine powder due to internal stresses. 鲁珀特水滴是长约50mm的蝌蚪形中空玻璃制品，其球根端逐渐变细为弯曲尾巴。它们是通过将一小滴完全熔化的玻璃滴入冷水中，并将其留置在水中直至冷却而成的。鲁珀特水滴可以承受巨大的外部压力而不破碎，但鲁珀特水滴的尾端一旦折断，整个鲁珀特水滴将在内应力的作用下大声爆炸成细粉末。
saddle bar 鞍座杆	A saddle bar is an iron bar that is fixed across leaded stained glass with ties to provide support to the glass panel. 鞍座杆是用绑带固定在打好铅补丁的彩色玻璃上，以为玻璃面板提供支撑的铁棒。
sang de boeuf 铜红釉	Sang de boeuf is French for oxblood. The term is used for a brilliant red glaze developed in China during the Qing dynasty. The colouring agent for this glaze is copper oxide fired in a reducing atmosphere. Sang de boeuf是牛血红的法语。该术语用于指清代创烧的一种的色艳亮丽的红色釉。该釉以氧化铜为着色剂，在还原气氛中烧成。
semi-synthetic fibre 半合成纤维	A semi-synthetic fibre is a fibre manufactured by the modification of a natural polymer. The most common semi-synthetic polymers, such as viscose, rayon, cellulose acetates and nitrate, are made from cellulose. 半合成纤维是由天然聚合物改性而制成的纤维，最常见的半合成聚合物，例如，粘胶、人造丝、醋酸纤维素和硝酸盐，都是由纤维素制成的。
sherd 碎片	A sherd is a fragment of pottery or glass. 碎片是陶器或玻璃的碎片。
sick glass 病态玻璃	Sick glass is a type of glass deterioration caused by the reaction of atmospheric water vapour with the alkalis in the glass mixture. It is recognisable at various phases of disintegration: formation of salts on the glass surface (making the glass appear cloudy); droplets of water on the surface (weeping or sweating glass); fine surface crazing (crizzling). The reaction results from an imperfect proportion of ingredients in the batch, notably too much alkali or an incorrect proportion of calcium oxide. The problem is neither infectious nor treatable, although further deterioration can be controlled through the use of correct climate control. It is most commonly found in glass from the late 17th century from England, Holland, Germany, China and Venice. See also crizzling and weeping glass. 病态玻璃是玻璃的一种衰变类型。它是因大气中的水蒸气与玻璃基体中的碱起化学反应而产生。其在玻璃衰变的各个阶段均可见，基本表现为在玻璃表面形成析出盐层，从而使玻璃呈现云雾状。在玻璃表面形成水滴（"玻璃出汗"）；表面裂痕（泛碱）。病态玻璃的起因多与玻璃本身配方比例不当有关，过多的碱性助熔剂或比例不当的钙质稳定剂都可能导致病态玻璃现象的出现。病态玻璃不会传染，但也无法修复，通过控制保存环境可以减缓衰变。病态玻璃在17世纪的英国，荷兰，德国，中国和威尼斯生产的玻璃中最常见。

silane	A silane is a silicon-carbon monomer, typically methyltriethoxy silane $Si(CH_3)(OC_2H_5)_3$ which is used in conservation for the consolidation of stone and ceramic objects. A silane coupling agent has groups which react with a polymer and a substrate in order to increase the durability of the adhesion between an adhesive and a glass surface.
硅烷	硅烷是硅碳单体，通常指甲基三乙氧基硅烷 $Si（CH_3）（OC_2H_5）_3$，用于保护石材和陶瓷物体的固结。硅烷偶联剂具有依次与聚合物和基材反应的基团，以增加粘接剂和玻璃表面之间的粘结耐久性。
silver staining	Silver staining is a technique for colouring glass. Silver sulphide is fired onto the surface to produce a deep yellow colour.
银着色	银着色是一种玻璃着色技术。将硫化银烧制到玻璃表面而生成深黄色。
sintering	Sintering of clay particles occurs when they have been heated sufficiently for components of the mixture to fuse at the contact points between the particles but without bulk liquification. At this point clay undergoes shrinkage and irreversible change to become a ceramic. The temperature at which this happens depends on the composition of the mixture, but is above 500℃.
烧结	粘土颗粒烧结发生于粘土被充分加热后，黏土中各个组分的颗粒在接触点产生融合但未出现整体液化的时候。此时，粘土会出现收缩和不可逆转的变化转换成陶瓷。烧结温度取决于混合物的组分，但一般高于500℃。
soda glass	Soda glass is glass in which the alkali constituent is soda (soda carbonate). Soda serves as a flux to reduce the fusion point of silica when making glass. Soda was traditionally obtained from Natron (Egypt) or sea plants. Egyptian, Roman, and Venetian glass were all soda glasses. Soda glass also contains some lime (approximately 15%) and is sometimes referred to as soda-lime glass.
苏打玻璃	苏打玻璃是碱成分为苏打（碳酸钠）的玻璃。苏打作为助熔剂，可降低玻璃制造时二氧化硅的熔点。玻璃制造中所用的苏打苏打传统上是从埃及泡碱或海洋植物中获得的。埃及，罗马和威尼斯玻璃均为苏打玻璃，而这些玻璃中同时还含有一定量的氧化钙（15%左右），故通常此类玻璃被称为钠钙玻璃。
solarisation (2)	Solarisation of a colourless glass is the development of a marked tint when the glass is exposed to sunlight for a long time. The tint is usually blue or purple and is caused by radiation damage leading to a reaction between iron and manganese oxide constituents in the glass.
过度曝晒 (2)	无色玻璃的过度曝晒是指玻璃长期暴露于太阳下而形成色调。色调显色通常为蓝色或紫色，是铁与锰的氧化物在阳光辐照下发生反应而导致的。
spinning process	Spinning is a technique used to produce a replica part, for instance in ceramic conservation. Wet plaster is shaped using a template on a turntable and then carved to incorporate fragments of the object.
旋压成型	在陶瓷修复中，旋压成型是一种制作器物缺失部分复制品的技术。先将湿石膏在旋转台上按模版塑形，然后再依据器物其他残片的特征对其进一步雕琢。

springing 弹变	Springing in a ceramic or glass object is the distortion resulting from the release of tension during breakage. The tension is usually created during initial manufacture by inadequate annealing. Springing can also result from tensions developed during deterioration, such as corrosion of metals. It can be seen either as a stepped crack or as the inability to make good joins during their reconstruction of a whole vessel. 陶瓷或玻璃物体的弹变是指陶瓷或玻璃材料断裂时释放张力所导致的变形。该张力通常是初始生产期间因退火不充分而产生的。劣化过程中产生的张力亦可导致弹变。也可以将其视为阶梯状开裂，或是容器重塑时未能较好连接所致。
static soak 静态浸泡	A static soak is a process which is carried out in order to desalinate an object. The object or its sherds is placed in purified water in a container. The soak water is changed on a regular basis and the salts are thus extracted. 静态浸泡是将某器物脱盐过程中的一道工序。将物体或其碎片置于容器中的纯净水中，定期更换水以析出器物中的盐分。
step 错位	A step on a join is the mis-alignment of the fragments during bonding. 错位指陶瓷碎片拼接过程中对接不准确导致的缺陷。
sticking order 粘贴顺序	Sticking order is the logical sequence in which sherds are bonded together to prevent locking out. 粘贴顺序是将器物碎片粘合在一起以防止出现碎片失位的逻辑顺序。
stoneware 炻器	Stoneware is a fairly coarse ceramic body which is partially vitrified by firing to ca 1250℃ but retains a degree of porosity. 炻器是一种较粗糙的陶瓷体，其烧成温度约为1250℃，其胎体已部分玻璃化，但仍会保留一定程度的孔隙率。
surface engraving 表面雕刻	See wheel engraving. 见车轮雕刻。
sweating glass "出汗"玻璃	See weeping glass 见"出汗"玻璃。
T-bar T型条	T-bars are horizontal iron or steel bars used to support stained glass panels onto which they are fixed with pins. T型条指用于支撑固定于其上的彩绘玻璃板的水平铁条或钢条。
tears 眼泪状气泡	Tears are air bubbles in the shape of tears, encased in the stem of drinking glasses or other glassware, or occasionally in a finial or solid knop. 眼泪状气泡指的是玻璃饮水器皿或其它玻璃器皿中包裹的气泡，有时也出现在顶端或实心球形装饰中。
terracotta 赤土陶器	Terracotta is low-fired, usually unglazed, red to buff coloured earthenware ceramic body. 赤土陶器是低温煅烧成红色至浅黄色的陶瓷体，通常不上釉。

thermal history 热历史	The thermal history of a ceramic object is the previous exposure to heat that the object has experienced, and which can be recovered through thermoluminescence dating. 陶瓷物体的热历史指陶瓷烧制过程中的受热情况，该热历史可通过热发光测年的方式予以确定。
thermal shock 热冲击	Thermal shock is a sudden change of temperature which causes stresses in a material. In glass and vitreous ceramics, the stresses may cause damage or breakage when released. The shock of hot water or hot air may be used to disassemble bonds from previous restoration. 热冲击指的是温度突然变化而引起材料的应力。在玻璃和玻璃陶瓷中，若使用此法，被释放应力可能导致物体损坏或破裂。可以使用热水或热空气的冲击来拆解开先前修复的粘结。
thermal stress 热应力	Thermal stress is internal forces in an object caused by the differential change of properties, typically size, resulting from a sudden change in temperature. 热应力是由于温度的突然变化导致的基体内某种性质的差异化改变（通常是尺寸），因而引起物体内部应力。
tie 连接	See rivet. 见铆钉。
travertine 石灰华	Travertine is a white calcium carbonate ($CaCO_3$) based sedimentary rock often used as building stone. 石灰华是一种基于白色碳酸钙($CaCO_3$)的沉积岩，通常用作建筑石材。
under glaze decoration 釉下彩	Under glaze decoration is a colour or design applied to a ceramic under the main glaze. 釉下彩是应用于主釉下陶瓷的一种颜色或设计。
Verre de Fougere 福格尔玻璃	See potash glass. 见钾玻璃。
vitrification 玻璃化	Vitrification is the conversion of a solid substance into its vitreous state by inducing heat, for example, ceramic becomes vitreous above 1100 C. 玻璃化是指通过加热将固体物质转化为玻璃态，例如，陶瓷在1100摄氏度以上变为玻璃质。
waldglas 森林玻璃	See potash glass. 见钾玻璃。
waster 废品	A waster is a defective ceramic discarded when removed from the kiln. 废品是指从窑中取出时，丢弃的有缺陷的陶瓷。
water white 水白色	A water white material is a material that has the lack of colour and opacity typical of water. Water white adhesives and casting materials are used particularly in ceramics and glass conservation. 水白色材料是指像水一样无色且透明的材料。水白色粘接剂和铸造材料特别用于陶瓷和玻璃保护。

weeping glass "出汗" 玻璃	Weeping glass is a stage in glass deterioration that manifests itself by droplets of moisture on the glass surface. Weeping is the result of chemically uncombined alkali being leached out by the action of water vapour. See also sick glass and crizzling. "出汗" 玻璃是玻璃劣化的一个阶段，表现为玻璃表面存在小水滴。"出汗" 是因水蒸气的作用引起的游离碱析出。另参见病态玻璃和泛碱。
wheel cutting 车轮切割	See wheel-engraving. 见车轮雕刻。
wheel-engraving 车轮雕刻	Wheel-engraving is a decorating technique of glass surfaces by the grinding action of a wheel, using disks of various materials and sizes. It is similar to glass cutting, but is more skilful. The technique has been in use since the medieval period in Egypt, Syria, Persia and Rome and sometime later in Germany and Bohemia. 车轮雕刻指的是使用各种不同材料和尺寸的圆盘，通过轮子的打磨作用对玻璃表面进行装饰的技术。它类似于玻璃切割，但技巧性更强。自中世纪以来，埃及、叙利亚、波斯、罗马及之后德国和波西米亚地区一直使用该技术。

09

建 筑
Architecture

action planning **行动计划**	In architectural conservation, action planning proposes major change to an area through development, redevelopment or improvement. Action planning can be the explicit result of institutional policy and professional philosophy. 在建筑保护过程中，行动计划建议通过具体措施对某个区域带来较大改变。行动计划可以是机构政策和专业理念明确体现的结果。
adobe **土坯**	Adobe is a Spanish term for mudbricks made of unfired, sun dried earth for buildings in arid climates. 土坯是西班牙语术语，指在干旱气候下用未烧制、晒干的泥土制成的泥砖。
aeolic erosion **风蚀作用**	Aeolic erosion is the surface attrition or wear of a material caused by wind blown abrasive powder, such as sand. 风蚀是指因风吹起的粗糙的粉末（如沙子）造成的材料表面磨损或损耗。
aggregate (1) **骨料/集料（1）**	In architectural conservation, an aggregate is the sand or gravel which is combined with an appropriate binding agent to make concrete, mortars, renders and plasters. 在建筑保护中，骨料是指与适当的粘合剂混合制成混凝土、砂浆、抹灰和灰泥的砂或砾石。
architect **建筑师**	An architect is a person professionally trained and accredited in the design and administration of building construction. 建筑师是在设计和管理建筑建造过程方面，受过专业训练和有专业资质的人。
architectural conservation **建筑保护**	Architectural conservation secures the long term survival or preservation of historic buildings, monuments and areas. 建筑保护确保历史建筑、纪念物和历史地段的长时留存或保存。
architectural conservator **建筑保护者**	An architectural conservator is an individual with knowledge and experience in the conservation of historic buildings, monuments and areas. 建筑保护者是在历史建筑、古迹和历史区域的保护方面具有知识和经验的个人。
architectural element **建筑要素**	An architectural element is one of the principal parts of a building, such as roof, wall, or floor. 建筑要素是建筑物的主要部分之一，如屋顶、墙壁或地板。
architecture **建筑/建筑学**	Architecture is the art and science of designing and administrating the construction of buildings or other structures. 建筑学是设计和管理建筑物或其他构筑物建造过程的艺术和科学。
artificial stone **人造石**	Artificial stone is a cast imitation of natural stone made of concrete which carries on its surface dust or chippings of the natural stone to be copied. 人造石是由混凝土铸成的天然石材的仿制品，其表面有复制的天然石材的灰尘或碎屑。
asbestos **石棉**	Asbestos consists of fibrous silicate minerals and was widely used in buildings and textiles for its heat resistance and insulating properties until its carcinogenic properties were discovered. 石棉由纤维状硅酸盐矿物组成，因其耐热性和绝缘性而广泛应用于建筑和纺织品中，后被发现具有致癌性。

asbestos board 石棉板	Asbestos board is a solid fibreboard consisting of asbestos fibres and binders, also including mineral fillers in the case of specific grades, intended for insulation, sealing and flame protection. It is virtually non-flammable. 石棉板是一种实心纤维板，由石棉纤维和粘合剂组成，也包括特定等级的矿物填料，用于绝缘、密封和防火。它几乎是不可燃的。
barium carbonate 碳酸钡	Insoluble barium carbonate ($BaCO_3$) is formed when a solution of barium hydroxide is applied to limestone as a consolidant. 当氢氧化钡溶液用作石灰石的固结剂时，会形成不溶性碳酸钡（$BaCO_3$）。
barium salt 钡盐	Barium salts, especially barium hydroxide [Ba(OH)2], are sometimes used as a consolidant for limestone. They react to form insoluble barium carbonate and barium sulphate. 钡盐，特别是氢氧化钡（$Ba(OH)_2$），有时用作石灰石的固结剂。它们反应生成不溶性碳酸钡和硫酸钡。
baryta water 氧化钡水	Baryta water is a saturated aqueous solution of barium hydroxide [Ba(OH)$_2$] in water. It is sometimes used as a consolidant for limestone to convert soluble calcium carbonate and gypsum into insoluble barium carbonate and barium sulphate. 钡水是氢氧化钡（Ba(OH)$_2$）在水中的饱和水溶液。它有时用作石灰石的固结剂，将可溶性碳酸钙和石膏转化为不溶性碳酸钡和硫酸钡。
basalt 玄武岩	Basalt is a dark volcanic rock which consists mainly of the minerals plagioclase, pyroxene and magnetite and forms characteristic polygonal columns. 玄武岩是一种黑色火山岩，主要由斜长石、辉石、磁铁矿等矿物质构成，形成独特的多边形柱体。
base moulding 底座线脚 / 底座线饰	A base moulding is a shape carved into the lower part of a column or plinth. It is also called bed moulding. 底座线脚是刻在柱子或柱基下部的形状。它也称为深凹饰。
bearing wall 承重墙	A bearing wall is a wall that provides support for a structural member (such as a beam) or element (such as a floor) in a building. 承重墙是为建筑物中的结构性构件（如房梁）或元素（如地板）提供支持。
bed "床" / 平面	A bed is the horizontal surface on to which bricks or stones are lain. "床"是放置砖石的水平表面。
black crust (1) 黑色结壳 (1)	A black crust is a crust which is coloured by smoke and similar pollution. 黑色结壳是一种被烟雾和类似污染物着色的外壳。
black crust (2) 黑色结壳 (2)	On limestones, a black crust is an encrustation of calcium sulphate (gypsum) caused by reaction with atmospheric sulphur oxides and smoke. 在石灰岩上，黑色的外壳是硫酸钙（石膏）与大气中的硫氧化物和烟雾反应形成的硬壳。

braced frame 支撑框架	In architecture, a braced frame is a number of straight lengths of material joined end to end to form a closed circumference with the addition of lengths across the interior to prevent its collapse. The materials used are typically wood, steel or concrete. 在建筑中，支撑框架是一系列笔直的材料末端连接在一起形成一个围合结构，在内部增加直线连接材料以防止坍塌。使用的材料通常是木材、钢筋或混凝土。
brick 砖	A brick is a cuboid of fired clay. Bricks can also be made of unfired clay, sand and lime, or concrete. 砖是烧制的粘土立方体。砖也可由未烧制的粘土、沙子和石灰或混凝土制成。
brickwork 砖砌	Brickwork is the orderly arrangement of bricks which are bonded together in the construction of walls and similar structures. 砖砌是在建造墙壁和类似结构时，将砖块整齐有序地堆砌在一起。
building 建筑物	A building is the result of a deliberate construction process. 建筑物是缜密的建筑过程达到的结果。
building code 建筑规范	A building code is national, regional or local legislation and/or guidance determining standards and approaches to construction. 建筑规范是确定建造标准和方法的国家、地区或地方立法和/或指南。
building material 建筑材料	Building materials are organic and inorganic materials used in the construction and subsequent repair or maintenance of buildings. 建筑材料是在建筑建造和后续修缮、维护中使用的有机和无机材料。
building survey 建筑勘察	A building survey is a detailed inspection of a building to determine its construction, related condition and internal environment. 建筑勘察是对建筑物进行详细检查，以确定其构造、相关条件和内部环境。
buildings at risk 濒危建筑	Buildings at risk are those deemed to be at risk from neglect and disrepair following a survey undertaken within a particular geographic area or of a specific building type. 濒危建筑是指在特定地段或特定建筑类型中调查后，被视为存在疏于照管和失修风险的建筑物。
built environment 建成环境	The built environment is those areas that are constructed, including buildings and roads. See also natural environment. 建成环境是指那些人工建造的区域，包括建筑物和道路。另见自然环境。
carbonate efflorescence 碳酸盐风化	Carbonate efflorescence is insoluble carbonate salts formed on porous materials such as brick. 碳酸盐风化是在多孔材料（如砖）上形成的不溶碳酸盐。
Carbowax® 碳蜡®	Carbowax is a water soluble wax based on poly(ethylene glycol). It has been used to consolidate decayed archaeological material such as wood, leather or glass. 碳蜡（商标名）是一种基于聚乙二醇的水溶性蜡。它被用来加固腐朽的考古材料，如木材、皮革或玻璃等。

cement 水泥	Cement is an inorganic powder which, after mixing with water, sets to a hard mass. Cement is normally mixed with aggregates such as sand or gravel to make concrete. See also Portland cement. 水泥是一种无机粉末，与水混合后凝结成硬块。水泥通常与砂石等集料混合制成混凝土。另见硅酸盐水泥。
cement mortar 水泥砂浆	Cement mortar is prepared from cement as the binding agent and sand as the aggregate. 水泥砂浆是以水泥为粘结剂、沙为集料配制而成的。
change control 变更控制	Change control is a decision making process imposed by regulatory authorities on proposed changes of building use. 变更控制是由监管机构对于建筑用途变更方案控制的决策过程。
change of use 用途变更	Change of use is the acceptance that a building is suitable for a use which is different from its initial or subsequent uses. 用途变更是指同意建筑适合于与最初或后续用途不同的其他用途。
clay 粘土	Clay is a weathering product of igneous and metamorphic rocks. It consists of hydrated aluminium silicates. 粘土是火成岩和变质岩风化的产物。它由水化铝硅酸盐组成。
clay minerals 粘土矿物	Clay minerals are aluminium silicates such as kaolinite [Al2Si2O5(OH)4] which can accommodate varying amounts of water between their plate-like crystals. 粘土矿物是铝硅酸盐，例如高岭土 [Al2Si2O5(OH)4]，它可以在板状晶体之间容纳不同量的水份。
concrete 混凝土	Concrete is a mixture made by mixing water, a binding agent (cement or lime), sands and larger aggregates. The mixture sets to form an amorphous material which is used for structural and non-structural uses. 混凝土是由水、粘合剂（水泥或石灰）、沙和体积更大的骨料混在一起的混合物。混合物凝固形成一种非晶态材料，用于结构和非结构用途。
consent 同意／许可	Consent is given as the formal approval or permission to undertake some task (such as the construction of a building). 许可是对开始执行某项任务（如建筑施工）的正式批准或许可。
conservation area 保护区	A conservation area is an area formally designated as being of special architectural or historic interest. 保护区是正式指定为具有特殊建筑或历史意义的区域。
conversion 改建	The conversion of a building is its alteration from one type or use to another. 建筑物的改建是指建筑物从一种类型或用途改为另一种类型或用途。
coursed stonework 层列砌石	Coursed stonework denotes stones or brick in a wall laid out horizontally in a continuous layer. 层列砌石结构表示墙壁中的砖石以水平方向逐层垒砌。

coursing joint 成行缝	A coursing joint (bed joint) is the horizontal mortar joint between adjacent layers of bricks or building stone in a wall. 成行缝（垫层缝）是指墙内相邻砖层或石层之间的水平灰浆接缝。
crust 结壳	On stone, a crust forms as a hard surface layer resulting from corrosion or surface deposit, typically in an aggressive or polluted environment. 在石头上，结壳是由于腐蚀或表面沉积而形成的坚硬表层，通常在具有侵蚀性的或污染性的环境中产生。
cryptoefflorescence 隐粉化	Cryptoefflorescence is a sub-surface deposition of soluble salts within porous material, such as brick and stone. 隐粉化是可溶盐在多孔材料（如砖和石头）中的亚表面沉积。
cultural landscape 文化景观	A cultural landscape is an expression of the aesthetic, historic, scientific or social significances and values associated with a particular natural or man-made landscape. 文化景观是与特定自然或人造景观有关的美学、历史、科学或社会意义和价值的表达。
dampproof barrier 防潮 / 屏障	A dampproof barrier is an impervious material included within the construction of a new building or inserted into an existing building to prevent the movement of moisture (typically from the ground). The barrier can be a solid membrane, such as lead, or a hydrophobic consolidant injected into the building element. 防潮屏障是在新建筑建造时纳入或现有建筑中添加的一层不透水材料，以防止潮气（通常来自地面）进入建筑物。屏障可以是固体薄膜，如铅，或者是注入建筑构件中的疏水性固结剂。
dampproofing 防潮	Dampproofing is the use or insertion of a dampproof barrier. 防潮是使用或插入防潮屏障。
daub 胶泥	Daub is an earth-based plaster applied to backing to form infill panels in timber-framed constructions. 胶泥是一种土基灰泥，用于支撑木结构建造中的填充板。
dead gypsum 硬石膏	Dead gypsum is calcium sulphate ($CaSO_4$)which has lost all its structural water through excessive heating. Unlike plaster of Paris, it will only rehydrate and set very slowly and cannot be used as gypsum plaster. 硬石膏是硫酸钙($CaSO_4$)，由于过度加热，它失去了所有的结构水。不像巴黎石膏，它的复水和凝结非常慢，不能用作石膏灰泥。
demolition 拆除	Demolition is the deliberate destruction of a built structure. 拆除是有计划的破坏已建成的建筑物。
derelict 废弃的	A derelict building is one that has been abandoned, neglected and is in need of considerable repair and maintenance. 废弃建筑物是指被遗弃、无人照管的需要大规模维修维护的建筑物。
design guidelines 设计导则	Design guidelines are guidelines concerning the design of buildings that are provided by national or local authorities. 设计导则是国家或地方政府提供的有关建筑设计的指南。

developer 开发商	A developer is a person or a company that undertakes development for financial gain. 开发商是为了经济利益而进行开发的个人或公司。
development 开发	Development is the making of any material change in the use of any building or other land, such as building, engineering, or mining. 开发是指对建筑物或土地的使用进行的重大物质改变（如建筑、工程或采矿等）。
distemper 水浆涂料	Distemper is an opaque paint made with a glue or casein binding medium frequently with a chalk pigment. It was often used in interiors. 水浆涂料是一种不透明涂料，由胶水或酪蛋白结合介质制成，通常与白垩颜料混合。它经常用于室内装饰。
dolomitic lime 白云石石灰	Dolomitic lime is lime prepared from dolomite which is a double carbonate of calcium and magnesium. 白云石石灰是由白云石制成的石灰，白云石是钙和镁的双重碳酸盐。
dry-grit blasting 干喷砂处理	Dry-grit blasting is a cleaning treatment which uses a strong air jet to blow abrasive onto a surface such as a wall. This method has frequently proved to be destructive and has caused damage to buildings. 干喷砂处理是一种清洁处理，使用强度很大的空气射流将磨料喷到建筑表面，如墙壁上。这种方法通常被证明具有破坏性，会对建筑物造成损害。
earthen floor 土质地面	An earthen floor is a ground floor made of compacted earth. 土质地面是由压实的泥土制成的地板。
efflorescence 粉化	Efflorescence is the surface deposition of soluble salts on porous materials, such as stone or brick, derived from the material itself or the surrounding environment. 粉化是可溶盐在多孔材料（如石头或砖）上的表面沉积，其来源于材料本身或周围环境。
enhancement 优化／提升	An enhancement is a deliberate change which raises or improves the appearance and character of a particular area or region. 提升是一种有计划的改变，以提高或改善某一特定区域的外观和特征。
expanding clay mineral 可膨胀黏土矿物	An expanding clay minerals is an unfired or low fired clay which is able to absorb water between the plate-like clay mineral crystals. The resulting expansion may cause damage to clay objects and to structures built on clay foundations. 可膨胀粘土矿物是一种未烧制或低温烧制的粘土，能够吸收板状粘土矿物晶体之间的水分。由此产生的膨胀可能会对粘土器物和建在粘土地基上的建筑物造成损害。
expansion joints 伸缩缝	Expansion joints are joints in a building which allow thermal expansion of the structure. 伸缩缝是建筑物中允许结构性热膨胀的接缝。

exploratory demolition 勘探性拆除	Exploratory demolition of a building is a documented and controlled demolition carried out in limited areas in order to provide information relating to the construction or condition of the building. 建筑物的勘探性拆除是在限定区域内进行的受控并有记录的拆除，目的是提供与建筑物的建造或整体状况有关的信息。
fabric (2) 构造 (2)	The fabric of a building or object is its overall construction and materials. 建筑或物体构造是其整体结构和材料。
fenestration 开窗 / 窗配列	The fenestration of a building is the arrangement of windows. 建筑物的开窗是指建筑中窗户的设计安排。
flashing 防水板	A flashing is a sheet of metal used to weather-proof joints on a roof. 防水板是安装于屋顶的防水接缝处的金属板。
floor load 楼面荷载	In a building the floor load is the force exerted on the floor. 楼面荷载是一栋建筑中施加在地板上的力。
Frenchman "法国人"（勾缝刀）	A Frenchman is a hand tool used to remove excess mortar from a masonry joint that has been repointed. It is constructed of a metal blade with a right-angled tip. "法国人"（勾缝刀）是一种手工工具，用来清除砖石砌体接缝上多余的灰泥。它是由一个带有直角尖端的金属刀片构成的。
frost damage 冻害	Frost damage is the damage caused to building materials such as porous stone, pipes by freezing water. On freezing, water expands by approx. 9 % which generates high internal pressures causing cracking and spalling. 冻害是指建筑材料如多孔石材、管道因水冻结而造成的损坏。冻结时，水体积会膨胀约9%，从而产生很高的内部压力，导致开裂和剥落。
frost heave 冻胀	Frost heave is the movement of foundations caused by freezing earth saturated with water. The expansion of the water may lead to damage to buildings and other structures. See also frost damage. 冻胀是由渗入水的冻结土引起的地基移动。水的膨胀可能导致建筑物和构筑物的毁损。另见冻害。
grade 级别	In England and Wales, historic buildings of special architectural or historic interest are listed with a grade, I, II* or II in decreasing order of importance. 在英格兰和威尔士，具有特殊建筑或历史意义的历史建筑按重要性的降序排列为一级、二级 * 或二级。
graffiti 涂鸦	Graffiti are texts or symbols painted or sprayed on buildings in acts of vandalism. 涂鸦是在建筑物上蓄意喷绘或涂写文字或符号。
grid-iron planning 正交网格规划	Grid-iron planning involves planning and constructing buildings in blocks within a regular network of roads and access ways. 正文网格规划涉及在棋盘般规整的道路街巷网络中规划和建造建筑组群。

ground (1) 底衬 (1)	A ground is a piece of timber built or inserted into a wall to provide a fixing point for furnishings. 底衬是建在墙上或插在墙上为装饰完工提供固定点的一个木片。
grout 灌浆	A grout is a thin mortar which is poured into the gaps within masonry. 灌浆是注入砌体缝隙中的一种薄灰浆。
grouting 灌浆 / 注浆	Grouting is the process of injecting grout into cavities of a wall. 灌浆是将水泥浆注入墙洞/缝的过程。
gypsum mortar (1) 石膏砂浆 (1)	A gypsum mortar is one made using calcined gypsum (calcium sulfate) binding agent with sands, aggregates and other materials. 石膏砂浆是用煅烧后的石膏（硫酸钙）粘结剂与砂子、集料等材料混合制成的砂浆。
gypsum mortar (2) 石膏砂浆 (2)	A gypsum mortar was a nineteenth-century patent cement based on gypsum and used for decorative plasters. 石膏砂浆是19世纪的一种以石膏为基料的专利水泥，用于装饰性石膏。
hardened mortar 硬化砂浆	Hardened mortar is mortar which has stiffened due to a reaction with atmospheric carbon dioxide (carbonation) and evaporation of water. This typically results in shrinkage of the mortar. 硬化砂浆是因与大气二氧化碳（碳化）发生反应和水蒸发而变硬的砂浆。这通常会导致砂浆缩水。
hawk "鹰"（抹泥刀）	A hawk is a hand tool used to hold mortar while repointing. It is constructed of a small board ca 30 cm square with a handle attached to the middle of one face. "鹰"（抹泥刀）是一种手工工具，用来在勾缝时保持住砂浆。它由一块约30平方厘米的小板构成，其中一面的中间附着一个把手。
high pressure water blasting 高压喷水清理	High pressure water blasting with water lances is a common stone cleaning technique in architectural conservation. 高压水枪喷水清理是建筑保护中常用的石材清理技术。
historic district 历史街区	A historic district is part of a rural or urban settlement that is considered and is often designated as being of special architectural or historic interest. 历史街区是被视为具有特殊的建筑或历史意义乡村或城市聚居区的一部分，通常有官方指定的保护称号。
historic environment 历史环境	A historic environment is an area or region having a recognised architectural or historic significance or value. 历史环境是具有公认的建筑或历史意义或价值的地段或区域。
historic layer 历史层	A historic layer of a historic building or area is the physical evidence of the development and growth over time that can be interpreted as separate from an adjacent layer. 历史建筑或区域中的一个历史层是指其发展演变与其他相邻历史时期有明显区别的物质证据。

historic site 历史遗址	A historic site is a specific rural or urban site that is considered and often designated as being of special architectural or historic interest. 历史遗址是特定的乡村或城市遗址，通常视为具有特殊的建筑或历史意义。
hydraulic cement 水硬性水泥	Hydraulic cement is cement that has the ability to harden and set by chemical reaction with water rather than by reaction with carbon dioxide. 水硬性水泥是一种能够通过与水的化学反应而非与二氧化碳反应而硬化和凝固的水泥。
hydraulic mortar 水硬性砂浆	Hydraulic mortar is mortar that has the ability to harden and set by chemical reaction with water rather than by reaction with carbon dioxide. 水硬性砂浆是一种能够通过与水的化学反应而非与二氧化碳反应而硬化和凝固的砂浆。
impermeable crust 不透水结壳	An impermeable crust is a surface accretion or deposit on a material (particularly stone) that does not permit the passage of liquids and gases. 不透水结壳是一种液体和气体无法通过的物质（特别是石质）表面的堆积或沉积。
jacking (1) 顶托 (1)	In architecture, jacking is the support or lifting of a fragile or collapsing structure by props. 在建筑中，顶托是用支柱支撑或抬升脆弱的或正在塌陷的构架。
jacking (2) 顶进 (2)	Jacking is the volumetric expansion of corroding ferrous metal embedded in masonry that causes displacement of masonry units. 顶进是嵌入石砌中的引起砌筑块材位移的腐蚀性含铁金属的体积膨胀。
joggle 榫接 / 啮合	A joggle is a distorted joint (such as in stone masonry) made so that one part cannot slide past the other. 啮合是一种扭曲的结合体（例如在石砌构造中），使得一部分不能滑过另一部分而得以固定。
joint (1) 接头 / 接缝 (1)	A joint in a building is the junction between horizontal and vertical elements. 建筑物中的接缝是水平构件和垂直构件的连接处。
land use 土地利用	Land use is the type of development or use to which land in a particular area or region may be put. Land use may be stipulated by a regulatory body. 土地利用是指对某一特定地段或区域的土地进行开发或利用的类型。土地利用可由监管机构规定。
landmark building 地标性建筑	A landmark building is a building that is recognised and designated as being of outstanding significance or value. 地标性建筑是指公认和被指定为具有突出意义或价值的建筑。
landscape 景观	Landscape is the natural or man-made setting to buildings and structures, incorporating both 'hard' (for example, paths or walls) and 'soft' (for example, trees or plants) elements and features. 景观是指建筑物和构筑物的自然或人造背景，包括"硬性"元素（如道路或墙体）和"软性"元素（如树木或植物）和特征。

landscape architect 景观设计师	A landscape architect is an architect who is professionally trained and experienced in the design and management of landscapes. 景观设计师是指在景观设计和管理方面受过专业训练和有专业经验的建筑设计师。
lime mortar 石灰砂浆	Lime mortar is a traditional mortar based on slaked lime with sands, aggregates and other materials. 石灰砂浆是一种传统的砂浆，以熟石灰为基料，加入沙子、集料和其他材料。
lime plaster 石灰泥	Lime plaster is a mix of slaked lime with sands, aggregates and other materials (such as tensile reinforcement) used to provide a covering to ceilings and walls. 石灰泥是熟石灰与沙子、集料和其他材料（如增强抗拉材料）的混合物，用作天花板和墙壁的覆盖层。
lime putty 石灰膏 / 油灰	Lime putty is a calcium hydroxide in water produced by the reaction of calcium oxide with water. It is used in mortars, renders, plasters and surface finishes. It reacts with carbon dioxide from the air to form the calcium carbonate which acts as a binding agent. See also slaked lime. 石灰膏是氧化钙与水反应生成的氢氧化钙。它用于砂浆、抹灰和表面处理。作为粘合剂，它与空气中的二氧化碳反应生成碳酸钙。另见熟石灰。
lime wash 石灰洗	Lime wash is a traditional surface finish for internal and external use based on a suspension of calcium hydroxide in water with or without colouring pigments. It is applied to walls as a protective surface coating. 石灰洗是一种传统的内外用表面处理剂，基于水中的氢氧化钙悬浮物，可能添加也可能不添加着色剂。它可作为一种保护性表面涂层用于墙壁。
lime water 石灰水	Lime water is a solution of slaked lime (calcium hydroxide) in water. It has been used as a surface consolidant for limestone. 石灰水是熟石灰（氢氧化钙）在水中的溶液，用作石灰石的表面固化剂。
liner 烟囱衬管	A chimney liner is an insertion into a degraded chimney structure to provide support or a gas impervious flue. The insertion may be a rigid ceramic or concrete tube, a poured concrete lining or a flexible metal tube. 烟囱衬管是插入老化烟囱结构中提供支撑或气体防水的插入物，可以是刚性陶瓷或混凝土管、浇注混凝土内衬或柔性金属管。
listed building 登录建筑	A listed building is one that is designated by a regulatory body as being of special architectural or historic interest. 登录建筑是指由一般管理机关指定的具有特殊建筑或历史意义的建筑物。
loss of detail 细节丢失	Building fabric suffers loss of detail when there is damage or erosion to finely carved or moulded detail. 建筑本体遭受细节丢失指其精雕或模制的细节部分被损毁或遭到侵蚀。

marly limestone 泥灰岩	Marly limestone is a limestone containing clay. 泥灰岩是一种含有粘土的石灰岩。
monument 纪念性建筑	a. A monument is a building or structure designed and constructed to commemorate a particular event or person. b. A monument is an ancient or historic building, structure or site, whether above or below ground and complete or in part, that is considered to be of particular quality or value. a. 纪念性建筑是为纪念某一事件或某个人而设计和建造的建筑物或构筑物。b. 纪念性建筑是指被认为具有特定品质或价值的古代或历史建筑、构筑物或遗址，无论其在地上或是在地下，是否完整。
mortar 砂浆	Mortar is a proportioned mix of water, binding agent (such as cement or lime) with sands, aggregates and other materials used to bed, joint and point walling materials (such as brick, stone). 砂浆是水、粘合剂（如水泥或石灰）与沙、集料和用于铺设、填抹和补墙缝材料（如砖、石）的其他材料按一定比例的混合物。
mudbrick 泥砖	A mudbrick is a brick made of unfired, sun dried earth for buildings in arid climates. 泥砖是用未烧制、晒干的泥土制成的砖，用于气候干旱地区的建筑物。
natural cement 天然水泥	A natural cement is based on naturally-occurring materials that will react with water. 天然水泥是与水可自然发生反应的水泥。
non-hydraulic cement 非水硬性水泥	Non-hydraulic cement is cement that hardens and sets by chemical reaction with carbon dioxide. 非水硬性水泥是通过与二氧化碳发生化学反应而硬化和凝固的水泥。
order 柱式	An order is a coherent set of features typically comprising base, column, capital and entablature, in Greek, Roman and Renaissance architecture. The commonly recognised orders are Doric, Tuscan, Ionic, Corinthian and Composite. 柱式是指希腊、罗马和文艺复兴建筑中一组连贯的特征，通常包括柱础、立柱、柱头和檐梁。常见的柱式有多立克柱式、托斯卡纳柱式、爱奥尼亚柱式、科林斯柱式和复合柱式。
pantile 波形瓦	A pantile is a heavy specially curved ceramic roof tile. 波形瓦是一种重型弯曲的特制陶瓷屋顶瓦。
percolating rainwater 渗透雨水	Percolating rainwater is rainwater penetrating into the fabric of a building. 渗透雨水是渗入建筑物本体的雨水。
photogrammetry 摄影测量法	Photogrammetry measures and records three-dimensional information from objects with the aid of stereoscopic photographs. It is typically used for the documentation of complex building facades and sculpture. 摄影测量法借助立体照片测量和记录物体的三维信息。它通常用于记录复杂的建筑立面和雕塑。

planning blight 规划缺陷	Planning blight is the detrimental effect of a development proposal (or lack of it), particularly on the value of land and buildings but also on the formulation of other uses of the land. 规划缺陷是指开发计划（或缺乏开发计划）的负面影响，尤其是对地价和房价的影响，也包括对其他土地用途的制定。
plaster (2) 抹灰 (2)	When you plaster a wall, you apply single or multiple layers of plaster. 在墙上抹灰时，是指涂抹一层或多层灰泥。
plaster object 石膏制品	A plaster object or coating is one made by applying plaster to a mould or armature. 石膏制品或涂层是在模具或支架上涂抹灰泥制成。
pointed architecture 尖拱式建筑	Pointed architecture is the Gothic architectural style. Variants are classified as first, second or middle, and third. 尖拱式建筑是哥特式建筑风格。变体分为一级、二级或中间级、三级。
pointing 勾缝	Pointing is the application of fresh mortar to the outer part of weathered masonry joints over the original bedding mortar. 勾缝是在原有垫层砂浆上，在已风化的砌体接缝的外部涂抹新砂浆。
Portland cement 硅酸盐水泥	Portland cement is cement which is made by roasting at ca 1400℃ clay or shale and limestone or chalk. It is widely used in mortars and concrete. It was patented by Joseph Aspdin in 1824 and named after its supposed resemblance to Portland limestone. 硅酸盐水泥是粘土或页岩、石灰石或白垩在1400摄氏度左右的温度中煅烧而成的水泥，广泛应用于砂浆和混凝土中。1824年，约瑟夫.阿斯普丁申请了专利，因其与硅酸盐石灰岩相似而得名。
pot life 活化寿命	The pot life of a recently mixed cement or two part adhesive is the period of time for which the material is sufficiently mobile to be workable. 新混合的水泥或双组粘合剂的活化寿命是指材料具有足够的流动性以使其性能正常的时间段。
pozzuolana additive 火山灰添加剂	A pozzolanic additive is a natural or synthetic material, such as volcanic ash and pulverised fuel ash, added to lime-based mortars, renders and plasters to produce enhanced performance characteristics, such as advanced setting times and early strength gain. 火山灰添加剂是一种天然或合成材料，如火山灰和粉状燃料灰，添加到石灰基砂浆、抹灰和灰泥中，以产生优化的性能特征，如提前凝固时间和早期强度增加。
preservationist 建筑文物保护者	A preservationist is a person who seeks to advance or achieve the preservation of buildings or structures. 建筑文物保护者是寻求推进或实现对建筑或构筑物保护的人。
pre-stressed concrete 预应力混凝土	Pre-stressed concrete is formed around embedded tensioned steel reinforcement that imposes a compressive force (or stress) on the concrete for enhanced material and structural performance. 预应力混凝土是在预埋的张拉钢筋周围形成的，它对混凝土施加压力（或应力），以优化材料和结构性能。

quicklime 生石灰	Quicklime is calcium oxide, a white caustic alkaline substance, obtained by heating limestone to ca 1000℃. 生石灰是氧化钙，一种白色碱性物质，通过将石灰石加热到约1000°左右制成。
raw casting 未加工铸件	A raw casting is a casted object that has not been worked to its final appearance. 未加工铸件是指尚未加工成最终外观的铸件。
refurbishment 翻修	The refurbishment of a building is work that brings it up to current acceptable standards for use. 建筑翻修是指使该建筑达到当前可接受的使用标准的工作。
regeneration 再生／复兴	The regeneration of an urban area results in improved cultural, economic, environmental and/or social conditions, through enhancement and investment. 通过优化和投资，城市/城区再生带来城市区域文化、经济、环境和/或社会条件的改善。
rehabilitation 整修	Rehabilitation of a deteriorated building or area is reparative work that brings it back to an acceptable state for continued use. 对毁损的建筑物或地区进行整修，使其恢复到可继续使用的可接受状态的工作。
reinforced concrete 钢筋混凝土	Reinforced concrete is concrete that is formed around embedded tensile steel reinforcement. It is used for structural uses in building. 钢筋混凝土是在预埋抗拉钢筋周围形成的混凝土。它用于建筑的结构性用途。
repoint 重新勾缝	You repoint a masonry wall by raking out the existing mortar in the joints to a depth of ca 25 mm and replacing with an appropriate mortar. 通过在接缝中挖出约25毫米的已有砂浆并替换为适当的砂浆，来再次在石砌墙上勾缝。
revive 复兴	A building or structure is revived by actions taken to extend its useful life. 复兴指建筑或构筑物通过采取具体措施延长建筑或构筑物的使用寿命。
sacrificial rendering 牺牲性抹面／底泥	A sacrificial rendering is a porous rendering applied to masonry walling either to draw out soluble salts or protect from external sources of salts. The rendering is designed to deteriorate and be removed in the future. 牺牲性底泥是用于涂抹在石砌墙的多孔底泥，用于提取可溶盐或防止来自外部盐的侵蚀。底泥设计为自然劣化，可在未来移除。
scaffold 脚手架	A scaffold is a temporary open structure on the exterior or interior of a building which allows to carry out building work at a high level. 脚手架是建筑物外部或内部的一种临时开放式结构，便于在高处进行建筑作业。
scheduled monument 列入名录古迹	A scheduled monument is one that has been designated by a regulatory authority to be of special archaeological, architectural or historic interest. 列入名录古迹是指政府监管机构指定的具有特殊考古、建筑或历史意义的古迹。

septarium 龟背石	A septarium is a calcareous clay nodule used as building stones and also used in the production of historic natural cements. 龟背石是一种钙质粘土，用作建筑石材，也用于生产历史悠久的天然水泥。
settlement 沉降	Settlement of a structure is the movement of the structure as a result of the movement of the foundations. The settlement may be of part of the structure, so causing disruption, or movement of the whole. 建筑沉降是由于地基的移动而引起的建筑的移动。沉降可能是结构的一部分，因此会造成整体断裂或移动。
slaked lime 熟石灰	Slaked lime is calcium hydroxide, a white substance made by reacting water with quicklime. 熟石灰是氢氧化钙，一种白色物质，由水和生石灰反应而成。
slater's ripper 瓦工除钉器	A slater's ripper is a hand tool used to remove the nails holding defective roof slates and shingles. It is constructed of a long flat steel blade with two sharp hooks at tip. The handle is hit with a hammer to cut or pull out the nail. 瓦工除钉器是一种手工工具，用来去除附在有缺陷的屋顶瓦板上的钉子。它由一个长形扁钢刀片构成，刀尖有两个钩子。用锤子敲打刀把，以切割或拔出钉子。
slicker 抹泥刀	A slicker is a hand tool used to apply mortar to masonry joints during repointing. It is constructed of a long flat steel blade which pushes the mortar into the joint, attached to a handle. 抹泥刀是一种手工工具，用于在勾缝时将砂浆涂抹在砌体接缝上。它是由一个长形扁钢刀片构成，可把砂浆推入接缝，刀片附在把手上。
spandrels 三角拱肩	Spandrels is the shaped additional inner structure filling the space between a rectangular frame and an oval or circular picture. It was in regular use from the second half of the 19th century. 三角拱肩是填充矩形框架结构和椭圆或圆拱之间空间的附加定型结构。自19世纪下半叶起被经常使用。
stacco 揭取	Stacco is the process of detaching a fresco painting from a wall by removing the pigment layer and the surface plaster. 壁画揭取是通过去除颜料层和表面灰泥将壁画从墙上分离出来的过程。
strappo 去除支撑	Strappo is the process of detaching a fresco painting from its substrate by taking off only the paint layer attached to a temporary support. 去除支撑是将壁画从其基底上分离出来的过程，只需去掉附着在临时支架上的油漆层。
structurally stable 结构稳定	A building or structure is structurally stable if it resists without damage the anticipated loads and forces acting upon it. 如果一座建筑或构筑物能抵抗作用在其上的预期荷载和力而不受损，则其结构是稳定的。
sulfate attack 硫酸盐侵蚀	Sulfate attack is the degradation of masonry and mortars due to reaction with sulfuric acid. This occurs particularly within chimneys, resulting in weakening of the structure. 硫酸盐侵蚀是由于与硫酸反应而导致石材和砂浆的劣化。这种情况尤其会发生在烟囱内，导致结构松动。

tell-tale 位移指示器	A tell-tale is a glass slip applied across a crack in a masonry wall in order to assess the amount and rate of movement of the crack. 位移指示器是在石质墙体的裂缝中加入玻璃滑片，以评估裂隙的程度和位移速度。
tie rod 系杆	A tie rod is a reinforcement to a building that resists the separation of the structures. Tie rods are made of materials that resist tension, typically steel, or reinforced concrete. 系杆是建筑物中的加固物，用来抵抗结构间的分离力。系杆由抗拉力材料制成，常见的有钢材或钢筋混凝土。
voussoir 楔形拱石	A voussoir is a wedge-shaped brick or stone forming part of an arch. 楔形拱石是构成拱门一部分的楔形砖石。
water jet 水射流	A water jet is used for cleaning masonry surfaces by forcing the dirt off. 水射流用于清除砖石表面的污垢。
weathering (2) 泻水坡 (2)	The weathering of a wall or other external building component is an angled finish applied to assist in shedding rainwater. 墙或其他外部建筑构件的泻水坡是一种成一定角度的饰面，用于帮助排出雨水。
weep hole 排水孔	A weep hole in a wall or other structure is a hole to allow the escape of collected water. 墙或其他结构中的排水孔是使收集的水排出的孔。
whitewash 石灰水	Whitewash is a paint made of lime mixed into water. 石灰水用石灰和水混合而成的涂料。
zoning (1) 规划分区 (1)	Zoning is the designation of different land use and development types within and around urban settlements. 规划分区指规划城市及其周边区域土地利用和开发的不同类型。

10

动植物材料
Animal and Plant Materials

acid deterioration 酸劣化	See acid hydrolysis. 见酸水解。
acid hydrolysis 酸水解	Acid hydrolysis of cellulose occurs when acids catalyse a reaction that breaks cellulose chains into smaller parts. This degradation weakens the overall strength of the cellulose and the materials made from it. The acids can originate from air pollution,production processes and material in contact with and/or applied to the paper surface. 纤维素的酸水解是指在酸性物质的催化作用下，纤维素分子链会分解成较小片段，导致纤维素制品强度下降的现象。诱发酸水解的酸性物质可能来自酸性污染气体、生产过程、接触和/或喷涂到纸面的材料。
actinomycetes 放线菌	Actinomycetes are prokaryotic heterotrophic microorganisms which are able to ferment carbohydrates and therefore play a role in the biological decay of wood and paper. 放线菌是具有丝状分支细胞的原核微生物，会使碳水化合物发酵，导致木材和纸张的腐烂。
alum tawed skin 明矾皮	Alum tawed skin is skin that has been prepared by processing with aluminium compounds and salt. This skin has not been tanned and is not resistant to water. 明矾皮是用铝化合物和盐加工而成的皮。这种皮没有经过鞣制，不耐水。
amber 琥珀	Amber is a transparent or translucent fossil (resin, exudet from coniferous trees. Its colour ranges from yellow to brown, orange and sometimes red. During corrosion it loses transparency and the surface becomes brittle over time. It was used for making decorative objects and as a binder in varnishes. 琥珀是一种透明或半透明的化石，来自针叶树分泌的树脂，颜色呈黄色、棕色、橙色和红色，可用来制作装饰品或是做清漆的粘合剂。随着时间推移，琥珀会逐渐变脆，透明度也会逐渐下降。
animal glue 动物胶	A kind of animal glue made directly from cattle hide, pig skin or bone. 动物胶是用牛皮、猪皮或骨等直接熬制而成的一种胶。
annual ring 年轮	An annual ring is the layer of wood formed every year during the growth of the stem of a tree. Sequences of annual rings are used in dating wooden objects. 年轮是多年生木本植物茎的横断面上的同心环纹，通常每年一轮，用于推算树木年龄。
archaeobotany 植物考古学	Archaeobotany is the study of vegetational remains from excavation sites. Its research object is the botanical environment and diet of humans in ancient times. 植物考古学是研究与考古学相关的植物遗存的学科，研究目标在于探索古代植物环境和古人类饮食习惯。
arsenic soap 砷肥皂	Arsenic soap is a mixture of arsenic oxide with soap that was used in preparing and preserving skin. 砷肥皂是氧化砷与肥皂的混合物，用于制备和保存皮。

back (2) 背衬加固	When you back a textile, you attach a fabric to its reverse by using stitching or an adhesive. This is done in order to add support or reinforcement to a weak and damaged textile. 纺织品的背衬加固，即采用缝线或粘合剂把一块背衬材料附在纺织品背面，其目的在于给脆弱和受损的纺织品提供支撑从而起到加固的效果。
battery jar 液体标本罐	A battery jar is a container for a fluid preserved specimen. It is a rectangular glass bottle cut off horizontally, onto which a flat sheet of glass is sealed as a lid. 液体标本罐是装有液体标本的容器。水平切割的长方形玻璃瓶，上面有一块平板玻璃作为密封盖。
benzene hexachloride 六氯化苯	Gamma-benzene hexachloride, g-C6H 6Cl6, (BHC) is a solid which was used as an insecticide on specimens. Its use has stopped because of the dangers to human health. γ-六氯化苯即 g-C6H 6Cl6，是一种固体物质，用作标本杀虫剂。由于会对人体产生危害，已停止使用。
borax 硼砂	Borax, sodium tetraborate, is a chemical which was used during the preservation of skins as an absorbant during drying of the animal and as a moth deterent. 硼砂又称四硼酸钠，是一种用途广泛的化学试剂，用于皮革保存，在动物标本干燥过程中用作吸湿剂，也可作为防蛀剂。
brown rot 褐腐病	Brown rot is the result of a fungal attack on wood, which attacks the cellulose component preferentially leaving the lignin behind. 褐腐病是真菌侵染木材导致的结果，这种真菌先攻击纤维素再攻击木质素。
Byne's disease 贝壳白化症	Byne's disease is an efflorescence on shells (usually marine), resulting from reactions of the calcium carbonate with organic acid vapours released from wooden cabinets and other storage materials. 贝壳白化症通常指海洋贝壳的风化，由碳酸钙与酸性物质反应而引发，酸性物质多来自木制橱柜以及其他储存材料中释放出的酸性气体。
calf skin 小牛皮	Calf skin is the raw hide of a calf. 小牛皮是小牛的生皮。
carbon dioxide 二氧化碳	Carbon dioxide is a gas which is used at ca 60% to kill insects, probably by dehydration. 二氧化碳是一种气体，浓度大约60%时可使害虫脱水而死。
carbonizing 碳化	Carbonizing is the conversion of organic, especially plant, material into a black residue mainly of carbon, by burning objects with reduced oxygen supply. 碳化是有机物尤其是植物在隔绝氧气条件下，燃烧生成黑色碳产物的过程。
card skin 卡片皮	See flat skin. 见平皮。

carpet beetle 地毯甲虫	The carpet beetle (Anthrenus verbasci) is an insect whose larvae cause mechanical damage to woollen and hair fibres and textiles by eating holes in them. Their excreta and pupae casings cause soiling. 地毯甲虫又称小圆皮蠹，是一种昆虫，其幼虫通过咬食羊毛、毛纤维和纺织品而对其造成机械损伤。它们的排泄物和蛹壳会造成污染。
celloidin 火棉胶	Celloidin is a 1% solution of cellulose nitrate in a di-ethyl ether/propan-2-ol solvent. It is used as an adhesive in conserving alcohol preserved fluid specimens. 火棉胶是硝酸纤维素溶于乙醚或异丙酮中而成的1%溶液，涂于物体表面溶剂迅速挥发，留下一层防水的坚韧薄膜，因此可用于液体标本的封护。
chamois 麂皮	a. Chamois is a soft, vegetable or oil tanned leather made from the skin of the chamois antelope. b. Chamois is an oil tanned leather made from split sheepskins. a、由羚羊皮制成的柔软的植鞣或油鞣皮革。b、由羊皮制成的油鞣皮革。
chestnut 栗树	Chestnut is a wood from the tree belonging to the Fagacee family. Chestnut was used as a support for wood panels especially in Portugal and Italy. 栗木属于山毛榉科，在葡萄牙和意大利曾被用作木板画的支撑材料。
clothes moth 衣蛾	The clothes moth (Tineola bisselliella, Tinea pellionella and Trichophaga tapetzella) is an insect whose larvae cause mechanical damage to protein fibres and textiles by eating holes or tunnels in them, or grazing their surface. Their excreta, cocoons and webbing adhere to the textile and cause soiling. 衣蛾是一种昆虫，包括幕谷蛾、附袋衣蛾和毛毡衣蛾，其幼虫通过蚀洞或啃食织物表面，对蛋白质纤维和织物造成机械损伤。它们的排泄物、茧和网状物粘附在纺织品上，造成脏污。
collagen 胶原蛋白	Collagen is a fibrous protein which swells in water and is used to make glue. It is found in animal connective tissues such as bone and skin. 胶原蛋白是一种纤维状蛋白质，在水中溶胀，可用来制造胶水。胶原蛋白存在于动物的结缔组织中，如骨骼和皮肤。
collodion 火棉胶	Collodion consists of nitrated cellulose (gun cotton) which is dissolved in ether and alcohol. It was used as image layer in the Wet Collodion Process and collodion P.O.P. Until the end of 19th century (in the graphic arts industry until the middle of 20th century), it was the preferred binder for negative plates. 火棉胶是将硝化纤维素（火棉）溶于乙醇和乙醚的混合液而制得的胶液。当其涂在物体表面，溶剂迅速挥发，留下一层防水的坚韧薄膜，因此在湿法胶棉工艺和胶棉工艺中，常用作成像层。19世纪末至20世纪中期的平面艺术行业中，火棉胶是负片的首选粘合剂。
colophony 松香	Colophony is the solid material remaining after the evaporation of the volatiles from pine exudates. 松香是松树分泌物经蒸馏除去挥发性物质后的固体树脂。

common furniture beetle 家具窃蠹	The common furniture beetle is a small insect, Anobium punctatum, whose larvae eat soft and hardwoods (especially sap wood), and paper causing extensive tunnelling. The adult beetles leave oval flight holes 2 mm in diameter. 家具窃蠹是一种小昆虫，学名Anobium punctatum，幼虫嗜食软木和硬木（特别是边材）。纸张一旦被窃蠹啃食，则会留下密集虫眼，虫眼呈直径2毫米的椭圆形。
contact insecticide 接触杀虫剂	A contact insecticide is a solid or liquid insecticide that kills an insect after touching it. The insecticide can be a poison or may cause physical damage. These insecticides are used to prevent the spread of insects around a building. 接触杀虫剂多呈固体或液体，具有毒性，会造成身体伤害，昆虫接触后死亡。这类杀虫剂用于防止昆虫在建筑物周围散步。
coprolites 粪化石	Coprolites are the fossilized faeces of animals and humans. 粪化石是动物和人类粪便的化石。
corrosive sublimate 氯化汞 (II)	See mercury (II) chloride. 见氯化汞(II)。
Danish jar 丹麦瓶	A Danish jar is a glass container used for storing fluid specimens. It has a PE clip-on-top which degrades and fails after 10-20 years. 丹麦瓶一种储存液体标本的玻璃容器，顶部有一个聚乙烯夹盖，10-20年后会退化和失效。
DDT 二氯二苯三氯乙烷	DDT is an acronym for the dichlorodiphenyltrichloroethane, IUPAC name 1,1-bis(4-chlorophenyl)-2,2,2-trichloroethane. It is an insecticide that was widely used on museum specimens before being banned because of its long term effect on wildlife. DDT是二氯二苯三氯乙烷的缩写，IUPAC的名称为1,1-双（4-氯苯基）-2,2,2-三氯乙烷。它是一种杀虫剂，曾被广泛用于博物馆标本。因其对野生动物有长期的影响而被禁用。
DDVP 敌敌畏	See dichlorvos. 见敌敌畏。
death watch beetle 红毛窃蠹	Death watch beetle, Xestobium rufovillosum, is a dermestid insect pest. Its larva makes galleries ca 3mm diam in wood. 红毛窃蠹是一种皮蠹害虫，学名Xestobium rufovillosum，其幼虫在木材中的虫室直径达到3毫米。
degreasing 脱脂	Degreasing is the process of removing fats and oil from skin and bone during preservation or later conservation. Techniques used include scraping, washing with solutions of detergents, and solvent cleaning. 脱脂是通过挂削、表面活性剂或有机溶剂清洗等技术，将油脂从皮肤和骨骼中除去的过程。

demineralise 去除矿物质或盐	A primarily organic object is demineralised by the leeching out of an inorganic component, such as the removal of calcium phosphate from bone in an acidic environment. 一个主要为有机物的物体是通过无机成分渗出的形式来去除矿物质，例如在酸性环境中从骨骼中去除磷酸钙。
denatured 变性	A denatured organic material is one that has changed or broken down sufficiently so that it can no longer take part in physiological functions. 变性是有机物已经被改变或分解，不再具备原有的生理功能。
Dermestid 皮蠹	Dermestids are a family of beetles, of which the hide and carpet beetles are pests. 皮蠹是甲虫的一个科，其中白腹皮蠹和红缘皮蠹都是害虫。
dermestidarium 虫噬法	A dermestidarium is a colony of dermestid beetles which are kept to eat the flesh off bones intended for an osteology collection. 虫噬法是通过皮囊甲虫取食骨骼上的肉来收集动物骨骼标本的方法。
dichlorvos 敌敌畏	Dichlorvos, 2,2-dichlorovinyl dimethyl phosphate, is a fumigant which is gradually released into an enclosed atmosphere and kills insects at high concentrations. 敌敌畏，2,2-二氯乙烯基，是一种熏蒸剂，可逐渐释放到封闭的空气中，在高浓度下杀死昆虫。
dovetail 燕尾榫	A dovetail is a join where the tenon and the corresponding mortise are cut into the shape of a dovetail. See also butterfly key. 燕尾榫是将榫和相应的卯切成燕尾形状的连接节点。另见butterfly key 蝴蝶榫。
dry leather 干燥皮革	It is a kind of leather in which moisture and grease are almost lost.The collagen fibers of leather were adherent and fragile, and lost their flexibility。 干燥皮革是处于水分和脂类几乎流失条件中的皮革，胶原纤维粘结、脆弱，并丧失柔顺性。
ebonized 仿黑檀木	An ebonized surface finish is one acquired by painting or staining and then polishing in order to give the appearance of ebony. 仿黑檀木工艺是对表面经过涂漆或染色，再抛光后得到类似黑檀木效果的工序。
enzyme preparation 酶制剂	The biological products with catalytic function after purification and processing are mainly used for degreasing cortical and cleaning organic pollutants. 酶制剂是经过提纯加工的生物制品，具有催化功能，主要用于皮质脱脂和有机污染物的去除。
ethylene oxide 环氧乙烷	Ethylene oxide is a fumigant biocide. 环氧乙烷是一种熏蒸杀菌剂。
fat burn 脂肪燃烧	Fat burn of a preserved animal is damage to skin resulting from the oxidation and movement of fats remaining in the animal. Fat burn frequently results in hair and feather loss. 脂肪燃烧是指动物标本内残留脂肪的氧化和移动对动物皮毛造成的损害。脂肪燃烧经常导致毛发和羽毛脱落。

fixative (2) 固定剂 (2)	A fixative for animal preservation is a chemical that denatures protein by coagulating it or by chemically combining with it. 固定剂是动物标本制作过程中使用的一种化学物质，通过凝固蛋白质或与之化学结合使蛋白质变性。
flat skin 平皮	A flat skin is an animal skin that has been preserved by being stretched over an insert made of card, wood, or wire, then air dried. 平皮是将动物皮在由卡片、木头或金属丝制成的衬垫上展平、风干形成的皮。
flesh side 皮里	The flesh side of leather is the surface where the skin was connected to the body of the animal. 皮里是皮与动物身体相连的面。
fluid preservation 液体保存	Fluid preservation is the preservation of an animal or plant specimen in a liquid. Preservative liquids include 70% ethanol, propan-2-ol, and 10% formaldehyde. 液体保存是将动物或植物标本保存在由70%的乙醇、丙二醇和10%的甲醛配比而成的防腐液中。
formaldehyde 甲醛	Formaldehyde, CH_2O, is a chemical which reacts with proteins and is used as a fixative. 甲醛即 CH_2O，可与蛋白质发生反应，可用作动物标本的固定剂。
formalin 福尔马林	Formalin is a solution of formaldehyde in water. 福尔马林是甲醛的水溶液。
frass 蛀屑	Insect frass is faecal material often used as evidence of insect damage. Characteristic size and shape can be used to identify the insect species 蛀屑是昆虫的排泄物，常被用作虫害的证据。根据特征大小和形状可以用来鉴别昆虫种类
fumigant 熏蒸消毒剂	A fumigant is a vaporised biocide that is used in fumigation. 熏蒸消毒剂是用于熏蒸的汽化杀菌剂。
fur 毛皮	Fur is a skin which has been preserved with its attached hair. 毛皮是连带毛发被一起保存下来的动物皮。
gallery (1) 虫室（1）	A gallery is the pattern of channels in an object caused by wood boring insects. 虫室（或虫房）是害虫在木头上钻孔留下的通道。
gelatin 明胶	It is a kind of macromolecular hydrocolloid, which is the product of partial hydrolysis of collagen. It is soluble in hot water and insoluble in cold water. It is used for bonding and strengthening. 明胶是一种大分子的亲水胶体，是胶原部分水解后的产物，可溶于热水，不溶于冷水，用于粘合加固。
glycerol 甘油	Its chemical composition is glycerin, colorless, odorless and sweet. Its appearance is clear and viscous. It is an organic substance used for moisturizing and softening leather. 甘油的化学成分为丙三醇，无色、无臭、味甜，外观呈澄明黏稠液态，用于皮革保湿软化。

goatskin 山羊皮	Goatskin is the raw hide of a goat. 山羊皮是山羊的生皮。
grain (2) 纹理	The grain of leather is the follicle pattern, naturally present or artificially produced. 皮革的纹理主要体现为毛囊的形貌特征，有天然纹理和人工纹理之分。
grain side 皮面	The grain side of leather is the outer-most side of the leather where the hair implant (follicle pattern) is visible. See also hair side. 皮面是皮革的最外层，可见毛囊。另见毛面。
graining 仿木纹	Graining is the simulation of the grain of wood with paints and glazes applied over an undercoat. 仿木纹工艺是指通过油漆和釉料模仿出木材纹理的工序。
ground glass jar 磨砂玻璃罐	A ground glass jar is a glass container used for storing fluid specimens. It has a glass top whose join with the top is a conical ground joint, usually lubricated with petroleum jelly. 一种储存液体标本的玻璃容器。顶部为玻璃，与磨砂接头相连，通常用凡士林润滑。
Gutta percha 马来乳胶	Gutta percha is transpolyisoprene obtained from a number of plants. It is a thermoplastic which can be modelled after being softened in hot water. It was used in the nineteenth century as a moulding material and is still used as a sealing material for bat 马来乳胶来自植物，主要成分是异戊烯的反式聚合体，具热塑性，在热水中软化后可用于塑模成型。
hair fibre 毛纤维	A hair fibre is a keratin protein fibre usually obtained from angora and cashmere goats, camels, alpacas and fur bearing animals. Hair fibres are used for making textiles and objects. 毛纤维是一种主要成分是角蛋白的蛋白质纤维，通常从安哥拉山羊和开士米山羊、骆驼、羊驼和毛皮动物中获得。毛纤维用于制造纺织品和羊毛制品。
hair side 皮革粒面	See grain side. 见皮面。
hemi cellulose 半纤维素	Hemi cellulose is a form of cellulose that has shorter and less linear chains. It will dissolve in alkalis and is therefore washed out of chemical pulps. When present in paper, it increases folding endurance. 半纤维素是一种具有较短和较少直链的纤维素形式，可溶于碱，因此在化学纸浆中能够被洗脱。半纤维素用于造纸可增加纸张的耐折性。
herbarium folder 标本纸夹	A herbarium folder is a folded, acid-free card in which pressed and mounted botanical specimens are stored. 标本纸夹是一种可折叠的无酸卡纸，用来保存已经压制和装裱好的植物标本。

herbarium packet 植物标本包	A herbarium packet is a small envelope for holding small herbarium specimens. It is made by folding paper so that the sheet can be opened out flat to reveal the specimen. 植物标本包是存放小型标本的信封，由纸张折叠而成，以便平展后露出标本。
hide 兽皮	In leather technology, hide is the skin of a large animal which has been flayed. 在皮革技术中，兽皮指被剥下的大型动物的皮毛。
hide beetle 白腹皮蠹	A hide beetle is an insect of the Dermestes species which is a pest in museums. 白腹皮蠹是一种皮蠹属昆虫，是博物馆常见的害虫。
house longhorn beetle 家天牛	A house longhorn beetle is a dull black or brown beetle, Hylotrupes bajulus, whose larva eat softwoods such as roof and floor timbers forming extensive tunnelling. The adult beetles leave oval flight holes 5 to 7 mm in diameter. 家天牛是一种暗黑色或棕色的甲虫，学名 Hylotrupes bajulus，其幼虫以软木材（如屋顶和地板）为食，形成大面积的虫道，成虫会造成直径5到7毫米的椭圆形虫道。
infestation 感染	Infestation is the presence of active insect, fungal or bacterial activity in an object. 感染是在物体中存在活跃的昆虫、真菌或细菌的现象。
insect pest 害虫	An insect pest is one which harms objects usually by feeding on the materials but also by soiling them. 害虫是对器物有害的虫子，通常是以器物材料为食且使其受污染。
insect pins 昆虫标本针	Insect pins are steel pins of various thickness which are used for the mounting of insect specimens. In textile conservation, they are used to hold textiles and backings in place during stitching treatments and to block out wet textiles. 标本针是粗细不同的钢针，一般用于制作昆虫标本。在纺织品文物修复中，亦可在缝合过程中固定纺织品和背衬，并阻隔潮湿的纺织品。
insecticide 杀虫剂	An insecticide is a biocide that kills insects and their eggs, larvae and pupae. It can be applied as a powder, a sprayed-on solution, a gas or slowly evaporating solid. We can distinguish between knockdown, with immediate short term effect, and residual insecticides, with prolonged effect. Some forms of insecticides also repel insects. 杀虫剂是杀灭昆虫及其卵、幼虫和蛹的制剂，包括粉末、喷涂溶液、气体或缓慢蒸发的固体。残余的杀虫剂也有灭虫效果，一些杀虫剂亦可驱虫。
Kaiserling solution 凯氏溶液	The Kaiserling solution is a preserving solution for animal specimens whose colour preservation is important. 凯氏溶液常用于保存对维持色彩有较高要求的动物标本。
knot (2) 木瘤	A knot is the remains of a branch within a plank of timber. It frequently contains a large amount of resin. 木瘤是木材生长枝桠的突起物，通常含有大量树脂成分。

lacquer 大漆	Oriental lacquer is a coating or binding medium made from exudates from a number of tree species. Different countries use local names for the lacquer: urushi from Japan, China and Korea from Rhus verniciflua, yun from Burma from Melanorrhoea usitate, with similar materials used in Thailand, Vietnam, and Indonesia. 大漆是一种取自树木的涂料或胶结材料，在不同国家和地区有不同的名称。在日本它被称为urushi，中国和韩国是Rhus verniciflua（漆），缅甸是yun，马来西亚是usitate，类似的材料也被用于泰国、越南和印度尼西亚。
lanolin 羊毛脂	A kind of oil secreted on wool. It is a light yellow or brownish yellow ointment. It is sticky and greasy, with weak and specific odor. Soluble in chloroform or ether, soluble in hot ethanol, slightly soluble in ethanol. 羊毛脂是附着在羊毛上的一种分泌油脂，为淡黄色或棕黄色的软膏状物，黏性而滑腻，具有特别的气味。在氯仿或乙醚中易溶，在热乙醇中可溶，在乙醇中微溶。
leather 皮革	Leather is the skin of an animal which has been tanned with compounds that crosslink and stablise the collagen structure. Tanning compounds may be vegetable (for example, oak bark), mineral (for example, chromium salt), or fats and oils dressed into the skin. Tanning changes the skin irreversibly. 生皮经过鞣制，其胶原蛋白结构发生交联并稳定，即可得到皮革。鞣剂取自植物（如橡树皮）则为植鞣，鞣剂取自矿物（如铬盐）则为铬鞣，鞣剂取自油脂则称油鞣。鞣制是不可逆的。
leather dressing 皮革敷料	A leather dressing is a mixture, of natural waxes and synthetic lubricants, applied to leather in order to make it more flexible. Some dressings are applied to leather in order to protect it from chemical deterioration. 皮革敷料是天然蜡和合成润滑剂的混合物，涂在皮革上可使皮革更柔软，防止其化学变质。
leather orthopedic 皮革矫形	The process of leather returning to normal shape used molds and tools. 皮革矫形是使用模具和工具使皮革物品恢复正常形状。
Lindane® 六氯化苯	See benzene hexachloride 见六氯化苯。农药商标名"林丹"。
lipid leaching 油脂浸出	Lipid leaching in an animal fluid specimen is the deterioration and release of fats from the tissue into the fluid. 油脂浸出是保存在液体中的动物标本脂肪发生组织降解并释放到液体中的过程。
lubricant 润滑剂	a. A lubricant, such as a natural or synthetic wax or oil, is a substance that is applied as an emulsion in water to leather in order to restore flexibility. b. A lubricant, such as oil or grease, is used on sliding parts in machinery to reduce friction. a、乳状液，涂在皮革上可以恢复皮革弹性，如天然的或合成的蜡或油。b、用在机器的滑动部件上以减少摩擦，如油或润滑脂。

lumen (1) 细胞的内腔 (1)	The lumen of a cell is space that is typically filled with water or air and not with protoplasm. 细胞的内腔是一个空间，通常充满水或空气，而不是原生质。
maceration 浸泡法	Maceration is a method of removing flesh from a skeleton by soaking in water, hot or cold, for extended periods. Chemicals such as sodiium perborate or enzymes can be added to the water to speed up the reaction. 浸泡法是通过长时间的热水或冷水浸泡，达到清除骨骼上的肉的方法。向水中加入过硼酸钠或酶等化学物质可加速反应。
magnesium carbonate 碳酸镁	Magnesium carbonate, $MgCO3$, is a powder which is used in the degreasing and cleaning of fur and feather on animal skins. There are two varieties, light and heavy which is absorbant and used in the degreasing and cleaning. 碳酸镁是一种用于皮毛或羽毛去油和清洁的粉末，包括轻质碳酸镁和重质碳酸镁。
mercury (II) chloride 氯化汞 (II)	Mercury (II) chloride is a toxic chemical which was used as a poison against fungal and insect attack for museum objects. It deteriorates to evolve mercury metal and vapour. Its use has been discontinued because of the damage to specimens and dangers to human health. 氯化汞是一种的有毒化学物质，曾经用于治理博物馆藏品的真菌和虫害，因其生成汞蒸气危及藏品和人员安全，现已禁用。
methyl bromide 溴甲烷	Methyl bromide is a gaseous fumigant which may cause damage to proteins. 溴甲烷是一种气体熏蒸剂，可能对蛋白质造成损害。
microbiological damage 微生物损害	Microbiological damage is damage caused by bacteria and microfungi such as mildews and moulds, which flourish under certain conditions of heat and moisture over time. Bacterial damage is invisible to the naked eye. Mildew usually causes a black discolouration. 微生物损害是在一定的温湿度条件下，细菌和真菌等微生物在物体表面不断滋生，对物体造成破坏。一般情况下，细菌造成的危害难以觉察。真菌中的霉菌会产生黑色霉斑。
mildew 霉	Mildew is small scale fungal activity found on the surface of an object in the form of dark growths. 霉是小范围的真菌活动，黑色，滋生于物体表面。
mineral tanning 矿物鞣革	Mineral tanning is tanning using chemicals such as chromium-, aluminium-, and zirconium salts. This process is very fast and produces very water-resistant leathers. Mineral tanned leather is not suitable for bookbinding. 矿物鞣革是用铬、铝和锆盐等化学物质对皮革进行鞣制的过程。此过程极快，生产出的皮革防水性强。矿物鞣制的皮革不适合用于书籍装帧。
mineralised 矿化	An organic material is mineralised when it becomes impregnated with, or replaced by, inorganic salts. For instance, a textile fragment can be mineralised by corrosion products arising from an adjacent metal object. 矿化是有机材料被无机盐浸渍或被无机盐取代的过程。例如织物碎片可以被邻近金属物体产生的腐蚀产物矿化。

mineralized leather 矿化皮革	a kind of leather form in which organic compounds are transformed into inorganic compounds when leather is immersed in soil microorganisms or inorganic salts. 矿化皮革是皮革在埋藏环境中，被土壤微生物或无机盐浸渍，内部的有机态化合物转化为无机态化合物的一种皮革形态。
mortise-and-tenon 榫卯	A mortise-and-tenon joint between two pieces of wood is made by cutting the end of one piece as a male (tenon) to fit into a corresponding female (mortise) in the other. 榫卯是两个木制构件的连接方式，通常是凹凸部分相结合，凸出部分叫榫，凹进部分叫卯。
mother of pearl 珠母贝	See nacre. 见珠母贝。
mould (1) 霉菌	Mould is a downy or furry fungal growth, which may occur on organic materials in the presence of excess moisture. 霉菌是绒毛状真菌，环境湿度过高时有机材料会滋生霉菌。
mould stain 霉斑	A mould stain is a discolouration on the surface or within an object. It is caused by some fungi which produce coloured waste products. 霉斑是由于真菌分泌的色素使物体表面或内部发生变色。
mount (3) 支架	In taxidermy, a mount is an internal structure used to give the specimen its shape before the skin is attached. 在动物标本剥制术中，支架是一种内部结构，用于在附着皮肤前给标本定形。
museum beetle 博物馆甲虫	A museum beetle is an insect pest, Anthrenus museorum, in museums. 博物馆甲虫是博物馆中的一种害虫，也叫Anthrenus museorum。
museum jar 博物馆标本容器	A museum jar is a round version of a battery jar. 博物馆标本容器是圆形的液体标本罐。
nacre 珠母贝	Nacre, also known as shell or mother of pearl, is a whitish, iridescent, hard material which forms the inner part of the shell. It is built up in interleaved layers of aragonite and organic substances. 珠母贝又称珍珠母，是一种具有白色珠光的坚硬材料，由文石层和有机层交错叠加而形成贝壳的内面。
natural resin 天然树脂	A natural resin is one that is derived by simple purification from a plant (usually) or animal source. Most natural resins are composed of terpenoid compounds. They will dissolve in organic solvents, rather than water. 天然树脂是动植物（植物来源为主）分泌物经过简单纯化提取而成的物质，大多数天然树脂的主要成分是萜类化合物，溶于有机溶剂，不溶于水。
nomenclature 命名法	A nomenclature is a standardised system for naming, defining and identifying specimens. 命名法是一套命名、定义和识别标本的标准化系统。

oil tanning 油鞣	Oil tanning is tanning using animal or plant oils such as fish oil. Oil tanned leather is called chamois. 油鞣是用动物油（如鱼油）或植物油对动物皮革进行鞣制，油鞣革被称为麂皮。
open joint 接口间隙	An open joint is a gap which has opened up between two pieces of wood, usually as a result of movement caused by moisture content changes. 接口间隙是由湿度变化而引起的两块木头相接之处的缝隙。
palaeobotany 古植物学	See archaeobotany. 见植物考古学。
papyrus 纸莎草 / 纸莎草纸	a. Papyrus is a reed plant of the sedge family (Cyperus papyrus). b. A papyrus is a writing support made of two layers of the pith from papyrus strips laid crosswise. It was mainly used in ancient Egypt. c. A papyrus is an ancient manuscript that is written on papyrus. a.纸莎草是一种属于莎草科的芦苇植物。b.纸莎草纸是古埃及人广泛采用的书写载体，由两层垂直交错的纸莎草条制成。c.一种写在纸莎草纸上的古老手稿。
parchment 羊皮纸	Parchment is limed, de-haired and pumiced skin of a sheep, goat or other mammal. It is stretched upon drying, which renders the skin opaque. This process is reversible by removing the lime and swelling the parchment in water. It was used for writing on or as a book cover. See also vellum. 羊皮纸来自绵羊、山羊或其他哺乳动物的浸灰皮、脱毛皮和磨光皮。羊皮在干燥时被拉伸，使其变得薄透便于书写。一旦去除浸渍羊皮纸的石灰或将羊皮纸浸泡在水中，即可恢复原有性状。它用于书写或作为书的封面。另见牛皮纸。
peat 泥炭	Peat is a layer of dead vegetable matter in variyng degrees of decay. It results from the accumulation of remains of vegetation in swamps or bogs. 泥炭是沼泽发育过程中，草木本植被腐烂堆积的产物。
petroleum ether 石油醚	A light petroleum product. It is a mixture of low molecular weight hydrocarbons (mainly pentane and hexane). It is a colorless transparent liquid with kerosene smell and is used for grease treatment. 石油醚是一种分子量相对较低的轻质石油产品，主要成分是戊烷和己烷，无色透明液体，有煤油气味，用于油脂处理。
pheromone 信息素	Pheromone is a hormone released by animals, especially to attract the opposite sex. Pheromones are used in insect traps. 信息素是一种动物释放的吸引异性的激素，可用于捕虫器。
phosphine 磷化氢	Phosphine is a gaseous fumigant which may cause corrosion of metals. 磷化氢是一种气体熏蒸剂，可引起金属腐蚀。
pig's bladder 猪脬	A pig's bladder is the bladder of a pig which is used for sealing a museum jar. 猪脬是猪的膀胱，用来密封博物馆标本容器。

poplar 杨树	Poplar is a wood from the tree belonging to the Salicacee family. It was widely used in Southern Europe and especially Italy as support for paintings on wooden panels. 杨树隶属杨柳科，在南欧尤其是意大利被广泛用于木板画的支撑材料。
powderpost beetle 粉蠹虫	A powderpost beetle is dark red to black beetle, Lyctus brunneus, whose adults and larvae feed on the sapwood of hardwood. The adult beetles leave oval flight holes 2 mm in diameter. 粉蠹虫是一种暗红色发黑的甲虫，它的成虫和幼虫以硬木边材为食。成虫会留下直径2毫米的椭圆形蚀行孔。
preparation (1) 准备 (1)	See ground. 见底层。
preparation (2) 制作标本的 准备工作 (2)	Specimen preparation of an animal is the process carried out to preserve the specimen. Depending on the animal to be preserved, the stages are: the removal of parts that will not be retained; drying; and supporting the remaining parts. 制作动物标本是保存该标本的过程。根据制作对象的状况，制作过程大致包括去除无需保留的部分、干燥、支撑成形。
preservative 防腐剂	A preservative for an animal specimen is a material to stabilise the skin and deter insect attack. 防腐剂用于动物标本的防腐，包括稳定标本的皮、预防虫害。
pressing 压制	Pressing is a method of preserving plants by drying. The specimen is placed between sheets of absorbant paper and corrogated cardboard. A moderate pressure is applied. Air is circulated and the paper is replaced as necessary until the plant is dry. 压制是一种让植物标本得以干燥保存的方法。将植物标本放置在吸水纸和瓦楞纸板之间，给予适度压力，放置在通风处，根据需要更换纸张直至干燥。
propylene phenoxetol 丙烯苯氧基乙醇	Propylene phenoxetol is a chemical which is used as a 1% solution in water as a preservative for previously fixed fluid specimens. 丙烯苯氧基乙醇是一种化学物质，其1%的水溶液可用作已经固定好的、液体保存的标本的防腐剂。
protein 蛋白质	A protein is a natural organic polymer which consists of amino acid monomers. Amino acids contain the group $NH_2CHCOOH$. There are two types of protein incorporated in objects: fibrous proteins (e.g. collagen, keratin and fibroin) which have an important structural function and colloidal proteins (e.g. albumin). Mammals provide wool and hair (keratin) and skin and tendon (collagen). Spiders and some moths produce silk (fibroin). Albumins include egg-white, milk and blood which are used as pigment binders. Enzymes are catalytic proteins used in conservation cleaning treatments. 蛋白质是由氨基酸单体组成的天然有机聚合物。氨基酸含有 $NH_2CHCOOH$ 基团。物体中含有两种类型的蛋白质：纤维蛋白（如胶原蛋白、角蛋白和丝素），它们具有重要的结构功能和胶体蛋白（如白蛋白）。哺乳动物提供羊毛和毛发（角蛋白）以及皮肤和肌腱（胶原蛋白）。蜘蛛和一些飞蛾产生丝（丝蛋白）。白蛋白包括蛋清、牛奶和血液，它们被用作色素粘合剂。酶作为具有催化性能的蛋白质经常用于文物清洗。

protein fibre 蛋白质纤维	A protein fibre is a natural organic polymer comprising amino acids. Wool, hair and silk are protein fibres. See also protein. 蛋白质纤维是包含氨基酸的天然有机聚合物。羊毛、毛发和丝绸都属于蛋白质纤维。另见蛋白质。
raised grain 木质波纹	Raised grain is the surface of wood whose fibres have swelled unvenly due to absorption of water. 木质波纹是木材纤维因含水率差异而产生的表面纹理。
raw hide 生皮	Raw hide is defleshed skin that has been preserved by drying. 生皮是指从动物身上取下、干燥保存的皮。
red rot 赤腐病	Red rot in leather is a symptom of deterioration caused by the interaction of sulfuric acid (from polluted air or manufacturing process) with vegetable tanning agents which leaves the leather friable, with a brick red surface. 赤腐病是皮革中的植物鞣剂与硫酸（来自空气污染物或制造过程）相互作用而导致的病害，皮革表面呈砖红色且易碎。
rehydration 复水	The rehydration of a dried out fluid specimen is a treatment which reintroduces water into the tissues without causing disruption. Solutions with surfactants and physiological salts are used. 复水是通过使用表面活性剂和生理盐水，将水重新引入脱水液体标本中的方法，此过程不会对其造成破坏。
riven board 裂板	A riven board is a plank of wood that has been made during the conversion of a log by splitting the log radially. 裂板是径向劈开原木后得到的平板木材。
rosin 松香	See colophony. 见松香。
round skin 填充用皮肤	A round skin is an animal skin that has been preserved with padding to simulate approximately the original shape of the animal. 填充用皮肤是用以填充保存的动物皮肤，模拟为动物的原始形状。
rubber 橡胶	Rubber is a thermosetting polymer that can be stretched elastically and then recover its shape. All rubbers are cross-linked in order to achieve the reversible elasticity. Natural rubber is derived from a tree (Hevea braziliensis) and usually cross-linked sulfur. Synthetic rubbers are made from a wide variety of polymers with a low Tg, typically less than -40℃, cross-linked in many ways. 橡胶是一种热固性聚合物，具有高弹性，拉伸后可回复原形。所有橡胶都可交联，以达到可逆的弹性。天然橡胶提取自巴西橡胶树，通常与硫交联。合成橡胶由多种聚合物制成，玻璃化转变温度较低，一般小于-40℃，交联方式很多。

rubber latex 胶乳	Rubber latex is the exudation from a tree (Hevea braziliensis), composed of a dispersion in water of cis-(1,4,)-polyisoprene. When used in conservation, the dispersion is stabilised with ammonia and the polymer cross-linked with sulfur. It has been used in making flexible moulds. 胶乳是由橡胶树割胶流出，主要成分为顺（式）-1,4-聚异戊二烯的水分散体，该分散体用于文物修复时，需用氨稳定，与硫会发生交联反应。它被用于制造柔性模具。
scale 鳞片	The hard lamellar structure derived from the skin surface of some animals has protective effect. 鳞片是一些动物皮肤表面衍生的硬薄片状结构，有保护作用。
scale angle 鳞片翘角	The angle between the scale and the hair fiber axis measured by the lateral projection (or axial section) is the angle of the scale rising from the hair stem, 通过侧面投影（或轴向切片）测得的鳞片与毛纤维轴间的夹角，即鳞片翘离毛干的角度。
sheepskin 绵羊皮	Sheepskin is the raw hide of a sheep. 绵羊皮是绵羊的生皮。
shelfback 背衬加固	See back (2). 见背后加固。
silverfish 衣鱼	A silverfish is a small wingless insect, Lepisma saccharina, that that is a pest of mouldy starch based materials such as the adhesives and glazing on paper. The insects trhive in damp, dark conditions and adults can reach 12.5 millimeters in length. 衣鱼是一种小型的无翅昆虫，学名 Lepisma saccharina，喜湿惧光，嗜食纸张中的淀粉类粘合剂和填充剂，成虫长度可达12.5毫米。
skin (1) （兽）皮 (1)	Skin is the external protective organ of any mammal, fish or reptile. It is made up of three layers, an outer epidermis, a middle dermis with a proteinous three-dimensional network of collagen fibres, and the inner subcutaneous tissue which has fat globules and connections to the underlying body of the animal. （兽）皮是所有哺乳动物、鱼类或爬行动物的外部保护器官。它由三层组成，最外层是表皮，中间层是由三维的胶原蛋白纤维结构组成的真皮，最内层是有脂肪细胞的皮下组织，与皮下动物的身体相连。
skin (2) 皮 (2)	In leather technology, a skin is the outer covering of a small animal which has been flayed. 在皮革技术中，皮是从小型动物体表剥离的一层表面组织。
skiver 薄皮革	Skiver is the thin grain side of tanned leather, which has been split from the skin. It is between 0,25 and 1 millimetre thick. It is used for labels and spine coverings. 将鞣制皮革分层切割可得的薄皮革粒面，厚度在 0.25 到 1 毫米之间，可用于制作标签或包裹书脊。

soft rot 软腐病	Soft rot is the damage to wood caused by a number of fungal species, which leave wood in a wet spongy state. 软腐病是木材感染多种真菌而造成呈湿海绵状的病害。
spirit specimen 液体标本	See fluid preservation. 见液体保存。
split (2) 分层 (2)	You split a skin or piece of leather when you separate it into layers parallel to the surface. 分层是将一块皮或皮革分离成数层的过程。
starch 淀粉	Starch is a high molecular weight polyglucose which is found as the food store in many plants. Starch is extracted as granules which swell and dissolve in hot water. It contains two major components, amylose (a linear polymer) and amylopectin (a highly branched polymer) with different solution and film properties. Different plants have starches with different proportions of these components. Typical plant sources are wheat, maize, rice, tapioca and potatoes. 淀粉是植物体内储存的高分子碳水化合物，由葡萄糖分子聚合而成，主要成分为直链淀粉（线性聚合物）和支链淀粉（高度聚合物）。被提取的淀粉可溶胀于热水。它包含两种主要成分，淀粉糖（一种线性聚合物）和淀粉果胶（一种高度支化的聚合物），具有不同的溶液和薄膜特性，不同植物的淀粉中这些成分的比例不同。典型的植物来源是小麦、玉米、大米、木薯和马铃薯。
sticky trap 捕虫器	A sticky trap is a small container incorporating a self-adhesive surface for attracting and holding insect pests. It is sometimes baited with a pheromone attractant or food and is used to monitor pest activity in an area. 捕虫器是一种吸引和捕捉害虫的黏捕器，有时以信息素或食物为诱饵，可监测一个地区的害虫活动。
stitching 缝制	Stitching of a herbarium specimen is the process of attaching that specimen to a herbarium sheet using thread which is tied under the sheet. 缝制标本是用线将标本固定在台纸上的过程，同时线要在台纸的背面打结。
strapping 捆扎	Strapping of a herbarium specimen is the process of attaching that specimen to a herbarium sheet with a tape of paper, fabric or polymer which passes over the specimen and is stuck to the sheet. 捆扎是用纸带、布条将植物标本固定在台纸上的过程。
study skin 修复皮	See round skin. 见填充用皮肤。
syntan 合成鞣剂	Organic tanning agents with similar properties to vegetable tanning agents were synthesized from simple organic compounds. 合成鞣剂是由简单的有机化合物人工合成、与天然植鞣剂具有相似性能的有机鞣剂。

tan 鞣皮	When you tan a skin to make leather, you react the skin with chemicals to stabilise the collagen structure and create a flexible sheet. 把皮鞣制成皮革，即采用化学物质以稳定胶原蛋白结构并使其变软的过程。
tawing 明矾鞣制	See alum tawed skin. 见明矾皮。
taxidermy （动物标本）剥制术	Taxidermy involves the cleaning and preservation of the skin of an animal, usually vertebrate, and its re-mounting on a framework or model simulating the skeletal and muscular structure of the animal. 剥制术是指对动物（通常是脊椎动物）的皮进行清洁和保存，并将其重新附着在动物骨骼和肌肉结构的仿真框架或模型上，获取动物标本的过程。
urea formaldehyde 脲醛	A urea formaldehyde plastic is a thermosetting polymer that is formed by the reaction of urea and formaldehyde by condensation. 脲醛塑料是由尿素和甲醛缩合反应形成的热固性聚合物。
urushi 漆蜡	See lacquer. 见大漆。
vegetable tanning 植鞣	Vegetable tanning is tanning using extracts from plant materials such as oak bark and sumak. 植鞣是利用橡树皮和漆树皮等植物原料的提取物进行鞣制。
wet leather 饱水皮革	It is a kind of leather in which moisture content is too high,The collagen fibers of leather were dispersed and swelled. 饱水皮革是处于水分含量过高条件中的皮革，胶原纤维疏解和溶胀。
wet rot 湿腐病	Wet rot is fungal attack on wood which occurs in aerobic wet conditions, leaving the wood weak and spongy. 湿腐病是木材在有氧潮湿的环境下感染真菌而导致木材腐烂软化呈海绵状的病害。
white rot 白腐病	White rot is a fungal attack on wood which attacks the brown lignin component, leaving behind the lighter cellulose. 白腐病是指真菌侵害木材中的棕色木质素，留下颜色较浅的纤维素，导致木材色泽发白的病害。
wiring 布线	Wiring of a herbarium specimen is the process of attaching that specimen to a herbarium sheet using non-rusting wire which is tied to the specimen. 布线是用不锈的金属丝将植物标本固定在台纸上的过程。
wood boring insects 蛀木虫	A wood boring insect is a pest, such as Annobium punctatum (common furniture beetle) and Xestobium rufovillosum (Death Watch Beetle), whose larvae make channels in wood, because, for example, wood is a food source. 蛀木虫是一种害虫，例如常见的家具窃蠹（Annobium punctatum）和红毛窃蠹（Xestobium rufovillosum），又称（Death Watch Beetle），它们的幼虫咬食木材，留下虫洞。

woodworm 木蛀虫	See common furniture beetle. 见家具窃蠹。
wool fiber shedding 脱毛	a. The removal of hair and epidermis from animal skin by chemical, physical, or biological techniques. b. Due to the influence of environment, fur products naturally shed off and thin hair and other diseases occur. a. 利用化学,物理或生物技术脱去动物皮上的毛。b. 因受环境影响, 皮毛制品上的毛自然脱落, 产生其他病害。
worm channels 蛀洞	Worm channels are the loss of original material due to the action of wood-boring insect or other pest. These channels may be on the surface or internal. 蛀木虫或其他害虫咬食木材, 形成蛀洞。木材表面或内部都可能存在蛀洞。

11

修复材料
Conservation Material

Ablebond (342-1)® 双组分环氧树脂	Ablebond (342-1) was a two component epoxy resin used in ceramic and glass conservation. The hardener is polyoxypropylene diamine and the resin is a diglycidyl ether of bisphenol. This resin was first manufactured in 1979 and its production ceased in the late 1980's. Ablebond (342-1)（商标名）为双组分环氧树脂，用于陶瓷和玻璃保护。固化剂为聚氧丙烯二胺，树脂为双酚二环氧甘油醚。该树脂最早生产于1979年，二十世纪八十年代停产。
abrasive cloth 砂布	See abrasive paper. 见砂纸。
abrasive paper 砂纸	An abrasive paper (or cloth) is a paper (or cloth) onto which an abrasive powder has been bonded. It is used to remove material from a surface layer. 砂纸（或砂布）是指粘有研磨粉的纸（或布），用于去除表面层材料。
abrasive powder 磨粉	An abrasive powder is a hard mineral that has been crushed and sorted into a uniform size. It is used with wet or dry surface cleaning techniques. 磨粉是压碎并制成均匀大小的矿石，以湿或干态用于表面清洁。
absorbent 吸收的	An absorbent material is capable of drawing into itself liquids such as water or other solvents. 吸收材料是能够将水或其他溶剂吸收的材料。
absorbent clay 粘土吸收剂	Particularly absorbent clays are used to make poultices in order to remove surface staining or draw soluble salts out of contaminated porous materials. Examples of these clays include sepiolite, kieselghur and Laropal. 特殊的粘土吸收剂可制成膏状物，以清除表面污渍或者将可溶性盐从受污染的多孔材料中排出。此类粘土的例子包括海泡石、硅藻土和醛树脂。
acrylic fibres 腈纶纤维	Acrylic fibres are fibres made from polyacrylonitrile polymers. They have been in use since 1945. 腈纶纤维的原料是聚丙烯腈聚合物。自1945年起，腈纶纤维一直被使用。
acrylic paint 丙烯酸涂料	An acrylic paint is an acrylic resin medium mixed with pigments. 丙烯酸涂料是掺有颜料的丙烯酸树脂。
acrylic polymer 丙烯酸类聚合物	An acrylic polymer is one derived from acrylate, methacrylate and acrylonitrile monomers. These can be made into resins, dispersions, fibres and moulding compounds. 丙烯酸类聚合物是由丙烯酸酯、甲基丙烯酸酯和丙烯腈单体制成的，可制成树脂、分散剂、纤维或成型材料。
Acryloid® 丙烯酸树脂®	Acryloid was the American tradename for Paraloid®. 一种丙烯酸树脂（美国商标名），即Paraloid®。
activated carbon 活性炭	Activated carbon is carbon that has a high surface area which has been treated to be particularly absorbent. It is used to remove gaseous pollutants. 活性炭是一种具有高比表面积的炭，经处理后具有很强的吸附性，主要用于去除气态污染物。

adhesive film 粘性胶膜	An adhesive film is a layer of adhesive which is unattached to a substrate. In textile conservation, films are placed under the area to be adhered, then made sticky with heat or a solvent. 粘性胶膜是有一层胶粘剂的膜，胶膜独立于基质。在进行纺织品保护时，胶膜应置于要粘贴的区域下方，然后加热或使用溶剂使其粘合。
adhesive tape 胶带	An adhesive tape is a tape support that has an adhesive applied to one or both sides. The support may be of paper, polymer, metal or cloth. The adhesive may be water activated, typically a gum, or be pressure sensitive. 胶带是一种单面或双面涂有胶粘剂的胶带支撑物，支撑物可以是纸、聚合物、金属或者布料。胶粘剂可以是水活化型，如树胶，也可以是压敏型。
aerosol silica 气溶硅胶	Aerosol silica is a kind of very finely divided silica of various forms that can be used as matting agent or thickener for media. See also fumed silica. 气溶硅胶是一种极细、形式多样的二氧化硅，可用作介质的消光剂或者增稠剂。另见气相二氧化硅。
agar 琼脂	Agar is a polysaccharide derived from seaweed (Rhodophyceae). It dissolves in hot water forming a solution which gels on cooling. It has been used as a consolidant. 琼脂是从海藻（红藻科）中得到的多糖。琼脂在热水中将溶解形成溶液，冷却后形成胶体，曾被用作加固剂。
aggregate (2) 骨料 (2)	An aggregate is inert particles added to a resinous material, for instance, in the production of fills for ceramics. 骨料是添加到树脂类材料中的惰性粒子，例如，陶瓷生产中的填料。
AJK dough AJK 面团材料	AJK dough was a strong, lightweight material used for filling ceramics and similar. It was made by mixing Alvar (a polyvinyl acetal), jute and kaolin with organic solvents and water. It suffered from both short and long term shrinkage, so its use has reduced. AJK 面团材料是用于填充陶瓷及类似物的高强度轻质材料，由 Alvar（聚乙烯醇缩醛）、黄麻和高岭土与有机溶剂和水混合而制成。因其无论是短期和长期的收缩都会使其质量变差，所以人们已减少使用。
alcohol 酒精	Alcohol is an organic compound that has a hydroxyl group. 酒精是有羟基的有机化合物。
Araldite 2020® 环氧树脂2020®	Araldite 2020 is a two-part epoxy system used for the bonding of glass and high fired ceramic objects. 环氧树脂2020（商标名）是用于粘结玻璃和高温陶瓷制品的双组分环氧树脂体系。
Araldite® 环氧树脂®	Araldite is the trademark for a range of two-part epoxy systems. Varieties used in conservation include the epoxy resin AY103 and amine hardener HY956, which are primarily used for consolidation of wood and casting in moulds. 环氧树脂是一系列双组分环氧树脂体系的商标。用在保护领域的品种包括环氧树脂 AY103 和胺固化剂 HY956，主要用于加固木材和铸制模具。

Arboflex 500® Arboflex 500®	Arboflex 500 is a butyl rubber and one of the more stable hydrocarbon elastomers. It resembles modelling clay in consistency and is used to fill the gap between the glass and the lead in stained glass panels. It does not set but will become brittle over time due to oxidation. Arboflex 500（商标名）是一种丁基橡胶，也是一种较为稳定的碳氢化合物弹性体。它的延展性类似造型/建模粘土，用于填充染色玻璃面板中玻璃和铅框之间的间隙。它不会硬化，但随着时间的推移会因氧化而变脆。
Archeoderm® 聚氯乙烯®	Archeoderm was a poly(vinyl chloride) used for the consolidation of archaeological objects. It replaced Derm-o-plast in the 1970's. 聚氯乙烯（商标名）用于加固考古器物。其在20世纪70年代取代了聚氯乙烯(Derm-o-plast)。
archival (1) 档案 (1)	An archival material is one that is intended to survive in perpetuity. 档案材料是指永久留存的材料。
attapulgite 硅镁土	Attapulgite is the name of a group of fibrous clay minerals (hydrated magnesium aluminium silicates) capable of absorbing large quantities of liquid without increase in volume. 硅镁土是一组纤维状粘土矿物的名称（水合铝镁硅酸盐），在体积不增加的情况下能够吸收大量液体。
backing glass 背板玻璃	A backing glass is a piece of modern glass used to support fragile stained glass by plating. The modern glass is cut to the same size as the old glass, both are sealed at the edge and held together with an extra wide lead. 背板玻璃是一块用于支撑易碎彩色玻璃的辅助用玻璃。将此玻璃切割成与原玻璃相同的大小，并都在边缘密封，用超宽铅条结合在一起。
beeswax 蜂蜡	Beeswax is a mixture of long chained esters with which bees make the walls of their honeycomb. Beeswax is used as a binding agent, polish and adhesive. 蜂蜡是长链酯的混合物，蜜蜂用其制作蜂巢壁。蜂蜡被用作粘结剂、上光剂和胶粘剂。
Beva 371® 醋酸乙烯酯®	Beva 371 is an thermoplastic adhesive film which consists of two ethylene-vinyl acetate co-polymers and contains resin and solvent components. Beva 371 is supplied as a solution or as a film. 醋酸乙烯酯（商标名）为热塑性粘附膜，由两种乙酸乙烯酯共聚物组成，包含树脂和溶剂组分。醋酸乙烯酯产品一般是溶液或薄膜。
biocides 生物杀灭剂	Biocides, such as fungicides and insecticides, are intended to eradicate the cause of a process of biodeterioration. 生物杀灭剂，如杀菌剂和杀虫剂，旨在从根源上去除生物腐蚀。
bone glue 骨胶	Bone glue is a glue made by degrading and solubilising the collagen in bones. It is sold in granular form. 骨胶是通过降解和溶解骨头中的胶原蛋白制成的胶。其产品为颗粒状。

bubblewrap 气泡膜	Bubblewrap is a packaging and cushioning material made of two sheets of polyethene laminated with bubbles of air trapped between. 气泡膜是一种包装缓冲材料，由两片层压气泡的聚乙烯制成。
buffer (2) 缓冲剂（2）	A buffer is any chemical, usually a salt, added to a solution that will stabilise the pH of that solution while the solution is being used or diluted. 缓冲剂是添加到溶液中的任何化学物质，通常是盐，在使用或稀释溶液时，起稳定溶液pH值的作用。
bulking agent (2) 膨胀剂 (2)	A bulking agent is an aggregate added to a synthetic resin in order to increase its volume and possible also its strength without significantly altering the resin's other properties. 膨胀剂是添加到合成树脂中的骨料，旨在增加其体积及强度，而不明显改变树脂的其他性质。
Butvar B-98® 聚乙烯醇缩丁醛®	Butvar B-98 is a poly(vinyl butyral) which has been widely used as a consolidant for textiles. Butvar B-98（商标名）为聚乙烯醇缩丁醛，已广泛用作织物的加固剂。
butyl rubber 丁基橡胶	Butyl rubber is a copolymer of isobutylene and isoprene that is more stable than natural rubber and has a low gas permeability. 丁基橡胶是异丁烯和异戊二烯的共聚物，比天然橡胶更稳定，透气性较低。
Calgon® 加尔贡®	Calgon is a commercial water softener that contains sequestering agents capable of forming complexes with unwanted metal compounds in hard water. In the past, its main active constituent was Sodium hexameta phosphate $(Na(PO_3)_6$. In the 1990's this was replaced with Zeolite compounds. Calgon has been used in porcelain conservation to improve the cleaning power of detergents. It has also been used to aid in the removal of calcium concretions on archaeological objects. Calgon has been shown to damage earthenwares and fragile glass or glaze surfaces. 加尔贡（商标名）为商用软水剂，含有螯合剂，能够在硬水中形成含有害金属化合物的配合物。在过去，其主要活性成分为六偏磷酸钠 $(Na(PO_3)_6$。在20世纪90年代，它被沸石化合物所取代。Calgon被用于瓷器保护，以提高洗涤剂的清洁能力。它也被用来帮助去除考古物品上的钙质凝结物。Calgon已被证明会损坏陶器和脆弱的玻璃或釉面。
carnauba wax carnauba 蜡	Carnauba wax is a kind of natural wax which is collected from the surface of the leaves of a palm, Copernicia prunifera, and is composed largely of myricyl cerotate $C_{27}H_{53}O_2.C_3OH_6$.It is one of the hardest and has one of the highest melting points (83-86℃) of the natural waxes. carnauba 蜡是从棕榈树叶子表面收集的一种天然蜡，如巴西蜡棕榈，主要由蜡酸蜂花酯 $C_{27}H_{53}O_2.C_3OH_6$ 组成。它是硬度最高、熔点最高的天然蜡之一，熔点达83-86℃。
casting medium 铸型材料	A casting medium is the liquid material used to produce a cast from a mould. 铸型材料是用于从铸具中制作铸件的液态物质。

cellulose acetate butyrate 乙酸丁酸纤维素	Cellulose acetate butyrate is a thermoplastic polymer made by reacting cellulose with acetic anhydride and butyric acid. It is used to make films with added plasticisers. It hydrolyses slowly to evolve acetic acid. It is used as film base. 乙酸丁酸纤维素是由纤维素、乙酸酐和丁酸反应而成的热塑性聚合物，缓慢水解会生成乙酸，添加增塑剂后可用于制作胶片基。
clay pack 粘土吸附材料	A clay pack is poultice using clay as the absorbent material. 粘土吸附材料是一种膏状物，用粘土作为吸水材料。
consolidant 加固剂	A consolidant is the reinforcing material deposited in an object in the process of consolidation. 加固剂是在加固过程中沉积在物体内的增强材料。
Correx® Correx®	Correx is a fluted or corrugated plastic board made of extruded polypropylene (PP). It is used to make supports and packaging for the storage of objects. Correx（商标名）为有沟槽或瓦楞的塑料板，由挤出的聚丙烯(PP)制成。其用于制造存储物体的支撑物和库房器物包装材料。
cotton wool 脱脂棉	Cotton wool is a loose felt of long cotton fibres, which is used as an absorbent and slightly abrasive material for holding liquids during cleaning. 脱脂棉是松软的长棉纤维，用作吸收和轻微的摩擦材料，可在清洁过程中保留液体。
cure 固化	A medium cures when it converts from its liquid to solid state by cross-linking. 固化指的是介质通过交联剂作用从液态转化为固态。
cyanoacrylate 氰基丙烯酸	A cyanoacrylate monomer, typically ethyl-2-cyanoacrylate, will polymerise in the presence of water to form a very high molecular weight polymer. This reaction is used to form adhesive joins, so it has been used for ceramics and stone. It can degrade under the influence of alkalis such as on unstable glass. 氰基丙烯酸单体，特别是氰基丙烯酸乙酯，会在有水时聚合形成极高分子量的聚合物，该反应用于形成粘合，因此用于陶瓷和石头的粘接。它可在碱的影响下降解，例如在不稳定的玻璃上。
cyclododecane 环十二烷	Cyclododecane ($C_{12}H_{24}$) is a volatile binding medium. 环十二烷($C_{12}H_{24}$)为易挥发的胶结介质。
dammar 达玛树脂	Dammar is a plant resin exuded from Dipterocarpaceae trees. Dammar varies depending on the country and tree from which it is derived. It is a pale yellow and brittle natural resin which dissolves in polar hydrocarbons and other organic solvents. It has been widely used in picture varnishes since described by Lucanus in 1829. It oxidises and yellows over time. 达玛树脂是从龙脑香树中渗出的植物树脂。达玛树脂因国家和所提取的树种的不同而不同，是浅黄色较脆的天然树脂，可溶解于极性烃类等有机溶剂中。自1829年Lucanus提及其以来，它被广泛应用于绘画清漆中。随着时间流逝它会氧化变黄。

deionised water 去离子水	De-ionised water is partly purified water in which the anions and cations have been exchanged with hydrogen and hydroxyl ions. This is achieved by passing water through an ion exchange resin. 去离子水为部分净化的水，其中的阴离子和阳离子在氢离子和羟离子的作用下发生交换。当水流经离子交换树脂即可实现这一过程。
denatured alcohol 变性酒精	Denatured alcohol is ethanol which has been adulterated with noxious substances to make it unfit for human consumption. Typical additives are methanol and propanol. 变性酒精指的是已经掺入有害物质，无法供人食用的乙醇。典型的添加剂为甲醇和丙醇。
dental impression compound 牙印模化合物（材料）	Dental impression compound is a material used to make semi-permanent moulds of small areas for replication. It has been adopted from the dental profession. It may be soft wax, a silicone rubber or other cross-linking resin. 牙印模化合物是一种用于制作半永久型小面积复制模具的材料，已被牙科专业采用。其可以是软蜡、硅橡胶或者其他交联树脂。
dental wax 牙科蜡	Dental wax is wax used in thin sheets which may be shaped after gentle warming and used as a support in the process of gap filling. It has been adopted from the dental profession. 牙科蜡是以薄片形式使用的蜡，在温和加热后可塑形，在间隙填充过程中用作支撑物。其已被牙科专业采用。
Derm-o-plast® 聚氯乙烯®	Derm-o-plast was a poly(vinyl chloride) used before the 1970's for the consolidation of archaeological objects. It has been replaced by Archeoderm. Derm-o-plast（商标名）为20世纪70年代之前使用的聚氯乙烯用于加固考古器物。其已经由Archeoderm取代。
detergent 洗涤剂	A detergent is a material, either a pure surfactant or with a mixture of other components, that is added to water to aid cleaning during washing. See also surfactant. 洗涤剂是指洗涤时添加到水中起辅助清洁作用的一种材料，可以是纯粹的表面活性剂，或是表面活性剂与其他组分的混合剂。另见表面活性剂。
dispersion (1) 分散体系	A dispersion is a mixture of fine particles which are held stable in a continuous medium. Examples of dispersion are mist (droplets of water in air) and wax polish (wax particles in organic liquid). 分散体系是在连续介质中保持稳定的细颗粒混合物。例如，分散体系为薄雾（空气中的小水滴）和上光蜡（有机液体中的蜡晶粒）。
dissolve (2) 溶解 (2)	In chemistry, a soluble compound dissolves in a liquid by separating into its component molecules or ions which are distributed through the liquid. 在化学上，可溶性化合物溶解于液体中，通过分散到液体的分子或离子，分布在整个液体中。

distilled water 蒸馏水	Distilled water is partly purified water from which the non-volatile impurities have been removed by first boiling and then by condensing the water. 蒸馏水是部分净化的水，其中的非挥发性杂质已通过首次沸腾和水冷凝去除。
DM5 DM5	DM5 is a co-polymer dispersion of vinyl acetate and butyl actylate. It has a Tg of 20℃. See also Mowilith®. DM5为醋酸乙烯酯和丙烯酸丁酯（丁基乙酰化物）的共聚物分散液，玻璃化转变温度为20℃。另见Mowilith®。
DMC2 DMC2	DMC2 is a co-polymer dispersion of vinyl acetate and di-n-butyl maleate. It has a Tg of 100℃. See also Mowilith®. DMC2为醋酸乙烯酯和马来酸二正丁酯的共聚物分散液，玻璃化转变温度为100℃。另见Mowilith®。
dry 干燥	a. You dry an object or its environment by removing water from it. b. A medium dries when it converts from its liquid to solid state by the evaporation of a dispersant or solvent. a. 通过去除器物或环境中的水可使其变干燥。b. 当分散液或溶剂蒸发使介质从液态转化为固态时，就可使其变干燥。
dry cleaning sponge 干洗海绵	A dry cleaning sponge is a soft, vulcanised rubber sponge originally designed to clean objects soiled by soot and smoke. It is used to remove surface soiling not easily removable by brushing or vacuum cleaning. See also Wish-ab®. 干洗海绵为柔软、硫化的橡胶海绵，最初是为了清洁被烟灰或烟污染的物体。用于通过擦拭或者真空除尘清除不易去除的表面污物。另见Wish-ab®。
Duco Cement® 杜科水泥®	Duco cement is a commercial adhesive, formulated from plasticised cellulose nitrate. In the past it was used for the conservation of ceramics. 杜科水泥（商标名）为商用胶粘剂，由塑化的硝荃纤维素配制而成。在过去，其用于陶瓷保护。
Durofix® Durofix®	Durofix is a commercial adhesive formulated from cellulose nitrate. It is primarily used for the bonding of ceramics and glass. Durofix 为商用胶粘剂，由硝荃纤维素配制而成，其主要用作陶瓷和玻璃的粘结。
EDTA 乙二胺四乙酸 (EDTA)	EDTA is ethylene diamine tetraacetic acid, a sequestering agent used for cleaning metal ions from objects such as calcium or iron deposits. It is normally used as one of the sodium salts, depending on the metal ion to be solubilised. EDTA是乙二胺四乙酸，一种用于从器物上清除金属离子，如钙或铁沉积物，的螯合剂。通常使用二钠盐。
elemi 榄香脂	Elemi is a type of resin exuded from a number of trees, currently principally Canarium indicum. The term has been used for resins from a changing list of trees over the centuries. Elemi is soluble in alcohol and benzol and was often used as an additive for wax-resin lining. 榄香脂是从树中渗出的一种树脂，目前主要是爪哇橄榄。几个世纪以来，尽管树种不断变化，榄香脂一词一直被使用。其可溶于酒精和苯，常常用作添加剂。

emulsifying agent **乳化剂**	An emulsifying agent is a type of surfactant added to aqueous washing solutions in order to form stable dispersions of hydrophobic materials such as greasy soiling. 乳化剂是一种添加到水性清洗剂中的表面活性剂，旨在使油脂等疏水材料稳定分散。
emulsion (1) **乳液 (1)**	An emulsion is a colloidal dispersion of a liquid in another liquid, such as milk in cream. 乳液是一种液体在另一种液体中的胶态分散体，如牛奶在奶油中。
enzyme **酶**	An enzyme is a protein that acts as a catalyst in physiological reactions. Enzymes are used very selectively to react with and remove insoluble contaminants from objects. They survive and react only in conditions similar to their natural physiological conditions. A number of different enzymes are used for dissolving binding agents, adhesives and varnishes. 酶是一种在生化反应中起催化作用的蛋白质。通常会非常有选择性地用于和物体中的不溶性污染物发生反应以将其去除。其只有在与自身的自然生理（生化）条件类似的条件下，才会存在和发生反应。一些不同的酶被用于溶解结合剂、粘合剂和清漆。
epoxy resin **环氧树脂**	An epoxy resin is a cross-linking polymer. It is made up of two parts: a component containing epoxide groups and a hardener that reacts with the epoxide and cross-links the molecules. Epoxy resins have been widely used in conservation since the 1950's as consolidants and gap-fillers on ceramics, glass, stone, wood and metal. 环氧树脂是一种交联聚合物，由两部分组成：含有环氧基团的组分、与环氧化物发生反应并交联分子的加固剂。自20世纪50年代以来，环氧树脂作为陶瓷、玻璃、石材、木材和金属的巩固剂和填充剂被广泛用于保护。
eraser **清洁擦**	An eraser is a material that is used to remove particulate contaminants from surfaces by rubbing with a tacky material that holds dirt and disintegrates into powder. Typical materials are natural rubbers and soft vinyl polymers. 清洁擦是一种用于从表面去除微粒状污染物的材料，主要通过粘性材料的摩擦将污物粘揭，并使其分解成粉末。典型材料为天然橡胶和软乙烯基聚合物。
erasing powder **擦除粉**	Erasing powder is made of ground eraser rubber or factice. It is used in the surface cleaning of paper. 擦除粉由粉状擦除橡胶或油膏组成，用于纸张的表面清洁。
ethylene vinyl acetate **乙烯醋酸乙烯酯**	Ethylene vinyl acetate (EVA), is a waxy thermoplastic polymer which is used in hot melt adhesives, such as Beva 371. 乙烯醋酸乙烯酯(EVA)为蜡质热熔性聚合物，用于如 Beva 371 等热熔胶。
facing adhesive **面层胶粘剂**	A facing adhesive is used to attach a facing to a surface. 面层胶粘剂用于将面层附着到物体表面上。

filler (2) 填充剂 (2)	A filler is a fine powder added to a paint which causes no appreciable changes in shade or hue. 填充剂是指添加到油漆中的细粉，其不会引起可察觉的颜色深浅或色调变化。
finish (1) 面漆 (1)	The finish is the final layer in surface decoration, such as varnish or lacquer. 面漆是表面装饰的最后一层，如光油或清漆。
fish glue 鱼胶	Fish glue is glue made from fish material. 鱼胶是用鱼作为原材料制成的胶。
fly ash 粉煤灰	Fly ash is a waste product precipitated in the flues of power stations. It is used as a pozzuolanic additive in mortars and grouts. It is also known as pulverised fly ash (PFA). 粉煤灰是电厂烟道内沉淀的废产物，用作砂浆、泥浆中的火山灰质混合料，也可以称为PFA。
French polish 法国抛光漆	French polish is a shellac coating which is applied to wood in many layers by rubbing a solution of shellac in alcohol onto the wood and allowing each layer to dry. 法国抛光漆是涂敷到木材上的多层虫胶涂料。方法是将虫胶酒精溶液抹到木材上，使其一层层变干。
fumed silica 气相二氧化硅	Fumed silica is a very finely divided colloidal form of synthetic silica, manufactured as a product of burning silicon tetrachloride. It is used as a bulking agent for epoxy fillers in glass and ceramic restoration and has been shown to improve the adhesive properties of some resins. It is also used as a matting agent for retouching media. It comes as a very fine powder and is available in a hydrophilic or hydrophobic form. See also aerosol silica. 气相二氧化硅是合成二氧化硅的一种非常精细的胶体形式，是四氯化硅燃烧生成的产物。在玻璃和陶瓷修复中用作环氧树脂填料的填充剂，以改进其粘接性。它也被用作修饰用消光剂。它是一种非常细的粉末，有亲水性或疏水性两种形式产品。另见气溶胶二氧化硅。
fungicide 杀真菌剂	A fungicide is a substance used to prevent, control or eradicate fungi, such as moulds and mildew. 杀真菌剂是用于预防、控制或根除霉菌等真菌的物质。
gel 凝胶	A gel is a jelly like material, which is a suspension of a liquid in a solid matrix in which the solid has created a more or less firm network holding the liquid in place. A gel is typically prepared by cooling a solution. 凝胶是一种胶状材料，是液体在固体基质中的悬浊液，其中的固体已经形成出一种大致稳定的网络结构，以使液体保持在固定位置。凝胶通常通过将溶液冷却来配制。
gelatine 明胶	Gelatine is degraded collagen which is carefully extracted from a collagen containing substrate. It is used as an adhesive, consolidant, fixative, size, thickening agent and as a coating for photograpic paper and film. 明胶是降解的胶原蛋白，从凝胶基质中精心提取而出。明胶被用作胶粘剂、加固剂、固定剂、上浆剂、增稠剂以及相纸膜和胶片膜。

Genklene® 金克林®	Genklene is a chlorinated hydrocarbon solvent (1,1,1-trichloroethane), which was used in solvent cleaning of objects. The use of 1,1,1-trichloroethane is now banned because it depletes ozone in the stratosphere. 金克林（商标名）为氯代烃溶剂（1,1,1 三氯乙烷），用于物体的溶剂清洁。1,1,1 三氯乙烷如今被禁用，因其会消耗平流层的臭氧。
gilding water 贴金水	Gilding water is a mixture of water and alcohol to which size may be added. It is used to attatch gold leaf to a surface during water gilding. 贴金水是含粘接剂的水和酒精的混合剂。用于在水法贴金时将金箔贴附到器物表面。
glass fibre 玻璃纤维	Glass fibre is glass that has been melted and drawn or blown into fibres. It is available in a variety of compositions and thicknesses. The fibres are used as reinforcement for resins or woven into textiles. 玻璃纤维是已经熔化并拉伸或者吹炼成纤维的玻璃，有多种组分和厚度可供选择。纤维用于强化树脂或纺织品。
glassfibre reinforced plastic 玻璃纤维增强塑料	Glassfibre reinforced plastic (GRP) is a polymer, usually derived from a polyester resin, which has had glass fibre incorporated in order to increase its strength and toughness. 玻璃纤维增强塑料 (GRP) 是一种聚合物，通常是聚酯树脂，其中加入了玻璃纤维用于增加其强度和韧度。
glue 胶	Glue is degraded collagen which is derived from boiling animal connective tissue (bones, skin and hoofs). It contains fat and other impurities. Different types are bone glue, rabbit glue, skin glue and fish glue. Glues made from mammals are usually applied in a warm (65-80℃) solution of water because it sets to a jelly at lower temperatures. Fish glue solution can be applied at room temperature. The final adhesive bond is formed by the evaporation of the water. 胶是从煮沸的动物结缔组织（骨头、皮肤和蹄）中提取的降解胶原蛋白。它含有脂肪和其他杂质。有骨胶、兔胶、皮胶和鱼胶。由哺乳动物制成的胶通常用在温水（65-80℃）的溶液中，因为它在较低的温度下会变成凝胶。鱼胶溶液可在室温下使用。最后的粘合键合是由水蒸发形成。
gum 树胶	A gum is a water-soluble exudate from plant material. Most gums are polysaccharides and used as binding media when creating artefacts. 树胶为植物体的水溶性分泌物，大多数胶为多糖，在制作人工制品时用作胶结材料。
gum arabic 阿拉伯树胶	Gum arabic is a water-soluble exudate of the north African Acacia arabica. It is used as an adhesive for print mounting and as image binder in gum-dichromate prints. 阿拉伯树胶为北非阿拉伯金合欢的水溶性分泌物，用作相片装裱的胶粘剂，以及树胶重铬酸盐印刷的图像粘结剂。
gummed paper tape 胶纸带	Gummed paper tape is an adhesive tape coated on one side with a water activated adhesive, usually a gum mixture. 胶纸带为一面涂有水活化胶粘剂的胶带，通常为树胶混合物。

hard water 硬水	Hard water is water that contains soluble compounds of ions, such as calcium and magnesium, that can precipitate on objects during wet cleaning and react with soaps to form insoluble scum. 硬水是指含有可溶性离子（如钙和镁）化合物的水，会在湿法清洁时沉淀到物体上，并与肥皂反应形成不溶性浮垢。
heat activated （**adhesive**） 热活化胶粘剂 （热熔胶）	A heat activated adhesive contains a thermoplastic that softens on heating, becomes sticky and sets on cooling. An example is Beva film. 热活化胶粘剂含有热塑性树脂，可在加热时软化并有粘性，在冷却时固化。例如Beva膜。
H.M.G.® H. M. G. 防水粘合剂	H.M.G. Waterproof Adhesive is a commercial adhesive that is primarily used for porous materials, notably ceramics. It is formulated from cellulose nitrate, plasticised with dibutyl phthalate. H.M.G.防水粘合剂是一种商用粘合剂，主要用于多孔材料，尤其是陶瓷。它由硝酸纤维素制成，用邻苯二甲酸二丁酯增塑。商标名。
homopolymer 均聚物	A homopolymer is a polymer composed of only one monomer type. 均聚物是指仅由一种单体类型组成的聚合物。
hook and loop fastener 魔术贴	A hook and loop fastener, commonly known as Velcro®, is a reversible fastening system in which two flexible nylon tapes are pressed together. One tape is covered with tiny, flexible hooks that hook onto the tiny, hard loops of the other tape. They can be easily pulled apart to release the fastening and then be fastened again. It has many applications, such as to hang tapestries on the wall. 魔术贴是两个柔韧的尼龙带按压在一起形成可逆的紧固系统，通常称为Velcro®（商标名）。一个尼龙带布满微小、柔韧的钩子，用于钩住另一个尼龙带上的小硬环。因其使用简便且可重复，得到了广泛应用，如将挂毯挂在墙上。
Hostaphan® Hostaphan®	Hostaphan is a film made of polyester. Hostaphan®是由聚酯纤维制成的一种薄膜。
Hostapon T® Hostapon T®	Hostapon T is an anionic surfactant of fatty acid methyl taurides manufactured by Hoechst. Taurides are formed from fatty acid chlorides and amino alkane sulfonic acids (usually with the sodium salt of methyl taurine). Hostapon T（商标名）为脂肪酸甲基牛磺酸的阴离子表面活性剂，由赫斯特公司生产。牛磺酸由氯化脂肪酰和氨基烷磺酸（通常用甲基牛磺酸钠盐）制成。
hot melt adhesive 热熔胶	A hot melt adhesive is an adhesive which is solid at room temperature, melts on heating and resolidifies upon cooling, for example Beva film. 热熔胶是一种在室温下呈固态的胶粘剂，加热时会熔化，冷却时会再凝固，例如Beva膜。
humectant 湿润剂	A humectant is a substance added to an object that attracts and retains water. 湿润剂是添加到物体中起吸水和蓄水作用的物质。
impregnant 浸渍剂	An impregnant is the fluid material introduced into an object during burial or as part of a treatment. 浸渍剂为在埋藏或处理过程中渗入物体中的一种液态物质。

Incralac®	Incralac is the commercial name of an acrylic resin which contains the corrosion inhibitor benzotriazole and is used as a protective coating for metal. Incralac® 是一种丙烯酸树脂的商品名，含有阻蚀剂苯并三唑，用作金属的保护涂层。
industrial methylated spirits (IMS) 工业甲基化酒精 (IMS)	Industrial methylated spirits (IMS) is the UK grade of ethanol which has been denatured with ca. 5% methanol. It is colourless. 工业甲基化酒精 (IMS) 为 UK 级乙醇，加入大约 5% 的甲醇变性，无色。
inhibitor 缓蚀剂	An inhibitor is a chemical substance or combination of substances which prevent or reduce chemical change in a material. For example, a corrosion inhibitor is applied to a metal to reduce corrosion. 缓蚀剂为一种化学物质或多种物质的组合，用于预防或减少材料的化学变化。例如，应用于金属制品上的缓蚀剂以减少金属腐蚀。
isolating barrier 隔离层	An isolating barrier physically separates an object from a potentially harmful agent. 隔离层可将物体与可能有害的制剂进行物理隔离。
ketone resin 酮树脂	A ketone resin is an oligomer formed by the condensation of polycyclohexanones. Ketone resins have been used as picture varnishes because of their similarity in properties to natural resins like dammar. 酮树脂为聚环己酮缩合形成的低聚物，因其性质类似于达玛树脂等天然树脂，故曾经用作画作上光油。
Klucel® Klucel®	Klucel is a hydroxypropylcellulose polymer which is soluble in water and some solvents. Klucel is made in different grades, based on the degree of polymerisation. In textile conservation, the grade of Klucel G is used as an adhesive and consolidant. Klucel（商标名）为羟丙基纤维素聚合物，可溶于水和其他溶剂。根据聚合程度，Klucel 被制成了不同的等级。在织物保护领域，等级为 G 的 Klucel 用作胶粘剂和加固剂。
kraft paper 牛皮纸	Kraft paper is a strong paper made of chemical pulp using the sodium sulphate alkaline process. Kraft paper is brown in colour and has to be bleached to obtain a lighter colour. In painting conservation, strips of kraft paper are stuck to the edges of the canvas painting to facilitate the stretching and flattening of the painting in a temporary working frame. 牛皮纸是采用硫酸钠碱法工艺用化学纸浆制成的、强度很高的纸，呈棕色，须漂白以获得较浅的颜色。在绘画保护中，将牛皮纸条粘在布上油画的边缘，以方便画作在临时工作框架中的拉伸和压平。
Lascaux 360® Lascaux 360®	Lascaux 360 is a thermoplastic adhesive that is a dispersion of an acrylic polymer, manufactured by Lascaux. Lascaux 360（商标名）为热塑性胶粘剂，是丙烯酸类聚合物的分散液，由 Lascaux 公司生产。

levelling 自流平	The levelling of a coating during setting is its flow from high points to low points which reduce the unevenness left during application by brushing or spraying. 涂层固化时的自流平是其从最高点流向最低点，以降低用刷子涂敷或喷涂时造成的不匀。
mastic 乳香脂	Mastic is a pale yellow triterpenoid resin exuded from a shrub, Pistacia lentiscus. When dissolved in solvent it gives a light yellow varnish has traditionally been used as a picture varnish, and becomes yellower and increasingly polar with ageing. It was important as picture varnish until the discovery of dammar resin. 乳香脂为从乳香黄连木灌木丛中渗出的浅黄色三萜系化合物树脂。当溶解于溶剂中时，会产生淡黄色清漆，传统上用作画作上光油，黄色会加深，随着老化会逐渐变得更深。在发现达玛树脂之前，它一直是重要的画作光油。
matting agent 消光剂	A matting agent is one added to a binding agent in order to reduce its sheen or gloss when set. 消光剂为添加到粘合剂中的制剂，用于降低其凝固时的光泽。
Melinex® film Melinex® film	Melinex is a registered brand name for polyethylene terephthalate film, a polyester film manufactured by ICI. It is most commonly used in the conservation of paintings utilizing the low-pressure table/ vacuum hot table. It is similar to Mylarfilm. Melinex 为聚乙烯对苯二酸盐薄膜的注册商标名称，是由 ICI 公司生产的聚酯膜。其最常用于画作保护，用于低压真空热桌。其类似于 Mylarfilm。
menthol 薄荷醇	Menthol ($C_{10}H_{19}OH$) is a volatile binding medium. 薄荷醇($C_{10}H_{19}OH$)为挥发性粘合剂。
methacrylate resin 甲基丙烯酸树脂	A methacrylate resin is a thermoplastic polymer made from methacrylate monomers. These resins are particularly resistant to yellowing and have been widely used as coatings, consolidants and adhesives in conservation. 甲基丙烯酸树脂是由甲基丙烯酸酯单体制成的热塑性聚合物，具有优异的耐黄变性能，广泛用作保护领域的涂料、加固剂和粘合剂。
methylcellulose 甲基纤维素	Methylcellulose (MC) is a cellulose ether. It is a non-ionic polymer. The white powder is water soluble. It is used as an adhesive, size, thickener, consolidant, fixative and as an emulsifier. 甲基纤维素(MC)为纤维素醚，是非离子型聚合物。其白色粉末可溶于水。用作粘合剂、上浆剂、增稠剂、加固剂、固定剂以及乳化剂。
microballoon 空心球	A microballoon is a small hollow sphere made of glass, ceramic or polymer. Microballoons are used as fillers to reduce weight and increase workability of the solidified fill. 空心球是有玻璃、陶瓷或者聚合物制成的空心小球，被用作固化填充料，以减轻重量、增加可加工性能。

microcrystalline wax 微晶蜡	Microcrystalline wax is wax that is made up of branched chain hydrocarbons. Microcrystalline waxes of various grades are extracted from crude oil. 微晶蜡是由支链烃组成的蜡，不同等级的微晶蜡是从原油中提取出来的。
mineral spirit 矿物油 / 石油脑 / 矿物油精 / 石油醚	A mineral spirit is a hydrocarbon liquid obtained by distilling natural oil. It is available in many boiling ranges, grades and purities. Mineral spirits are used as solvents. 矿物油是由石油所得精炼液态烃的混合物，有不同的沸点、分子量和纯度。矿物油被用作溶剂。
mobile liquids 流性液体	Mobile liquids are liquids that have low viscosity. 流性液体是指粘度较低的液体。
moisture barrier 防潮材料	A moisture barrier is an impermeable or semi-permeable material that prevents the ingress of water or water vapour. 防潮材料是指为防止水或水蒸气进入的一种不可渗透或者半渗透材料。
monomer 单体	A monomer is a small molecule that can be reacted chemically with other monomers to form a polymer or oligomer. 单体是指可与其他单体发生化学反应并生成聚合物的小分子。
Mowilith® Mowilith®	Mowilith is a range of vinyl acetate co-polymer dispersions made by Hoechst. The grades DMC2 and DM5 are used in a mixture as a thermoplastic adhesive in textile conservation. Mowilith（商标名）是一系列醋酸乙烯共聚物分散液，由赫斯特公司生产。DMC2 和 DM5 两个等级混合起来作为热塑性胶粘剂用于织物保护。
Mowital® Mowital®	Mowital is a poly(vinyl butyral). Mowital has been used widely in conservation as a consolidant and as an adhesive. Mowital（商标名）为聚乙烯醇缩丁醛，其作为加固剂和胶粘剂已广泛应用于保护领域。
Mylar® film Mylar 薄膜	Mylar film is a polyester film manufactured by DuPont. It is similar to Melinex film. Mylar 薄膜（商标名）为杜邦公司生产的聚酯薄膜，类似于 Melinex 膜。
Nitromors® Nitromors®	Nitromors Green is a commercial water washable paint stripper whose main component is dichloromethane ($CH_2.CL_2$). It comes in a gel form and is used in ceramic conservation to remove old areas of retouching and break down old bonds made with adhesives such as epoxies, shellac, polyesters and acrylics. Nitromors Green（商标名）为商用可水洗型油漆去除剂，其主要成分为二氯甲烷($CH_2.CL_2$)。其以凝胶形式存在，用于陶瓷制品保护领域以去除旧的补釉区域，并破坏胶粘剂制成的旧的粘合。例如环氧树脂，胶，聚酯和丙烯酸树脂。
non-drying oil 不干性油	A non-drying oil is oil that contains insufficient unsaturated groups to form a coherent film by oxidation. See also oil and drying oil. 不干性油是指含有不充分的不饱和基团，无法经氧化形成一致膜的油。另见油与干性油。

nylon 尼龙	Nylon is a synthetic thermoplastic polyamide made from various monomers. It is made into fibres and solid resin forms. There are many types of which nylon 6,6 and nylon 6 are the most commonly used. Nylon 6,6 is made from adipic acid and hexamethylene diamine. nylon 6 is made from cyclic caprolactam. nylon has been in use since 1940. 尼龙是由多种单体合成的聚酰胺类化合物，具热塑性，可制成纤维和固态树脂等形式，自1940年以来就开始使用尼龙，其中尼龙6,6和尼龙6最常用，尼龙6,6由己二酸和六亚甲基二胺制成，尼龙6由环己内酰胺制成。
oil 油	a. Oil is a mixture of hydrocarbons which is refined from crude oil extracted from the ground. It is typically used for lubrication. b. Oil is a naturally occurring triglyceride ester of fatty acids derived from animals and plants. See also drying oil and non-drying oil. a. 油是烃类混合物，从地下开采出的原油中提炼而来，通常用于润滑。b. 油是从动植物中提取的脂肪酸中天然存在的甘油三酯。另见干性油。
oligomer 低聚物	An oligomer is a substance which is formed from only a few (up to 10) monomer units. 低聚物是指仅由少量（最多10个）单体单元形成的物质。
Opticon UV 57® Opticon UV 57®	Opticon UV 57 is an acrylic resin used for the bonding of glass, which cures in ultra violet light. Tests in the 1970's showed it to have poor physical properties. Opticon UV 57（商标名）为用于玻璃黏合的丙烯酸树脂，在紫外线作用下会固化。20世纪70年代的试验表明其物理性较差。
Orvus® Orvus®	Orvus is an anionic surfactant of fatty alcohol sulphate. Orvus（商标名）为脂肪醇硫酸盐的阴离子表面活性剂。
paraffin wax 石蜡	Paraffin wax is a hydrocarbon wax of straight chain alkanes, ca C22-C36, normally extracted from crude oil, though synthetic analogues are now also made. It is available in a number of grades, from relatively weak low melting point waxes to tough microcrystalline waxes. 固体石蜡为直链烷烃的烃蜡，约为C22-C36，通常从原油中提取，尽管现在也有合成的类似物。有许多等级可供选择，从相对较弱的低熔点蜡到坚硬的微晶石蜡。
Paraloid B-67® Paraloid B-67®	Paraloid B-67 is an acrylic polymer, poly(isobutyl methacrylate) (PiBMA). Paraloid B-67 in solution is used in conservation predominantly as a retouching and varnishing medium. Although it is stable, it is known to crosslink with time. Paraloid B-67（商标名）为丙烯酸聚合物，即聚甲基丙烯酸异丁酯(PiBMA)。Paraloid B-67溶液在保护领域主要作为补饰和清漆介质。尽管其较稳定，但现已知其会随着时间的推移而交联。
Paraloid B-72® Paraloid B-72®	Paraloid B-72 is an acrylic co-polymer, poly(ethyl methacrylate/methyl acrylate), PEMA/MA. Paraloid B-72 in solution is widely used in conservation as a consolidant, adhesive and varnish. It has been in use for 50 years and in tests has proved to have good ageing pnoperties. Paraloid B-72（商标名）是一种丙烯酸共聚物，聚甲基丙烯酸乙酯/丙烯酸甲酯，PEMA/MA。溶液中的Paraloid B-72作为一种固化剂、粘合剂和清漆/封护剂被广泛应用于文物保护。它已经被人们使用了50年，经测试具有良好的老化性能。

patch 补丁/补片	A patch is a piece of thin material attached to an object in order to conceal or repair a hole. In time, a patch may form a distorting impression on the object such as the front of a canvas. 补丁/补片是指附着到物体上的一片薄材料，用于掩盖或修补小洞。最终补丁/补片会在器物上（如帆布前面）形成一个失真的印痕。
plastic (1) 塑料 (1)	A plastic is a synthetic polymer that is formed into shapes primarily by moulding. It may be a thermoplastic or thermosetting polymer. 塑料是以热塑性或热固性单体聚合而成的高分子化合物，可模制成型。
Plasticine® 塑胶黏土®	Plasticine is a modelling material composed of petroleum jelly, fatty acids and whiting. It is used to model missing areas in glass and ceramic objects prior to the making of moulds. 塑胶黏土（商标名）是一种由凡士林油、脂肪酸和白涂料组成的塑形材料，用于在制作模具前仿造玻璃和陶瓷制品的缺失区域。
plasticiser 增塑剂	A plasticiser is a liquid added to a material in order to reduce its brittleness or improve its working properties. 增塑剂是一种添加到材料中的液体，用于降低其脆性，或者改进其工作性能。
Plastogen G® Plastogen G®	Plastogen G is an acrylic polymer used for gap filling in glass conservation. It consists of a PMMA powder containing an initiator and an MMA liquid which, when mixed together, set to a translucent solid. Plastogen G（商标名）为玻璃保护领域用作间隙填充的丙烯酸聚合物，由含有引发剂和MMA流体的PMMA粉末组成，当混合起来时，就固化为半透明固体。
Plexigum® Plexigum®	Plexigum is an acrylic polymer (iBMA) of medium molecular weight, used for the consolidation of various materials. Plexigum（商标名）为具有中等分子量的丙烯酸聚合物(iBMA)，用于不同材料的加固。
poly(ethylene glycol) 聚乙二醇	Poly(ethylene glycol), PEG, is a thermoplastic made by polymerising ethylene oxide with a Tg of -55℃. The grades used in conservation are viscous liquids or waxy low molecular weight materials. PEG is soluble in water and some polar organic solvents such as alcohol and toluene. In solution in water, PEG has been used as a consolidant for waterlogged wood since the 1950's and as a lubricant for leather and basketry. 聚乙二醇（PEG）是由环氧乙烷聚合而成的热塑性高分子材料，可溶于水和一些极性有机溶剂，玻璃化转变温度为-55℃。依分子量不同而性状不同，用于保护领域的PEG为无色无臭黏稠液体至蜡状固体。PEG可溶于水和一些极性有机溶剂，如酒精和甲苯。自1950年以来，聚乙二醇水溶液的一直被用作饱水木材的脱水剂、皮革和编制物的润滑剂。
poly(methyl methacrylate) 聚甲基丙烯酸甲酯	Poly(methyl methacrylate), PMMA, is a thermoplastic made from methyl methacrylate monomer. The polymer is water white and rigid with a Tg of 105℃. It is widely used as a glass substitute. 聚甲基丙烯酸甲酯树脂（PMMA）是由甲基丙烯酸甲酯单体聚合而成的热塑性高分子材料，呈水白色、质硬，玻璃化转变温度为105℃，被广泛用作玻璃的替代品。

poly(vinyl acetate)	Poly(vinyl acetate), PVAC, is a thermoplastic made from methyl methacrylate monomer. The polymer is water white and flexible with a Tg of 25℃. In conservation, it is used as an adhesive and consolidant. In its pure form, it has been shown to be stable to yellowing on light ageing. It has been used in conservation since the 1950's and is widely used as a co-polymer in making polymer dispersions.
聚醋酸乙烯酯	聚醋酸乙烯酯（PVAC）是由醋酸乙烯酯单体聚合而成的热塑性高分子材料，呈水白色，有韧性，玻璃化转变温度为25℃。高纯度状态下稳定性较好，在光老化时很稳定，不会变黄。因此自20世纪50年代以来，在保护领域被用作粘合剂和加固剂，并被广泛用作制造聚合物分散体的共聚物。
poly(vinyl alcohol)	Poly(vinyl alcohol), PVAL, is a thermoplastic derived by hydrolysing poly(vinyl acetate). The polymer is water white and many grades are soluble in water though it will react by cross-linking through the hydroxyl groups. It has been used as an adhesive and consolidant, particularly in textile and paper conservation. It is freequetly incorporated in PVAC dispersions.
聚乙烯醇	聚乙烯醇（PVAL）是通过水解聚醋酸乙烯酯得到的热塑性化学物，呈水白色，虽然会通过羟基发生交联反应，但多溶于水。在纺织品和纸张保护方面，聚乙烯醇溶液可用作粘合剂和加固剂。
poly(vinyl butyral)	Poly(vinyl butyral), PVB, is a thermoplastic polymer made by reacting poly(vinyl alcohol) with butyraldehyde. It has a Tg of 45-63℃ (depending on the extent of reaction with butyraldehyde) and is soluble in alcohols.
聚乙烯缩丁醛	聚乙烯醇缩丁醛（PVB）是由聚乙烯醇和丁醛反应制成的热塑性聚合物，玻璃化转变温度为45-63℃，具体取决于与丁醛的反应程度，可溶于醇类。
poly(vinyl chloride)	Poly(vinyl chloride), PVC, is a thermoplastic made from vinyl chloride monomer. The polymer is water white and rigid with a Tg of 95℃. It is widely used as a glass substitute and in plasticised form as a flexible film. Because of its instability to degradation, it is no longer used near museum objects.
聚氯乙烯	聚氯乙烯（PVC）是由氯乙烯单体制成的热塑性聚合物，呈水白色，质硬，玻璃化转变温度为95℃，被广泛用作玻璃的替代品，在塑化状态下亦用作柔韧性薄膜。因其在劣化过程中不稳定，目前不再用于博物馆藏品。
pressure-sensitive tape	A pressure sensitive tape is one that uses a semi-liquid adhesive that will adhere to a surface when pressure is applied. The tape is used as a temporary support for fragments whilst one applies a final adhesive or to carry out a dry run. The most commonl used adhesives are rubber or acrylic based, many of which cause staining and are unstable. In general the adhesives used are not suitable for conservation treatments.
压敏胶带	压敏胶带是指使用半流体粘合剂的胶带，在施以压力时会粘附到表面上。当涂敷最后的粘合剂或者进行干燥操作时用作碎片的临时支撑。最常用的粘合剂是基于橡胶或丙烯酸的，其中许多会导致染色和不稳定。一般来说，所使用的胶粘剂不适合用于保护处理。

Primal® WS **(-12,24,or 50)** 水溶性丙烯酸树脂	Primal WS is an acrylic resin in an aqueous dispersion. It is used as a consolidant for wall paintings and newly excavated materials including glass. It is especially suitable for friable, waterlogged materials, due to its dispersion in water and neutral pH. There have been questions as to its long-term stability. Primal WS（商标名）为水溶性丙烯酸树脂用作壁画和新发掘材料（包括玻璃）的加固剂。因其水溶性和中性pH，尤其适用于易碎、饱水材料。其长期稳定性一直存疑。
protease 蛋白酶	A protease is an enzyme that catalyses the degradation by hydrolysis of proteins. 蛋白酶是指通过蛋白质水解加速降解的酶。
protective coatings 保护涂层	Protective coatings are thin surface films which are applied to an object as a measure of preventive conservation to slow down deterioration. 保护涂层是指涂敷到物体上起预防性保护作用的表面薄膜，以减缓器物劣化。
purified water 纯净水	Purified water is water from which contaminants such as cations, anions, dissolved organic matter or gases have been removed. The type and degree of purification is usually specified by the purification technique. Purified water is the preferred water to use when treating objects, in order to avoid adding contaminants. 纯净水是指已去除阳离子、阴离子、溶解的有机物质或气体等杂质的水。纯化的类型和程度通常由纯化技术决定。纯化水是处理器物优选的水，以避免处理过程中增加污染物质。
rabbit skin glue 兔皮胶	Rabbit skin glue is a strong adhesive made from rabbit skin. 兔皮胶是由兔皮制成的强力胶。
regular gold 标准金	Regular gold is 22ct gold. 标准金即22克拉黄金（俗称22K金）。
removable fill 可去除式填充物	A removable fill is cast into place with a release agent applied along the break edges, allowing the treatment to be readily reversed. 沿着器物断裂边缘涂抹脱模剂后，再将可去除式填充物浇注到位，以使得处理可逆。
resin (2) 树脂 (2)	An animal resin is a solid material with properties like those of resin (1). The resin is usually produced as protective coating. Shellac is the most used animal resin. 动物树脂是指性质像树脂(1)的固态物质。树脂通常用于制作保护涂层。虫胶是最常用的动物树脂。
resin (3) 树脂 (3)	A synthetic resin is a material which possesses similar solid properties to resin (1). However, most synthetic resins have much higher molecular weights. Examples are acrylic resin and epoxy resin. 合成树脂是具有与树脂(1)类似的固体性质的材料。然而，大多数合成树脂具有高得多的分子量。例如，丙烯酸树脂和环氧树脂。

resin disintegrator 树脂去除剂	A resin disintegrator is a liquid applied to a resin or paint surface in order to swell and disrupt it, as precursor to its removal. Resin disintegrators can incorporate penetrating organic solvents or aqueous alkaline solutions. 树脂去除剂是一种涂敷于树脂或油漆表面使其膨胀并分解裂的液体，是去除树脂前的预处理。树脂去除剂是能够吸收渗透有机溶剂或碱性水溶液。
resoluble 可溶解的	A resoluble material is one which remains soluble in the solvent used to apply it as part of a treatment to an object. 可溶解材料是保持可溶于应用时使用的溶剂中的材料，作为器物处理的一部分。
sacrificial coating 牺牲性涂层	A sacrificial coating protects the underlying object by degrading in preference to the underlying material. 牺牲性涂层通过优先降解来保护下方的物体。
Santocel® 硅酸盐®	Santocel is a silica matting agent which is mixed with silicon rubber in order to produce a putty-like consistency when making moulds. Santocel（商标名）为一种二氧化硅消光剂，当它和硅橡胶混合可在制造模具时产生油灰一样光滑的质感。
separation layer 分离层	A separation layer is a coating or layer that is used to distinguish, physically or visually, between an original part of an object from material added for restoration or support purposes. 分离层为涂层或膜，用于物理或视觉区分物体的原有部分与添加的修复部分或支撑材料。
sepiolite 海泡石	Sepiolite is a mixture of clay like hydrated magnesium silicates. When ground into a powder, sepiolite is very absorbant and is used in making poultices. 海泡石为粘土状含水硅酸镁的混合物，研磨成粉末的海泡石吸水性很强，常用于制作敷剂。
silicone 硅胶	A silicone polymer is one based on $(S_iR_2 \cdot xH_2O)$ monomer units. Silicones are used as solvents, oils and rubbers. Because silicones have a very low Tg (-123℃) and very low surface tension, they are frequently used as release agents, water repellents and mould making rubbers. These properties also result in silicones being very difficult to remove, especially from porous surfaces. 硅胶是由 $(S_iR_2 \cdot nH_2O)$ 单体制成的聚合物，具有较低的玻璃化转变温度 (-123℃) 和表面张力。这种特性，一方面使之可用作脱模剂、防水剂和制模剂，另一方面会导致其一旦施加到到多孔表面上则难以去除。
silicone release film 硅酮分隔膜	Silicone release film is a paper or fabric impregnated with a silicone polymer. It is used as a substrate for casting adhesive films and preparing adhesive impregnated backing fabrics. It is also used as a non-stick barrier in the application of linings using hot-melt adhesives. 硅酮分隔膜是用硅酮聚合物浸染过的纸或纤维。它被用作浇铸胶膜和制备浸胶背衬织物的基材。在使用热熔胶的衬里应用中，它也用作不粘屏障。

silicone rubber 硅橡胶	Silicone rubber is a synthetic rubber based on polysiloxane chains. It is used for making moulds and for sealing. 硅橡胶是基于聚硅氧烷链的合成橡胶，可用于制作模具或密封材料。
Skala® 斯卡拉®	Skala is an industrial polyester sewing filament. It is used as a more durable alternative to silk filament and is available in many colours. 斯卡拉（商标名）是一种工业聚酯缝纫丝线，用作比桑蚕丝更耐用的替代品，有多种颜色可供选择。
soil suspension agent 土壤悬浮剂	A soil suspension agent holds soiling in a water during wet cleaning so that it can easily be rinsed away instead of re-depositing on the textile. In textile conservation, sodium carboxy methylcellulose is frequently used as a soil suspension agent. 在湿法清洁期间，土壤悬浮剂可使污物悬浮在水中，以便能够轻易被冲掉，而不是再沉积到织物上。在织物保护领域，羧甲基纤维素钠常用作土壤悬浮剂。
soluble nylon 可溶性尼龙	Soluble nylon is a nylon modified to enable its solubility in common solvents. The soluble nylon met with in conservation is Calaton CB®, a N-methoxymethyl nylon 6,6. It is soluble in hot ethanol but on ageing, especially in acid conditions, it becomes increasingly insoluble and cross-links. It was used as a fixative for pigments during washing and in conservation as an adhesive and consolidant, but it is no longer used because of its poor ageing and physical properties. 可溶性尼龙是改性后可溶于常见溶剂的尼龙。保护领域使用的可溶性尼龙为Calaton CB®，一种N-甲氧甲基化尼龙66。其可溶于热乙醇，但老化后，特别是在酸性条件下，它变得不相融和产生交联。在洗涤和保存过程中，它被用作颜料的固定剂，作为粘合剂和固化剂，但由于其老化和物理性能较差，已不再被使用。
Sovol Autosol® Sovol Autosol®	Sovol Autosol is a commercial chrome abrasive made up of a mixture of kieselguhr (hydrated silica SiO2), white spirit, distilled water and fatty acids. It is used to remove dirt from marble and non-porous ceramic surfaces as well as to polish epoxy or polyester fills in ceramic and glass objects. Sovol Autosol（商标名）是一种商用铬磨料，由硅藻土（水合二氧化硅SiO2）、白酒、蒸馏水和脂肪酸的混合物组成。它用于去除大理石和非多孔陶瓷表面的污垢，以及用于陶瓷和玻璃物体中环氧树脂或聚酯填充物的抛光。
Stabiltex® Stabiltex®	Stabiltex is the older name for Tetex®. Stabiltex（商标名）为Tetex®的旧称。
steel wool 钢丝绒	Steel wool is very fine wire which has sharp edges. It is used as an abrasive. It is available in a number of grades from very fine (0000) to coarse (2). 钢丝绒为极细有锐利边缘的钢丝，用作磨料。可供使用的等级很多，从极细(0000)到粗糙(2)都有。

sticky threads 粘线	Sticky threads are short lengths of threads or filaments which have been coated with an adhesive. In textile conservation, they are used to secure or support damaged areas when the application of a backing is not appropriate. 粘线是指涂有胶粘剂的较短的线或细丝。在织物保护领域，当不太适合使用背衬时，可用其保护或支撑受损区域。
stoddard solvent 斯托达德溶剂	Stoddard solvent is the USA term for a hydrocarbon solvent which is used for solvent cleaning in textile conservation. Stoddard solvent has a boiling point of 177-210℃. It is usually a solvent of low quality and purity. See also mineral spirit and white spirit. 斯托达德溶剂是烃类溶剂的美国术语，用于织物保护领域的溶剂清洁。其沸点为177-210℃，通常为低质量低纯度溶剂。另见矿物油。
sulfur difluoride dioxide 二氟二氧化硫	Sulfur dioxide difluoride (SO_2F_2) is a gaseous fumigant, which may cause corrosion of glass and metals. 二氟二氧化硫(SO_2F_2)为气态熏蒸剂，可造成玻璃和金属腐蚀。
support (1) 支撑物 (1)	A support is the underlying material or structure used to impart physical stability to an object. 支撑物是指用以给予物体物理稳定性的底层材料或结构。
support (2) 支撑材料 (2)	A secondary and temporary material is used as a support when it prevents forces on an object from causing damage while the object is, for instance, being manipulated, or on display. 在操作或者展示物体时，为防止物体上的作用力造成损坏，会将使用辅助和临时材料用作支撑材料。
support (4) 支撑 (4)	You support an object by adding additional material or structure to impart physical stability. The material is usually in a form that can be easily removed without affecting the object. 通过增加附加材料或者改变结构来支撑器物，以赋予其物理稳定性。附加材料通常为可轻易移除但对器物没有影响的材料。
suspension 悬浊液	A suspension is a liquid which contains finely dispersed solid particles. 悬浊液是含有细分散固体颗粒的液体。
Synperonic N® Synperonic N®	Synperonic N is a non-ionic surfactant made of a nonyl phenol ethoxylate. In textile conservation, it is used to wet clean textiles. The use of nonyl phenol ethoxylate has been banned in some countries because it is not biodegradable. Synperonic N（商标名）为非离子表面活性剂，由壬基苯酚乙氧基化物制成。在织物保护领域，其用于湿法清洗织物。壬基苯酚乙氧基化物已被一些国家禁止使用，因其不可生物降解。
tack (1) 粘合 (1)	A tack applied during reconstruction of a fragmentary object is the minimum amount of adhesive join required to hold the fragments in their correct position while the whole object is being reconstructed. The tack may be reversed as needed to allow for the adjustment of the fragments during the reconstruction process. Once the reconstruction has been finalised, another adhesive is used to make the final joins. 在重建一个残缺物体的过程中，粘合是在整个物体重建过程中，使碎片保持在正确位置所需的最小粘合量。在重建过程中，为了调整碎片，粘合要具有可逆性。重建完成后，使用另一种粘合剂进行最终粘接。

tack (2) 粘性 (2)	The tack of an adhesive in liquid form is its ability to create an instantaneous bond to the substrate. 液态形式胶粘剂的粘性指其与基质产生的瞬时键合能力。
Technovit 4004® Technovit 4004®	Technovit is a mixture of a powdered poly(methyl methacrylate) PMMA, with its monomer whose polymerisation is catalysed on mixing the components. Technovit is predominately used to make gap fillings in glass conservation. Technovit 粉末状聚甲基丙烯酸甲酯PMMA的混合物，其单体的聚合通过混合组分来催化。其主要用于制作玻璃保护领域的间隙填充剂。(商标名)
Tetex® Tetex®	Tetex is a lightweight, transparent fabric woven in plain weave with fine polyester filaments. Tetex（商标名）为轻质、透明的用细聚酯丝平纹梭织而成的平织布。
thermoplastic polymer 热塑性聚合物	A thermoplastic polymer is one that will soften, flow and be shaped when heated. Many thermoplastic polymers are soluble in solvents. 热塑性聚合物是指受热后会软化、流动并塑形的聚合物。许多热塑性聚合物都能溶于溶剂中。
thermosetting polymer 热固性聚合物	A thermosetting polymer is one that sets to a solid which cannot be remelted on heating. 热固性聚合物是指已固化的固体在受热后不会再融化的聚合物。
thixotropic liquid 触变液体	A thixotropic liquid is one which flows after being stirred, but which forms a non-flowing gel on standing. 触变液体是指搅拌后会流动，但不动时会形成不流动凝胶的液体。
tissue paper 薄绵纸	Tissue paper is a thin sheet of paper, typically less than $25g/m^2$, used for protection and cushioning. Acid free tissue paper is normally used in conservation. 薄绵纸是一种很薄的纸，通常小于$25g/m^2$，起保护和缓冲作用。无酸绵纸通常用于文物保护。
tricyclene 三环烯	Tricyclene ($C_{10}H_{16}$) is a volatile binding medium. 三环烯($C_{10}H_{16}$)为挥发性粘合剂。
turpentine 松节油	Turpentine is a volatile liquid produced by distilling the exudate from pine trees. It is composed of cyclic monoterpene hydrocarbons. It oxidises rapidly and accumulates non-volatile oxidation products which are deposited from solution causing long term contamination and initiation of further oxidation reactions. 松节油是从松树的渗出物中蒸馏提取出的挥发性流体，由循环单萜烯组成。其会迅速氧化并积聚非挥发性氧化产物，沉积于溶液中，造成长期的污染并引发进一步的氧化反应。
UHU Hart® UHU Hart®	UHU Hart is a commercial adhesive that is used in the conservation of porous ceramics. It is a solution of cellulose nitrate plasticised with dibutyl phthalate. UHU Hart（商标名）为用于有孔陶瓷保护的商用胶粘剂，是用邻苯二甲酸二丁酯塑化的硝基纤维素溶液。

Vel-mix® Vel-mix®	Vel-mix is a material similar to dental plaster, but somewhat more durable and harder. It has been used as a filling and supporting material for heavy objects including glass stacks. Vel-mix（商标名）为类似于牙科石膏的材料，但更耐用、更坚固。其已被用作重物（包括堆叠玻璃）的填料和支撑材料。
Viacryl®SM 564 Viacryl® SM 564	Viacryl is an hydroxyl containing acrylic polymer which is mixed with Desmodur to make a polyurethane. It was used as an adhesive and consolidant and to create a protective layer on stained glass. Viacryl（商标名）是含羟基的丙烯酸聚合物，与聚氨基甲酸酯类粘合剂混合后制成聚氨酯。其用作胶粘剂和固定剂，以在彩色玻璃上用作保护层。
Vinamold® Vinamold®	Vinamold is a plasticised poly(vinyl chloride) moulding material which is used in its hot molten state to make a mould. The use of such hot-melt moulding materials can cause damage to objects due to thermal shock. Vinamold（商标名）为塑化的聚氯乙烯模具材料，在热熔状态下用于制作模具。此类热熔模塑材料的使用会因热冲击对器物造成损伤。
Vinamul 6815® Vinamul 6815®	Vinamul 6815 is a poly(vinyl acetate) dispersion used primarily to consolidate waterlogged archaeological materials. Vinamul 6815（商标名）为聚醋酸乙烯酯分散液，主要用于加固饱水考古材料。
volatile binding medium 挥发性粘合剂	A volatile binding medium is a temporary coating or consolidant that is removed by sublimation. 挥发性粘合剂是指可通过升华作用去除的、暂时性涂层或者加固剂。
walnut shell 核桃壳粉	Walnut shell powder is used as mild abrasive and absorbent. It is applied in air abrasive equipment. 核桃壳粉用作柔和磨料和吸收材料，被用空气喷磨设备中。
white spirit 矿物油	White spirit is the UK and Australian term for a mineral spirit which is used in solvent cleaning. White spirit has a boiling point of 155-210℃. It is usually a solvent of low quality and purity. See also Stoddard solvent. 矿物油(White spirit)是矿物油(mineral spirit)的英国和澳大利亚术语。它是一种清洁溶剂，沸点为155-210℃，通常为低质量低纯度溶剂。另见斯托达德溶剂。

12

修复方法与工具
Conservation Treatment and Tool

abrasive cleaning 机械清理	Abrasive cleaning is a treatment which involves removing part of the surface of an object by mechanical action. 机械清理是通过机械作用去除器物表面一部分的处理方法。
air abrasion 空气喷砂（干喷砂）	Air abrasion is a method of removing material from a surface by using small abrasive particles in a jet of compressed air. 空气喷砂是通过在压缩气流中使用小颗粒磨料去除表面材料的方法。
air abrasive (1) 空气喷磨	An air abrasive treatment is one that uses air abrasion to clean objects. 空气喷磨是通过空气喷磨来清洁器物的处理方法。
air abrasive (2) 空气喷砂	Air abrasive equipment is a tool comprising an air compressor, a hopper to store abrasive powder and a small nozzle, which are all linked through a control unit. 空气喷砂设备是一种将空气压缩机、存储研磨粉的料斗和小喷嘴组装在一起的设备。
Airbrasive®unit	An Airbrasive® unit is an equipment manufactured to control air abrasive treatment. Airbrasive®unit是用于控制空气研磨处理的一种设备。
air drying 自然干燥	Air drying is the process of drying an object by allowing the water to evaporate from it, generally in a humidity controlled environment. 自然干燥是在控制湿度的环境中，通过水分蒸发来干燥器物的过程。
alkalisation 碱化	Application of an alkaline agent which reacts with acids in the paper and leaves in paper an alkaline reserve capable of reacting with acids in the future. See also deacidification. 碱性试剂与纸张中的酸发生反应，留下碱性成分，后续可与酸发生反应。另见脱酸（基本概念组）。
aqueous treatment 水处理	Aqueous treatment is any treatment that involves the application of water to an object. 水处理是用水来对器物进行处理的过程。
archival (2) 档案盒法	An archival method is one which is intended to prevent short or long term changes in the material to which it is applied. 档案盒法是旨在防止档案盒中物品发生短期或长期变化的方法。
assemble 组装	You assemble an object when you bring together its component parts into their proper positions. 器物的组装是把一个器物的组成部分放在适当的位置。
bandaging 绷带法	When you use bandaging to support an object, you wrap around it strips of textile often strengthened by the addition of plaster of Paris. Bandaging is frequently applied to archaeological objects before lifting. 绷带法是用绷带支撑器物，即用条状织物将器物包裹起来，通常会使用熟石膏增加强度。考古器物在搬运前经常使用绷带法。

blast cleaning 喷砂清理	Blast cleaning is a treatment which involves the use of an abrasive in a high speed air or water jet to remove deposits from wall and other surfaces. It is frequently damaging to the underlying material. 喷砂清理是在高速空气或水射流中使用磨料清除墙壁和其他表面的沉积物的处理方法。此法通常会对底层材料造成损害。
cast (1) 铸件	A cast is a negative copy of an object made by introducing a liquid into a mould. The cast is formed when the liquid solidifies. 铸件是将液体注入模具而制成的器物的负模。铸件在液体凝固时形成。
cast (2) 铸造	When you cast an object, you make a mould from the object and then take a negative copy from the mould. 铸造是用器物制作一个模具，然后从模具上得到器物的负模。
caulk 填缝	When you caulk a join between two components of an object, such as boat timbers or a metal tank, you push in a material that stops the penetration of water. This may be an oily fibre or a non-setting mastic. 用填料密封一个器物两部分的连接处，比如船木或金属槽，可以向其填入一种防止渗水的材料，例如油性纤维或非固化油灰。
clamp (1) 夹具	A clamp is a tool used to hold parts of an object together under compression during treatment. 夹具是一种工具，在处理过程中，通过压力将器物的各个部分固定在一起。
clamp (2) 夹持	When you clamp an object, you use a tool to hold it immobile. 夹持是用工具固定住一个器物。
conductivity meter 电导率仪	A conductivity meter is an instrument that measures the ability of a material, usually a solution, to conduct electricity. 电导率仪是一种用于测量材料（通常是溶液）导电能力的仪器。
conservation technique 保护技术	A conservation technique is an established procedure used in conservation treatment. 保护技术是在保存处理中使用的既定程序。
consolidation 加固	Consolidation is a treatment which aims to increase the mechanical strength of a flaking, unstable or fractured object by the introduction of a liquid or vapour material which hardens in situ. 加固是一种处理方法，目的是通过引入原位硬化的液体或气相材料来提高易剥落、不稳定或易断裂器物的机械强度。
copper foil technique 铜箔技术	The copper foil technique is a technique for bonding broken stained glass. Self-adhesive copper foil is rubbed onto the glass edges and the foil-covered edges of the glass are then soldered together. It is used as an alternative to unsightly mending leads or if adhesives cannot be used. 铜箔技术是一种粘结破碎彩色玻璃的技术。将自粘铜箔涂在玻璃边缘，然后将覆盖铜箔的玻璃边缘焊接在一起。使用此技术可避免修补导致的不美观引线，不能使用粘合剂的情况下亦或使用该技术。

dental drill 牙钻	A dental drill is a machine tool used for abrading or boring fine holes. It has been adopted from the dental profession. It has a handset for holding the drill bit which is driven by a remote power source. 牙钻是一种用于打磨或钻细孔的机械。由牙科专业引入。牙钻具有一个手柄，用于固定由外接电源驱动的钻头。
dental pick 牙探针	A dental pick is a hand tool with a single sharp prong used to remove material from cavities. It has been adopted from the dental profession. 牙探针是一种一端具有锋利尖头的手持工具，用于从孔洞中剔除物质。由牙科专业引入。
disinfestation 杀虫	Disinfestation is the process of eliminating, destroying or killing harmful insects in or from objects. 杀虫指在器物内部或外部消灭或杀死有害昆虫的过程。
dowelling 榫接	Dowelling is the joining detached parts of an object by using a dowel. 榫接是指用暗榫连接器物分离的部分。
drill 钻	A drill is a machine used for boring holes. 钻是用来钻孔的机器。
dry cleaning 干洗	Dry cleaning is a treatment for removing undesirable material from an object without using a liquid. See also solvent cleaning and surface cleaning. 干洗是在不使用液体的情况下，从器物上清除不需要的物质。另见溶剂清洗和表面清理。
dry cleaning sponge 干洗海绵	A dry cleaning sponge is a soft, vulcanised rubber sponge originally designed to clean objects soiled by soot and smoke. It is used to remove surface soiling not easily removable by brushing or vacuum cleaning. See also Wish-ab®. 干洗海绵是柔软的硫化橡胶海绵，专为清洁受到油烟和烟雾污染的器物而设计。它被用于清洁用刷子或真空清洗都无法去除的表面污渍。另见Wish-ab®。
English paring knife 英式削薄刀（平刃）	An English paring knife is a paring knife with a flat cutting edge. 英式削薄刀是平刃的削薄刀。
evacuate (2) 排空	When you evacuate, you remove as much air or gas as possible from or out of an object. 排空是指尽可能多地从器物中排出空气或气体。
fan 风扇	A fan is an electrical device which produces an unheated current of air. In textile conservation, it is used to speed the drying of wet textiles. 风扇是一种电气设备，可产生未加热的空气流。在纺织品保护中，用于加速湿纺织品的干燥。
finishing (1) 涂饰	Finishing is the final process in conservation treatment, such as the application of a wax coating to a surface. 涂饰是保护处理的最后一道工序，例如在表面涂上一层蜡。

finishing (3) 修整	Finishing is the process of preparing a fill to receive re-touching, for instance in ceramic conservation. 修整是准备填充物以接受补釉的过程，例如应用在陶瓷保护中。
French paring knife 法式削薄刀（圆刃）	A French paring knife is a paring knife with a rounded cutting edge. 法式削薄刀是圆刃的削薄刀。
fumigation 熏蒸	Fumigation of an object is the treatment of an infestation using a biocide in vapour phase and in an enclosed space. See also vacuum fumigation. 熏蒸是在气相和封闭空间内使用杀虫剂处理虫害的处理方法。另见真空熏蒸。
German paring knife 德式削薄刀（圆刃）	A German paring knife is a paring knife with a rounded cutting edge ground at an angle. 德式削薄刀是一种刃口沿着一定角度磨圆的削薄刀。
gilder's cushion 金箔垫	A gilder's cushion is a soft padded cushion often covered with skin. Gold leaf is cut on this before being applied to the surface to be gilded. The cushion may have a parchment shield to prevent the gold leaf from blowing away. 金箔垫是一种带皮的软垫。表面镀金前，需要把金箔先放在金箔垫上切割。金箔垫上有时还要放置一张羊皮纸，以防金箔被吹跑。
gilder's knife 金箔切刀	A gilder's knife is a long bladed knife used to cut gold leaf to the required size. 金箔切刀是一种长刃刀，用于将金箔切成所需尺寸。
gilder's mop 贴金圆刷	A gilder's mop is a fat round brush made with hairs of squirrel, badger or pony. It is used for patting gold leaf into contact with the prepared ground then brushing off the waste pieces of gold leaf. 贴金圆刷是一种用松鼠、獾或小马的毛制成的圆形刷子。用于拍打金箔，使金箔与表面贴合，然后刷除多余的金箔。
gilder's tip 贴金平刷	A gilder's tip is a brush made from long animal hairs set between two pieces of cardboard. It is used to transfer gold leaf from the gilder's cushion to the surface being gilded. 贴金平刷是将动物的长毛夹持在两片硬质薄板之间制成的刷子。用于金箔从金箔垫转移到待贴金的物体表面。
glass bead peening 玻璃珠喷砂	Glass bead peening is the process of firing glass beads with the aid of air abrasive equipment in order to burnish a surface. 玻璃珠喷砂指利用空气研磨设备喷射玻璃珠来进行抛光的过程。
glass fiberbristle brush 玻璃纤维毛刷	A glass fibre bristle brush is used in cleaning to abrade and remove unwanted surface material by abrasion. 玻璃纤维毛刷用于清理、磨去或去除不需要的表面材料。

gold-beaters skin 动物肠衣	Gold-beaters skin is the treated large intestine of oxen. It is very thin and strong. Gold-beaters skin is used to interleave gold leaf while it is beaten to its desired thickness. It is also used to repair vellum and parchment. 动物肠衣是经处理加工的牛大肠，薄且强度高。动物肠衣用来在金箔被敲打到所需厚度时隔开金箔，也用于修复牛皮纸和羊皮纸。
grindstone 磨石	A grindstone is made of sandstone and used for shaping materials or sharpening edged tools. 磨石由砂岩制成，用于打磨材料或磨砺具刃工具。
heated spatula 加热抹刀	A heated spatula is a hand-held, electrically heated, tool used to soften or shape heat sensitive conservation materials, such as resins or waxes in processes such as filling and re-inforcement. 加热抹刀是一种手持的电加热工具，用于在填充和加固过程中，树脂或蜡等热敏性保护材料的软化或塑形。
hot table 热台	A hot table is a table made with a heated metal plate whose temperature can be controlled. It is used to apply backings to paintings and flat textiles by using thermo-plastic adhesives. 热台是配备了可加热金属板的工作台，其温度可以控制。通过热塑性粘合剂将底材施加到绘画和平整的纺织品上。
hot vacuum table 真空热台	A hot vacuum table is a hot-table with a perforated metal surface and an adjustable suction applied through the perforations. It is used to apply linings to paintings and flat textiles by using thermo-plastic adhesives. 真空热台具有开孔的金属表面，通过孔洞可以调节吸力。它通过热塑性粘合剂将背衬施加在油画和平整的织物上。
impregnate 浸泡	You impregnate an object when you make a fluid material, such as a consolidant in solution, biocide or inhibitor, flow into it through its existing porous structure. 浸泡器物是指使一种流体材料（如溶液中的固化剂、杀虫剂或抑制剂）通过器物的多孔结构流入器物内部。
impregnation 浸泡	The impregnation of an object is the process of introducing a fluid material into its pores. 浸泡是将流体材料引入器物孔隙的过程。
infill 填充	An infill is the area of replacement or simulation of a lacuna of an object using a sympathetic material. 填充指用合适的材料替代或模拟器物的空隙区域。
inject 注入	You inject a fluid into a material by forcing the fluid into its structure using a hypodermic syringe or similar. 注入指使用皮下注射器或类似设备将液体注入材料的结构中。
integration 补全	During restoration, the integration of an object is the addition of parts in order to achieve its aesthetic completeness. 在修复过程中，器物的补全是为了实现审美完整性而增加器物缺失的部分。

intervention 干预	Intervention in conservation is any treatment that involves the removal from or addition of material to an object or changes its nature through chemical action. See also active, passive, preventive and remedial conservation. 干预指移除或添加材料或通过化学作用改变物体性质。另见主动、被动、预防性和抢救性保护。
irreversible 不可逆的	An irreversible treatment of an object is one whose effects cannot be undone, perhaps because of changes to the object or because an added material cannot be removed. 对一个器物的不可逆处理指其效果无法撤消，可能是因为器物发生改变或是添加的材料无法移除。
isinglass 鱼胶	Isinglass is a pure fish glue made from the collagen of the air bladders of sturgeon fish. 鱼胶指由鲟鱼鱼鳔中的胶原蛋白制成的一种纯鱼胶。
jacket 护套	A jacket is a layer of reinforcement applied to a fragile object to prevent internal distortions when being lifted or moved. 护套是一层施加到易碎器物上的防护层，以防止在提取或移动时内部发生变形。
join (1) 接缝	A join is the line along which fragments or component parts are adhered. 接缝是碎片或组成部分的结合处形成的线。
join (2) 连接	You join fragments or component parts of an object together when you attach them. 连接指将器物的碎片或组成部分固定在一起。
laminate (2) 托裱	You laminate a sheet material such as paper by adhering it on one or both sides to a supporting sheet. 托裱是将纸等薄层材料的一面或两面粘贴到支撑片材上。
lamination 托裱	Lamination is treatment of a sheet material which involves the sheet being adhered on one or both sides to a supporting film. 托裱是一种对片材的处理方式，一般将片材的单面或双面粘上支撑膜。
low pressure table 低压台	A low pressure table is a surface through which a suction is applied. It is a development of a vacuum hot table. Vacuum pumps are used to remove the air and moisture while the air pressure presses the painting to the table. It enables the controlled use of moisture and pressure in the conservation of paintings. 低压台是施加吸力的表面，是真空热台发展的产物。通过使用真空泵将画作压到低压台台面的方式，去除空气和湿气。在绘画保护中，此法使得湿度和压力可控。
manipulate 操作	You manipulate an object when you touch the object with your hands, for instance during examination or handling. 操作是指在检查或处理过程中用手触摸器物。
marine archaeological conservation 海洋考古保护	Marine archaeological conservation deals with the preservation of finds from sea water environments. 海洋考古保护指保存来自海水环境的发现物。

mass treatment 批量处理	Mass treatment is simultaneous treatment of large numbers of objects in one batch as opposed to the handling of individual items. 批量处理指在一个批次中同时处理大量器物，而不是处理单个文物。
mechanical cleaning 机械清理	Mechanical cleaning is removal of part of the surface of an object using tools. 机械清理指用工具清除器物表面的一部分。
microblasting 微喷砂	Microblasting is a delicate abrasive surface cleaning technique. Various fine powders and other materials are blown in a jet of air to remove deposits from, for example, statuary, stone, archaeological objects and stained glass. 微喷砂是一种精细的磨料表面清洁技术。气流中带有各种细粉和其他材料，以除去雕像、石头、考古器物和彩色玻璃上的沉积物。
micrometer 测微计	A micrometer is an instrument used to measure very small lengths, often in conjunction with a microscope. 测微计是一种测量微小长度的仪器，通常与显微镜一起使用。
microscope 显微镜	A microscope is an instrument for magnifying small objects, thus revealing details invisible to the naked eye. 显微镜是将小物体放大的仪器，可以揭示肉眼不可见的细节。
minimum intervention 最小干预	Minimum intervention in the treatment of an object is the smallest amount of alteration to an object required to ensure its survival in a given situation for a specified time. 处理一个器物时的最小干预指确保器物在特定情况下、在规定时间内留存下来所需的最小改变量。
mini-suction apparatus 微型抽吸装置	A mini-suction apparatus applies a vacuum over a small area though an small porous pad or perforated metal sheet. It is used for local treatment where extraction or pressure are required on a small area of a painting or paper sheet. 微型抽吸装置通过小的多孔垫或穿孔的金属板在较小的区域上施加真空。适用于在绘画或纸张的小面积上进行抽气或加压的局部处理。
mis-alignment 错位	Mis-alignment is the incorrect positioning of component pieces during reconstruction. 错位指在复原过程中部件的定位不正确。
model (1) 模型法	A model method is an exemplar which assists in developing practical methods to be applied. 模型法指设置范例来帮助人们开发实际应用方法的方式。
model (2) 翻模	When you model a replacement for a missing part of an object, you create a new form in a plastic material which subsequently hardens. 翻模指为器物的缺失部分塑造一个替代品，即采用可硬化的塑性材料制作一个新部件。
mould (2) 模	A mould is a shape from which a copy is made in reverse. Liquid material is poured into the mould, allowed to harden and then removed, thus producing the reverse copy. 模是用于制作负模的模型。将液态材料倒入模中，硬化后取出，可以制得反向的复制品。

muller 研磨器	A muller is a heavy small flat slab with a handle in the middle of one side used for grinding pigments or other material on a larger slab. Mullers were often made of stone though glass is now more common. 研磨器是一种重的小型厚板，一侧正中有个把手，用于在较大的厚板上研磨颜料或其他材料。研磨器过去通常用石头制作，现在常用玻璃制作。
pretreatment 预处理	A pretreatment is used to stabilise or prepare an object before a longer or more complex treatment can be carried out. 预处理用于在进行更长或更复杂的处理之前稳定或制备物体。
refiring 复烧	Refiring ceramics is the process of filling a lacuna with clay, then heating in a kiln to convert the clay to ceramic. 复烧陶瓷是用粘土填充空隙，然后在窑中加热，使粘土转化为陶瓷的过程。
reintegration 重组修复法	Reintegration is a restoration treatment which aims to recover the aesthetic unity of an object by replacing a loss or a lacuna. 重组修复法是一种修复处理方法，旨在通过弥补损失或空白来恢复器物的审美统一性。
remedial conservation 抢救性保护	Remedial conservation is treatment undertaken to stabilise an object and/or rectify previous deterioration. See also interventive conservation. 抢救性保护为了稳定器物和/或纠正先前的劣化而进行的处理。另见干预性保护。
reverse 逆向	When you reverse a treatment on an object, you take the object back to the identical state before the treatment was started. This is probably physically impossible to achieve in practice, so each description of reversing a treatment needs to be qualified by specifying the extent of the reversibility. 对器物进行逆向处理时，会将该器物恢复到开始处理之前的相同状态。实际上，这在物理上是不可能实现的，所以每一个关于逆向处理的描述都需要通过明确可逆的程度来限定。
reweave 补织	When you reweave a textile, you introduce new threads which follow exactly the original weave structure. Reweaving is applied to holes or areas where warps or wefts are lost. It is a traditional restoration technique and can be found mostly on tapestries. 补织指在织物中引入新的线，完全遵循原来的编织结构，在经线或纬线缺失的孔或区域进行重织。这是一种传统的修复技术，主要见于挂毯。
scribe 划线	You scribe a line by marking a piece of material, usually rigid such as wood or metal, to be added in order that it can be fitted exactly to another surface. 划线即在坚硬材料（如木头或金属）划出一条线，以使之能够精确地贴合到另一个表面上。
shot blasting 喷丸清理	Shot blasting is a powerful method of air abrasion using iron or steel particles. 喷丸清理是利用钢或铁颗粒进行空气磨损的一种强力处理方法。

solvent dehydration 溶剂脱水	Water is removed from an object by solvent dehydration using a water miscible solvent to displace the water. 溶剂脱水是通过使用水溶性溶剂置换水，从而从器物中除去水。
spatula 抹刀	A spatula is a small hand tool with a flattened end used for modelling or applying a filling material. 抹刀是一种小型手工工具，末端扁平，用于塑形或施加填缝材料。
sponge 海绵	In textile conservation, you use a sponge to apply a pumping action during wet cleaning and solvent cleaning and to remove surface soiling by absorption. Sponges can be natural, such as a sea sponge, or synthetic, such as the ones made from foamed latex. 在纺织品保护中，可以用海绵在水洗和溶剂清洗过程中抽吸，通过吸收去除表面污垢。海绵可以是天然的，例如天然海绵；也可以是人造的，例如由发泡乳胶制成的海绵。
spotting 局部预处理	Spotting is the localised pre-treatment of a stain prior to solvent cleaning used by the commercial dry-cleaning industry. Aqueous or solvent cleaning solutions are applied in combination with mechanical action. 商业干洗行业使用溶剂清洗之前对污渍进行的局部预处理。水溶液或溶剂清洗溶液与机械作用结合使用。
stove 烘烤	When you stove a coating, you heat it together with the object to which it is applied, in order to cure or cross-link the medium. 烘烤涂层即将器物和所施加的涂层一起加热，以便固化或交联介质。
sublimation 升华	Sublimation is the process of evaporation directly from the solid state. 升华是直接从固态蒸发的过程。
surface application 表面处理	An object has received a surface application when a liquid material for treatment has been applied extensively over the surface. 表面处理是将用于处理的液体材料完全涂于器物表面。
surface cleaning (1) 表面清理 (1)	Surface cleaning an object is the removal of the soiling that lies on the surface of the object. Surface cleaning makes use of mechanical techniques, with or without water or solvents. The major types of surface cleaning are swabbing, vacuuming, brushing or cleaning by using absorbent materials such as sponges. 对器物进行表面清理指清除器物表面的污物。表面清理使用机械技术，可使用也可不用水或溶剂。主要的表面清洁方式有擦拭、吸尘、刷除或使用海绵等吸水材料进行清洁。
surface cleaning (2) 表面清理	In paper conservation, surface cleaning is the process of removing any unwanted soiling form paper objects using a brush, an eraser and/or powdered gum. 在纸张保护中，表面清理指用刷子、橡皮擦和/或粉末清除纸张表面上的污物。
surface coating 表面涂层	A surface coating is a coating applied to the surface of an object in order to protect or enhance it. 表面涂层是为了保护或增强器物表面而施涂的涂层。

total cleaning 全面揭露	Total cleaning is the complete removal of a surface layer from an object, usually in order to make its display or interpretation easier. 全面揭露是将器物表面的一层完全去除，使其更易于展示或阐释。
treat 处理	When you treat an object, you make physical changes to the object with the intention to preserve it. 处理器物即为保护器物而对其做物理上的改变。
treatment 处理	A conservation treatment is the process of changing an object in order to preserve it. 保护处理是为保存器物而改变它的过程。
two-part stick 拼接	Two-part stick is a technique used to bond sprung ceramics, in which the distorted sections are aligned under a degree of pressure and then dry-stuck in sequence. 拼接是一种用于粘结断裂陶瓷的技术。在一定压力下将变形部分对齐，然后按顺序粘接。
ultrasonic bath 超声清洗	When you treat an object using an ultrasonic bath, you place it in a liquid which is excited by ultrasonic vibrations, above 16,000Hz. 使用超声清洗处理器物，是指将器物放置在由16,000Hz以上的超声波振动激发的液体中进行处理。
ultrasonic cleaner 超声波清洗机	An ultrasonic cleaner is a machine that cleans objects immersed in a liquid by inducing high frequency cavitation. 超声波清洗机是一种通过高频空化作用来清洁浸没在液体中物体的机器。
vacuum dry 真空干燥	You vacuum dry a paper or textile object that is sensitive to large amounts of water by sucking the water from the object using controlled suction on a vacuum table. 纸张或纺织品对水敏感，对它们进行真空干燥就是通过控制真空工作台来吸干其中的水分。
vacuum fumigation 真空熏蒸	Vacuum fumigation is fumigation carried out in a vacuum to enhance the penetration of the fumigant into the object. 真空熏蒸是在真空中进行熏蒸，以增强熏蒸剂对器物的渗透。
vacuum table 真空工作台	A vacuum table has a plate of perforated stainless steel through which an adjustable vacuum can be drawn. A vacuum table is used for wet and solvent cleaning and for stain treatments of paper and textiles. 真空工作台具有穿孔的不锈钢板，由此可以调节抽吸的真空度。真空工作台用于纸张和纺织品的水洗和溶剂清洗，以及污渍处理。
vibrotool 振动工具（如刻字笔）	A vibrotool is an electrically powered vibrating needle held in a small hand set which is used to remove hard concretions from a surface. 振动工具是在一个小手柄上安装振动针的电动工具，用于从表面去除凝结物。

wet cleaning **湿法清洗**	Wet cleaning is the process of cleaning an object that involves the use of water. The cleaning solution may contain a surfactant and a soil suspension agent to assist the removal of insoluble dirt. The dirt and cleaning additives are then removed from the object by repeated rinsing in clean, preferably purified, water. 湿法清洗是用水清洗器物的过程。清洁溶液含有表面活性剂和土壤悬浮剂，以帮助清除不溶性污垢。然后，通过在干净的、最好是纯水中反复冲洗，以去除物体上的污垢和清洗添加剂。
Wish-ab®	Wish-ab is a dense, rubber sponge of various grades of hardness. It is designed for the mechanical surface cleaning of wallpaper. In textile conservation, it is used to mechanically surface clean textiles such as wall coverings. See also dry cleaning sponge. Wish-ab®（商标名）是一系列硬度等级不同的致密橡胶海绵。用于墙纸表面的机械清洁。在纺织品保护中，用于纺织品表面的机械清洁，例如墙面材料。另见干洗海绵。
Zettler process **赛特勒法**	The Zettler process is an old technique for restoring damaged stained glass, in use in the first quarter of the 20th century. The process involved the sprinkling of fusible glass on the surface of the damaged stained glass and refiring at 400 C. 赛特勒法是修复受损彩色玻璃的一种古老技术，在20世纪初就开始使用。这一工艺包括将易熔玻璃点在受损的彩色玻璃表面，并在400℃下复烧。

13

分析方法
Analysis

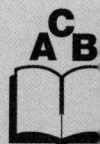

abundance 丰度	Abundance is a relative quantity or number present in relation to a total number. 丰度指在总数中的相对质量或数量。
accuracy 精度	In any kind of measurements accuracy means the absence of errors and the degree of precision. 在各种类型的测量中，精度代表低误差和精确程度。
acidic 酸性的	An acidic organic object, for example, one made from textile or paper, has a pH under 7. A textile may become acidic due to ageing, chemical treatments, soiling or atmospheric pollution. 酸性有机物（如由纺织品或纸制的有机物）的 pH 值低于 7。纺织品可能会因老化，化学处理，污染或大气污染而呈酸性。
activity coefficient 活度系数	The activity coefficient describes the active concentration (activity) of ions in a salt solution. In concentrated solutions the activity may be different from the actual concentration because ions may form aggregates. 活度系数指盐溶液中离子的活度浓度（活度）。在浓溶液中，因为离子可能会形成聚集体，所以其活性可能与实际浓度不同。
analysis 分析	Analysis is the investigation of an object using physical and chemical techniques. It is performed in order, for instance, to identify component materials or methods of manufacture. 分析指使用物理和化学技术对目标对象开展调查。调查过程需要有序开展，比如为识别材料成分或制造方法。
anisotropic 各向异性	An anisotropic property of a material is one which varies depending on the direction in which it is measured. 材料的各向异性是一种随其测量方向而变化的特性。
aromatic 芳香族	An aromatic organic compound has at least one benzene ring in the molecule. 芳香有机化合物的分子结构中至少有一个苯环。
atomic absorption spectroscopy 原子吸收光谱	Atomic absorbtion spectroscopy analyses the amount of substance dissolved in a solution by measuring the amount of radiation absorbed, usually in the ultra violet or visible regions of the electromagnetic spectrum. 原子吸收光谱指通过测量紫外线或可见光范围中的辐射吸收量，来确定溶液中的物质含量。
autoradiography 放射自显影法	Autoradiography is an examination method for paintings, used since late 1970s. A painting is first exposed to a low level of ionising radiation which activates some pigments. Images of the radiation emitted from these pigments are subsequently recorded on radiographic plates. By this method one can detect some underdrawings, specific pigments and enhance the visibility of dark areas on a painting. 自 20 世纪 70 年代后期，放射自显影法被用来检查书画。首先，将书画置于低剂量的电离辐射下，激活书画中的某些颜料，之后记录下颜料发出的辐射图像。通过这种方法可以检测出一些底图、特定的颜料，并提高绘画中暗区的可见度。

bar 巴	A bar is a unit of air pressure where 0.980665 bars is equal to 1 atmosphere. 巴是空气压强的单位，0.980665巴等于1个大气压。
birefracting 双折射	When examining a thin section of paint under the microscope using polarized light, birefracting pigment particles appear as bright points against a dark background. This property is used to identify pigments. 当用偏光显微镜检查较薄的漆层切片时，双折射颜料的颗粒在深色背景下显示为亮点，这一特性可被用于辨别颜料。
blue wool standards 蓝色羊毛标准	The British Standards Institution blue wool standards (BS EN ISO 105-B08:1999) are a set of 8 blue dyed wool fabric samples which fade at different rates on exposure to light and UV. The rate of fading of the standards is compared with the rate of fading 英国标准协会蓝色羊毛标准（BS EN ISO 105-B08：1999）在耐光色牢度试验中，为评定染色物的色牢度级别，将试样与8块不同褪色程度的标准蓝色羊毛标准，进行比较，以评定试样耐光色牢度等级（耐光稳定性）。
bond strength 粘合强度	Bond strength is the strength of the join formed when two or more fragments are adhered together. 粘合强度是两个或多个片段粘合在一起时形成的连接强度。
Brinell-hardness 布氏硬度	Brinell-hardness is a method of measuring the hardness of materials using a standardised press to force a steel ball on the surface of the material tested and measure the press in. 布氏硬度是一种测量材料硬度的方法，用标准化压力机将钢球压在待测材料的表面以计算所施加的压力。
burn test 燃烧测试	A burn test is a simple method of identifying the type of a bundle of fibres by applying a naked flame to it and examining the burning process and odour as well as the appearance of the burnt remains. The fibre types of cellulose, protein and many synthetics can be easily determined by using this method. 燃烧测试是一种简单的辨别方法，通过明火来辨别纤维束种类，检查燃烧过程和气味，观察残渣外观。纤维素，蛋白质和许多合成物的纤维类型可以通过此方法来轻松识别。
bursting strength 抗破裂强度	The bursting strength of paper is the resistance of paper against pressure which is applied to it locally. It is a measure of the tensile strength and elasticity of the paper. 抗破裂强度是纸对局部受力的抵抗力，用来衡量纸张拉伸强度和弹性。
capillary 毛细管	A capillary is an open pore of a small cross section within a porous material. 毛细管是多孔材料中横截面的开口气孔。
capillary rise 毛细上升	Capillary rise is the extent of the upward movement of liquid within a porous material (such as masonry). The extent of the rise is a balance between the upward force caused by surface tension against downward gravitational force. 毛细上升指液体在多孔材料（如砖石）中上行的程度，其上升程度取决于克服重力后，所产生表面张力大小。

capillary suction 毛细吸收	Capillary suction is the force acting over an area of liquid which is being drawn up into a porous material (such as stone) due to the effects of surface tension. It is measured by applying an equal and opposite force under air pressure. 毛细吸力指由于表面张力而被吸入多孔材料（如石头）中的对液体的作用力。通常在气压下，施加相等且相反的力可以测量毛细吸力的大小。
capillary tension 毛细管张力	Capillary tension is the force of attraction between a liquid and a solid that affects the movement of liquid within the pore structure of a porous material. 毛细管张力是液体和固体间的吸引力，影响着多孔材料中孔隙结构的液体流动。
capillary water 毛细水	Capillary water is the amount of water present within the pore structure of a porous material. 毛细水是存在于多孔材料孔结构中的水量。
chroma 色度	In describing a colour using the Munsell and similar colour systems, the chroma is the perception formed as a result of the intensity of wavelengths of light in the colour. The chroma of a colour can vary from zero (for example, white or black) to full saturation, which is the maximum possible perception of the hue. 在使用Munsell和类似的颜色系统描述颜色时，色度是指对颜色中的光的波长强度的感知结果，色彩的色度可以从零（例如白色或黑色）到完全饱和，也就是对色调的最大感知程度。
chromatography 色谱法	Chromatography is a method of separating mixtures by passing the mixture over a static adsorbant. The components of the material are separated by differential adsorption. The technique was originally used for coloured materials whose components could be identified visually but now a wide variety of materials is analysed using very different separation media and detectors. The stationary phase can be paper, alumina, oil, or glass. 色谱法利用不同物质在不同相态的选择性分配，以流动相对固定相中的混合物进行洗脱，混合物中不同的物质会以不同的速度沿固定相移动，最终达到分离的效果。该技术最初用于分离通过肉眼进行识别的有色物质，现在用不同的分离介质和检测器进行分析更多的材料。固定相可以是纸、氧化铝、油或者玻璃。
chromophore 发色基团	A chromophore is a functional group in an organic molecule that absorbs light. It is usually an unsaturated group. 发色基团是有机分子中吸收光的官能团，通常是不饱和基团。
CIELab CIELab 色彩空间系统	The CIELab system is a widely used uniform colour space developed by the CIE. CIELab色彩空间系统系统由 CIE（Commission International de l'éclairage）开发，是一种应用广泛的统一颜色空间。
coefficient of saturation 饱和系数	The coefficient of saturation of a porous material is the amount of solute present in a porous material as a proportion of the maximum possible under specific conditions. 多孔材料的饱和系数指在特定条件下多孔材料中溶质的最大饱和数值。

coefficient of thermal expansion 热膨胀系数	The coefficient of thermal expansion describes how much a material expands in length when its temperature is increased by 1 Kelvin. 热膨胀系数用来描述固态物质温度改变摄氏度1度时，其某一方向上长度的变化量。
cohesion 粘聚力	Cohesion is the degree to which molecules, particles or layers stick together, usually without any added material. 粘聚力指在不添加任何材料的一般情况下，分子，颗粒或各层间的粘合程度。
colour 色彩	A colour is the perception of light as different from the white light produced by a natural light source. The coloured light may come from a light source such as a lamp or by reflection from an object. Colour is measured by a number of different systems, each of which uses a different notation to specify a colour. 色彩是与自然光源产生的白光对比形成的色彩差异认知。彩色光的来源可以来自电灯等类似光源，也可来自物体反射，目前有很多颜色系统可以定义颜色，每种系统都使用不同的符号来表示颜色。
colour fastness 色牢度	Colour fastness is the ability of a colouring material to resist change under a specific influence, such as that of light, acids or alkalis. 色牢度是着色材料在特定影响下（如光，酸或碱等）抵抗变色的能力。
colour rendering 显色性	The colour rendering quality of a light source is the closeness of perception of a colour under that source to the perception under a standard source. The colour rendering quality can be estimated by eye or by calculation of the spectra. 光源的显色质量指该光源与标准光源下呈现颜色的接近程度。通过肉眼或计算光谱可以估算出显色质量。
colour rendering index 显色指数	The colour rendering index is the measure of how nearly an artificially produced light matches that produced by a natural source such as daylight or candle. The CIE colour rendering index is on a scale of 1-100, with 100 being a perfect match with natural 显色指数是衡量人造光源与自然光源（如日光或蜡烛）匹配程度的指数。CIE的显色指数范围为1-100，其中100非常接近日光。
compressive strength 抗压强度	The compressive strength of a material is the maximum pressure (compressive force per area unit) which can be applied to a specimen in a standardized test before it fails. 材料的抗压强度指外力施压力时的强度极限（每单位面积的压力）。
contaminant 污染物	A contaminant on an object is a material that can cause the object to deteriorate or, in the case of analysis, give misleading results. 物体上的污染物可能导致物体劣化或在干扰分析结果的物质。

correlated colour temperature 相关色温	The correlated colour temperature (CCT) of a light source is the estimation of the temperature in K of a reference light source that produces the perceptible colour reflected from a surface. For temperatures above 5000K the reference source is daylight and below that is a black body radiator. 光源的相关色温（CCT）是通过使物体表面反射光而产生的可察觉颜色的参考光源色温（K），得到的估算值。参考光源的色温（K）色温高于5000K时，参考光源为日光，低于5000K的温度，参考光源为黑体。
corrosion potential 腐蚀电位	The corrosion potential is the real electric potential measured on the surface of a corroding material in either an electrolytic or a galvanic cell. 电解池或原电池中的腐蚀电位指在腐蚀材料表面测得的实际电位。
corrosion rate 腐蚀率	The corrosion rate of a metal describes how fast its oxidation proceeds in a specific environment. It is often given as the thickness of material lost to corrosion per year or the weight lost per area and time unit. 金属的腐蚀率代表在特定环境中生成金属氧化的速度，通常以每年或单位面积和单位时间上因腐蚀而损失的材料厚度或重量来表示。
couple 电偶	In electrochemistry a couple is a combination of two different metals in electrical contact between which a potential difference (a voltage) can be measured. 在电化学中，电偶指由两种不同金属组成的组合，在电流的作用下人们可以测量它们之间的电位差（电压）。
coupon 模拟试样	A coupon is a small sample replicate that is used in an experiment studying change. 模拟试样指在实验中用于研究的模拟小样品。
covering power 遮盖力	The covering power is the ability of a paint layer to conceal a lower layer. It is a result of both the pigment and binding medium properties. 遮盖力指涂料上层掩盖下层的能力，是颜料和粘合介质共同作用的结果。
critical humidity 临界湿度	Critical humidity is the minimum humidity required for the deliquesence of a specific salt. This is therefore the lowest humidity that the salt will promote the corrosion of a metal. It is also the lowest humidity at which the salt will be able to migrate through a porous material. 临界湿度是特定盐潮解的最低湿度。因此在最低湿度下，盐将促进金属的腐蚀。这也是盐能够通过多孔材料迁移的最低湿度。
cross-section 剖面	a. A cross-section is made when an object or sample is cut at right angle to the surface in order to reveal its internal structure. b. A cross-section is the imagined appearance of the internal structure of an object as if cut along a plane. a.剖面指将与物体或样品表面成直角切割后，显示出其内部结构的一面。b.剖面指沿对象平面切开的内部结构图像。

cumulative exposure 累积曝光量	The cumulative exposure is the amount of light to which an object has been exposed. It is calculated by integrating the exposure to light over the period of exposure. This is usually achieved by measuring the illuminance level at the surface of the object at regular intervals and averaging over time. The common unit of measurement is the lux-hour. 累积曝光量指物体在光线下的曝光总量，通过对曝光时间内的曝光量进行积分计算获得。一般通过在一定时间间隔测量物体表面的光照度，取测量结果的平均值实现检测。常用的计量单位是勒克斯-小时。
D6500 D6500	D6500 is a mathematical description of the spectrum of standard daylight with a colour temperature of 6500K. Standard descriptions of daylight with other colour temperatures are available. D6500是色温为6500K的标准日光光谱的数学性描述，此外，还有对其他日光色温的标准描述。
decision tree 决策树	A decision tree is a method of analysing the processes of taking a decision to arrive at a number of possible outcomes. 决策树是一种分析决策过程的方法，可以得到一系列结果。
decomposition potential 分解电势	The decomposition potential is the electrical potential required to start and maintain the reaction in a galvanic cell which leads to the electrochemical decomposition of one of the materials present in the cell. 分解电势指在原电池中开始和维持反应所需的电势，该电势将导致电池中的某种材料发生电化学分解。
degree of polymerisation 聚合度	The degree of polymerisation (DP) of a polymer is the average number of monomer units in a polymer molecule. See also molecular weight. 聚合物的聚合度（DP）指聚合物分子中单体单元的平均数目。另见分子量。
dendrochronology 树木年代学	Dendrochronology is the method of determining the age of wood by counting its annual growth rings. 树木年代学是通过计算木材年轮来确定木材年龄的方法。
densitometer 光密度计	A densitometer is a machine which measures optical density. 光密度计是一种测量光密度的设备。
deposition velocity 沉积速度	The deposition velocity of a pollutant is a measure of the rate of reaction of the pollutant with a surface. The larger the number means that the rate of reaction is greater. 污染物的沉积速度是污染物与表面反应速率的衡量指标，数字越大，反应速率越快。
dew point 露点	On cooling a sample of air, the dew point is the temperature at which liquid water precipitates out. 冷却空气样本时，露点是水蒸气凝结为液态水的温度。

diagnosis 诊断	A diagnosis is a hypothesis which explains the causes of a particular defect, deterioration or decay which affects a material. It is achieved through analysis and evaluation of known facts, symptoms and collected data. 诊断是一种推测，它解释了影响材料的特定缺陷，劣化或衰减的原因，通常通过分析和评估已知事实、状态和收集数据，来进行诊断。
dichroism 二向色性	Dichroism is the optical effect when a glass object shows different colours, depending on the angle of the light falling on it. This is often achieved by the addition of small amounts of colloidal gold to the glass batch. The glass appears red by transmitted light and olive green by reflected light. 二向色性是玻璃物体因入射光的角度不同而产生不同颜色的光学效果。通常原因在于玻璃材料中添加了少量的胶体金。这类玻璃材料在透射光下呈红色，在反射光下呈橄榄绿。
differential scanning calorimetry 差示扫描量热法	Differential scanning calorimetry (DSC) is an analysis technique where a small sample of a material is heated in a container and the heat input required to raise the temperature is recorded, in comparison with an empty container. It has been developed into a highly sensitive analysis of the state of organic materials. 差示扫描量热法是在程序温度控制下，测量试样与参比物之间单位时间内能量差随温度变化的一种分析技术。它在有机材料测量领域已发展成为一种高灵敏度的分析方法。
dispersion (2) 色散 (2)	In physics, dispersion refers to the separation of visible light or other electromagnetic waves into different wavelengths. 在物理学中，色散是可见光或其他电磁波在不同波长内的分离现象。
disruptive stress 破坏应力	Disruptive stress is an applied force capable of causing fracturing of a material. 破坏应力指能够引起材料破裂的作用力。
dosimeter 剂量计	A dosimeter is a device that measures the exposure in a specific position to an influence. Dosimeters are used to gauge the exposure of an object to a number of environmental influences such as light, UV and pollutants. Dosimeters usually react chemically in a reproduceable way that can be extrapolated to the extent of exposure. 剂量计是一种测量物体在特定环境下的受影响程度的设备。剂量计用于测量物体暴露在多种环境因素下的受影响程度，例如光，紫外线和污染物。剂量计通常以可重复的方式进行化学反应，这种反应可以推算出受影响的程度。
elasticity 弹性	Elasticity is the property of a material to return to its original shape and size after being distorted. 弹性指材料变形后恢复其原始形状和尺寸大小的属性。
electrochemical potential 电化学势	The electrochemical potential of a metal describes its strength as an oxidising agent. Potentials are always measured as voltages (potential differences) between two different metals in an electrochemical cell. Measuring against a standard hydrogen electromotive force of a metal. 金属的电化学势表示其作为氧化剂的强度。电势始终以电化学电池中两种不同金属之间的电压（电位差）来衡量。以金属的标准氢电势进行测量。

electromagnetic radiation 电磁辐射	Electromagnetic radiation are waves of varying electrical and magnetic fields, which can also be expressed as quanta of energy. The radiation can be highly energetic such as g-rays through x-rays, UV, light, IR, microwave to lower energy radio waves. 电磁辐射由电场与磁场的交互变化产生，也可用能量量子表示。辐射可以是通过X射线的g射线、紫外线（UV）、光、红外线（IR）这样的高能辐射，也能是像微波以及能量较低的无线电波。
electromotive force 电动势	The electromotive force of a metal describes which voltage (electrode potential) reduces metal ions to their metallic state under standard conditions relative to a standard hydrogen reference electrode. 金属的电动势是在标准条件下相对于标准氢的参比电极，它能指出在多少电压下（电极电势）金属离子会被还原为金属状态。
electromotive force series (EMF series) 电动势系列 （EMF系列）	Different metals can be listed according to their electromotive force potentials (reduction potentials), giving the EMF series. Noble metals such as gold have high (positive) EMF potentials, base metals such as magnesium or aluminium have low (negative) EMF potentials. 根据电动势（还原电势）不同可以有不同的金属，从而得到EMF系列。贵金属（如金）具有高（正）EMF势，基本金属（例如镁或铝）具有低（负）EMF势。
electron probe microanalysis 电子探针显微分析	Electron probe microanalysis (EPM) analyses a very small quantity of substance. A very fine beam of electrons is focussed onto a sample which produces a characteristic x-ray spectrum of the elements present. It can be used for the quantitative analysis of elements with atomic numbers in excess of 11. 电子探针显微分析（EPM）通常用于分析含量极少的物质，将极细的电子束聚焦在样品上后，会产生所含元素特征的X射线光谱。它可用于原子序数大于11的元素的定量分析。
electron probe microbeam analysis 电子探针微束分析	Electron probe microbeam analysis (EPMA) is a method for the microscopic quantitative elemental analysis of materials with a scanning electron microscope. The instrument determines the composition of microscopic areas on the specimen from the energy and intensity of X-rays generated by the interaction between electron beam and specimen. 电子探针微束分析（EPMA）是一种用扫描电子显微镜对材料进行微观元素的定量分析方法。该仪器根据电子束与试样相互作用产生的X射线的能量和强度来确定试样上微观区域的组成。
electronegative potential 阴电势	Metals with an electronegative potential (that is, a negative EMF potential) such as tin, iron or zinc are placed below hydrogen in the EMF series and therefore can be oxidised by protons (hydrogen ions, H+) under standard conditions. As a result these metals dissolve in non-oxidising acids such as hydrochloric acid. 阴电势（即负EMF势）的金属（例如锡，铁或锌）在EMF系列中位于氢之下，因此在标准情况下会被质子（氢离子，H＋）氧化。因此，这些金属溶解在非氧化性酸中，如盐酸。

electropositive potential 阳电势	Metals with an electropositive potential (that is, a positive EMF potential) such as gold, silver or copper are placed above hydrogen in the EMF series and therefore cannot be oxidised by protons (hydrogen ions, H+) under standard conditions. As a result these metals do not dissolve in non-oxidising acids such as hydrochloric acid. 阳电势（即正EMF势）的金属（如金，银或铜）在EMF序列中高于氢，因此在标准情况下不会被质子（氢离子，H＋）氧化。因此，这些金属不溶于盐酸等非氧化性酸中。
ell 厄尔 （织物宽度的单位）	An ell was a unit of measurement used to indicate the width of a fabric. A Flemish ell in the 17th century was 69 cm., an English ell 114 cm. 厄尔是用于测量织物宽度的单位。17世纪时，1佛兰德厄尔相当于69厘米，1英国厄尔相当于114厘米。
embedding medium 包埋剂	An embedding medium is a liquid into which a sample is placed and which solidifies to support the sample securely. An embedding medium is typically used to hold a small sample from an object to enable its analysis, such as during thin sectioning. 包埋剂是一种浸入样品的液体，起到硬化和加固样品的作用。包埋剂通常用于小型样本以进行分析（如在切片过程中）。
equilibrium potential 平衡电势	The equilibrium potential between the electrodes in a galvanic cell is the voltage measured in the absence of an electric current, no ongoing electrochemical reaction and no electrode polarisation. To maintain a reaction an overvoltage must be applied. 原电池中电极之间的平衡电势是在无电流，无正在进行的电化学反应和无电极极化的情况下测得的电压。为延续反应，必须施加过电压。
evaluate 评估	When you evaluate a material or process, you determine its appropriateness or efficacy. 在评估材料或其过程中，人们会确定其合适性或有效性。
fission track dating 裂变径迹年代测定法	Fission track dating is a method of estimating the age of glass and other mineral objects by observing the tracks in them made by the fission fragments of the uranium nuclei that they contain. By irradiating the objects with neutrons to induce fission and comparing the density and number of tracks before and after irradiation, it is possible to estimate the time that has elapsed since the object solidified. 裂变径迹年代测定法是一种通过观察玻璃和其他矿物材料中含有的铀原子核的裂变碎片轨迹，来估算材料年龄的方法。通过用中子辐照以引发裂变，比较辐照前后的径迹密度和数量，就可以估计出物体固化后的时间长度。
fluorescence 荧光	When a material is excited by a form of radiation, fluorescence is the resulting emission of electromagnetic radiation, usually light or UV radiation. 当材料被某种形式的辐射激发后，荧光就是残生的次级电磁辐射（通常是光或UV辐射）。

folding endurance 耐折度	The folding endurance of paper is the number of double folds a paper can take before breaking along the fold line. It measures the strength of the paper fibres and their internal bonding. 纸张的耐折性是纸张在被折断前，沿折线进行的双次折叠的次数，耐折度被用来测试纸纤维的强度及其内部粘合力。
forensic science 法医学	Forensic science is the application of science to legal problems. 法医学是用来解决法律问题的应用科学。
freeze-thaw cycle 冻融循环	A freeze-thaw cycle is repeated solidification and melting of water at temperatures around 0℃. This cycle is particularly destructive for porous stone and similar materials because freezing water expands by approx. 9%. See also frost damage. 冻融循环指在0℃左右反复冻结和融化的水。由于水结冰，体积会膨胀约9%，因此该循环对多孔石材及类似材料具有很大危害，另见冻害。
FTIR 傅立叶变换红外光谱	Fourier Transform Infrared spectroscopy 利用干涉谱的傅立叶变换技术获得红外光谱的光谱学方法
galvanic series 电势序	The galvanic series is the relative hierarchy of metals arranged according to their corrosion potentials. 电势序是根据金属的腐蚀电位排列的相对等级。
gas chromatography 气相色谱法	Gas chromatography (GC) is an analysis technique where a small sample of an organic material, which has been vapourised usually from a solution, is carried by a gas stream through a column containing an adsorbent coating. The components of the material are separated by differential adsorption and detected at the end of the column. The speed of passage of the component through the column is diagnostic of the specific compound. 气相色谱法（GC）是一种用于检测有机材料的分析技术，溶液中气化的少量有机物质由气流搭载通过含有固定相的色谱柱。材料的不同组分由于吸附作用的差别在色谱柱的末端得到分离和检测。流动相通过色谱柱的不同速度对应不同的物质成分。
gas-liquid chromatography 气液色谱法	Gas-liquid chromatography (GLC) is a method of analysis, by which the components of a mixture are separated in a machine that carries the components in a gas stream through a column coated with a liquid in which the components are slightly soluble. 根据所用固定相的不同可分为两类：固定相是固体的，称为气固色谱法，固定相是液体的则称为气液色谱法。
gel permeation chromatography 凝胶渗透色谱法	Gel permeation chromatography (GPC) is an analysis technique where a small sample of an organic material, usually a polymer in solution, is carried by a solvent through a column containing a microporous gel. The smallest components of the material penetrate deeper into the gel and are held longer, so separating the mixture by molecular weight. 凝胶渗透色谱法（GPC）是一种分析技术，一小部分有机材料的样品（通常是溶液中的聚合物）由溶剂载着通过包含微孔凝胶的色谱柱。材料中最小的成分渗透到凝胶中更深的地方并保持更长的时间，因此按分子重量来分离混合物。

glass transition temperature 玻璃化转变温度	The glass transition temperature of an amorphous material is the temperature at which on heating it starts changing from a glassy state to a plastic, or rubbery, state. 非晶态材料的玻璃化转变温度是其在加热后从玻璃态转变为可塑或橡胶状态的温度。
gloss (1) 光泽度 (1)	In technical terms, gloss is the amount of specular reflection from a surface and is measured by standard methods, for example, ISO 2813. 光泽度是用标准方法（例如ISO 2813）测量出的物体表面镜面反射总量的术语。
Gran's potentiometric method 格兰电位滴定法	Gran's potentiometric method for chloride analysis is an electrochemical titration technique for the quantitative determination of chlorides in solution. 格兰对氯化物的电位分析方法是一种电化学滴定技术，可用于定量测试溶液中的氯化物。
hardness (1) 硬度 (1)	The hardness of a material is the susceptibility of its surface to marring or indentation. There are a number of definitions and techniques for assessing hardness. 材料硬度指其表面抵抗破坏的能力，目前有许多测试方法和硬度标准可以用来评估硬度。
hardness (2) 硬度 (2)	The hardness of water is the amount of alkaline earth salts in solution that react with soaps. Salts such as calcium hydrocarbonate cause temporary hardness, because they precipitate on heating. Salts such as calcium sulphate cause permanent hardness, because they remain in solution on heating. 水硬度是溶液中与肥皂发生反应的碱土金属盐的总量。以酸式碳酸盐形式存在于水中的部分会因遇热形成沉淀而被除去，这被称为暂时硬度；而像硫酸钙这样的盐因其性质较为稳定，并不能通过加热去除，故称为永久硬度。
Herzberg stain 赫尔茨贝格染色测试	The Herzberg stain is a chemical spot test, named after the German paper scientist W. Herzberg, which is used to establish whether a paper is a chemical pulp or contains lignin. It colours fibres differently. For example, it colours chemical pulp red, chemical pulp containing lignin yellow-brown and groundwood fibres bright yellow. 赫尔茨贝格染色是以德国纸张科学家赫尔茨贝格命名的一种在现场进行的化学测试，用来确定纸张是化学纸浆，还是含有木质素。不同纤维的纸张会被染上不同颜色，如化学纸浆会被染成红色，含有木质素的化学纸浆会被染成棕黄色，磨木纸浆则呈现出亮黄色。
hue 色度	In describing a colour using the Munsell and similar colour systems, the hue is the perception formed as a result of the wavelengths of light in the colour. For instance, yellow and green are different hues. 在用孟塞尔（Munsell）和其他类似的颜色系统来描述颜色时，色度指不同波长的光对人眼产生的感觉，比如黄色和绿色就具有不同的色度。

humidity indicator card 湿度指示卡	A humidity indicator card is a piece of paper impregnated with a cobalt chloride salt mixture, designed to change colour at a specified humidity value. 湿度指示卡是一块浸有氯化钴盐混合物的试纸，在指定湿度下指示卡的颜色会发生变化。
hysteresis 滞后现象	A material displays hysteresis of a property when the equilibrium state of the property is different depending on the direction from which the equilibrium is approached. For example, hysteresis can be seen in humidity changes around paper objects: cellulose absorbs water more quickly than it will desorb it. Consequently, there is more water in paper at a given RH on drying than there is before humidification. 当接近饱和状态的方向发生变化时，处于饱和状态的属性就会改变，导致包含该属性的材料表现出滞后现象。例如，周围湿度发生变化后，纸张就会发生滞后现象：纤维素吸收水分的速度比解吸水分的速度快。因此，在给定的相对湿度下烘干时，纸张中的水分比加湿前的水分要多。
identification 鉴定	Identification establishes what an object is, its component materials or causes of degradation. 鉴定指辨别物体属性，组成材料或劣化原因。
identify 鉴定 / 鉴别	You identify an object (or material or cause of deterioration) by giving it a name, distinguishing it from similar objects or putting it in context. 鉴别物体，或材料或损坏原因的确认包括命名，与相似事物进行区分；或确定周围关系的关联。
illuminance 照度	Illuminance is the amount of light falling on a surface. It is frequently measured in lux. 照度指落在物体表面上的光量，通常以勒克斯为测量单位。
Image-Interaction-Test 图像交互作用测试	The Image-Interaction-Test is part of the Photographic Activity Test. It uses an emulsion of collodial silver in gelatine on polyester film with as a detector for image silver damaging substances. 图像交互测试是一种摄影活性试验，使用聚酯胶片中明胶的胶性银乳剂用来检测损害银盐图像的有害物质。
indicator 指示剂	An indicator is a detector of a component of a mixture. Indicators usually change colour when the component is present is sufficient concentration. Indicators are used in packaging as a visual check that the object is in appropriate environmental conditions. Examples are RH indicators for metals and acid indicators for plastics. 指示剂用于检测混合物的成分。在被测成分达到一定浓度，指示剂颜色能发生改变。指示剂可用于包装业，用肉眼检查对象是否处于适当的环境下。例如针对金属测试相对湿度的指示剂，针对塑料的酸度指示剂。
inductively coupled plasma atomic emission spectrometry (ICP-AES) 电感耦合等离子体原子发射光谱法 (ICP-AES)	ICP-AES is a method for the quantitative elemental analysis of inorganic materials. The instrument uses solutions which are vaporised and ionised in a gas plasma. The ionised sample is analysed in an emission spectrometer to determine its composition. ICP-AES 是一种无机材料的元素定量分析方法。仪器中的溶液能在气体等离子体中被汽化和离子化，之后用放射光谱仪对被离子化的物质进行分析，确定其组成成分。

inductively coupled plasma mass spectrometry 电感耦合等离子体质谱法	Inductively coupled plasma mass spectrometry (ICP-MS) is a method for the quantitative elemental analysis of inorganic materials. The instrument uses solutions which are vaporised and ionised in a gas plasma. The ionised sample is analysed in a mass spectrometer to determine its composition. 电感耦合等离子体质谱法是一种无机材料的定量元素分析方法。仪器中的溶液会在气体等离子体中被气化和离子化。电离样品在质谱仪中分析以确定其成分。
infra red 红外	Infra red electromagnetic radiation occurs beyond the red end of the visible spectrum, 0.75 to 1000μm 红外电磁辐射的波长在可见光谱的红色光之外，范围为 0.75 至 1000μm。
infra red photography 红外摄影术	Infra red photography is carried out as part of the documentation process used to reveal features not visible in light. It requires specialist cameras, film or digital processing. 红外摄影术是档案记录的一部分，用于揭示在自然光下不被发现的特征。红外摄影需要专业相机，胶卷或数字处理方法。
infrared reflectogram 红外反射图	An infrared reflectogram is a photographic or digital image of the infrared reflection from a painting. 红外反射图指在书画中利用红外反射制作出来的照片或数字图像。
infrared reflectogram assembly 红外反射图模块	An infrared reflectogram assembly is a mosaic of images taken with an infrared camera. 红外反射图模块是用红外成像仪拍摄的区域图像，多张区域图像可以用来组合成一张整体图像。
infrared spectrophotometer 红外分光光度计	An infrared spectrophotometer is an instrument for measuring absorbances in the infrared region of the spectrum. 红外分光光度计是一种用于测量光谱红外区域中吸光度的仪器。
inspection 视察	An inspection is a formal examination whose findings are documented. 视察是对结果进行归档记录的正式核查。
investigation 调查	Investigation of an object is physical examination carried out prior to and during treatment to discover information, for record purposes and to guide decisions. 调查是指在修复前和修复中对目标进行的调查，可用来探索信息、记录其用途和指导决策。
investigative cleaning 调查性清洁	Investigative cleaning is the removal of part of an accretion layer or deteriorated original material in order to reveal details. This type of cleaning aims at leaving as much of the object intact as possible. 调查性清洁指为观察细节而去除部分积垢层或劣化的初始材料。清洁原则要求最大可能地保障物体完好无损。

iso-electric point 等电位点	The iso-electric point of an amino acid is the pH where the anionic and cationic species are in balance. For proteins, there is no single pH but an iso-electric range. 氨基酸的等电点是其阴离子和阳离子处于平衡状态时的pH值。蛋白质没有单一pH值，而是具有等电范围。
light fastness 耐光性	Light fastness is the ability of coloured materials to resist fading when exposed to light. 耐光性代表有色材料暴露在光线中抵抗褪色的能力。
light intensity 光强度	The light intensity is the degree of illuminance found in a specific situation. 光强度指在特定情况下的光照度。
load 荷载	The load of a structure denotes the forces exerted by its own weight. 结构荷载是由其自身重量施加的力。
logger 记录器	A logger is an electronic recorder for keeping physical data aquired from sensors, such as humidity, light, or vibration. 记录器是一种电子记录器，用于保存从传感器获取的物理数据，如湿度，光线或振动等。
loupe 手持低倍显微镜	A loupe is a low-magnification hand lens, often used in preliminary examinations of paintings. 手持低倍显微镜是一种低倍手持镜头，通常用在书画检测的初级阶段。
lumen (2) 流明 (2)	A lumen (lm) is a unit of luminous flux, which is, in practice, the amount of light falling on 1m2 at a distance of 1m from a light source emitting one candela. 流明（lm）是光通量的单位，实际上指在距离发出一个坎德拉（1cd）的光源1米远的地方落在1平方米上的光通量。
luminance 亮度	The luminance of a surface is the intensity of light emitted from a surface. 亮度指从物体表面发出的光的强度。
lux 勒克斯	Lux is a standard unit of illuminance, lumen/m^2. 勒克斯是照度的标准单位，用lumen/m^{2}表示。
mass spectroscopy 质谱法	Mass spectroscopy (MS) is an analysis technique where a material is heated in a vacuum chamber, separated into compounds of different molecular mass and detected. The heating frequently causes the chemical to disintegrate and the resulting pattern of daughter fragments is used as a characteristic of the material being analysed. 质谱法（MS）是一种分析技术，将材料放在真空室内加热，之后对分离出的不同分子量的化合物进行检测。材料加热后经常导致化学物质分解，由此产生的子体碎片作为被分析材料的特征。
material safety data sheets (MSDS) 化学品安全技术说明书 (MSDS)	Material safety data sheets are a data collection of potential hazards associated with a material or substance. 化学品安全技术说明书指材料或物质相关的具有潜在危害的数据集合。

metallography 金相学	Metallography investigates the microstructure of polished and etched metal surfaces to determine composition and manufacturing techniques of an object. 金相学研究抛光和蚀刻金属表面的微观结构，以确定物体成分和其制造技术。
metamerism 同色异谱	Metamerism occurs when two materials appear to be the same colour under certain lighting conditions, but different under others. It occurs when the apparently similarly coloured materials have different absorption spectra in the visible region. 当两种材料在某些光线下看起来颜色相同，但在其他光线下却表现出不同的颜色时，这就是同色异谱现象。当表面看上去颜色相似的材料吸收可见区域中的不同光谱时，同色异谱现象就随之发生。
micron 微米	One micron is a unit of length equal to one-millionth of a meter. It is commonly used in the measurement of cross -sections. 微米是长度单位，是1米的百万分之一，通常用于剖面的测量。
millibar 毫巴（气压单位）	One millibar is one thousandth of a bar. 1毫巴是1巴的千分之一。
mired 微倒度	A Mired is 1/106K and is used in calculating the correlated colour temperature. 微倒度（Mired）为1/106K，用来计算相关色温。
moisture content 含水率	The moisture content of a material is the weight of water contained in the material in proportion to the dry weight of the material. See also regain. 材料的含水率是材料中所含水分与材料的干重之比。另见饱水率。
molecular weight 分子量	The molecular weight of a molecule is the sum of the relative atomic masses of the constituent atoms. The IUPAC preferred usage is relative molecular mass (Mr). For a polymer which has a random mixture of molecules of varying sizes, average molecular weights are used to describe size of molecules. Number average, weight average and viscosity average molecular weights are different measures of the size distribution of the polymer molecules. 分子的分子量是组成原子的相对原子质量的总和。IUPAC的首选应用相对分子质量（Mr）。对于具有不同尺寸分子的随机混合物的聚合物，用平均分子量来描述分子的大小。数平均、重量平均和粘均分子量是衡量聚合物分子量分布的不同方法。
Mottle-Test 斑点测试	The Mottle-Test is part of the Photographic Activity Test. It uses a polyester film with an emulsion of collodial silver in gelatine as a detector for image silver damaging substances. 斑点测试是一种摄影活性试验，使用聚酯胶片和明胶中的胶体银乳剂来检测损害银盐图像的有害物质。
Munsell colour system 孟塞尔色彩系统	The Munsell colour system is a collection of coloured samples arranged in a three dimensional theoretical colour space, with the axes of hue, value and chroma. 孟塞尔色彩系统是排列在三维理论色彩空间中的色彩样本的集合，具有色相，明度和色度。

mushiness-test 抗划痕测试	A mushiness-test is a scratch-resistance test for wet photographic material. 抗划痕测试指对湿性感光材料的耐刮擦性能的测试。
nanometer 纳米	A nanometer, nm, is one billionth of a meter, 10-9m. It is the unit normally used to measure the wavelengths of electromagnetic waves from x-rays to infra-red radiation and the sizes of molecules. 纳米（nm）是10-9m的十亿分之一米，通常用于表示从X射线到红外辐射的电磁波波长和分子大小。
Natural Colour System 自然色彩系统	The Natural Colour System is a collection of coloured samples arranged in a three dimensional theoretical colour space, with the axes of hue, blackness and chromaticness. 自然色彩系统是排列在三维理论色彩空间中的彩色样本的集合，具有色相，黑度和色度。
neutron activation analysis 中子活化分析	Neutron activation analysis (NAA) is a method for the quantitative elemental analysis of inorganic materials which are irradiated from a neutron source and become radioactive. From the radiation emitted by the sample its composition can be determined. The method is suitable for trace element analysis but cannot analyse lead. 中子活化分析（NAA）指无机材料用反应堆、加速器或同位素中子源产生的中子作为轰击粒子的活化分析方法，是确定物质元素成份的定量分析方法。是通过鉴别和测试式样因辐照感生的特征辐射，进行材料的组成成分分析。该方法适用于微量元素分析，但不能检测铅元素。
non-destructive 无损的	A non-destructive investigation is one which uses remote sensing techniques to understand internal structure. The most common non-destructive methods used on paintings are X-radiography, infrared and ultraviolet photography. 无损调查指使用非接触分析方法来了解物体的内部结构。最常见的检测书画的无损方法是X射线照相，红外和紫外线照相技术。
non-destructive analysis 无损分析	Non-destructive analysis involves determining the composition or properties of an object without any sampling or cleaning of the surface. 无损分析指对对象表面不进行任何取样或清洁的情况下，确定对象成分或属性的分析方法。
non-destructive testing 无损检测	See non-destructive analysis. 另见无损分析。
Oddy test Oddy 测试	The Oddy test is a method of assessing the corrosiveness of display and storage materials on metals. It is carried out according to strict protocols. Oddy测试是根据严格规程执行，检测展览和库房中的材料对金属的腐蚀程度的方法。
opacity (1) 不透明度 (1)	Opacity is the extent to which a material prevents the transmission of light. 不透明度是衡量材料阻止光透过的程度。
opacity (2) 不透明度 (2)	Opacity is the reciprocal of the transmission ratio. It is used as the basis for density measurements of photographic materials. 不透明度是传输比的倒数，是摄影材料测量密度的基础。

pedology 土壤学	Pedology is soil science. 土壤科学是研究与土壤相关的科学。
petrology 岩石学	Petrology is the science of the rocks that form the crust of the earth. 岩石学是形成地球外壳的岩石科学。
phase diagram 相图	A phase diagram describes which phases form in a system in thermodynamic equilibrium under given conditions (temperature, overall composition of the system). In reality, the phases may be quite different if the system is not in equilibrium. 相图指在给定条件（温度，系统的综合成分）下在热力学平衡状态下系统中形成的相图。如果系统处于非平衡状态，那么其相位可能会完全不同。
pH-indicator 酸碱指示剂	A pH-indicator is a substance that will change to a specific colour as a result of the alkalinity or acidity of the medium to which it is exposed. The colour of the substance is compared with a chart of known colours at specific pH-values of the indicator, in order to find the approximate pH-value of the measured medium. 酸碱指示剂会随其接触介质的酸碱度而产生颜色变化，将接触介质后的酸碱指示剂同已知的色卡进行对比，可确认介质的酸碱度，以求得被测介质的近似pH值。
Photographic Activity Test 摄影材料活性测试	The Photographic Activity Test is a standardised (ISO 14523:1999), qualitative test to determine chemical inertness of (conservation) materials regarding image silver and discoloration effects of photographic fibre base paper. See also Image-Interaction-Test, Stain-Test and Mottle-Test. 摄影活性试验是一种标准的（ISO 14523：1999）定性测试，用于确保修复材料的图像银和照相纤维原纸变色效果的化学惰性。另见图像交互作用测试，染色试验和斑点测试。
photomicroscopy 显微照像术	Photomicroscopy is a method of photographing a surface through a microscope. 显微照像术是一种利用显微镜拍摄物体表面的方法。
PIRA test 皮革印刷工业研究 协会测试	The Printing Industries Research Association test of leather is carried out to assess the sensitivity of thvegetable tanned leather to acids. 皮革印刷工业研究协会为评估鞣制的皮革对酸的敏感性，进行的皮革测试。
polarization resistance method 极化电阻法	The polarization resistance method is a method used to determine experimental corrosion rates by measuring the change of polarization as a function of the applied overvoltage. 极化电阻法指随施加的过电压函数的变化，来测量极化强度，并确定腐蚀速率的方法。
potentiodynamic 动电位的	Potentiodynamic technique varies the potential between the working and reference electrodes at a constant rate while the resulting current density is measured. 动电位技术以恒定速率改变工作电极和对照电极间的电势，并在同时测量其电流密度。

potentiostatic 恒电位的	Potentiostatic technique keeps the potential between working and reference electrodes constant. 恒电位技术维持着工作电极和对照电极间的电势恒定。
Pourbaix diagram 布拜图（电位-pH图）	A Pourbaix diagram illustrates the electrode potentials of a given metal in solutions of various oxidising power, hydrogen potential and ion concentration. These diagrams are used to investigate the likelihood of corrosion. 电位-pH图表明了给定金属在不同氧化能力，产氢潜势和离子浓度下溶液中的电极电势，该图可用于观察金属发生腐蚀的可能性。
pressure test 压力测试	A pressure test is a method of measuring the leakiness of a building by blowing air into the building and measuring the resulting pressure rise. 压力测试是一种测量建筑物是否漏气的方法，将空气吹进建筑物并测量其压力的升高变化。
radiation 辐射	Radiation is a physical phenomenon which acts over long distances and may penetrate solid matter. Examples are electromagnetic waves (X-rays, light, microwaves, radio waves) or particle radiation (radioactive α - and β -radiation). 辐射是一种可长距离发射，并可能穿透固体材料的物理现象，如电磁波（X射线，光，微波，无线电波）或粒子辐射（放射性 α 辐射和 β 辐射）。
radiography 放射线照相术	Radiography is the use of high energy radiation to produce an image of an object. The radiation penetrates the object and produces a shadow image of the internal structure on photographic film or an electronic imaging screen. The radiation used is usually X-rays, but may also be γ -rays or neutrons, in which case radiography is referred to as X-radiography, γ -radiography, and neutron radiography respectively. 放射线照相术是利用高能辐射产生物体图像的方法。辐射穿透物体后，会在胶片或电子成像屏幕上显现出物体内部结构的阴影图像。使用的射线通常是X射线，但也可以是 γ 射线或中子，相应的放射线照相术分别称为X射线照相术、 γ 射线照相术和中子照相术。
raking light 侧光	Raking light is light that illuminates an object at an oblique angle in order to emphasise textural effects or damage. 侧光指用倾斜角度照射物体，以强调纹理效果或损伤物体的光。
reduction 还原反应	Reduction of a substance is a reaction that typically results in the loss of oxygen or the addition of hydrogen. In conservation, reduction is carried out in order to convert a metal compound back to the metal, or to destroy a chromophore that relies on the oxygen component to absorb the light. reduction is the opposite of oxidation. 物质的还原反应通常会导致氧气减少或氢气增加。在保护中，还原反应是为了将金属化合物转换回金属，或者破坏依靠氧成分吸收光的发色团。还原与氧化相反。

refraction 折射	Refraction is an optical phenomenon where a beam of visible light which crosses a boundary between two substances with different optical properties changes direction from its original path. 折射是一种光学现象，当光穿过具有不同光学特性的两种介质的交界处时，光束的原始方向会发生改变。
regain 保水率	Regain is the weight of water held by a textile at equilibrium with its environment under a specified relative humidity and temperature. It is expressed as a percentage of the weight of the textile when in a state of total dryness. 保水率指在特定的相对湿度和温度下，纺织品内的水分与所处环境达到平衡时所含水的重量，它还代表在完全干燥的状态下占纺织品重量的比例。
research 研究	Research is a critical study undertaken to discover new facts in a body of knowledge. 研究是为探索知识体系中的全新认知而进行的重要研究。
risk assessment 风险评估	A risk assessment is an informed judgement made about particular risks. 风险评估是对特定风险做出的知情判断。
risk evaluation 风险判断	A risk evaluation is a judgement taken after a risk assessment about the severity and consequences of possible harm, weighed against other risks. 风险判断指对可能发生危害的严重程度、后果和其他风险进行的判断。
risk management 风险管理	Risk management involves assessing, planning for, responding to and monitoring potentially adverse influences to an object, collection or building. 风险管理涉及对某一器物、藏品和建筑物进行的评估、计划、和对潜在的不利因素采取的行动和监测。
sacrifice 样品	A portion of an object is sacrificed to obtain information by being removed and destroyed during analysis. See also sample. 在分析过程中，为了获取信息，取走或牺牲文物的一小部分作为样品来获取更多信息。另见样本。
sample 样本	A sample is a portion of an object that has been removed for examination, analysis or separate archiving. Care has to be taken that the sample taken is characteristic of the material to be analysed. 样本是为进行检查，分析或单独归档而从目标器物上取的一小部分。值得注意的是，提取样品的特征必须能够代表被取样的器物。

scanning electron microscope 扫描电子显微镜	A scanning electron microscope (SEM) is a form of microscope that uses a beam of electrons to form an image of a very small object. The beam of primary electrons scans the specimen and those that are reflected, together with any secondary electrons, are collected. This current is used to modulate a second electron beam in a TV monitor, which scans the screen at the same frequency, consequently building up a picture of the specimen. The resolution is limited to about 10-20 nm. A SEM usually requires that the object be placed in a high vacuum, but an environmental SEM allows the examination at air pressures near to atmospheric. 扫描电子显微镜（SEM）是一种利用电子束分析较小物体的显微镜，扫描电子显微镜的制造是依据电子与物质的相互作用。当一束高能的入射电子轰击物质表面时，被激发的区域将产生二次电子等电磁辐射。扫描样品的电子光束和被反射的光束与二次电子，一起被收集。电流被用来调制电视监视器中的第二个电子束，它以相同的频率扫描屏幕，从而形成一幅样品的图像。分辨率控制在10-20纳米左右。扫描电子显微镜通常要求将物体置于高真空中，但环境扫描电子显微镜允许在接近大气压状况下进行检查。
smoke test 烟雾测试	A smoke test is the introduction of smoke into a building or cabinet and applying a pressure. The places where the smoke is pushed out reveals the air leakage paths. 烟雾测试指将烟雾引入建筑物或展柜后，再施加压力的测试方法。有烟雾排出的地方就是气体泄漏的路径。
softening point 软化点	The softening point is a specific point in the viscosity of melted glass. It occurs at 6 x 106 Nsm-2. The working range of glass is the difference in temperature between the softening point and the working point (10 3 Nsm -2). 软化点是玻璃软化时的一个具体年度值，它发生在6 x 106 Nsm-2。玻璃材料的工作温度范围位于软化点与工作点之间（10 3 Nsm -2）。
specimen 标本	A specimen is an object chosen for preservation and study by a natural scientist. 标本是自然科学家选择保存和研究的对象。
spectrometer 光谱仪	A spectrometer is an instrument for measuring the energy emitted or transmitted by a material at different wavelengths of electromagnetic radiation. 光谱仪可以测量不同的电磁辐射下，某种材料发射或传输能量的仪器。
spot test 斑点测试	A spot test is a wet, micro-chemical identification for a component of an object. The test can be carried out by applying the solution to the object or on a small sample. 斑点测试是对器物进行湿化学显微鉴别的方法，一般将溶液涂在物体或小样上来进行测试。
stain (1) 染色剂 (1)	A stain is a dye which is applied to a cross-section in order to colour the different components differentially. 染色剂指施加在断面上，对不同组件进行着色的染色剂。

Stain-Test 染色试验	The Stain-Test is part of the Photographic Activity Test. It uses a piece of white, undeveloped but fixed, photographic fibre base paper to detect substances capable of staining photographs. 染色试验是照相活性试验的一部分。它使用一张白色未显影但定影的照相纤维原纸来检测能使照片染色的物质。
strain gauge 变形测量仪	A strain gauge is a sensor that responds to very small shape changes with electrical property changes. It is used in conservation to measure the forces on objects, for instance on paintings and buildings. 变形测量仪是一种对随电性能变化、显微形变做出反应的传感器，它在修复中被用来测量物体（如书画和建筑物）上的力。
structure 结构	The microscopic structure of a material is the spatial arrangement of its atoms, ions or molecules and determines its macroscopic properties. 材料的微观结构是其原子，离子或分子的空间排列，微观结构还决定其宏观属性。
Tafel diagram 塔菲尔图	A Tafel diagram is used to determine experimental corrosion rates. It is a plot of overpotential (electrolytic polarization) as a function of the logarithm of current density. 塔菲尔图用于确定腐蚀速率，它是电流密度的对数与过电势（电解极化）作图。
Tafel line 塔菲尔直线	The Tafel line is an extrapolated line in a Tafel diagram which allows the calculation of corrosion rates. 塔菲尔直线是塔菲尔图中的外推线，用于计算腐蚀速率。
Tafel slope 塔菲尔斜率	The Tafel slope is the slope of the curve in a Tafel diagram. It allows the calculation of corrosion rates. 塔菲尔斜率是塔菲尔图中曲线的斜率，可以用来计算腐蚀速率。
tear resistance 抗撕裂性	The tear resistance of paper is the force required to tear a given piece of paper. The tear resistance in the machine direction is different from that in the cross-grain direction. 纸张的抗撕裂性指撕裂特定纸张所需的力。纵向的抗撕裂性与横向的抗撕裂性不同。
template 试板	A template is a thin sheet cut into a shape which measures, records or reproduces characteristic curvature. 试板是被切成特定形状的薄片，可用来测量，记录或复制特征曲率。
tenacity 韧性	Tenacity is the measure of the tensile stress that has to be applied to a fibre in order to break it. Tenacity is expressed in grams per tex. 韧性指施加在纤维上使其断裂的拉伸力的衡量标准，韧性用克/特克斯表示。
tensile strength 抗拉强度	The tensile strength of paper is the strength required to rupture a strip of paper lengthwise. 纸的抗拉强度是使纸条纵向断裂所需的强度。

thermography 热成像法	Thermography is a method to assess the thermal insulation of a building through infrared photography. 热成像法是一种通过红外照相技术评估建筑物隔热效果的方法。
thermohygrograph 温湿度数据图	A thermohygrograph measures, then produces an output on paper showing, the change in air temperature and humidity over time. 温湿度数据图是先用温湿计测量，然后再给出显示空气温湿度随时间变化的结果。
thermohygrometer 温湿计	A thermohygrometer measures the change in air temperature and humidity over time. 温湿计是测量空气中温度和湿度随时间变化的工具。
thermoluminescent dating 热释光测年	Some minerals in pottery produce small amounts of light when heated, with the amount produced increasing with time since the last heating. Thermoluminescence dating measures the light produced in order to estimate the age of a piece of pottery of unknown 陶器中的某些矿物质在最后一次加热后，再次遇热时会产生少量的光，光的总量会随时间不断累积增加。实验人员利用热释光测量所产生的光量来对陶器进行时代判断。
Threshold Limit Value 阈限值	The Threshold Limit Value (TLV) of a substance is the concentration of its vapour in air that can be safely breathed over a normal working week. TLV is the measure used in the USA. 物质的阈限值（TLV）是某种气体在空气中的含量小于这一阈值时，在一个工作周期充分且持续暴露于该环境中工人的健康不会受到危害。TLV是美国使用的度量。
time weighted average 时间加权平均值	The time weighted average concentration of a substance in air is worked out by measuring the concentration measured in successive intervals and taking the average of the concentrations over a specified period. 空气中某一物质浓度的时间加权平均值可通过计算测量连续间隔中的浓度，和提取特定时间段内浓度的平均值而得出。
tracer gas 示踪气体	A tracer gas is a gas which is released into a space and whose concentration is then measured over time. This measurement is used to estimate the air exchange rate of a building or cabinet. 示踪气体指释放到某一空间，在一定时间内测量该气体的浓度变化。这项指标可以用来评估建筑物或展柜的空气交换率。
transmission ratio 透射率	The transmission ratio of a transparent material is the ratio of the transmitted light to the incident light. 透明材料的透射率是透射光与入射光的比率。
transmitted light 透射光	The transmitted light through a material is that portion of the impinging light which passes through. 透射光是指穿过材料的那一部分入射光。

ultrasonic test 超声波测试	Ultrasonic testing is a non-destructive method for the detection of voids and cracks within the structure of an object or building. 超声波测试是一种无损方法，用于检测器物或建筑物结构中的空隙和裂缝。
ultra-violet radiation 紫外线辐射	Ultra-violet radiation is electromagnetic radiation having wavelengths (4-400 nm) between that of violet light and long x-rays. In painting conservation, ultraviolet radiation is used in investigations to study varnish layers and earlier retouchings. It is used to irradiate the object, causing the fluorescence in pigment and varnish layers which occurs in the visible range of electromagnetic radiation. 紫外线辐射是一种电磁辐射，波长在紫光和X射线间（4-400 nm）。紫外线辐射在光油层层和早期全色的研究。它对物体进行辐照，使颜料和漆层产生荧光，这种荧光是可见光范围内的电磁辐射。
uniform colour space 均匀色度空间 （CIE1960色度空间）	A uniform colour space is a theoretical model for expressing a colour sensation where an equal numerical change indicates the same degree of perceptible difference in colour across the space. 均匀色度空间是传递色彩感觉的理论模型，相同的数值变化表示整个空间中颜色的可变色差相同。
UV fluorescence 紫外荧光	UV fluorescence is the emission of ultra violet radiation by a substance following excitation by energy source other than heat, typically an electron beam. 紫外荧光是指物质受到紫外光（通常是电子束激发后产生的）照射后激发出的光谱。
UV photography 紫外线摄影术	UV photography is the creation of an image of an object illuminated by UV radiation. The image may be obtained from reflected UV or from the light fluorescence excited in the object. 紫外线摄影术指由紫外线照射而产生的荧光图像，图像是反射的紫外线或激发出的荧光形成的。
value (1) 色度值 (1)	In describing a colour using the Munsell and similar colour systems, value is a measure of the amount of light reflected. 在孟塞尔（Munsell）和其他类似的颜色系统中，色度值是被用来描述反射出的光量。
viscosity 黏度	The viscosity of a fluid is its resistance to flow. 流体的黏度是其抵抗流动的性能。
working electrode 工作电极	The working electrode in an electrochemical cell for the quantitative determination of corrosion properties is the electrode made of the material to be tested. 工作电极是由测试材料制成的电极，可用于对电化学电池中腐蚀性能的定量测定。
x-radiograph X射线照相图	An x-radiograph is an image made by the effects of x-rays on a photographic plate. The resulting image is lighter where the rays have been absorbed by denser material and darker where the rays pass through. X射线照相图是X射线在照相底片上生成的图像。当光线被密度较高的材料吸收时，所得图像较为明亮；当光线穿过时，所得的图像较暗。

x-radiography x 射线照相术	X-radiography is the use of x-rays to produce images of objects. X射线照相术通过使用X射线制作物体图像。
x-ray x 射线	X-rays are electromagnetic radiation of short wavelength, ca 10-3 to 10nm, able to pass through bodies opaque to light. X射线是波长很短、能穿过不透光的物体的电磁波，波长约为10-3至10nm。
x-ray crystallography x 射线晶体学	X-ray crystallography determines the structure of crystals or molecules by the use of x-ray diffraction. x射线晶体学是借助X射线在晶格中的衍射得到的图案来推断出晶体或分子结构的学科。
x-ray diffraction x 射线衍射	X-ray diffraction is preferential reflection of x-rays in specific directions by a crystal. This is the basis of x-ray crystallography. 当一束单色X射线入射到晶体时，由于不同原子散射的X射线相互干涉，在某些特殊方向上产生强X射线衍射，这是X射线晶体学的基础。
x-ray fluorescence x 射线荧光	X-ray fluorescence is the emission of x-rays from atoms excited by the impact of high-energy electrons on the surface of an object. The energies of the fluorescent x-rays are characteristic of the excited atom. 物质受X射线或其他光子源照射，受激产生次级的特征X射线(X光荧光)，而进行物质成分分析和化学态研究。
x-ray fluorescence spectroscopy x 射线荧光光谱	X-ray fluorescence spectroscopy analyses the x-rays excited in an object to prepare a chemical analysis of the object. It is widely used in scanning electron microscopes and electron microprobes. X射线荧光光谱指利用X射线或其他光子源照射物体，产生次级的特征X射线，从而对物体进行化学分析的光谱学分析方法。这种方法被广泛应用于扫描电子显微镜和电子微探针分析中。

14

其他
Others

AATA	AATA is the acronym for Art and Archaeology Technical Abstracts. It is an abstracting journal published by the GCI Los Angeles and the IIC London. AATA 是《艺术和考古技术摘要汇编》的简写，它是盖蒂文物保护研究所和国际文物保护修复协会的出版物。
AIC	American Institute for Conservation of Historic and Artistic Works, Washington, USA. 美国历史和艺术品保护研究所，位于美国华盛顿。
Athens Charter 雅典宪章	The Athens Charter for the Restoration of Historic Monuments is a charter that was adopted at the 1st International Congress of Architects and Technicians of Historic Monuments in Athens in 1931 and published by the International Office of Museums in 1933. 《雅典历史遗迹修复宪章》是1931年在雅典举行的第一届国际历史古迹建筑师和技师大会上通过的宪章，1933年由国际博物馆办公室出版。
ANSI	American National Standards Institute 美国国家标准学会
Burra Charter 巴拉宪章	Burra Charter is The Australia ICOMOS Charter for the Conservation of Places of Cultural Significance adopted by Australia ICOMOS and published in 1979, with revisions in 1981, 1988 and 1999. 《巴拉宪章》由国际古迹遗址理事会澳大利亚委员会在 1979 年发布，并于1981、1988和1999 年修订。
C. C. I.	Canadian Conservation Institute, Ottawa, Canada. 加拿大文物保护研究所，位于加拿大渥太华。
C. I. E.	Commission Internationale de L'Eclairage (International Commission of Illumination). 国际照明委员会
CACTCH	China Association for Conservation Technology of Cultural Heritage 中国文物保护技术协会
CHIN	CHIN 是加拿大遗产信息网络(Canada Heritage Information Network)的缩写。它是由位于渥太华的加拿大遗产部主办的，提供关于文物保护和修复信息的网站，网址是 https://www.canada.ca/en/heritage-information-network.html
CMA	Chinese Museums Association 中国博物馆协会
CMA-CC	Chinese Museums Association Committee for Conservation 中国博物馆协会藏品保护委员会
COoL	COoL 是文保在线的缩写，是美国斯坦福大学主办的提供文物保护和修复信息的主流网站，网址是https://cool.culturalheritage.org/
ECCO	European Confederation of Conservator-Restorers Organisations 欧洲修复师联盟

ENCoRE	European Network for Conservation-Restoration Education 欧洲文化遗产保护修复教育网络
European Architectural Heritage Year 1975 1975年欧洲建筑遗产年	European Architectural Heritage Year 1975 was planned to stimulate public awareness and concern for the richness of Europe's architectural heritage, and raise awareness for the challenges and losses faced by member countries. 1975年欧洲建筑遗产年的设立旨在激发公众对欧洲建筑遗产丰富性的认知和关注，同时提升对成员国面临的相关挑战和损失的意识。
Getty Conservation Institute (GCI)	The Getty Conservation Institute (GCI) is an American foundation associated with the J. Paul Getty Museum in Los Angeles, which carries out and funds conservation research projects. 盖蒂文物保护研究所（GCI）位于美国洛杉矶，与保罗·盖蒂博物馆同属于盖蒂基金会，负责开展和资助文物保护研究项目。
ICCROM	International Centre for the Study of the Peservation and Restoration of Cultural Property 国际文化遗产保护及修复研究中心
ICOM	International Council of Museums 国际博物馆协会
ICOM–CC	International Council of Museums - Committee for Conservation 国际博物馆协会藏品保护委员会
ICOMOS	International Council on Monuments and Sites 国际古迹遗址理事会
ICOMOS CHINA	Chinses National Committee for the International Council on Monuments and Sites. 中国古迹遗址保护协会
IIC	International Institute for Conservation of Historic and Artistic Works,London,UK. 国际文物保护学会，位于英国伦敦。
ISO	International Standards Organisation 国际标准化组织
NCHA	National Cultural Heritage Administration 国家文物局
NICAS	荷兰保护·艺术·科学学会 （NICAS，Netherlands Institute for Conservation+ Art+ Science）
Principles for the Conservation of Heritage Sites in China	Principles for the Conservation of Heritage Sites in China writen by ICOMOS China in collaboration with the Getty Conservation Institute and the Australian Heritage Commission and published in 2000. 《中国文物古迹保护准则》于2000年由国际古迹遗址理事会中国国家委员会（中国古迹遗址保护协会）与美国盖蒂保护所、澳大利亚遗产委员会合作编制。2015年修订。

SPAB	Society for the Protection of Ancient Buildings. 古建筑保护学会
SPNHC	Society for the Preservation of Natural History Collections 自然历史藏品修复学会
UKIC	United Kingdom Institute for Conservation of Historic and Artistic Works, London UK. 英国历史文献和艺术品保护研究所，位于英国伦敦。
VDR	Verband der Restauratoren - Confederation of Conservators - Restorers. Union of seven professional organisations in Germany in April 2001. 文物修复师联盟2001年4月在德国成立，是由七个专业修复机构组成的联盟。
Venice Charter	The International Charter for the Conservation and Restoration of Monuments and Sites (known as the Venice Charter) was approved at the 2nd International Congress of Architects and Technicians of Historic Monuments in Venice in 1964 and adopted by the General Assembly of ICOMOS. 《保护和修复古迹遗址国际宪章》（简称《威尼斯宪章》）于1964年在威尼斯举行的第二届国际古迹建筑师和技师大会通过，并在国际古迹遗址理事会全球代表大会上正式颁布。

编后记

近年来，我国博物馆与世界各国博物馆的专业交流日渐增多，通过这些专业交流，提升和拓宽了我国博物馆相关从业人员的专业水平与研究视野。中国博物馆协会为加强博物馆从业人员的专业能力建设做出了诸多努力，举办了多次国际学术交流活动。从与国际博协、故宫博物院共同组织的每年两期国际博物馆培训班，与美国盖蒂领导力学院共同资助国内博物馆管理者参与的"博物馆领导力项目"，到2019年资助国内博物馆青年代表参与国际博协京都大会，我们都能感受到博物馆从业人员，尤其是新一代博物馆人出色的专业水平。同时，我们也发现，一部分人在尝试翻译或撰写一些英文专业材料时，会遇到一定的障碍，出现中外使用专业术语不对称现象，造成专业交流不畅的情况。

有鉴于此，在参与筹备国际博物馆协会藏品交流委员会（ICOM-CC）第19届大会的过程中，编者获得了ICOM-CC编译的藏品保护多语种电子词典。这些词典中的术语包括英语、法语、希腊语、德语、意大利语、荷兰语、匈牙利语，却唯独没有中文。我国尚没有类似的专业术语词典，本着向ICOM-CC第19届大会参会人员尤其是中方参会人员提供一份参考的初心，我们开始着手分类和翻译工作。

本手册绝大多数的英文词条来自ICOM-CC藏品保护电子词典。翻译、编辑本手册的过程也是重要的研习之旅。由于涉及到了藏品保护工作的方方面面，为保证术语的准确性和易于理解使用，编译过程中，除了翻译之外，更多的工作是查阅相关资料、思考、提出问题、咨询专家并反复修改，整个过程持续了一年之久。由于在很多类别中，中外术语并不能一一对应，本手册只是提供了一种更贴近实际情况的表述方式。

本手册的编译工作得到了国家文物局和中国博物馆协会的大力支持，编译过程中，多位国内馆藏文物保护专家也提供了无私帮助。各章审校专家更是逐字逐句对文稿进行了专业审校，织物和绘画章、专家还在原有词条的基础上，添加了部分重要词条。山东大学文化遗产研究院马清林教授亲自担任了本手册的专家顾问，为手册的分组、专业词汇的拣选和整体把关提供了重要的专业意见。在此，谨对各位专家的支持表示衷心地感谢！

特别感谢中国博物馆协会刘诗琦在本手册最后的编辑工作中对各个词条文字的整理修改，感谢山东大学文化遗产研究院龙莎莎、阚颖浩的校对工作。

由于编者水平有限，本手册中列词条的翻译难免出错，敬请读者批评指正。

艾静芳

2021年3月

致　谢

国际博协藏品保护委员会（ICOM-CC）大会是国际藏品保护人员、专家学者及机构重要的学术和技术交流平台。本手册绝大多数的英文词条来自 ICOM-CC 编译的藏品保护电子词典。为迎接即将于 2021 年 5 月在北京召开的 ICOM-CC 第 19 届大会，ICOM-CC 及各相关关机构免费提供了该电子词典的版权。在此，专门感谢 ICOM-CC 以及藏品保护电子词典编纂专家。

The book would not have been possible without the generosity of the free authorization from all the institutions and persons from these institutions, who originally were part of this project.

Deep appreciation to all the contributors who made original contributions, especially:

TEI of Athens, Greece: Georgios Panagiaris, Vasilike Argyropoulos

Fachhochshule f ü r Technik und Wirtschaft Berlin, Germany: Matthias Knaut

The Manchester Museum, UK: Velson Horie

Netherlands Institute for Cultural Heritage, The Netherlands: Steph Scholten

EVITech Institute of Arts and Design, Finland (Metropolia UAS): Rikhard Hördal, Tannar Ruuben

P.K. Net Informatics Ltd., Greece

University of Athens, Department of Informatics, Greece: Dracoulis Martakos

And appericiation to the editor of the English Version: Velson Horie.